John B. Connally
Portrait in Power

—*Shelly Katz*

John B. Connally
Portrait in Power

Ann Fears Crawford
and Jack Keever

Jenkins Publishing Company
Austin, Texas / 1973

Design
Larry Smitherman

for Robert M. Crunden
a.f.c.

for Cindy, Graham, and Erin
j.k.

Preface

Texans have always reveled in politics. The adventurous frontier years, the unique days of the Republic, and the exciting years of early statehood were peopled with lusty politicians who often became leaders by blending backwoods intuition with public presence. The twentieth century also has contributed its share of eccentric and extraordinary politicians: from James Stephen Hogg to Lyndon Johnson, Texans have left their mark on the political scene in bold script.

No one is more of a Texas phenomenon of the 1960s and the 1970s than John Bowden Connally who, with Lyndon Johnson, stands as the major influential politician in the state during the era.

John Connally's political story is typically Texan. He was born and reared in a small town, where men lived off the land and prayed for sons to help with the labor. Early poverty and his Methodist upbringing have influenced Connally. His lifestyle reflects the family virtues of sobriety and hard work. College was the bridge to a political career. The friends he made at The University of Texas during the 1930s paid off a quarter of a century later in his first campaign for governor and they could continue to pay dividends in national politics.

Connally followed in the tradition of other Texas politicians on the rise by aligning himself with a prominent officeholder—Lyndon Johnson, who gave him a political foothold. Connally used his talents for the mutual benefit of both men. Throughout the 1960s Johnson and Connally together wielded enormous and unprecedented power in Texas. However, Connally's natural inclinations carried him far to the right of Johnson. The roots of Populism planted during Johnson's youth and his humanitarian concern for people were missing in Connally.

Connally's political conservatism and economic ideas have been influenced by wealthy men, chiefly by Texas millionaire Sid Richardson, and his own efforts to achieve wealth; Connally decided early in life that he never wanted to be financially dependent on anyone. His shift to the right in political and economic thinking culminated in his switch to the Republican party in 1973—a move that would have almost certainly ended the career of other twentieth century Texas politicians. But not only has Connally survived his departure from the Democratic party, he has prospered as a new Republican.

The assassination of John F. Kennedy, Connally's friendship with Lyndon Johnson, and his association with Richard Nixon's administration have kept Connally in the presidential spotlight for a decade. Despite his prominence in high political circles for so long a time, people continually ask: Who is Connally? Where did he come from? Where is he going? He remains both a charismatic and an enigmatic figure, and as stories circulate that he will be a presidential candidate in 1976, the interest in Connally grows.

This political biography sketches Connally's formative years and the influence they have had on his life and his personality. The authors have tried to show how Connally established a provincial power base in Texas from which, at his whim, he steps up to one of national importance.

The authors wish to acknowledge many people who granted interviews and allowed their remarks to be recorded. Most of the material for the book has been gathered from interviews and newspapers. The authors also relied on personal experiences. Jack Keever reported politics for the Associated Press at the capitol during Connally's administration, and Ann Fears Crawford was on the research staff of the Institute of Texan Cultures during HemisFair '68. They also have been acquainted with close personal friends of Connally's for a number of years.

The authors are particularly indebted to the late President Lyndon Johnson for his remarks on Connally. Johnson's written remarks were forwarded to the authors a short time before the president's death, and may have been the last evaluation Johnson made of another politician.

A debt of gratitude goes to the members of the Connally family. Mrs. Wayne Connally was most helpful in researching birthdates for Connally's ancestors and background on the family's early days in Texas. Merrill Connally spent hours with the authors, showing them the Connally lands and providing material and pictures for the book. Other members of the family who contributed their reminiscences were Carmen Connally Hicks and her husband D. W. "Speedy" Hicks; Golfrey Connally; Wayne Connally; and Blanche Connally Kline.

Among those interviewed were the following: George Christian; the late Crawford Martin; former lieutenant governor Ben Barnes; Larry Temple; Mike Myers; United States Representative Charles Wilson; former United States Senator Ralph Yarborough; former Secretary of State Bob Bullock; United States Representative J. J. "Jake" Pickle; Ronnie Dugger; Land Commissioner Bob Armstrong; National Democratic Chairman Robert Strauss; Will Davis; Walter Caven of the Texas Railroad Association; Dick Cory of the Texas Brewers' Institute; former governor Preston Smith; Roy Evans, former president of the Texas AFL-CIO; O'Neil Ford; Henderson Shuffler, director of the Institute of Texan Cultures; Kyle

Thompson; Bill Carter; Nick Johnson; Maurine Ray; Bill Berger; Dr. Joe Neal; Jerry Hall; former state representative Randy Pendleton; and Joe and Sarah Terry. Numerous others were interviewed in connection with the book.

The authors also wish to express their gratitude for information supplied by Herb Klein, former Director of Communications for President Nixon, and Karen Elliott and Peggy Simpson, Texas reporters in Washington. We also wish to express our appreciation to syndicated columnist Joseph Kraft and author David Halberstam for sharing their views on Connally with us.

In gathering material on Connally, the authors relied on professional help from the numerous libraries. We particularly wish to thank the staff of the *Texas Observer* for allowing us to use their files and pictures. Our thanks also go to J. C. Martin and his staff at the Texas Newspaper Collection; the Texas Legislative Library; The Austin-Travis County Collection of the Austin Public Library; the Texas Archives, Barker History Center; W. H. Crain, Curator, The Hoblitzelle Collection, Humanities Research Center, The University of Texas; Archives, Texas State Library; Joe Ed Manry, The Department of Drama, The University of Texas; the Sam Fore Jr. Collection, Wilson County Library.

The authors wish to express their appreciation to the following: Cynthia Pendergrass Keever for editorial suggestions; Richard West for content suggestions; Marilyn Palmer for help with research; Elizabeth Davis for preparing the manuscript for publication; Kevin Crawford and Natalie Newell for helping with indexing; Julian Read for advice.

Ann Fears Crawford
Jack Keever
Austin, Texas
15 September 1973

Contents

John B. Connally
Portrait in Power

"A Deep Love for the Land"

1

The rolling land stretches southward toward the Rio Grande. It is a rough land marked with live oaks, scrub oaks, huisache, and mesquite. Once the hunting ground of the mighty lords of the plains, the Comanche, the Apache, and the Tonkawa, the land once rang with the jangle of the silver spurs of the Spanish conquistadors. In 1718 Martin de Alarcon, governor of the province of Texas and founder of Villa de Bexar (present-day San Antonio) led an expedition across the land en route to Espiritu Santo Bay. The kings of Spain sent their viceroys and inspectors Pedro de Rivera and the Marquis de Rubi to explore it as part of the Spanish frontier.

The early settlement of the area that is now Wilson County in south central Texas is credited to the Mexican cattle barons. In 1830 Francisco Flores de Abreyo established the first hacienda in the area. His descendants still live in the town of Floresville, which bears his name.

Manuel Barrera secured a land grant in 1833, and the old alcalde of Bexar, Erasmo Seguin, settled in the area in the late 1830s. The influx of settlers in the 1840s and 1850s increased, swelled by German farmers from Guadalupe County and Poles from Karnes County. The Mexican vaqueros and the Anglo farmers soon mixed, giving the area the ethnic character indigenous to southwestern ranch and farm lands.

Watered by the San Antonio and Cibolo rivers, the sandy loam and black soil of the area were good for both the raising of livestock and farm produce. Water was plentiful and grass grew in abundance. Soon peanuts, grains, corn, melons, and vegetables were rivaling the livestock industry. When the Englishman James Charles Wilson marched off to a Mexican prison with the members of the ill-fated Mier expedition,[1] managed to escape, and returned to his adopted state to serve in the legislature, Wilson County had its name. The bell that sits atop the old county courthouse has rung only three times—once when World War I ended, once when the county celebrated its centennial in 1950, and the last time when her native son, John Bowden Connally Jr., was inaugurated governor of Texas.

A man's roots can run deep beneath the sandy soil of Wilson County, and Connallys and Wrights[2] have lived in the area for four generations. The Connallys came to the United States from their native Ireland with the great swell of immigrants escaping the Irish potato famine in the nineteenth century. The first American Connally, Charles P. Connally, John's great-grandfather, migrated to Texas from Alabama, settling near the Gonzales area in the south central part of the state. John Connally's grandfather, John Wesley Connally, was born near Gonzales on January 4, 1849. Family legend records that he carries the same name as the famous Texas gunslinger, John Wesley Hardin. Hardin's father and Connally's great-grandfather lived near one

1. The last raiding expedition from Texas into Mexico during the days of the Republic of Texas.

2. Connally's maternal ancestors.

2

another and were good friends. The two boys were born in the same year, and the two fathers named their sons for the great Methodist preacher John Wesley.

In his adult years John Wesley Connally settled in the Nocernut community between Floresville and Nixon. John Bowden Connally was born April 18, 1889, and was named for his father. His middle name was derived from his maternal grandmother's maiden name. On January 27, 1908, John Bowden Connally married Lela Wright from the neighboring Fairview community. The newlyweds settled near Floresville, and the following year on February 9, 1909, their first child, a little boy named Wyatt, was born. One day Mrs. Connally was out in the yard washing clothes in an iron pot over a log fire. The little boy toddled too close to the open fire and was burned severely. He died soon thereafter.

The Connallys' second son, Stanford Wright, was born on March 22, 1911, and a daughter, Carmen, followed on January 27, 1914. Another son was born on February 27, 1917, and was christened John for his father. He was not given the middle name of Bowden, but he adopted his father's middle name sometime after his high school years. Family members differ in their opinion of when Connally actually began using the Bowden name. Brother Merrill believes that John adopted the name just before joining the Navy following Pearl Harbor. ''He just couldn't face the prospect of going through the Navy as plain Johnnie Connally,'' Merrill states. His wedding announcement, however, carries the middle initial ''B,'' and college friends recall his using the ''Bowden'' name.

The Connallys rounded out their family at regular two-year periods after John's birth. Golfrey Michael, now an economics professor at San Antonio College, was born on January 17, 1919. Merrill Lee, former Wilson County judge and commissioner, followed on April 9, 1921, and the last son, Wayne Wright, former state senator and one-time candidate for Texas lieutenant governor, was born on March 19, 1923. Blanche, the baby of the family, was born February 24, 1925. During the children's younger

3

years the Connally family made their home on a rented farm near Floresville.

Floresville, the county seat of Wilson County, is still primarily a livestock and farming area. Farmers began planting peanuts in large numbers in the 1930s, and today they are a million-dollar crop. Several thousand acres of the surrounding farmland are planted in pecan trees. Watermelons, blackeyed peas, corn, and truck produce make up the diversified farm crops of the area, and Floresville is now the largest supplier of dairy cattle for the San Antonio milkshed.

Since its beginnings Floresville has been composed of both Mexican American and Anglo families, with an equal measure of Germans, Swedes, and Poles. The town centers around its main square, where automobiles now park and men in Western dress still lounge lazily. Several blocks off the main square stand the ruins of the once magnificent houses known as ''silk stocking row.'' The bankers and lawyers—the Houstons and the Browns—used to run the town, according to Merrill Connally, although many of their families have moved from Floresville. Now and then a descendant will return and restore one of the old houses to its former glory and settle down once again.

However, the lifeblood of the area now focuses around the outlying agricultural and ranching country. Many of the stores stand abandoned around the town square, and the city of Floresville boasts neither a hotel nor a motel. The newest building in town is the bank, with adobe structure and hanging lanterns in the Mexican style. Life is homey and folksy in Floresville, and anyone on the street can tell you about the Connallys, although the local newspaper doesn't even have a picture of its most famous citizen in its files.

The land around Floresville is ''Connally Country.'' John Bowden Connally Sr. and his wife, Lela, bought the original Connally homesite five miles west of Floresville in June 1932. The present house was on the site, but the Connallys have added to it and improved it. A trim white picket fence surrounds the rambling white wooden farm-

4

house. An adjoining block building that originally served as an old beer cooler now serves as a smokehouse. Ice was brought from the railroad, which first reached Wilson County in 1886, to cool the home brew. The Connally family home now sits in a grove of over one hundred pecan trees and is presently tenant farmed by Tony Griago, who also serves as foreman of the Connally ranch, and Esaquel Talamentes.

The Connally homestead of 1,013 acres has over two hundred acres planted in velvety-green coastal bermuda grass. The lands belonging to the Connally brothers, John, Merrill, and Wayne, are also planted in the lush and hardy grass that is capable of grazing more cattle per acre than any of Texas' native grasses. Fort Worth millionaire Sid Richardson first introduced coastal bermuda to the Connallys, and now thousands of acres of the soil-conserving grass cover Connally lands. Many experts consider the Connally brothers as pioneers in grassland farming in south central Texas.

Sid Richardson also encouraged Connally to stock his ranch with the Galiceno horses, brought to Yucatan from the Galicia country of Spain by Cortes and other Spanish conquistadors. Both Sid Richardson and Dallas millionaire Clint Murchison stocked the wiry ponies, and Richardson gave Connally a filly and a stallion to begin the herds now used to corral cattle on the Connally ranches. Small ponies with a great deal of stamina, the Galicenos are ideal stock ponies, tough but not mean.

John and his brothers, Merrill and Wayne, raise registered Hereford and Santa Gertrudis cattle commercially. The brothers' ranches, including John's Sandhill and Picosa ranches, have been cleared, retaining the best of the live oaks and eliminating the cactus, hackberry, and scrub oak that once grew wild over the land. Connally remarked to reporters at the press showing of the ranch house that, "Blowing sand was piled fence high on some of this country you're looking at right now. The mesquite was so thick it would take days to round up cattle. You could even lose a tractor in some of the gullies. I guess we've cleared 2,500 acres of family land and put it all in coastal bermuda.''

Each of the Connallys ranch a spread of several thousand acres. Their distinctive homes stand out from the small farm houses that dot the south Texas countryside. Merrill's is a brick house set in a clump of live oak trees and backed by a swimming pool, tennis court, and private lake. Wayne's is a recently constructed two-story structure of pinon and East Texas pine, designed by San Antonio architect O'Neil Ford and furnished with Victorian antiques that his wife Kay has collected through the years.

John Connally's Sandhill and Picosa acreage are justifiably the most breathtaking spreads in the area. Sandhill covers 2,400 acres, and Picosa 1,200. Another ranch, the Four C belonging to Connally's children and named for them, encompasses 1,200 acres, and Connally owns another 500 acres in the area. In addition, Connally bought 250 acres of his family's homestead, with brother Merrill purchasing the remainder. In 1965 Connally bought the Tortuga Ranch[3] in Zavala and Dimmit counties, 14,270 acres from the Delhi Properties, for about $300,000.

The Connally ranch house at Picosa, designed by architect John Linn Scott of Austin, took over a year to build and was completed in 1964.[4] Cars with license plates from as far away as New York state often travel Farm Road 2579 heading out of Floresville toward Pleasanton to let visitors to Texas take a look at Connally's ranch. The sprawling house sits atop a hill where Connally can survey almost every acre of his land. Constructed of native Lueders stone, the two-story home contains approximately seven thousand square feet of space and is a mixture of English, French Provincial, and informal Texas ranch styles. The cost of construction has been estimated at approximately $200,000 to $250,000 and Connally has commented that, ''Frankly, we spent too much!''

---

3. Connally sold the Tortuga property in 1972.

4. Connally received criticism from Texas labor for using non-union labor to build his ranch house.

The ranch house is the first house that John and Idanell Connally built, and Connally remarked that, "We planned to build a larger house with guest rooms, but started cutting down when we got the price estimates." Guests at the Picosa Ranch will have to bed down in a camp house which started as a hunting cabin, with its mounted deer heads and colorful Indian blankets. It will sleep fourteen guests. Idanell and John Connally planned their eleven-room house for themselves and their children. The central two-story unit contains a large living room and dining room in the Georgian style, the family room with its twenty-eight-foot high cathedral ceiling, the kitchen area, and a maid's bedroom and bath.

A single-story wing contains four bedrooms, one for each of the three Connally children and a master suite for John and Idanell. Eight bathrooms, a large library and study, and Connally's office and study complete the elegant ranch house. The back of the house curves around the native oak trees, and a forty-four foot swimming pool graces the back-yard. [5]

Both the Connallys are enthusiastic antique collectors, and their home reflects their interest in antiques and in Western art. The walls of their home display the work of such Southwestern artists as Melvin Warren, Frank Tenney Johnson, and Porfirio Salinas. The first painting of their new ranch home was presented to the Connallys in January 1965 by Mr. and Mrs. Roger Zeller of San Antonio, who commissioned the Spanish-born painter Jose Vives-Atsara to do a painting of the house. The paintings reflect the warm oranges and greens of the decor, the wood and stone of the interiors.

Collecting the furnishings for their new home was a six-year project for the Connallys. Connally flew to Abilene with his architect to choose the limestone for his home. The Georgian living room is graced with a marble mantle and black Brazilian granite flooring that the Connallys bought in

5. After retiring as secretary of the treasury, Connally began planning extensive additions to the Picosa ranch house.

South America. They imported eleven handcarved doors, a staircase railing of antique brass and iron, and a marble dining room floor from an eighteenth-century London mansion. Two of the teakwood doors weighed 360 pounds each. In Bastrop, Texas, the Connallys found two silver kerosene carriage lamps from the historic Pease Mansion in Austin.[6] Crystal chandeliers and furniture were bought at Samuel Hart Gallery's auction of the Yount[7] estate, and a large Oriental chandelier was bought in New Orleans. Connally remarked that, "We hawked auctions. Ninety-five percent of the furniture was bought at auction." Mrs. Connally remarked that Connally was an often overly enthusiastic collector. "I'm the only wife who's had to say, 'No, we don't need that.'"

Connally commented on the outlet for creativity that furnishing and landscaping his ranch home gave to him and his wife. "We're planning to landscape the area around our ranch house. . . . Obviously, we could hire a landscape architect to do it but we want to do it ourselves. We want to plan it and plant the trees." However, politics and his law practice claim much of his time. The time he spends at his ranch is precious to him.

Whenever Connally is in foreign countries, his interest in livestock is apparent. Merrill recalls that in the spring of 1972, when Connally traveled to eighteen countries in South and Central America, he constantly inquired about livestock and the conditions for breeding cattle. "He has the type of mind that he can remember facts and statistics . . . a world of information that you wouldn't think he would have time to even observe, much less remember. He noted that in Uruguay, for instance, they have three meatless weeks out of every month; and in Argentina, one of the great beef-producing countries in the world, they can't legally eat

---

6. "Woodlawn," the historic Pease mansion in Austin, was once the home of former Texas Governor E. M. Pease and is now the home of former Texas Governor Allan Shivers.

7. M. F. Yount, a Beaumont millionaire, made his fortune from Texas' famed oil strike at Spindletop. A former member of The University of Texas Board of Regents, he left a sizeable estate including antique furniture.

meat but for two weeks out of every month."

Merrill believes that John's love of the land and of the cattle it can produce was fostered in the years he worked on the family farm. "During the summer months, we had the responsibility for the care of the cattle, even to doctoring them for screwworms. None of this is foreign to John—he was part and parcel of it all." Connally's older sister Carmen, wife of rancher D. W. "Speedy" Hicks of Bandera, states that, "John has a deep love for the land. He also has a deep respect for people who work with their hands or who work the land." And John Connally affirms his ties to the land of south Texas where he was born and reared. In commenting to a *Time* magazine reporter planning a cover story on him in 1964, Connally stated, "One of the things that meant the most to me was breaking the land with a turning plow. Believe it or not, that's a fine sensation. You get under a layer of turf with a plow and it's got sort of a crackle as it breaks loose. I used to take off my shoes because the soil behind the plow just felt good to walk in. It had a good feel, good smell. It had sort of life to it."

—*Texas State Archives*

"An All-Around Boy and Good Son"

2

When Governor John Connally escorted reporters around his newly completed Picosa ranch home in 1964, he commented on the technological improvements that machinery had brought to the farm and ranch area. "Farm life is not what it used to be. . . . When Merrill and I were boys we spent many a day in the hot field stacking hay. Now look how easy they do it." Farm life was hard for the Connally family during the 1920s and depression years of the 1930s. John's mother, Lela Wright Connally, had been one of a family of nine children who helped hoe and pick cotton to support the family after their father died of appendicitis. She managed to complete high school, earn a teaching certificate, and teach in a country school, before marrying John Bowden Connally Sr. She resolved early in life that education and hard work would be the making of her children.

All the Connally children worked on the farm the Connallys leased in the 1920s and later at the homestead the family purchased in 1932, while John Connally Sr. supplemented the farming money by working as a butcher and a barber. Connally's younger brother Golfrey recalls that, "We were growing up at the end of the age of 'King Cotton,' and we did all the chores and worked in the fields with Dad, pulling those big cotton sacks down the rows. I was pretty small then, but I pulled a flour sack right alongside my older brothers. We learned the value of hard work early in life."

Wayne Connally also affirms that, "We were all made to understand that we had to work to earn our way in the world, and each had to contribute his own in a family way to make ends meet. We learned to work together at every job on the farm from working cattle to hoeing peanuts, pitching hay, and harnessing mules. We all had to go in and do our share, depending on our age at the time and what jobs we were capable of doing." In speaking to the National Rural Electric Cooperative Association in Dallas in March 1964, Governor Connally pointed out that, "Our small ranch was a living for a large family, and it took long, hard hours of work by every member of my family to make ends meet. We plowed behind a mule, got our water from a hand-pump, studied by kerosene light, and learned to appreciate the nice things in life."

Working the farm had its lighter moments, too, for the Connally boys. Wayne recalls that Johnnie's—the name he was known by as a boy—particular chore was to milk the cows early in the morning. One wet, cold Texas morning, the future governor was shivering and milking away. When the milk bucket was about half full, the cow put her foot in the bucket, spilling milk in every direction. John lost his temper and picked up a two-by-four and hit her across the neck. It crimped the cow's neck, and John thought he had killed her.

Johnnie's notorious temper got him into trouble with older brother Stanford over corn pulling, which ended in a fight that sent John limping back to the farm house in tears. Wayne remembers that the brothers were pulling corn on the "Back 40," a mile or so from the ranch house. Wayne was driving the team of mules, with Johnnie pulling corn on one side, Stanford on the other, and Golfrey and Merrill in the back of the wagon. It was just at sundown as the wagon was loaded for the trip home when one of the boys threw an ear of corn over the side of the wagon. It hit one of the others, and then the corn really began to fly! It ended up in a corn fight between Johnnie and Stanford, with Johnnie taking the worst end of the deal—a heavy ear of corn on the side of the head. He took off for home, walking all the way, and vowed he'd never go near the corn field again.

Work around the farm precluded the boys' participating in sports after school. There were chores to be done. "None of us every played on a football or basketball team," Merrill recalls. "There was never an ironclad rule against our participating in intramurals, but when school hours were over, we went home, and we went to work. It was awfully hard to keep bread and beans on the table, particularly for a family with seven children." The Epworth League, the Methodist young people's group, however, provided ample opportunity for social functions. On one memorable occasion a planned kidnapping staged by Johnnie Connally and his adventurous cousin and schoolmate Phlemon Wright almost ended in tragedy. Wright remembers that, "Johnnie did his share of devilment. He just didn't get caught." Carmen Connally Hicks remembers the occasion as one party the entire family talked about for some time to come.

The Epworth League had planned a Sunday night hayride with a picnic supper at the Connallys' artesian well—a delightful place for a party. Johnnie and Phemon Wright decided to stage a holdup disguised as Mexican desperadoes with guns and masks. Johnnie slipped his father's old .45 thumbbuster out of the house, and, having no blanks at his disposal, loaded it with real bullets. The two cousins took one of the girls into their confidence and warned her to sit on one particular corner of the wagon where she could be easily kidnapped. Unfortunately, a great-granddaughter of Sam Houston, Catherine Q. Paulus, and her escort, Cullen Archer, slipped into the designated spot, and the two desperadoes, with Spanish threats and the firing of the old gun, kidnapped the wrong girl! Johnnie managed to haul Catherine off under one arm with the horses raring and young people screaming. In the confusion, the sponsor of the Epworth League, seeing one of her charges being abducted by Mexican bandits, jumped off the wagon right into a number two washtub full of picnic sandwiches, and "Juanito" Connally, Mexican bandit, dropped the girl. It took several hours to round up all the League members from behind the bushes and cactus and to get the party going again.

The Connally clan was a closely knit one, where both work and play were shared. The Christian virtues of hard work and sobriety were stressed, and, in a community where home brew graced most of the tables, neither beer nor whiskey was allowed. Even today the Connallys abstain from alcohol, John taking a glass of sherry or wine and sipping it from time to time. In Austin political circles, former Senator Wayne Connally is well known for his "big Texas-size Cokes." After Texas governor Price Daniel, who also abstains from alcohol, abolished the cocktail party at the Austin Country Club that traditionally preceded the inaugural ball, Connally never reinstated it.

During their growing-up years, the Connally children were never encouraged to dance, although they attended parties and socials given by the Epworth League. Carmen Connally Hicks recalls that, "Dad was such an old-fashioned dad that I didn't go to many parties without an escort, and John was the one who had to go. Stanford, being my older brother, wouldn't go, but John fit in well."

John Connally Sr. was not a churchgoer, but Lela Connally's family had attended church activities and meetings all their lives. The Connally children attended Sunday school at the First Methodist Church in Floresville and the Epworth League on Sunday evenings. "We were not allowed to miss church unless there was just some real emergency," Wayne Connally recalls. Carmen, John, and Golfrey often played instrumental trios for Epworth League socials—Carmen on the trombone, John on the saxophone, and Golfrey on the violin. The Connally children were also appointed speakers for league meetings.

The Connally children remember both their father and mother as strict disciplinarians, although the spankings were given by Mrs. Connally. "John and I got our share of spankings," Carmen states; and her husband, "Speedy" Hicks claims, "People used to say there were never any branches on the peach trees over at the Connally place. They'd all been used for switches." Carmen remembers: "Every once in a while Dad would come in from town and tell us that some man had stopped him on the street and told him what a fine family he had. They just never did hear anything bad about the boys or any devilment they were into. And Dad always gave Mother the credit."

Although John Connally Sr. had quit school after the sixth grade to begin working, he was as ambitious as his wife was for his children's education. His children recall that Dad Connally wanted them to go to college and hoped that each would have a professional education. "He wanted a doctor, a lawyer, and an engineer," Golfrey laughs. "And he almost succeeded. I started out in engineering at The University of Texas, but found out that I wasn't really suited for it. Having had the opportunity to take a couple of elective courses in the social sciences, I switched over to economics. But John fulfilled Dad's ambition for a lawyer, and even knew what he wanted from his early days."

Connally's brothers and sisters remember that he would always have a ready answer for adults who asked him what he wanted to be when he grew up. He always said that he wanted to be a cowboy, a lawyer, and a preacher. One Christmas he asked for a gun, a rope, and a Bible. When Connally was governor of Texas, he spoke at the dedication of a new church in Bandera, home of Carmen and Speedy Hicks. When Carmen introduced her brother, she told the audience of his early ambitions, adding that he owned a ranch and got to "play cowboy," he was governor of the state and a lawyer, and that in giving the speech for the church dedication he was getting his chance to "be the preacher."

Although the Connallys gave up their rented farm and moved into San Antonio in 1926, Johnnie returned to

Floresville in the summers to work for his winter spending money. He picked cotton and hoed peanuts on the Wright farm in Fairview, and his cousin Phlemon worked side by side with John in the peanut fields. "We worked barefoot in the sandy fields and by the time the sun got overhead, we were looking for two kinds of weeds, one to chop and another big enough to stand in its shade and cool our feet," Phlemon later recalled. One summer Connally worked as a batch weigher, computing amounts of cement for bridges and asphalt for roads for the Texas Highway Department.

When the family lived on the south side of San Antonio, young John helped a neighbor boy "jump" a milk route each afternoon. John was not paid for his services, but every now and then he would receive extra milk for his help. Carmen recalls that, "He'd bring that milk in, and was he ever proud of it! He wasn't being paid for it, but he felt he had earned it. As far as I know, John has never in his life been bored." When he entered The University of Texas, he hawked gum, mints, and other candy for the Beech-Nut Chewing Gum Company, washed dishes in his rooming house, and picked up jobs as caretaker for his fraternity house.

When Connally Sr. moved his seven children to San Antonio, John entered the sixth grade and continued at Harlandale High School. The family remained there until June 1, 1932. The senior Connally operated the independent Red Ball bus line in partnership with T. L. Perry from Corpus Christi. The line, the forerunner of such major companies as Greyhound and Continental, originally ran from San Antonio to Corpus Christi, and later extended from Corpus Christi to Laredo and from Houston to Corpus.

Connally and Perry obtained a permit from the Texas Railroad Commission to operate the line, and used seven-passenger Oldsmobile automobiles as public conveyances. Equipped with jump seats, the automobiles made the route from San Antonio to Corpus Christi, and then would return often with an eighth passenger squeezed in the crack between the jump seats. Lela Connally sewed triangular pieces of canvas with a red felt ball in the center for her husband's "buses," and Connally attached them to the front fenders, where they would flap in the breeze as the Oldsmobiles made their daily routes. Merrill recalls that most of the children were too young to drive for their dad, but that Stanford, who was eighteen, once drove the route from San Antonio to Corpus. He made it out of San Antonio, but he had to ask one of the passengers the way to the coastal city, as he had never been there.

Connally Sr. operated the bus line for eight years, until the pressure from the major companies became so great that he was forced to sell out. Merrill recalls that those years were the times when the major companies played "rough pool" and would send hired muggers out to attack the drivers and inflict physical violence on the passengers. Many of the men who owned the smaller independent lines wanted to hold out against the majors, but Connally and Perry soon sold their line to Greyhound.

During the San Antonio years, young John developed his ability in dramatics, debate, and extemporaneous speaking that he had begun in Floresville. Carmen Connally Hicks remembers that Mrs. Lucille Lang Duffner, who taught Connally in the fifth grade, seemed to sense that John was a little something special, and encouraged him in declamation. Connally chose Joaquin Miller's "The Defense of the Alamo" for his selection and won with the poetic selection time and time again. He took additional speech lessons from a coach in San Antonio and continued his public speaking during his high school days at Harlandale and during his senior year at Floresville High School.

Sister Carmen would help him at home, and the young orator would declaim Patrick Henry's "Speech Before the Virginia House of Delegates," and the rafters would ring with the fiery patriot's immortal lines, "I know not what course others may take; but as for me, give me liberty, or give me death!" When Connally was president of the Curtain Club at The University of Texas, he was invited back to Harlandale High School to deliver the commencement address. Carmen attended the commencement and remembers that Connally's speech was quite impressive but

17

also quite long. "It was a wonderful speech," she says, "but it just went on, and on, and on. He just couldn't seem to find a place to stop. I just wanted to say, 'John, stop right there!'"

Not all John's public speaking experiences were pleasant ones. His brother Merrill recalls that, after the family moved back to Floresville in 1932, John entered a speech contest against one of the city boys, a member of the so-called "elite" families of Floresville. "Of course, we were the country kids—poor white trash to many of the people," Merrill recalls. "We were really second-class citizens in effect. It's hard to conceive of its existing today, but it did. The country kids were looked on in one way, and the city kids in another. The city parents ruled the roost—the politics, the government, and the society. And in this case the speech contest."

With the whole community—students and parents as well—assembled in the school auditorium, the two boys gave their declamations. When the judges announced that the city boy had won over Johnnie Connally, the country boy, Merrill recalls that there was a "dead hush" in the auditorium. "Everyone was hesitant to believe that John had not won. Not because of who he was, but because he was by far the better of the two speakers. It was the same old story. The superintendent of schools was beholden to the district judge, who was part and parcel of the county unit. There was nothing we could do. It was a closed corporation. Of course, John went on to prove what a good speaker he was. And the fellow who won the contest never went any further than that day."

Connally's high school classmates dubbed the future governor "Senator," and his speaking ability led the editors of his Floresville high school annual to include a one-sentence description of Connally in the annual—"They always talk who never think." Connally's concern with his appearance also gained him the following remark from the annual editors: "What would happen if Johnnie lost the part in his hair?" His concern for his appearance began at fourteen or fifteen when he started to notice the girls, and his slicked-down hair led his brother Stanford to give him the nickname "Don Juan." In later years Stanford dropped the "Don," and Connally is often called "Juan" by his brothers.

Connally's high school dating years caused his younger brothers and sisters some hardship. "John was old enough to drive," Merrill recalls, "and he had the privilege of the car. On Saturday night, all of us younger ones wanted to go to the picture show. But, of course, John was slicking his hair down and going on a date. John would drop us off at the show and go to pick up his date. The show would be over, of course, about nine or ten o'clock, but Blanche, Wayne, and I would have to wait on the street corner until midnight for John." Wayne adds that, "We had a four-door Chevrolet sedan, either a 1934 or 1935 model, and between John and Golfrey, they wore that one out in two years."

Carmen remembers John as a great tease. "I can remember on one occasion chasing him around the house. I don't know why, because I never could catch him. He was always faster. I'd usually end up taking my shoes off and throwing them at him." Her most pleasant memories of John are of the Christmas most of the family was sick with influenza. No one had been able to do the shopping, and there was very little money to spend for Christmas presents for the younger children. "Mother sent John to town with what money there was, and John bought each person in the family a present, wrapped it, and put it under the tree. The next morning he was the first one up, just as excited as he could be about Christmas even though he had done all the work. The only present he had bought himself was a little knife."

During the years that the family lived in San Antonio, both the Connallys dreamed of bringing their children back to Floresville to live. Connally Sr. saved the money from the bus line to buy and stock the Floresville farm he had coveted. For years he had wanted one particular piece of farm and ranch land, and early in the depression days, when land was cheap and many ranches were being turned back to the bank, the Connallys were able to buy the property they desired. "When we left we were tenant farmers,"

Merrill recalls, "and when we returned, we owned one of the choice pieces of property in the area."

The purchase of the property did not endear the Connallys to the leadership of the community. Many of the larger ranchers were creating giant spreads by buying up little farms and leasing them out. The so-called "leaders" had already picked out a new owner for the land, and they were incensed that the Connallys had acquired the property. When the family was able to gather around the large kitchen table with its kerosene lamp, there was much cause for heart-felt thanks.

Although the subjects for discussion centered on crops, livestock, and the activities in town, soon the talk focused on politics. The Connally children cut their teeth on political campaigning when Connally Sr. joined with several other members of the community to beat the incumbents, the "courthouse crowd," in the county elections. Connally Sr. ran for county clerk on the reform ticket, devoted to straightening out the county funds. An audit had revealed that the local funds were short, and the reform ticket waged a campaign to bring good government back to the courthouse.

Connally Sr. took Carmen and John to nearby Stockdale to campaign for him. He instructed the youngsters to go from door-to-door, introduce themselves to the people, and hand out his cards. Carmen remembers that it seemed to impress people that the candidate's children were out working for him. She did most of the knocking, and John did most of the talking.

Merrill recalls that during the campaign there were a number of highly suspect voting procedures: "Wilson County was always a political hot potato." Illegal absentee voting was common, as well as the practice of removing boxes from the courthouse to count the ballots. During the first primary in July, John Jr. and Charlie Fuller, son of the candidate for chief deputy, were sent by their fathers to keep an eye on the absentee voters in the county clerk's office. The peace officers assigned to the election confronted the boys and ordered them out. John and Charlie came out and told their fathers that they were not allowed in. Connally Sr.

and Fuller ordered the two boys back inside the courthouse. "Make them carry you out. That's the only way you're coming out of there!" the candidates told their sons. Eventually the illegal election practices ceased, and Connally Sr. served as county clerk from January 1, 1937 through December 31, 1942.

The talks around the old kitchen table beneath the kerosene lamps made a deep impression on the Connally boys. And they caught the fever of political life during their father's campaign days. John Connally began developing his politically vital ability to remember everyone's name—first and last. John Connally Sr.'s philosophy of hard work and determination also fired his son's ambition, as did his mother's belief in education for all her children.

Carmen Connally Hicks recalls that her parents looked amazingly alike—often being mistaken for brother and sister instead of husband and wife—and they thought alike. There was no work too hard to do; there was no hour too early to get up and start. Both parents had a great deal of pride in themselves and in their children. They instilled in their children the belief that they could do anything with their lives that they wanted to. "They taught us that we were not better than anyone else," Carmen states, "but no one else was better than we were. We could be just as good or just as important as we wanted to be."

John Connally was influenced by his father's determination and his mother's sense of humor. "John looks more like Mother than Dad," Carmen feels, "and the expressions around his eyes are definitely Mother's. She has a quick wit about her, and her eyebrows go up and down when she talks, just like John's."

Lela Wright Connally, who now resides in a Bandera rest home owned by Carmen and Speedy Hicks, is justifiably proud of her famous son but asserts to family and friends that, "I've got five sons and two daughters and I'm proud of them all." But her pride in her famous son is obvious when she recalls his childhood—"He was always an all-around boy and a good son."

"Critic-at-Large of Things as They Are"

3

When John Connally arrived at The University of Texas in 1933, his burning ambitions were to become a lawyer and to make a name for himself. He immediately entered into the active life of the campus, and the experience he had gained in public speaking at Harlandale High School in San Antonio stood him in good stead. He joined the Wesley Players, the University Methodist Church's dramatic group, and eventually became president. It was his association with the campus drama organization, the Curtain Club, however, that provided a creative outlet for his dramatic talent and brought him into contact with a brunette coed, Idanell Brill from Austin, who would become his wife.

The University of Texas boasted no organized department of drama when Connally arrived on the campus. However, the Curtain Club had been organized on January 7, 1909, by a young professor of English, Stark Young.

Twenty young men met with Professor Young to read and discuss plays, and on March 2, 1909, the all-male group produced Ben Jonson's *The Silent Woman*. The production was so popular that the group produced *The Miser* in 1911 and toured the production throughout college campuses in Texas. In 1912 *The Drama*, national theatre magazine, called the Curtain Club the "leading dramatic club in the south." By 1916 the club had opened its doors to women, and by 1925 the group had a written constitution and a board of governors. Eventually, students interested in stage management, costuming, and lighting joined the actors; and the year that Connally joined the organization, Hogg Memorial Auditorium was complete with equipment and stage that would allow the Curtain Club to produce such plays as *Marco Millions, R.U.R.,* and *Biography.*

Under the direction of James H. Parke, the Curtain Club during the 1930s claimed many members who made their mark on the dramatic world—Eli Wallach, Zachary Scott, Brooks West, husband of Hollywood actress Eve Arden, and television personality Allan Ludden.

On the nights of October 29, 30, and 31, 1935, Connally played the captain of the waiters in Kaufman and Hart's *Merrily We Roll Along,* with Idanell serving on the property crew. In 1936 the aspiring actor appeared as Radius, a robot, in Karl Capek's futuristic drama, *R.U.R.,* and took the role of the "richly dressed man" in Fernac Molnar's *Liliom,* with Eli Wallach in the title role. Once again Connally shared his backstage experiences with freshman Idanell Brill, who served as prompter for the production.[1]

According to Connally's sister, Carmen, Connally had been dating a number of older girls, including one in

---

1. In 1934 Connally had performed in various capacities for the Curtain Club. Programs listed him as in charge of tickets and box office for *Another Language* and as a member of the stage crew and doorman for Noel Coward's *Hay Fever.* In 1935 he served on the ticket committee for *The Ninth Guest,* while future television commentator Walter Cronkite served on the publicity committee. Connally joined Eli Wallach on the backstage committee for *She Stoops to Conquer,* and both were listed as members of the cast of *Both Your Houses.* Idanell Brill is listed as one of the understudies.

Floresville, before he met Idanell. With his dark hair and good looks he made quite a hit with the ladies, and many of his law fraternity brothers often quipped that, "John comes home from a different direction every night!" Texas Congressman J. J. "Jake" Pickle recalls that Connally had enough money from home to make him a "wheeler dealer." His fraternity brothers never knew to what party or what function he was going but only that he would come in at odd hours. "One night he'd go out all dressed up in a Homburg and spats, the next night it'd be blue jeans and a Stetson, and the next night just a pair of sports pants and a sports shirt," Pickle remembers. Connally was enchanted by the petite brunette, Idanell, a Bluebonnet Belle nominee in her freshman year at the University. One of Connally's classmates recalls that Idanell was actually John Singleton's girl and that Connally took her away from him: "She was courting Singleton on campus and John backstage at Curtain Club!" [2]

Idanell, the daughter of Mr. and Mrs. Arno Brill of Austin, came to The University of Texas with dreams of becoming an actress. In later years she remarked that, "I'm really a frustrated thespian." She joined the Curtain Club and served as secretary when Connally was president, and, when the College of Fine Arts was formed, she became a fine arts major. However, many honors outside the acting field came to her during her university years. She was chosen a Bluebonnet Belle, one of the Ten Most Beautiful during her freshman year, queen of the Texas Relays during her sophomore year, and Sweetheart of the University during her junior year.

Idanell stated that the night she became Sweetheart of the University and the night she met John Connally were the high points of her university years. Although John and Idanell were active in Curtain Club, they only played together in two plays, one the club's production of S. N. Behrman's *Biography* in November 1936. In the production

2. Singleton is now a federal judge in Harris County, appointed by President Lyndon B. Johnson. He was also appointed by Connally to the Texas Depository Board.

John played Richard Kurt, described by the student reviewer as an effective, aggressive personality, to Jack Sucke's timid Leander Nolan. John's program picture shows the set mouth and the arched eyebrow that later became his trademarks. The program noted that Connally's favorite food was green grape pie and his pet hate was turnip greens. "John lives on a ranch and says he loves to ride horses. His ambition 'is to be critic-at-large of things as-they-are.'" Idanell played the part of Slade Kennicott, the role played by Una Merkel in the motion picture production.

Austin insuranceman Jack Sucke remembers starring with Connally in *Biography* and comments that, "John had a great deal of stage presence, and if he hadn't chosen a role in politics, he would have made a fine actor." W. H. Crain, another Curtain Club member at the same time as the Connallys and currently curator of the University's Hoblitzelle Library Theatre Collection, notes that, "Connally was a born actor. He could play any part that he wanted, and could have made a career of the theatre if he had chosen to." Austin builder Nash Phillips, who played in numerous Curtain Club productions with both John and Idanell, remarks that, "Just to watch him [Connally] on the stage, you knew he was marked for destiny. He was a true leader of men."

From 1936 to 1938 Connally was very active in Curtain Club productions [3] and received awards for his dramatic work. An event of the 1937 season for Curtain Club members was the arrival of William Lee, Metro-Goldwyn-Mayer director and official, who conducted screen test auditions on the stage of the downtown Paramount Theater. Lee selected seven university students, among them John Connally, to appear for screen tests. The October 6, 1937, edition of the *Daily Texan* carried Connally's picture along with that of Alma Rae Holloway,

---

3. In 1936 he played the part of Captain Bluntschli in George Bernard Shaw's *Arms and the Man.* The picture of Connally on the program shows him brandishing a pistol, with a lock of hair falling rakishly over one eye. In 1937 Connally won the coveted role of cowboy Curley McLaine in Lynn Riggs' *Green Grow the Lilacs*, the play on which the musical *Oklahoma!* was later based.

another Curtain Club member, with the caption, "Will They Go Hollywood?" In September 1937 Connally was elected to a full term as president of the Curtain Club by unanimous vote of the thirty members.

On May 6, 1938, Connally was reelected Curtain Club president, and Idanell was elected to serve as secretary for the upcoming year. At the club's annual banquet on May 14, 1938, John received awards for the best use of voice and the best interpretation of character, while Idanell received awards for the best sense of timing and the best interpretation of character.

When Connally became president of the Student Assembly, he resigned as president of Curtain Club to devote himself to his political office. On November 10, 1938, the members of the Board of Directors of Curtain Club accepted Connally's resignation, and club members elected J. Pat O'Keefe to fill the vacancy created by Connally's resignation. O'Keefe, who served as the organization's president from 1938 to 1940, later was appointed executive director of the State Democratic Executive Committee by Governor John Connally and also headed the governor's Texas Fine Arts Commission.

Connally's election as president of the Curtain Club and his numerous appearances in campus productions gave him wide recognition at the university. Before running for president of the Student Assembly, he had practiced his oratorical powers and affiliated with other organizations, giving him a power base from which to make his campaign. He was elected a member of the Hildebrand Law Society and served as president of the Athenaeum Literary Society, a stepping stone to campus politics.

Mother + Dad—
I'll love you
always,
Johnnie.

"Remember That Always: 'The Eyes of Texas' Are Upon You"

4

During John Connally's years at The University of Texas, politics was the "meat and potatoes" of campus life. Students expected colorful and hard-fought campaigns for student body offices. During legislative sessions, legislators often spoke on the campus. The proximity of the university to the capitol and the long-standing political and financial interest of the state legislature in university affairs sparked the controversies that often embroiled university officials and the board of regents with the legislature.

In 1936 the Texas House of Representatives conducted an investigation into the influence of communism and atheism on the university campus. Amid cries of "influence" and "red-baiting," hearings were held at the capitol, with faculty and tutors called to explain the teaching of so-called "subversive doctrines" before an investigative committee of house members. The house voted 67 to 39 to clear the university professors of the charges, but tempers ran high during the investigation. Also, during the campaign year of 1936, many university students were actively involved in campaigning for the Roosevelt-Landon presidential race.

On October 3, 1936, John Connally filed for a position on the Student Assembly, the lawmaking body of the university student government, from the School of Law. He listed his qualifications as president of the Athenaeum Literary Society, president of the Wesley Players, winner of the 1934 intersociety oratorical contest, member of the Curtain Club board of directors, vice-president of the 1935 freshman law class, member of the Hildebrand Society[1] and member of Delta Theta Phi, legal fraternity.[2]

Connally's record as president of the Athenaeum, prestigious debating society at the university, gave him a foot in the door to a position on the Student Assembly. During the 1930s the political life on the campus was divided between three factions on the university campus—the fraternities, the independents, and the old debating societies. Athenaeum was the most powerful of the three societies and the oldest, being formed the day before The University of Texas opened. The Reagan and Hogg societies, named for United States Senator John H. Reagan and former Texas Governor James S. Hogg, shared the political forum with the Athenaeum, and a great rivalry existed between the members of Athenaeum and Hogg.

It was a tradition of Athenaeum that the members voted to impeach their president toward the end of his term in office. Impeachment was considered an honor and a sign that the president had been an effective and strong leader. During the impeachment proceedings, the president was allowed to make a rebuttal, which was traditionally greeted with hissing and catcalls from the members.

When the motion was made to impeach Connally, the entire membership of the society voted for his impeach-

1. A voluntary moot court sponsored by the students.

2. Connally was later elected to membership in the Friars, an exclusive honorary men's service association.

ment. When Connally was impeached, he stood before the group shocked, with tears streaming down his face. He left the room crying, and some members of the group met across the street at Hilsberg's Cafe to decide what action to take. They decided that Connally had taken the impeachment so hard that they would reelect him. However, Connally showed up at the next meeting in his usual manner and pretended that the impeachment had never taken place.

A controversy between law school officials and the members of the society came to a head during Connally's term as president of the organization. For a number of years Dean Ira Polk Hildebrand and other members of the law school faculty had tried to move the society's meetings from the law building to the Student Union, as the rowdy meetings often disturbed classes and other students at work in the building. The members, standing on the precedent that the organization had always met in the law building, steadfastly refused to move their headquarters. The faculty of the law school would often go to such extremes as barring the door, but the resolute members would crawl through the lower windows and hold their meeting in triumph.

When Dean Hildebrand began to pressure the group to make the move, the members voted to send Connally to the dean to represent their views. They armed him with their most persuasive speeches, and expected him to return victorious, but Connally told them that he had discussed the issue with Dean Hildebrand and was convinced that it would be a good idea if they moved. With the typical high emotions of young orators, the members were incensed that their chosen advocate had "lost his case" and had given in to the administration without a fight. They dubbed their president John "Bow Down"[3] Connally, and among the members of the society the name stuck for the remainder of his term of office.

In his race for a seat on the Student Assembly, Connally's name appeared last on the ballot. Two seats were open, and others filing for the position were Jack Plunket,

3. A reference to Connally's use of "Bowden" as his middle name.

Charles C. McDougall, John Dawson, and Bill Francis. Connally refused to go on record on the important issue of censorship of the student newspaper, the *Daily Texan*, a recurring battle that the student body had to fight every ten years or so. Most of the candidates came out against censorship, and the majority of the students at the university voted against any form of censorship. With the backing of his law fraternity, Connally won a seat on the assembly with 210 votes, second to Francis' 236 votes.

With spring in the air, the Forty Acres was again alive with political action. On February 21, 1937, the *Daily Texan*'s political column "Viewing with Alarm" noted that seven campus politicians had been bitten with the vice-presidential bug. In the "independent" camp there were three possible candidates, the first and foremost being John Connally backed by Delta Theta Phi legal fraternity, which was also backing Jake Pickle for president of the Student Assembly. Quoted the *Daily Texan*: "John Connally is generally well-liked with strong Independent support, fairly strong sorority support, and scattered fraternity support. And with Pickle behind him, clique clouds would not be too rosy."

Pickle, now a United States congressman, was Connally's political mentor during their university days, and the two young men helped pull together an effective "political machine" based on their legal fraternity, called by its members "Dollar Thirty Five." Pickle and Connally, along with many of their fraternity brothers, had worked to elect Jimmie Brinkley, an independent, defeating the fraternity-backed candidate the year before.

When Jake Pickle decided to run for president of the Student Assembly, he appointed Connally as his campaign manager and began to work actively to garner the votes of all students—fraternity and independent alike—on the campus. The fraternity groups were divided into two cliques —the "Big Clique" and the so-called "People's Party." The fraternities had a candidate, Ramsey Moore, that they were pushing for the presidency, and Pickle chose to run as an independent. Robert Eckhardt, now a congressman from

Houston, also decided to run as an independent candidate, and Pickle soon realized that the independent votes would be split. Knowing that the two independent candidates would be pitted against one fraternity man, Connally advised Pickle to call for a referendum that provided for a runoff between the two candidates with the most votes.

Congressman Pickle recalls that many students on the campus began to feel that the fraternity and sorority vote was being used to manipulate the student presidential election, and, of course, his campaign workers stressed the need for an impartial administration. "We found out early in life that an issue was sometimes more important than the candidate, and certainly if you put them together, you could make a winning combination. We passed out petitions in every dormitory, every boarding house, every beanery—we even invaded some of the sororities and fraternities. We found out who had mimeograph machines hidden in what basement, who could write, and who could work, and who were the best contacts. We did such a good job that we had the campus seething by election day. We had to have a runoff!"

Campaigning was hot and heavy in the final days before the election, with Pickle calling for a reconciliation between fraternities and independents and for responsibility in the student government. Speaking on Pickle's behalf on April 4, Connally stated that, "Everyone who knows Pickle knows that a fair and impartial administration will be seen." When the general election results were in, Pickle and Moore faced a runoff, with Pickle winning a plurality. In the runoff election, held on April 9, Pickle was elected with a total of 2,992 votes.

Pickle's administration was considered an excellent one, and Delta Theta Phi, wanting to use the power base they had formed for Pickle's campaign, chose Connally to make the next president's race. Pickle recalls that Connally had wanted to run when Pickle ran, but that he told Connally that he was the better man to run first. "I had served on the Student Assembly from Arts and Sciences, and I had also served as chairman of the Judiciary Committee. I had two campus-wide elections under my belt, and Connally had none. I was at my peak on campus, and I had to run then or not at all. I had decided earlier that I wouldn't run because I wanted to go on to law school and I didn't think I had time for any more politics on campus. But the fraternity thought I was the logical one to run, as I had branched out from my independent stand to gather in some fraternity support.''

When the question came up the next term as to whom Delta Theta Phi would support, Pickle did not recommend that Connally run, although many students would later accuse Connally of ''sliding into office on Pickle's coattails.'' Pickle remembers: ''I did not hand pick Connally. You don't hand pick John Connally. In fact, I felt it would be very difficult to run another person from the same organization for the same office two years in a row. It had never been done. I questioned whether we could do it. But we had the organization, we had the contacts, and we had the candidate. And John wanted to run. He said, 'We can beat them. I don't care if any organization has never run two candidates in a row and won. I can beat them!' I finally said, 'Well, all right. Let's go! Let's do it!' And Connally and I switched roles. This time I served as his campaign manager.''

Once again the Pickle-Connally machine rolled into action. ''We divided the campus into sections like precincts,'' Pickle recalls, ''and we covered the campus thoroughly. We out-organized and we out-politicked the opposition.'' Pickle attributes much of the success of the campaign to Connally's leadership abilities. ''John was then a natural leader. He'll make up his mind about something, and he'll have strong feelings about it, and he'll be positive about his position. He was positive that we could stir up the campus about my election, and he was positive that he could win the race for president. He became the leader of our group, and he did it without being just a 'hail-fellow-well-met.' ''

On March 19, 1938, Connally announced for president and was endorsed by Pickle. The political editor of the *Daily Texan*, under the picture of Mr. Manglewit, the stereotyped Southern politician with plantation hat and cigar, editorialized that, "Mr. Connally is the first presidential candidate to announce who is sponsored by a political machine. Mr. Jake Pickle is hoping to give the Old Guard a real battle in the race. . . . Mr. Pickle resents any implication that this organization and the Outlaws are all together in blissful union. But the fact remains that from those fraternities Mr. Pickle expects to get a good many votes. Add to them the faithful Little Campus crowd and the Inter-City Council, and, political organization or no, there's a lot of votes tied to Mr. Pickle's coattails. Which means that Mr. Connally will be a powerful presidential candidate."

The race began early to shape up between Connally and fraternity candidate Tom Law, son of an English professor at the university and later a prominent Fort Worth attorney. The *Daily Texan* commented that Law "dances well and may be seen frequently at some of the nicer night spots. His French is terrible." On March 29 the *Daily Texan*'s political editor also reported that, "The two early season strong candidates . . . are beating the bushes for votes . . . waging stiff campaigns. . . . Mr. Law [Tom] is in a secure position with the Old Guard behind him, but Mr. Connally [John] has Mr. Jake Pickle working for him which is of no less consideration." Later the political editor was forced to apologize to the Inter-City Council for implying that candidate Connally had their official sanction.

As the campaigning continued, Pickle called a meeting of the Student Assembly to consider a law to provide for a bond of from five to ten dollars that each candidate filing for a political office would post to signify that he was a serious candidate. The money would be used to defray the costs of election expenses, but critics of the proposal charged that it was a political move to keep the number of candidates filing for the president's race to a minimum and give Connally fewer opponents to beat. On March 30 the Student Assembly passed a law providing that each candidate was required to post a five-dollar bond to be forfeited if he did not poll at least two-hundred votes. However, on April 3, the Judicial Council by unanimous vote declared both the five-dollar fee and the bond unconstitutional.

Creekmore Fath, leader of the Associated Independent organization, also accused the Pickle-Connally machine of another political move designed to give their candidate a clear advantage. Fath claimed that Pickle and Sally Lipscomb, secretary of the Student Assembly, were trying to keep Connally in first place on the ballot by refusing to put back on the ballot names of several candidates who had filed, removed their names, and then decided to reenter. When the official ballot was printed, Connally's name appeared first in the field of seven candidates.

When the votes in the general election were counted on April 5, 1938, Connally came in second with 2,692 to Tom Law's 2,710 to pair the two in a runoff election. The vote was the largest in any student election in the history of the university.

In the April 8 runoff election, the efforts of the Pickle-Connally machine paid off. Connally won the race by a 1,100-vote margin over Law. One Connally observer recalls that after Connally was elected president a large party was held at the Varsity Inn. Connally merely sat at the end of the table, but refused to join in the traditional merrymaking. The observer says that many of the students who had worked for Connally felt that he lacked appreciation for their campaign efforts.

Connally received the happy news on April 27 that the Student Assembly had voted a thirty-dollar-a-month salary to the president, and many students felt that Connally ran for the presidency because of the salary. On April 29 Connally was officially installed as president of the Student Assembly and received new cowboy spurs as a symbol of the office.

At the end of the spring semester, Connally was elected one of the twenty-five outstanding members of the class of 1938. The office of Student Assembly president required a good deal of time, and Congressman Pickle recalls that both he and Connally had to supplement their incomes by working, Pickle by providing milk for his dormitory and Connally by hawking mints and gum. Connally had more financial help from home, however; ''If Pickle had a nickle, Connally had a quarter,'' Pickle states.

Meanwhile, Idanell's picture regularly graced the *Daily Texan*'s pages and she was elected to Tri Delta's ''Who's Who in Texas.'' In a preferential poll conducted by the Student Assembly on March 22, 1938, Idanell was listed on a five-name ballot for the runoff election for Sweetheart of the University. In addition to Idanell, Jetty De Long, Elva Johnson,[4] Mary Jo McAngus, and Lois Sager were candidates for the honor. After the runoff election, Idanell's victory was announced at the annual Round-Up Revue and Ball on April 7. On November 23, 1938, Connally and Idanell led the Grand March at the Thanksgiving Ball, held in Gregory Gymnasium. As president and sweetheart of the university, the *Daily Texan* reported that, ''To the coast-to-coast music of Anson Weeks and his orchestra, Connally with Miss Brill at his arm will climax the many-sided array of entertainments.''

One of the highlights of Connally's term of office was the *Daily Texan*'s campaign to clean up campus eating establishments. Working in cooperation with the State Health Department, the campus newspaper launched a crusade that investigated and led to twenty-one fraternity houses and restaurants bringing their kitchens in line with acceptable health standards.

For several months, The University of Texas had been without a president, and with the new year the board of regents announced their choice. On January 3, 1939, Dr. Homer Price Rainey was named president, inaugurating another era that was marked by political infighting between the members of the legislature and the university. It ended in 1944 with the removal of Rainey and the university's subsequent censure by the American Association of University Presidents. However, Rainey came to the university highly

4. Elva Johnson later married Jack S. Josey, Connally's political supporter and friend. The Joseys were among the guests the Connallys entertained in 1972 at their Jamaica home.

honored, and Connally welcomed him on behalf of the student body, "With such an administrator as Dr. Rainey for President, The University of Texas should make great progress in achieving national leadership along educational lines." Another exciting event took place on the university campus in January 1939, when Governor-elect W. Lee "Pappy" O'Daniel chose to have his inauguration in Memorial Stadium with flags flying and bands playing the strains of the melody he had composed, "Beautiful Texas."

In commenting on university personalities in his political column "Gone with Guinn," carried in the *Daily Texan*, Jack Guinn wrote, ". . . the University is interesting because it has some interesting citizenry. Take Mr. John Connally now. Mr. John Connally is the president of the Student Assembly. Mr. Connally presides when great and weighty matters are decided by that sterling body, the Assembly. Mr. Connally is indispensable. . . . Next we come to Miss Idanell Brill, who is the Sweetheart of the University. We have not yet decided the duties of the Sweetheart of the University in an organization this big, but we do know about the Sweetheart election. It is an annual affair in which women are given a chance to be women and slander each other and always, they say, the most deserving girls win. Then they all sigh and sit back and say, 'Gawd, how'd she ever get it?' "

On March 2, 1939, the anniversary of Texas' independence from Mexico, banner headlines in the campus newspaper carried the words, "John Connally Resigns as Students' Association President." In announcing his resignation, Connally cited the need to devote more time to "my sadly-neglected studies." Pickle recalls that Connally did not make the necessary grade points to hold the office. Connally announced that he was severing all official connection with any extra-curricular activity on campus and that he handed in his official resignation "with a feeling of bravery that I do not possess. I do so with a reluctance that only I can feel. Perhaps I can best explain by quoting Etan at Verdun, 'Here I stand, I can do no other.' " Connally stated that the office of president had taken so much time that he would need an extra year to finish law school. He cited his ambitions in taking office "'. . . to help in any small way that I could the molding of a greater University of Texas spirit and in whatever way I could to create a greater feeling of unity between the students themselves, and between the students and faculty.'' Connally also felt that "serving as your president [is] the greatest privilege of my life.''

In resigning as president of the Curtain Club to run for the presidency of the Student Assembly and again in resigning as president of the Students' Association, John Connally set a pattern he would revert to more than once in his political career. The challenge was presented to him, and in his own mind he met it. When the challenge no longer existed, Connally lost interest. The cause was important; the job uninteresting.

—*Mitch Greene*

"The Art of Achieving the Possible"

5

With his campaign for president of the Student Assembly and the taste of power the office brought him, John Connally was dedicated to a life in politics. His break came when he applied for a job through the state administrator of the National Youth Administration in Texas, an up-and-coming young politician named Lyndon B. Johnson. Sam Fore Jr., publisher of the Floresville newspaper, recommended Connally to Johnson as one of the college boys who needed a job to help him stay in school. With Johnson's help, Connally got a job working in the Supreme Court Library at the capitol in Austin, stacking and dusting books for seventeen cents an hour. "I had my eye on him partly because Mr. Sam Fore of Floresville had told me about him and thought so highly of him and his family," former President Johnson recalled.

When Johnson ran for Congress from the Tenth District in 1937, Connally helped out in the special election by running errands, stuffing envelopes, and doing other jobs a young college student could handle. Johnson liked Connally and recalled that, "I looked him over and decided to bring him to Washington as my Congressional secretary in the early part of 1939. I had been Congressman Kleberg's[1] secretary myself a few years before, so I thought I knew what qualities to look for in hiring a man of my own. That would include youthful aggressiveness, a dedication to work, accuracy in performing your work, and the ability to get along with people. He had all of these qualities in great abundance."

Connally gained additional experience in 1938 by campaigning for railroad commissioner Ernest O. Thompson in his gubernatorial race against W. Lee O'Daniel. Connally made his first political radio speech over station KNOW in Austin on behalf of Thompson. The statewide broadcast was timed with the traditional Fourth of July political activities across the state. Connally wrote to the Floresville newspaper imploring his friends in Wilson County to back Thompson's candidacy. In the release printed in the Floresville newspaper, Connally stated that Thompson is "one of the finest characters I ever knew— a clean man and a straight thinker. A man with a brilliant mind, wonderful education, and a wealth of experience. He talks horse sense and knows what it is to work hard to make a success. He is one of the hardest working men I have ever known—never stops. He is tolerant in his thinking, fair in all his dealings and positive in his convictions. He is truly a friend of the LITTLE MAN, and the farmers and stockmen of our state will have a real friend in Austin."

In 1939, when Johnson offered a Washington job to Connally, he dropped out of law school, deferring his final

1. Kleberg won a special election on November 24, 1931, to fill the vacancy caused by the death of Harry Wurzbach, a Republican from Seguin, in the United States House of Representatives. Johnson had managed the successful state senate campaign of Wally Hopkins of Seguin, and Hopkins asked Kleberg to take Johnson to Washington with him. Johnson stayed on Kleberg's staff until 1935, when President Roosevelt appointed Johnson director of the National Youth Administration in Texas. He quit the youth administration in 1937 to run for Congress in a special election created by the death of James Buchanan.

examinations until 1941.[2] Connally had already passed the Texas State Bar exam on December 19, 1938, but had not completed his course work. Connally became secretary to Congressman Johnson in August 1939, serving until February 1941. He later served as Johnson's administraive assistant for ten months when Johnson was elected to the United States Senate in 1949.

Former President Johnson recalled that from 1938 on, Connally ''either managed or worked actively in every campaign I ever ran, right up to 1964. . . . He is ambitious but has never let it get the best of him. He is the type of man people come to for help and advice, rather than the other way around. He doesn't ask for much but lets it come to him. . . . He has gained a reputation for standing up for his views. . . . He understands the art of achieving the possible.''

Working for Congressman Johnson proved invaluable to the young politician, and campaigning for the congressman gave Connally a knowledge of Texans around the state. He learned which newspaper publishers he could count on. He also learned the value of meeting people, and he perfected his talent for remembering their names. Congressman Pickle believes that during Connally's years in Washington with Johnson he learned how to organize and carry out a political campaign. ''I guess Mr. Johnson was the best organizer this country's ever seen. Connally learned how to answer letters, how to get things done, how never to take 'no' for an answer, and how to keep working at politics until all hours. In addition, Connally made contacts throughout this district. He also made contact with every congressman in Washington.''

Congressman Johnson returned to Austin with Connally during the Christmas season of 1940 to serve as best man when John Connally married Idanell Brill at the First Methodist Church in Austin on the evening of December

2. Connally obtained an LLB degree from The University of Texas in August 1941. The grade requirement for graduation from law school was lowered from 70 to 65 in 1941.

21. A letter written by Connally from Washington to his parents in Floresville, dated November 11, 1940, and in the possession of Blanche Connally Kline, tells of the young couple's marriage plans.

Dearest Mother and Dad,

You don't know how sorry I am that I don't write more. I know that I should and I really want to, because I think of you so much. It's just awfully hard ever to find time to do anything. That's hard to believe, I know. Idanell has been here, as you know, and I think for the first time she knows and understands how it is. She worked with us in the national campaign for two weeks. I was hoping that I could go home when they . . . went, but no such luck. Someday, however, I'm going to get there. I would very much like to see you and be with you and talk to you, but it seems that I'll have to write what I want to say.

Idanell and I plan to be married sometime in December—about the 21st—that I suppose is no great surprise to you, because I have been going with her for five years. I am sure of what I'm doing—so don't worry on that score, and I think she is equally certain —I just wanted you to know. First, naturally I hope that you approve and there's just one thing I want to ask of you all that I can't of anyone else—We are going to have a church wedding—a rather large one I imagine, and we no doubt will be ''present poor,'' so don't plan to give us anything like that.

If you do want to give us anything, just give us the money. What with a ring, a big wedding, etc., that will be more welcome than anything else, because we will probably have much more than we can ever use since we won't be able to settle down anywhere right now anyway! Will you do that?

And, Mom, please have Carmen, Mel, or someone to list all the kinfolks on both sides of the family and their addresses and send the list to Idanell at 713 West 14th Street, Austin, Texas, so that she can send them invitations. Do this as soon as you can.

Tell Blanche I got her letter, and I sure did love to hear from her just as I always love to get letters from you all. I would give anything to be home with you, and you just wait til I get there. I am going to give every one of you a big hug and kiss, including "Toota" [Wayne] and Dad. Tell my "Toota" he'd better have those horses in shape, cause I'm going to ride 'em plenty. You all be sweet and write me when you can, cause I love all of you and miss you more than I can tell you—but who wouldn't miss the finest Mom and Dad in the world?

Love,
Johnnie

On April 21, 1965, speaking to the Council of Bishops of the Methodist Church in Houston, Connally recalled for Bishop Kenneth Pope his marriage ceremony. "Dr. Pope may not remember every particular as well as I do, but more than twenty-four years ago he married Idanell Brill and John Connally. Dr. Pope, you might be pleased to know that the last time I checked, the knot was still secure."

In February 1941 Connally returned to Austin to enter private law practice. On March 18, 1941, he was appointed to the Board of Directors of the Lower Colorado River Authority, serving until he resigned on December 31, 1946. Jack Guinn, one of Connally's classmates at The University of Texas, wrote a profile of the youngest member of the LCRA board for the Austin *American*, speculating on Connally's political future.

John Bowden Connally, Jr. is six feet, two inches tall, has a wealth of black hair that waves over his head and ends in a senatorial twist at his neck. He probably needs glasses, because his eyes squint behind their shaggy black brows. He has a heavy beard, and although he keeps it cut, its blackness gives him that heavy-jowled look that belies his age, which is only 24. . . . There are a few who say the gentleman will run for Congress if Johnson seeks the senator's place again next election and there are those who say he won't.

45

For himself, Connally looks solemn and nods, "No," but at the same time looking reflectively at the toes of the cowboy boots he wears—probably remembering that at one time he wanted to be a Texas Ranger—but became an actor instead.

With the Japanese attack on Pearl Harbor and the United States' entry into World War II, Connally, a member of the naval reserve, volunteered for action. Connally was assigned to a desk job in Washington doing labor relations work and then in the office of undersecretary of the Navy James Forrestal. Speaking to a gathering in Texas when Connally was governor, President Johnson recalled that when Connally boarded a plane to join an aircraft carrier, Johnson had cried because he was afraid he would never see his friend again. Looking at Governor Connally, Johnson said, "I think you are the only man who ever made me cry. I never loved you more than I do now."

In March 1943 Connally went to North Africa as part of the staff of Robert Murphy, counselor to General Eisenhower. When he returned to Washington, he worked three months with the petroleum reserves corporation on an important Saudia Arabia oil deal. Connally continued to push for active duty, and drew an assignment for brief temporary duty on the *Franklin* in the radar room. In April 1945 he was assigned to the aircraft carrier *Essex*, a flagship for a task force of five carriers operating off the Japanese coast in the North Pacific.

Connally's job aboard the *Essex* was group combat information center officer, directing the fighter planes in actual combat. The *Essex* rode out three typhoons and a hit by a Japanese suicide plane. One day the admiral in charge of the squadron sent every fighter he could spare to escort a bombing mission. No planes were left to protect the task force, when suddenly Japanese bombers attacked in mass. Connally grabbed the microphone of the radio set and gave the Navy distress call, "Hey Rube!" The fighter planes immediately turned back to protect the endangered task force. The day was saved by Connally's quick action, and in the ensuing battle, Navy ace Commander David McCampbell chalked up nine Japanese planes to his credit.

This may have been the only time during World War II that the emergency distress call, ''Hey Rube! was actually given. If Connally had given the distress signal and had called the fighters back for less than an emergency, he could have been disgraced and court martialed from the Navy. Fortunately, his quick thinking and decision won him the Legion of Merit with nine battle stars and the Bronze Star, including a commendation from Admiral T. L. Sprague, who said that his ''work was in great part responsible for the success of the Task Group.''

Connally had risen in rank from ensign to lieutenant commander in the Navy when he was mustered out from the *U.S.S. Bennington* in November 1945. He returned to Austin to settle down to a new career in the radio industry. During his college years, he had worked for radio station KNOW as an announcer and disc jockey for their program devoted to campus activities at The University of Texas. When he returned to Austin, he worked for the Johnson-owned radio station KTBC. Then he and a group of ten veterans[3] organized radio station KVET in Austin, and Connally served as president and manager of the station for three years.

Connally borrowed $25,000 from the Capital National Bank in Austin to bankroll his share of the station. By law, radio station KVET was required to be in competition with KTBC, owned and controlled by the Johnsons. However, one of the principals in the Capital National Bank was Herman Brown, part owner of Brown and Root Construction Company in Houston, the primary financers of Johnson's campaigns for Congress and the presidency. One of Johnson's political opponents, Hardy

3. Among the organizers of the radio station were Connally's brother Merrill; Frank Yeagley, electronics engineer; J. C. Kellam, executive manager of radio station KTBC for the Johnsons; Sherman Birdwell, who became a member of the Texas Employment Commission and also worked for Johnson; Willard Deason, who managed the station after Connally retired; Pickle, who served as business manager; R. L. Phinney, former Austin postmaster and district collector of the Internal Revenue Service, who served as assistant manager and treasurer; Connally; and Edward Clark, Austin lawyer who referred to himself as a ''Johnson Democrat'' so long as the former president was alive.

Hollers, charged during Johnson's 1946 campaign for Congress that Johnson had cooperated with his (Johnson's) former associates in founding KVET. Although Connally made radio speeches defending Johnson against many of Hollers' charges, he never mentioned this one.

Pickle recalls that each of the men borrowed their funds and that the group spent some $40,000 to $45,000 to get on the air. "It didn't cost as much to go on the air then . . . that (sum) included buying the land, building a new radio facility, and installing billowing circular plywood forms that would send the sound off and back. We spent more money on our station than we should have, but we built a nice station. We all worked for practically nothing. My salary as business manager was $250 a month. I think Connally got a little more, but not a whole lot. The first couple of years that the station operated, we drew very little out, but we met our payments. And after the outbreak of the Korean War, business became better and we moved forward."

In a speech to the Texas Association of Broadcasters in Austin, Connally told of almost missing the opening of the new station. Austin lawyer Ed Clark had bet Mayor Tom Miller that Connally wouldn't make it on time for the formal opening, and Connally recalled that, "In the early fall of that year (1946) the lights burned late on Bradford Alley. All of us worked night and day to be ready for the day when KVET would take the air for the first time. . . . That morning finally came, just a few hours after we had called it a night. There at the front door well before six a.m., the designated air time, was Mayor Tom Miller, along with most of my associates. Everyone was there except John Connally, who had the only key. He had overslept—and KVET, after all our careful planning, went on the air late!" Connally had gone to bed at two in the morning, and had set his alarm to wake him at five thirty. When the alarm rang, Connally turned it off and went back to sleep. When his wife Nellie woke him at six, he sprinted for the station and arrived eleven minutes late, attired in a battle jacket, pants, and his house slippers.

When Lyndon Johnson went to the Senate in 1949, Connally went along as his administrative assistant, serving from January to October. Connally was the junior assistant, with Arthur Perry, distant relative of the Texas writer George Sessions Perry, serving as senior assistant to U.S. Senator Tom Connally. Walter Jenkins, Connally's classmate at the university, headed Johnson's Washington office staff. Margaret Mayer reported in the Austin *American,* "'Does anybody know where John is?' is a kind of joke among Lyndon Johnson forces. It refers, of course, to John Connally who may be easier to see than Harry Truman but is certainly harder to find and just as busy."

Connally resigned as Johnson's administrative assistant to return to Austin as a member of the law firm of Powell, Wirtz, and Rauhaut. His primary work with the law firm was to serve as legal counsel for the Rural Electrical Cooperatives, smoothing the passage of the Rural Telephone Cooperative Enabling Act of 1950 through the Texas legislature. In recalling the battle to get the legislation passed, Connally, speaking before the Natural Rural Electric Cooperative Association in 1964, stated, "Since I have been Governor, there have been some tough fights in the Legislature, such as regulating small loans and passing an equitable municipal annexation law. I got my training for these struggles when we battled for that telephone co-op bill fourteen years ago."

With his work for Powell, Wirtz, and Rauhaut, Connally once again aligned himself with Johnson supporters, as the partners of the firm were close both to Johnson and to George and Herman Brown, financers of Johnson's campaigns. (Ben Powell Sr. had previously served on the Texas Court of Civil Appeals.) In 1937 Alvin J. Wirtz,[4] a state senator, had arranged a meeting between a group of public utility owners and representatives of the Lower Colorado River Authority and Congressman Johnson to work toward harnessing the lower Colorado River

4. Lyndon Johnson once stated that Alvin Wirtz had taught him more about people than anyone he had ever known.

and bringing electric power to the small rural farmers throughout the area. Johnson's promotion of the LCRA helped make it one of the largest rural electrification developments in the United States. Wirtz remained one of Johnson's closest political advisors, and Johnson assisted in having Wirtz appointed as undersecretary of the Interior in 1940.

While Connally was with the law firm, he gained full exposure to corporate law, and at one time served as an attorney in conjunction with the law firm of Looney, Clark, and Morehead for Brown and Root, Inc., in their suit against the Texas State Federation of Labor. The construction company alleged that the labor organization had been in conspiracy against the Texas "right-to-work act" in discriminating against non-union labor. They also alleged that labor had made use of such illegal measures as secondary boycotts, pickets, and unfair lists. In addition, Connally expanded his growing acquaintance in both state and national political circles. Politicians began to recognize Connally as Johnson's right-hand man and accepted the fact that when Connally spoke, he reflected both the political views and the feelings of Lyndon Johnson.

The Texas delegation at the Democratic National Convention in 1940. Connally stands directly behind the Texas placard, House Speaker Sam Rayburn is in center, and Robert Strauss at right.

—*Texas State Archives*

"Have You Gone Over to the Enemy?"

6

Throughout the 1940s and into the 1960s Connally worked in Johnson's campaigns and at cementing and maintaining Johnson's contacts in Texas. By 1948 Connally had become one of Johnson's most valued advisers and a kingpin in the Johnson organization. In 1948 the Austin *Statesman* published a profile on Connally describing the way that Johnson worked on the young politician to bring him over to his side. If Connally failed to warm up to Johnson's suggestions, Johnson would begin to pace the floor, call on his other lieutenants to back him up, and make sly references to Connally's courage. Finally, if Connally still held firm, Johnson would ask, "Are you working with me, or have you gone over to the enemy?" The article concluded: "Through all this Connally keeps a cool head, until Johnson, failing to overpower his friend with arguments, stomps out of the room in high dudgeon. This doesn't bother Connally anymore. He has learned that a few days later Johnson will think it all a huge joke—and brag to friends how Connally set him back in the traces."

Connally ran Johnson's campaign for the Senate in 1948 that centered around the controversial Ballot Box 13 in Jim Wells County. Although Johnson carried the election by eighty-seven votes, winning for himself the nickname "Landslide Lyndon," the election tabulation remained in question for days and the State Democratic Executive Committee finally voted 29 to 28 to award Johnson the election and send him to the Senate. Connally later defended Johnson and the allegations that he had stolen the election with the comment, "All of the conversation about fraud and so forth was ridiculous."

The 1948 election for the Senate seat vacated by W. Lee O'Daniel saw Texas split along conservative and liberal lines, basically revolving around economic issues. The Texas Regulars in 1944 had splintered from the Democratic party in opposition to the New Deal and to the renomination of President Roosevelt. The "Regulars," composed of the extreme right-wing conservatives within the Democratic party, appeared on the ballot, but Roosevelt carried Texas. When former university president Dr. Homer P. Rainey, fired from his post by the conservative board of regents for his "super-liberalism," ran for governor in 1946, the former Texas Regulars were among his most vehement opponents.

O'Daniel had defeated Johnson in a special election in 1941 for the Senate seat vacated by the death of Senator Morris Sheppard, and Johnson was determined to win the 1948 contest. Johnson had gone into the Senate race in 1941 with Roosevelt's blessing, and had the tag of "New Deal" firmly applied to his political and economic views. His opponent in the 1948 race was the conservative, wartime governor of Texas, Coke Stevenson, called "Calculatin' Coke" for his habit of pondering decisions while puffing on his pipe. The campaign revolved around the issue of federal programs at the state level and the two candidates' stands on Taft-Hartley labor law, prohibiting the closed shop. Stevenson chose to run on his record and refused to comment on his stand on Taft-Hartley, while Johnson openly stood on his voting record for the law.

With Connally running the campaign for Johnson, the candidate swooped across the state by helicopter,[1] often surprising rural inhabitants by appearing "out of the blue" for the typical Johnson vigorous handshake and campaign oratory. Stevenson ran a rather lackluster campaign, confident of his ability to garner the conservative vote. With the primary vote in, Stevenson led Johnson by a vote of 477,077 to 405,617 and, with no clear majority, a runoff election was called for under Texas law. New Deal and Fair Deal politicians across the state worked tirelessly in Johnson's behalf, while Stevenson continued to bank on the anti-New Deal sentiment and the conservative vote across the state.

The runoff election was held on August 28, and for days the results were in doubt. Returns continued to give first one candidate a lead and then another. When Johnson went on the radio on September 2 with his victory speech, the Stevenson forces erupted, challenging the vote and crying "fraud." The controversy centered around the South Texas vote, an area predominantly Mexican American, where the vote was controlled by George Parr, the self-styled "Duke of Duval." Parr's political fiefdom, inherited from his father, former state senator Archie Parr, extended throughout Jim Wells, Brooks, Starr, and Duval counties. The first vote from the Twenty-seventh Senatorial District showed Stevenson ahead, but a "corrected vote" reported on September 3, showed Johnson with 202 additional votes and Stevenson with one additional vote in Precinct 13 in Jim Wells County. The "corrected vote" gave Johnson the eighty-seven vote lead he needed to win the election.

With the State Democratic Executive Committee meeting in Fort Worth within the week to certify the nominees to appear on the ballot for the general election in November, Stevenson challenged the vote. Vann Kennedy,

1. This was the first instance of a helicopter being used in a Texas political campaign.

secretary of the committee, said the returns would be "checked, double-checked, and rechecked." Connally went to San Diego, seat of the Parr empire, and Stevenson and his forces arrived to check the poll lists and the election returns throughout the district. Parr claimed that he had no knowledge of any election irregularities and that the election was "as clean an election as had ever been held." The Stevenson forces hurried into Jim Wells County to find the poll lists locked in the vault of the Texas State Bank, controlled by the "Duke of Duval." However, officials of the Jim Wells County Democratic Executive Committee reported to Stevenson that the 202 names reported as Johnson votes in the "corrected" totals had been written in alphabetical order in blue ink, while the names on the original list were in black.

As Parr's forces guarded the entrance to the bank with rifles, Governor Stevenson called on Texas Ranger Captain Frank Hamer to back up his campaign workers, Kellis Dibrell and Jim Gardner, in obtaining the poll lists. When the governor and Hamer, noted for his daring exploits in running down Clyde Barrow and Bonnie Parker, moved through the crowds surrounding the bank, the Ranger captain told the group "Git!" and they "got." Hamer ordered the armed men at the bank to allow Stevenson's men to enter the bank and inspect the poll lists without taking notes or removing them from the premises.

Stevenson's forces began checking the names in dispute, claiming that some of the voters' "last known address was the cemetery" and that many swore they had never voted for either candidate. Stevenson moved to call a meeting of the County Democratic Executive Committee with the hope of having Ballot Box 13 thrown out and his margin again restored. Connally immediately informed Johnson of the move, and Johnson obtained an injunction from Judge Roy Archer in Austin to block the meeting. Johnson said that the FBI would be the "disinterested and efficient agency" to make an investigation of the election returns, and Stevenson in turn accused Johnson of using "unusual proceedings" designed to keep the truth from coming out. The next step for Johnson was to persuade the State Democratic Executive Committee, meeting in Fort Worth with chairman Robert W. Calvert presiding, to accept the report of its subcommittee in Austin, which had ruled in Johnson's favor.

The committee's convention proceedings form one of the most dramatic episodes in Texas' flamboyant political history. One of Johnson's representatives before the com-committee was Jerome Sneed. When Sneed collapsed on the floor of Fort Worth's Blackstone Hotel, he signed his proxy over to former State Senator Alvin J. Wirtz. Former Governor James Allred came to Fort Worth to work the floor for Johnson, and former Governor Dan Moody flew into Fort Worth to mastermind Stevenson's strategy. Connally and the other Johnson lieutenants feverishly worked the meeting, presenting the Johnson case and trying to persuade the committee members to their point of view.[2] Charles I. Francis, former member of the legal firm of Vincent, Elkins, Weems, and Searls, lawyer for Brown and Root, and organizers of the gigantic Texas Eastern Transmission Corporation, argued the Johnson case before the delegation, with Austin attorney John D. Cofer pitching in. Moody and State Senator C. C. Small led the Stevenson forces. When the vote was taken on a roll call, the committee was split with 28 votes for Johnson and 28 for Stevenson. Mrs. Seth W. Dorbandt of Conroe attempted to withdraw her vote for Johnson in an attempt to throw the issue into the courts. C. C. Gibson, committeeman from Amarillo, made a dramatic appearance to break the tie. Gibson claimed he had been out of the room on the roll call, and shouted up to give Johnson the tie-breaking vote. And the convention awarded Johnson the nomination by a vote of 29 to 28. Johnson stated that his heart was "so full of gratitude there is no room for bitterness."

Johnson's forces immediately reported the official results to the secretary of state in Austin, so that Johnson's

2. Roy Evans, former president of the Texas AFL-CIO, recalls that, "He [Connally] was Johnson's bag man that year, but in a convention he was just Johnson's lieutenant. He was the person in charge of lining up people on the various issues. He was very effective at it."

57

name would appear on the ballot for the general election in November. Stevenson's forces moved to have a restraining order issued by Dallas District Judge T. Whitfield Davidson. Stevenson lieutenant C. C. Renfro drove to Davidson's farm near Jefferson in East Texas, and Davidson signed the restraining order at 6:25 a.m. Off the record, Davidson suggested that both names be entered on the ballot for the November election. Stevenson agreed, but Johnson, who had fought hard for his victory, refused. When Connally, as Johnson's chief campaign aide, was asked by newspaper reporters his opinion of the restraining order, he replied that he had no statement about the new move. He said that his part in the campaign was over; that the job could be handled by the Johnson lawyers.

When a write-in campaign between the two candidates seemed inevitable, President Harry S Truman, realizing the importance of Johnson's election to his Fair Deal, invited Johnson aboard his campaign train and called for the support of Democratic leaders across the state. Johnson appealed Davidson's restraining order directly to the Supreme Court, with Abe Fortas, Charles Francis, and Thurman Arnold representing him. Justice Hugo Black handed down a decision in Johnson's favor, and his name appeared on the ballot as the Democratic nominee. Disgruntled, Stevenson advocated that all Democrats support the Republican candidate, Jack Porter, in the general election. (Stevenson also supported Jack Cox, the Republican candidate, against Connally in the gubernatorial election in 1962.)

While working as a Johnson organizer during the national Democratic convention in Chicago in 1940, Connally met Fort Worth millionaire Sid Richardson, who was to have a profound effect on his life and his career. When Alvin Wirtz died, Connally resigned from the law firm of Powell, Wirtz, and Rauhaut and went to work for Richardson as legal counsel, political adviser, and expert in governmental affairs.[3]

3. Through his association with Richardson from 1952 to 1960, Connally became a director, vice president, and secretary of Sid Richardson, Inc.; director,

In an interview with Houston *Post* reporter Louis Hofferbert in 1962, Connally recalled that, "I went to Fort Worth and visited Mr. Richardson in his rooms at the Fort Worth Club. We talked most of the night. He invited me to join his organization, and he said: 'I can hire good lawyers and good engineers and good geologists, but it is hard to hire good common sense.' At the end of our talk he told me: 'I'll pay you enough so Nellie and the kids won't go hungry, and I'll put you in the way to make some money.'"[4]

In 1962 Connally estimated the size of the Richardson estate, of which he was an independent executor, at $100 million. However, in 1948, *Fortune* magazine estimated Richardson's fortune in the over-$150 million category. Other estimates have run as high as approximately $800 million. Richardson was a self-made millionaire, who began his business career in the little cotton town of Athens, Texas. Joe Terry, longtime employee of the Richardson enterprises and close friend of Connally, recalls that the gruff and outspoken Richardson would often comment on his oil and cattle deals, "I'm nothin' but a horse trader at heart!" A national magazine reported Richardson as saying, "I'll be tradin' when they bury me."

Fort Worth's "Bachelor Billionaire" began life as the son of the owner of a large peach orchard who taught the boy to trade by skinning him in his first deal. Young Sid was fired from his first job in a cotton compress for reportedly being lazy on the job, and spent the rest of his life laboring to accumulate a fortune. Sid became a friend of the Athens' bank president's son, Clint Murchison, and the two often collaborated in later life on their business deals—ranging across the nation from the Del Mar Race Track in California to the New York Central Railroad.

vice president, and secretary of Salt Water Control, Inc.; director, executive vice president, and secretary of Sid Richardson Carbon Company. In addition, he became director of other Richardson enterprises: the Amarillo Broadcasting Company, the Valley Broadcasting Company in McAllen, and the New York Central Railroad.

4. Connally said, "When I went to work for Mr. Richardson, we agreed that we would just try it and see how it worked. If he didn't like it, he could let me go in the morning. If I didn't like it, I could leave in the afternoon."

The two country boys first worked together on oil deals that were to make their fortune, and members of the Dallas and Fort Worth business community claim they can remember when "Mr. Sid" wore patches on his pants and often borrowed carfare to make the run between Dallas and Fort Worth. One businessman summed up the careers of both men, "Sid and Clint are both nice guys. They have only the simplest, most innocent desire in the world—to make money. All they want is more."

In his early years Richardson worked as an oil-well supply salesman, soon branching out into scouting and leasing. He wildcatted his first strike in Winkler County in West Texas in 1933, lost his fortune, and returned to his first love, cattle trading. When his herd was wiped out with tick fever, he borrowed money from the Athens bank to bankroll a new start. His second big oil strike brought him into "big money," and he returned to Athens driving a Cadillac, swung around the town square for the local folks to get a good look, and marched into the bank to pay back his loan.

The depression and fluctuating oil prices threatened to wipe Richardson out from time to time, and he was often unable to pay his office rent or his dues at the Fort Worth Club. When he brought in the Keystone field in 1937, Richardson commented, "It was luck. . . . I did it by jumping up in the air six feet and holding myself up by my own bootstraps." In 1943 the famous Ellenberger lime with reserves estimated at 250 million barrels was discovered on his leases, and Richardson moved into the class of the "big rich." After the war, Richardson expanded his operations into Louisiana and brought in another strike at Cox Bay, which propelled him to the top—the richest man in America.

With his single-minded devotion to making money, Richardson often commented about women, "They're all wantin' a landin' field, but mine's fogged in." His name was often linked with that of movie actress Joan Crawford, who came to Fort Worth to see him. Richardson refused to become involved in civic endeavors and avoided publicity about his philanthropic affairs. His political interests never led to the right-wing involvement that absorbed many wealthy Texans, and he showed no affection for the late Senator Joe McCarthy. He dined several times at the White House during the Roosevelt administration, largely because of his business association with Elliott Roosevelt in a Texas radio station, and he advised President Roosevelt on oil production during World War II. Roosevelt also visited with Richardson at his St. Joseph's Island retreat in the Gulf of Mexico, near Aransas Pass.[5] Richardson maintained a warm relationship with Speaker of the U.S. House of Representatives Sam Rayburn, and through Rayburn with Johnson.

Richardson's interest in politics came through a chance meeting with General Dwight D. Eisenhower on December 12, 1941. William H. Kittrell of Dallas, a Texas Democrat, was riding with Richardson in a private drawing room on a Washington-bound train, when Eisenhower's plane was forced down. The general boarded the train, and Kittrell, who knew the general, invited him to share the drawing room, while his berth was being prepared. Later, Richardson recalled that he never realized who Eisenhower was until after they had left the train in Washington.

In 1949, when Eisenhower was president of Columbia University, he and his wife visited with Richardson on his private island. The general hunted ducks and quail, while Mrs. Eisenhower rested and wrote letters. Richardson realized Ike's potential as a presidential candidate, and flew to SHAPE headquarters in Paris early in 1952 to convince Eisenhower to run for president—as a Democrat. When Adlai Stevenson, the Democratic presidential nominee, refused to support Texas' claims to the submerged oil lands off her coast known as the "tidelands," Richardson, along with other Texas millionaires, bolted the Democratic party and went with Eisenhower, the Republican nominee. Richardson is reported to have said to Ike, "General, there's no way out. You've got to do it. I'll

5. The noted Texas author J. Frank Dobie dedicated his book *The Longhorns* to Sid Richardson, who raised Longhorn cattle on St. Joseph's Island, where he allowed Dobie to write part of his book.

go with you any way you go, but if you go as a Republican it's going to be hard.'' Richardson, along with other Texas millionaires, bankrolled Eisenhower's campaign with untold thousands of dollars. His support and that of other Democrats for Eisenhower in Texas played a significant role in Eisenhower's election. Undoubtedly, Richardson's ability to lead the wealthy conservative element in Texas toward Eisenhower influenced Connally. He knew where he could get his support to lead the conservative element in Texas into the Republican column for Richard Nixon in 1972.

Connally proved invaluable to Richardson in Washington when legislation involving oil and gas was under consideration in Congress. Texas newspapers reported that Connally was often in Washington entertaining various congressmen. Connally failed to register as a lobbyist and was criticized for his activities. Other lobbyists noted Connally's activities and that he kept a suite at the Mayflower Hotel in order to entertain. When a rumor circulated that Connally would be denounced on the Senate floor, Johnson urged him to register. Connally replied that as he had gained natural gas holdings in Texas through his association with Richardson, he was in Washington representing his own interests and was not required to register as a lobbyist for Richardson.

As majority leader, Johnson introduced a bill in the Senate that would limit federal price control on the oil and gas industry in 1956. When the bill was voted out, a Republican senator, Francis Case from South Dakota, announced that a lobbyist representing the oil industry had approached him with a $2,500-bribe to vote in favor of the bill. Eisenhower vetoed the bill and strongly condemned the actions of the oil and gas lobby.

Connally had entertained members of the oil and gas industry in the majority leader's office until Johnson could arrive on the scene, and many of the industry's people considered him one of the prime lobbyists in favor of the bill. Connally let Washington before the bribery scandal broke. Newspaper columnist Drew Pearson linked Connally to one of the lobbyists implicated in the scandal and branded Connally "one of the most brazen lobbyists in Washington for the natural-gas bill." The effects of the scandal were felt again by Connally when his appointment as secretary of the navy was before the Senate and again when he was up for confirmation as secretary of the treasury. At that time Connally told the Senate, "I had no part in the incident any more than anybody else who was interested in the oil and gas business." [6]

Connally's association with Sid Richardson also brought him into contact with the "good life," represented by Richardson, his partner and nephew Perry Bass, the Eugene Lockes, and other members of the Dallas-Fort Worth society set. The Connallys soon joined two country clubs in Fort Worth, the Ridgelea and Shady Oaks. Connally often played golf at the clubs, and Joe Terry says that, "He could be a good golfer if he worked at it." Connally often played with the bookkeepers when the Richardson employees challenged one another—the bookkeepers versus the engineers. Terry recalls that Connally played to win and was constantly challenging the other players to compete. "John is a real competitor," Terry states. "He doesn't like to lose. When he plays golf, he plays to win."

While the Connallys were living in Fort Worth, their eldest child, Kathleen, was killed. "Kay Kay," as she was affectionately called by her friends and family, was a popular and well-liked sixteen-year-old junior at Arlington Heights High School in Fort Worth. Kathleen had been dating Bobby Hale, eighteen, son of I. B. Hale, the security chief at General Dynamics, and the couple were considered extremely serious about each other. Both were described as extremely good looking and popular by their classmates and Hale had "dreamy blue eyes" according to one of his classmates.

6 .Texas Attorney General Will Wilson stated in April 1962 that Connally was one of twenty-four men chosen in 1955 by the General Gas Committee to lobby on the gas bill that Eisenhower vetoed. However, Connally remarked that he had never been employed as a lobbyist nor had he ever hired anyone to lobby.

The young couple eloped and were married on March 16, 1959, in Ardmore, Oklahoma. They had gone to Tallahassee, Florida, to "make their own way" and were living in a tiny upstairs apartment across from the Florida Supreme Court Building. At the time of Kathleen's death, Hale was employed as a $70-a-week laborer for a boat company, and Kathleen was working in a five-and-dime store. Young Hale reported to the authorities that Kathleen had discovered that she was pregnant just two weeks before her death. Both the senior Hale and Connally had visited with the young couple since their marriage, and Connally stated at the inquest that the teenagers planned to return to Fort Worth the following September to finish high school.

Kathleen, according to the report her young husband gave to the authorities, had spent several nights away from their apartment, and the night before the shooting had spent the night in the neighboring apartment of Mrs. Ethel Hawes. She wrote a note to her husband telling him that she was "hurt in mind and soul," and Mrs. Hawes had delivered the note to Hale the next morning. Mrs. Hawes convinced Kathleen to return to the apartment, and Kathleen told Hale, "Bobby, I'm sick in my mind and I need help. I know now that no one can help me." Hale later found Kathleen on the sofa with a twenty-gauge shotgun. When he tried to take the gun from her, it discharged, striking the girl. Neighbors rushed to the scene and had to restrain Hale from jumping out of the second-floor window. The neighbors called the police at 12:15 p.m., but the girl was dead on arrival at the hospital.

Both families went to Florida and attended the coroner's inquest that ruled the girl's death accidental. In the investigation no fingerprints of Hale's were found on the gun, and Hale underwent a lie detector test that indicated his innocence. Kathleen's body was returned to Fort Worth, and funeral services were held for the young girl in the First Methodist Church. Lyndon Johnson cancelled an appointment with President Eisenhower to attend the funeral and to serve as one of Kathleen's pallbearers. After the tragedy, Connally refused to talk about the accident. Members of his family say that Kathleen was the child who most resembled him. Connally turned his attention to his other children, and observers report that he is quite affectionate toward them.

Friends of Connally's remark that he always enjoys having people around him and in his home. Sarah "Chich" Terry recalls that, "They always had company. Often, after dinner, the phone would ring and it would be Nellie saying 'The coffee pot's on. Come on over.'" Many nights they would play games such as Monopoly, but often they would only talk, with their conversation interrupted by the numerous telephone calls Connally received from politicians across the country. Connally's image on the Texas political scene was exceedingly low key during the years in Fort Worth. He was decidedly Richardson's man in Washington. Often the two couples would spend the evening listening to Connally's collection of old-time classical musical records. He was particularly fond of some of the recording stars such as Enrico Caruso. He shared his interest in music with his brother Wayne, and John was unusually fond of one particular tenor. "Chich" and Nellie Connally would moan and tease him, when he would say, "Let's get out the old records and listen to some Jussi Bjoerling (which he pronounced 'Juicy Berling')."

Connally had the leisure time in Fort Worth to enjoy hunting, and he enjoyed taking the men from his office to hunt deer and dove on his brother-in-law Speedy Hicks' ranch in Bandera. This became a yearly occasion, with Connally paying the first year's lease, and the other men chipping in for the remaining years. Joe Terry has many fond memories of the days spent on the deer lease and recalls that Connally was a "great guy" to be with on a deer lease. "He had a good sense of humor and enjoyed stories around the campfire just like the rest of the boys. He's at his best when he's informal." Terry recalls that Connally's favorite job was cooking fried potatoes, which soon became the featured specialty of the deer camp. "He was a great fry cook. He fried the greasiest potatoes in the world."

65

Terry also noted that Connally was interested in everything around him. "John is an observer and interested in anything and everything. We'd be driving to deer camp, and at every farm house we'd pass along the road, he'd want to know who owned it." He admires Connally both as a friend and as a politician, citing his strongest point as his ability to understand a problem and to grasp details. "John can study a problem and understand it immediately, even if it deals with abstract engineering concepts."

Terry has often been an observer of the famous Connally temper in action. "You can ruffle his feathers right quick. If a person says something to him he doesn't like, you can almost see him react. It's almost a physical thing."

The Fort Worth years were Connally's "money making" years, and he could afford to buy the elegant, and conservative, business suits and handsome ties that he became famous for as governor. "John was always well dressed and well groomed," Terry recalls. "Everything he has is the best, and if you don't believe it, he'll convince you of it." Connally bought his first Mercedes-Benz from Harry Harris in Fort Worth. Connally was quite proud of it and demonstrated it to everyone who would ride in it. When the men were on their way up to the deer camp, he made half of them ride half way with him, and the other group ride the rest of the way. "All the way," Terry remembers, "he was touting that Mercedes. He called it 'the finest engineered car in the world.'" Connally still drives a Mercedes, with his initials "JBC" on the license plates.

John Connally and Sid Richardson shared another interest besides politics and making money—a love of the land. Richardson invested extensively in Texas ranch land and cattle. Terry recalls that once Richardson and a group of men were driving by Fairview Farms, the oil man's extensive spread. Richardson surveyed the vast panorama before him and commented, "Looks like some rich old oil man owns it." Terry says that, "Mr. Sid loved cattle and grass. He liked to see red cows on green grass." He also feels that the two men influenced each other a great deal in every facet of their lives, and Connally became Richardson's closest associate through the land and development deals that they entered into.

Richardson became the man that Connally admired most, and Connally's economic philosophy moved far to the right of Johnson's through his association with Richardson. Before breaking with the Democratic party to support Eisenhower, Richardson had backed Democratic Senator Richard Russell of Georgia against Adlai Stevenson for the nomination. Both Johnson and Connally also backed the senator against the governor from Illinois, and Connally helped set up Russell's headquarters at the national convention in Chicago in 1952. When Richardson backed Eisenhower, Johnson, however, stood by his party loyalty and went with Stevenson. Although Texas liberals suspected Connally of defecting to the GOP during the 1952 race, Connally, in 1968, maintained that he had voted for and supported Democratic nominees in all state and national races.

With Johnson a probable nominee for the 1956 presidential race, Connally swung into action. He established headquarters for Johnson at the national Democratic convention, and the television public got their first glimpse of the famous Connally ''good looks,'' when Connally placed Johnson's name in nomination before the convention. Although Johnson claimed the votes of the Texas and Mississippi delegations and a smattering of other votes, Adlai Stevenson was nominated on the first ballot.

The 1956 presidential race also saw one of the famous Johnson-Connally ''spats,'' with Connally the winner, an occasion that didn't happen often when one dealt with Lyndon Johnson. Connally had set up a rally in Texas for Johnson, and the candidate objected to the arrangements. According to Ronnie Dugger, writing in *Atlantic Monthly*, Connally told Johnson, ''It's been done and we're not going to change it. You can either pick up and go on back to the ranch or come on in. What'll it be?'' Johnson didn't like it, but he came on in.

During the 1956 national Democratic convention the liberal *Texas Observer* reported that Connally shouted into a dead microphone in an attempt to get convention chairman Sam Rayburn of Texas to recognize the Texas delegation. With Adlai Stevenson holding enough delegate votes to carry the Democratic presidential nomination, Rayburn asked if any state desired to change its votes.

"Mr. Speaker," exclaimed Connally. Rayburn looked out over the vast assembly and did not appear to hear. "Governor Adlai Stevenson having received the majority of the votes, he is the nominee of the Democratic Party," said Rayburn. A great cheer arose. "Come on, Mr. Sam," cried out [Ben] Bock [a delegate] imploringly. "The chair recognizes the governor of Oklahoma," said Rayburn. "Hell," said Bock, whose coat sleeve was pushed back to his elbow from all the banner waving. Oklahoma moved that the nomination be unanimous. John Connally put his fists to the side of his head. A delegate who did not wish to be named said: "Did you ever see anyone get his throat cut with the back edge of a knife like John Connally did?"

Dugger says that Connally nominated Johnson for president at the 1956 convention, but, when the Texas liberals offered to help, Connally replied, "We've got the votes." But, of course, they did not, says Dugger.

Even as Stevenson of Illinois and Averell Harriman of New York struggled for the presidential nomination, there were numerous potential candidates, including Johnson, for the number two spot on the Democratic ticket. Johnson said several times he was not interested in being vice president, but Felix McKnight of the Dallas *Morning News* reported that Johnson was the top choice to run with Stevenson—it was the "strength" ticket the Democrats wanted.

McKnight said Johnson "was coolly waiting around for the explosion that might send him into presidential contention." But it never came, despite Connally's pledge that Johnson would "carry forward the fight for the people without fear or hesitation, a man to rely upon for fairness and justness and equality of treatment, and a man to prove by his personal conduct that a good Democrat places his country first.'' The nomination of Stevenson apparently changed Johnson's mind about the vice presidency—McKnight said he was ''reported ready to accept the position if he is asked.'' Instead, Stevenson told the delegates he would let them choose the vice president, and Johnson pulled out of the race, dramatically throwing Texas' 56 votes to ''that gallant young sailor who bears the wounds of war, Jack Kennedy.'' However, Senator Estes Kefauver of Tennessee won the nomination.

The state Democratic convention was held in Fort Worth in September 1956, and Johnson's former press secretary George Christian remembers meeting Connally there for the first time. Price Daniel had won the Democratic nomination for governor over Ralph Yarborough by 3,171 votes out of a total of 1,392,831, and Christian recalls that Johnson ''with John Connally's very strong help, had wrested control of the precinct conventions from Governor [Allan] Shivers, the incumbent, in a very brutal, bruising intra-party struggle. The bruises were still there in September, but at that time an informal coalition was undertaken among Daniel, Speaker Rayburn, and Senator Johnson, again with John Connally's help, to maintain control of the State Democratic Executive Committee and the convention against the forces of Mrs. Frankie Randolph, who at that time was heading the so-called loyalist forces. . . . He [Connally] was pretty well the manager for Johnson in all his political endeavors, whether it was running for office or involving himself in a convention.''

Connally served as the liaison between Johnson and Rayburn and the Daniel forces, and Christian recalls a meeting at Fort Worth's Texas Hotel at the 1956 convention. The meeting had been in progress for approximately thirty minutes when Connally appeared. ''When he came in,'' Christian recalls, ''the entire room welcomed him with, 'Well, here's the real words of wisdom. . . . We're thrashing around, but let's get Connally's view.' I remember Price Daniel's delight at having him arrive at the meeting, and Price immediately said, 'Here's John Connally. Let's hear what he has to say.' His relationship to Johnson was so close that everyone recognized that John Connally not only had a great deal of influence on Johnson's decisions, but when he spoke, he pretty well represented Johnson on political matters.''

By 1960 Lyndon Johnson was a serious contender for the presidential nomination, and Theodore White, in his book on the presidential race, asserts that Connally, ''the [Senate] majority leader's most important political lieutenant for many years,'' was one of only four men, besides Johnson, who ''counted'' in developing Johnson's strategy to get the Democratic nomination for president.[7] Austin attorney and long-time Democratic worker Will Davis asserts that, ''We [meaning Connally and others] were all working hand-in-glove trying to get Johnson the nomination against [John] Kennedy.'' Although Johnson and his organization were swept away by the tide of the Kennedy momentum at the convention in 1960, Connally did not lose his spot in the Johnson chain of command. Austin lawyer Bob Armstrong, now the state land commissioner, was campaigning for the Kennedy-Johnson ticket in 1960. One day he reported on the statewide campaign to the executive board of the campaign, whose headquarters were in the Littlefield Building in Austin. It was the first time that Armstrong had a chance to talk to Connally. ''He was very assertive,'' Armstrong remembers, ''and obviously relied upon by those who were there, some of them from Johnson's organization. In fact, it was principally Johnson's organization. . . . And he [Connally] was very warm, friendly, and full of the Democratic fight at the time.''

The Texans were better prepared for the 1960 convention at Los Angeles, ''doing all we could to round up votes,'' recalls Davis, but Johnson's supporters could not ''head off the Kennedy avalanche.'' At a press conference

7. The other three that White mentioned were Speaker Sam Rayburn; George Reedy, who became President Johnson's press secretary; and Irvin Hoff, on loan from Senator Warren Magnuson of Washington.

during the convention, Connally and Mrs. India Edwards, former chairman of the women's division of the Democratic National Committee, announced that Kennedy had Addison's disease and might be physically unfit for the presidency.[8] On the eve of the opening of the preliminary session, July 4, India Edwards stated that, "Doctors have told me he [Kennedy] would not be alive if it were not for cortisone." Mrs. Edwards said that the reason for the news release was that many of the Johnson supporters objected to Kennedy's "muscle flexing in boasting about his youth."

Pierre Salinger, Kennedy's press secretary, said the statement was one of "two crises we had not anticipated . . . the accusation went far beyond the latitude of fair play, even in the rough and tumble of convention politics." Salinger explained, "I met with the senator [John Kennedy] and Bob Kennedy, and it was their inclination to ignore the charge as being unworthy of a reply. Johnson himself had issued a statement denying advance knowledge of the Connally-Edwards charge and repudiating it in the strongest possible language."

In his book critical of John Kennedy, Victor Lasky wrote that Kennedy had "inadvertently dragged in the 'health issue' by declaring that the presidency demanded 'the strength and health and vigor of young men.'" Connally, described as the executive director of the Johnson forces, said he would be happy to submit Senator Johnson's medical record since his recovery from his 1955 heart attack and to have it compared to that of Senator Kennedy or any other contenders for the presidential nomination. Kennedy's supporters labeled the health issue a last-minute desperation attempt by Johnson.

8. In Theodore Sorenson's book on Kennedy, he said Kennedy had an adrenal insufficiency, but "he [Kennedy] avoided the term Addison's disease, which, though it was no longer a barrier to full life, had a frightening sound to most laymen and was interpreted differently by different physicians. Originally, before the newer adrenal hormones were available, Addison's disease carried implications wholly absent in the senator's case—including tubercular glands, a brownish pallor, progressive deterioration and death." Sorenson said a December 1958 examination showed "satisfactory adrenal function." Robert F. Kennedy explained to reporters that the nature of his brother's illness had been adequately explained in James McGregor Burns' book, *John F. Kennedy, A Political Biography.*

Almost six months later, after President-elect Kennedy had appointed Connally as secretary of the navy at $22,000 a year, Connally denied having said that Kennedy was in poor health. Connally said the subject of Kennedy's health had come up at a press conference at the Los Angeles convention, and he had made some comment about the senator's health which, according to the Associated Press, he "would not try to reconstruct now." Connally also denied having said that the convention had been rigged for Kennedy, although political editor Allen Duckworth of the Dallas *Morning News* reported that Connally had made the charge after National Democratic Chairman Paul Butler, a Kennedy supporter, had awarded half of Texas' visitor tickets to the convention to anti-Johnson liberals. Connally said it was an attempt to pack the galleries with Kennedy boosters.[9]

Johnson, buoyed by a crowd of three thousand Texans who had donated $170,000 to his convention campaign at a June rally in Austin, had great hopes as the convention started. He told a joint news conference that Kennedy had been absent during much of the civil rights debate. Kennedy replied that Johnson had been an excellent Senate majority leader and should keep that job. The Massachusetts senator won the nomination on the first ballot—as his brothers Robert and Ted had predicted—with 806 votes, forty-five more than he needed.[10] Johnson trailed with 409.

White says the vice presidency was offered to Johnson "coldly, not as if he were the second ablest man in the party or a man fit to qualify for the presidency, but in a manner that cast it as a cold deal, an index of Kennedy's

9. Connally also proposed that state delegations be allowed to caucus by secret ballot instead of by the open ballot. He implied that Johnson would have greater strength in New York if the ballots were not counted in the presence of such pro-Kennedy New York men as Mayor Robert Wagner, Averell Harriman, and Carmen De Sapio.

10. Kennedy was the wealthiest man the Democrats had ever nominated, according to the *Congressional Quarterly*, and also the first senator nominated since the Republicans had nominated Warren G. Harding in 1920.

need for a Southerner to balance a Catholic.''

Connally recalled Johnson's decision to accept the nomination in a 1967 article for *Life* magazine, leaving out any comments Connally might have made, even though he was Johnson's campaign manager at the 1960 convention: ''During the discussion, Mr. Johnson said very little. A deliberate, almost somber calm came over him. I had not seen him before so deeply in this mood . . . we came to understand that Mr. Johnson had no alternative but to accept the vice-presidential nomination. He agreed and thus had forged another link that bound Mr. Kennedy to Texas. But it had not been an easy decision. I remember Mrs. Johnson in tears at one point. She knew the sense of dismay their friends and supporters would feel. . . . They had committed themselves, emotionally and intellectually, to Mr. Johnson's campaign for the Presidency itself. For him to join Mr. Kennedy at the end seemed like going over to the enemy. . . . I think there is no doubt that the Democrats would have lost in 1960 without Mr. Johnson on the ticket.''

A close political associate who has sat in on innumerable discussions with Connally and others says, ''Connally was not for Lyndon Johnson taking the vice presidency, not at all. John Connally knew that if Lyndon Johnson didn't take the vice-presidential nomination, more than likely Jack Kennedy wouldn't win. He [Connally] knew that if he [Kennedy] didn't have Johnson to carry Texas and the South, that Jack Kennedy would be beat, and I'd say that John Connally wasn't for Jack Kennedy at that time. I know—I'll say it different—he was against Jack Kennedy at that time being president.'' Congressman Pickle claims that Connally thought Johnson ''deserved Kennedy's support in 1960—it was LBJ's turn—since LBJ had advanced Kennedy's candidacy for vice president in 1956.''[11]

11. Many Texas delegates were so mad at Johnson's accepting the vice-presidential nomination that they left the convention without even waiting to hear his acceptance speech. ''They crammed a civil rights plank down our throats,

National Democratic Chairman Robert Strauss had not begun his climb in the party hierarchy in 1960. He was just a successful Dallas lawyer trying to elect Johnson president by seeking convention votes in the Florida, New York, and New Jersey delegations. Although he and Connally had been in college twenty years earlier, they really just started getting to know each other [12] after the Los Angeles convention. Walter Jenkins, another Johnson aide, and his wife joined them. "I well remember, as we were having dinner," Strauss says, "Connally commented that, 'There is no point in us moping around. We just got the hell kicked out of us, and if we're smart, it should stand us in good stead because we're going to be around politics for a long time.'"

After the victory of the Kennedy-Johnson ticket in November 1960, Robert Baskin of the Dallas *Morning News* wrote of a "strong move [to] induce" Connally to run for Johnson's Senate seat. He mentioned that Connally reportedly was the "choice of a number of moderate and conservative Democratic leaders." Connally skipped that race, and, in the special election held in 1961, John Tower, a Republican who had tried to win the seat from Johnson in 1960, captured the job without much difficulty.

After Kennedy's election, the new president-elect began assembling his cabinet, his department heads, and his advisers. On December 27, 1960, Kennedy placed John Connally's name in nomination for the post of secretary of the navy. Many people thought that the nomination was a payoff to Johnson for helping carry the South for the Kennedy-Johnson ticket. Some speculated that Robert McNamara had suggested Connally for the post, but Connally later insisted that Sam Rayburn had placed his name before Kennedy. Rayburn commented that, "Con-

nominated a liberal for president and then asked us to help sell the deal to the South with Johnson's aid," a delegate protested.

12. After Connally became so popular as governor and everyone seemed to be telling "I knew him when" stories, Strauss remarked to an audience that he apparently was the only student at The University of Texas in the late 1930s and early 1940s who had not roomed with Connally.

nally is one of the ablest men of his age I have known. I think he is capable of doing a fine job in any position in which he is placed.'' When Connally was informed of the Kennedy appointment, he stated, ''I am flattered and honored. I have a deep admiration for the Navy as a service and for the personnel of the Navy.'' Connally's appointment was the highest appointive office given any Texan during Kennedy's administration.

Connally met opposition over his appointment from Senator William Proxmire, a Democrat from Wisconsin. Although the Senate overwhelmingly approved Connally's nomination, Proxmire pointed out that Connally's association with Sid Richardson and his position as one of three independent executors of the Richardson estate posed a conflict of interest. Although Connally resigned many of his corporate connections, he stated that he felt he would be letting down the trust Richardson had put in him if he should resign as an executor of the estate. In Senate debate, Proxmire described Richardson's business as ''one of the world's biggest private oil companies'' and the Texas oil men as a ''tough, hard, determined, militant bunch'' who knew how to get what they wanted from the federal government. Proxmire also felt that Connally's links with the oil industry should disqualify him from being in charge of naval oil reserves and for procuring petroleum for the armed services. However, Senator Richard Russell, chairman of the Armed Services Committee, answered that the handling of the oil reserves had to be approved by the Armed Services Committees of both houses of Congress. Russell also stated, ''I don't think that because he [Connally] has been a success in the oil business means that he is going to steal the oil reserves or any part of it.''

Proxmire also pointed out Connally's lobbying activities on behalf of Richardson in 1956 and stated that Richardson had been a stockholder in Transport Company of Texas, which held large Defense Department oil transport contracts. The senator demanded that Connally divest himself of an oil lease he held in Andrews County that yielded approximately $325 a month. Proxmire commented on Connally's income from the lease—"That's not peanuts!"

Proxmire objected to Connally's income as an executor of the Richardson estate. Under Texas law, executors of an estate are entitled to take 5 percent of the value of the property coming into the estate and 5 percent of the property going out of the estate. While Connally was secretary of the navy, the estate was managed by the other two executors, Perry Bass and Howell E. Smith. In an interview in the *Texas Observer*, Proxmire stated: "In this job, Connally has received between $40,000 and $80,000 per year in fees as a percent of the income and expenses of this $100 million bonanza. He will again get this income when he leaves the Navy. How much he earns then will, in my judgment, depend in part on the policies he follows as Secretary of the Navy. He also owns oil leases from which he will continue to receive an income of $4,000 per year while he is Secretary of the Navy." Proxmire also stated that since Connally "has only been in office a few days, he hasn't had time to try anything but you can bet your life I'll keep an eye on him."

When Connally was nominated for the post of secretary of the treasury by President Nixon, his financial gains from the Richardson estate once more became a controversial issue. During the Senate hearings, Connally admitted that he had received a fee of $750,000 from the foundation. The sum was paid over a ten-year period to avoid excessive capital gains taxes. Connally also admitted that he had received $575,000 during the time that he served as governor of Texas. The Senate investigation also revealed that Richardson and his partner, Clint Murchison, had diverted the profits of the Del Mar Turf Club to Boys Inc., a nonprofit organization. Connally served as one of the directors of the organization, and the state of California brought suit against Richardson and Murchison for tax evasion. The state and the federal government began taxing the receipts of Boys, Inc. However, a federal district judge in Dallas reversed the decision and ordered that taxes paid be refunded to the youth organization.

As soon as Connally had taken office as secretary of the navy, he was faced with his first emergency. The *Santa Maria*, a Portuguese ship, had been pirated by insurgents and was reported to be roaming the Caribbean. Connally immediately moved to find the vessel. He ordered the search force increased and kept close watch on the progress of the search, until the pirates released the ship.

Connally's naval experience gave him added status at the Pentagon, as many former secretaries had so little experience that one admitted he couldn't even operate a rowboat. Connally also had more personal contact with military personnel in the Pentagon, summoning them to meetings with him—an unprecedented move on the part of the secretary of the navy. One such meeting occurred on April 11, 1961, when Connally first took office. All Navy and Marine Corps officers serving in the Pentagon met with the new secretary at Constitution Hall. Speaking to the assembled officers, Connally expressed his views on the role of the Navy in the defense program. "I see no substitute for sea power," the secretary said. "Our most probable call to battle will be that resulting from the nibbling, tantalizing tactics of potential enemies. . . . And here—as we have for years—the Navy-Marine Corps air-sea-ground teams excel."

In his speech Connally also discussed the controversial subject of what military men might say in public. He stated, "I have a simple rule of thumb by which I hope you will govern your actions: Recognize and accept your own responsibility by insisting upon being quoted by name, rank, and billet. Your responsibility will then be fulfilled much the same as when signing the log for your watch. In short, if you are not willing to be quoted by name, you should not be speaking."

Connally received widespread recognition as the foremost Texan in the Kennedy administration. The Houston *Chronicle* ran a two-page spread on the new secretary in its magazine section on February 5, 1961, and numerous other Texas newspapers carried profiles on him. Texas politicos and long-time friends—some 1,500 strong

—packed Memorial Coliseum in Corpus Christi to pay tribute to Connally on his first visit to Texas since being named to the naval post. Robert M. Jackson, the editor of the Corpus Christi *Caller-Times*, reported that reservations were in such demand that the planning committee began turning away reservations the day before Connally's arrival. Many of Connally's Washington associates attended the function, including Congressman Joe Kilgore. Dolph Briscoe, another Texas rancher who became governor of Texas in 1973, presented Connally with a saddle especially made for him.

Connally was named the outstanding distinguished alumnus of The University of Texas for 1961 by members of the ex-students' association. On November 9, 1961, Connally spoke to the association at a dinner, attended by Vice President Lyndon Johnson. When former Governor Allan Shivers was named one of the four distinguished alumni the next year, the *Texas Observer* commented on the political nature of the process of choosing the university's distinguished alumni. Jack Maguire, the executive secretary of the association, told the *Observer* that politics should not be a consideration and that often the selections could be improved. He explained that each year the deans of the various colleges of the university were asked to nominate candidates from among their graduates. Although both Connally and Shivers were graduates of the university's law school, Dean Page Keeton made no nominations in 1961 or 1962.

Maguire explained that the selection of the candidates was made by a seven-man committee appointed by the association's president. A forty-four member council of the association ratified the nominating members' selection. Maguire admitted that the council had received criticism in the case of Connally's selection and assured the *Observer* that picking only one alumnus for each year would not be repeated. Maguire felt that Connally's selection was made ''right'' when Connally became secretary of the navy, and that the criticism came mostly from ''people who wondered why certain other people weren't picked.''

Although the method of nomination was changed after 1962 so that any member of the ex-students' association might make nominations, the association continued to be criticized for awarding its honors to professional and business "establishment" men, who often made gifts of money to the university. Texas writers, artists, and humanitarians, for the most part, are bypassed as distinguished alumni. In 1972, when the association was criticized for failing to honor women among its alumni, Nellie Connally was named a distinguished alumnus. Her nomination prompted one Texas liberal feminist to quip: ''Nellie Connally has been distinguished through marriage!''

Connally's tour through Texas at the time of his selection in 1961 included substituting for Speaker Sam Rayburn at a Veterans' Day program in Bonham, Texas, to commemorate the tenth anniversary of a veterans' hospital. Connally visited with the gravely ill Rayburn for five minutes before telling the audience at the dedication that an untroubled future in America depended on two things: "First, whether or not we recognize the nature of the threat; second, whether or not physically, emotionally and spiritually, we are sufficiently dedicated to our way of life and its institutions to be willing to undertake their total defense."

When Connally arrived at the airport in Austin, he was greeted by an honor guard of naval ROTC members. As Connally leaned forward to ask one midshipman his name, the naval man thought that the secretary wanted to inspect his rifle. He brought the rifle up sharply in the ''port arms'' position and struck Connally with the end of the rifle or sight, not with the bayonet attached to the rifle. Connally appeared at a banquet in his honor with a black patch over his injured left eye. When Connally arrived at the head table accompanied by Lyndon Johnson, he found that UT Chancellor Harry Ransom, Ramon Beteta, a Mexico City publisher and a distinguished alumnus of UT, and Maguire had also donned black eye patches.

Johnson, who was greeted with rousing applause, gave the speech in honor of Connally. He commented that Connally had often ''spoken in my behalf'' and described the secretary as "one of the most dedicated, most patriotic, most sincere and able young men of our state and nation." Connally forecast his return to the state by quipping to the audience, "You all certainly do look well. I'd like to live down here." However, when asked about rumors that he would run for governor, Connally answered, "I hope to be back in two or three weeks—certainly by next month." He also stated that he felt it inappropriate to "inject politics of any kind" into the festivities in his behalf.

When Connally resigned his post as secretary of the navy on December 11, 1961, to seek the Democratic nomination for governor, he commented that he was extremely pleased with the improved state of readiness developed in 1961 by the Navy-Marine Corps team. He stated, "We will shortly be turning out one Polaris submarine a month. We have increased amphibious lift from one and one-half to two divisions for the Marine Corps." Connally was credited with maintaining the Navy and Marine facilities on "ready call" during the atomic age and its daily threat of attack. In addition, Connally believed strongly that military servicemen should be indoctrinated against communism.

When the admirals first heard rumors of Connally's plans to run for governor, Rear Admiral Daniel F. Smith, chief of naval information, said, "I hope those folks down there don't decide to elect him governor or something. We need him here."

Connally's experience as secretary of the navy proved to be useful to him both in his role as governor of Texas and later as secretary of the treasury. While in Washington in the navy post, Connally observed the ways in which money was allocated for defense contracts and for other federal spending. Speaking in 1963, after he was governor, Connally said: "As I viewed the contracts for research in my former role as secretary of the navy, it was astounding to me how concentrated these contracts were. They were concentrated because of the capacity of certain institutions and research complexes to handle adequately the research task."

Connally's appointment as secretary of the navy presented a curious parallel. The link to the parallel was Sid Richardson, who persuaded President Eisenhower to appoint another Texan, Robert B. Anderson, as secretary of the navy in 1952. Anderson, born in Burleson, Texas, also received his law degree from The University of Texas. He served in the Texas legislature, as chairman of the State Board of Education, chairman of the Texas Unemployment Commission, and as a director and deputy chairman of the Dallas Federal Reserve Bank.

When Eisenhower appointed him as navy secretary, Anderson was serving as manager of the W. T. Waggoner estate in Vernon, Texas, like the Richardson estate, a vast Texas cattle and oil empire. Anderson also served as deputy secretary of defense and as secretary of the treasury from 1957 to 1961. Under Anderson's sponsorship the present oil import quota system was initiated. When McNamara was nominated as president of the World Bank, both Connally and Anderson were mentioned as possibilities for the position of secretary of defense. In 1965, while governor of Texas, Connally suggested that out-of-state members be appointed to the Board of Regents of The University of Texas. One name that Connally mentioned was that of Robert Anderson, then of New York.

The parallel continues, with Connally mentioned as a strong presidential contender in 1976. In 1964, when Eisenhower was considering potential presidential candidates to succeed him, he stated, "I firmly believe that the smartest man in this whole nation is Bob Anderson. He would be perfect for the job. Golly, that fellow can reduce the toughest problem to its bare essentials like nobody else I've ever known, and in damned short order, too. Trouble is, Bob's a Democrat." Anderson was fifty-three years old at the time that Eisenhower mentioned him as a possible presidential contender; Connally was fifty-six at the time that he was first considered a serious contender for the Republican nomination—and still a Democrat. Like Connally, Anderson had amassed a considerable fortune in Texas before entering political life. He is now a member of the prestigious banking firm of Loeb, Rhoades in New York and was instrumental in obtaining backing from John L. Loeb for Lyndon Johnson in his campaign for president in 1964.

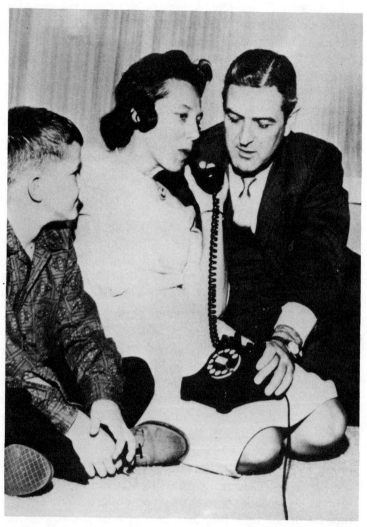

—Fort Worth Star-Telegram

The newly appointed Secretary of the Navy, his wife Nellie, and their youngest son Mark in their empty Washington apartment.

—Fort Worth Star-Telegram

Secretary of the Navy John B. Connally.

—Texas State Archives

Secretary of the Navy John Connally arrives in his home state.

JOHN CONNALLY
VICTORY SPECIAL

—*Austin American-Statesman*

GOVERNOR OF TEXAS 1962-1965

7

"I Asked the Permission of None"

As Lyndon Johnson's aide-de-camp in state and national politics and as secretary of the navy in the Kennedy administration, John Connally felt he had tested his mettle. At forty-four years of age, he wanted to be his own boss. "As governor, this is your state, you run the program, you give the directions, you've got pretty much a free hand," says Congressman Jake Pickle.

Connally's December 1961 announcement to run for governor was no surprise to his brother Merrill, who had accompanied John to the executive mansion two months earlier to talk to Governor Price Daniel about the possibility; nor to Dallas lawyer Robert Strauss. However, his younger brother, Wayne, says, "It was a big surprise . . . and I quite frankly thought it was a step backward in politics from secretary of the navy."

At the time that Connally was secretary of the navy, neither he nor Pickle had sought public office. Governor Daniel had appointed Pickle to the Texas Employment Commission, and Pickle was visiting his old friends, John and Nellie Connally, at their home in the District of Columbia suburb of Foxhall. "I was trying to tell him what a good job I was doing as employer representative on the Employment Commission," Pickle recalls. "I said I found out that you can do this and this, and I was telling them how to operate things; and he said, 'Let me tell you about all I'm doing.' And he'd take the conversation away from me and finally I said, 'Now which one of us is gonna get to brag first?' . . . But I knew very well from talking to him that he ran the Navy. He wasn't belligerent, but he wasn't taking any foolishness. He'd studied his lessons and he gave directions. He found out that . . . he could be a successful administrator over a big outfit like the United States Navy. And he felt that he could handle any type of job that came along. He didn't want to practice law and there he was, a very much recognized authority in the U.S. Navy. He had no future in Washington, particularly. . . . Where else could he go, except come back and maybe run for office himself? And he just made up his mind that he was a stronger and better man than the other people who were going to run, and he just appointed himself governor."

Connally didn't exactly "appoint" himself to the office. The 1962 governor's race, stretching over ten months, was the first major step in Connally's elective career. A June 1961 poll had given Connally only 1 percent of the vote in a governor's race, and a later sampling showed only 4 percent favored his running in 1962. "We knew he was an unknown to some extent," recalls Merrill Connally, "but we knew he was known by a vast number of people, particularly from two areas. One, those people with whom he had worked and been to school with at UT. . . . Many . . . had gone on to law school, had become leaders, and had gone back to their communities. They were county judges, district judges . . . people of some prominence and influence in most of the counties of the state. . . . In addition to that, he had the people he had worked with since school days from way back in the 1930s, all the way up through the many, many Lyndon Johnson races. He missed no conventions that I know of—precinct, county, state, or national—since World War II.'' George Christian was Daniel's chief aide in 1961, and he remembers the ''so-called establishment was worried about the governor situation, and that Connally was getting lots of encouragement.''

Governor Daniel had fought the sales tax, and Texas big businessmen were upset at him for opposing it. ''Some saw Connally as the wave of the future,'' says Christian. ''If Daniel had announced sooner, Connally might not have run, but Connally didn't think Daniel was going to run.''[1] It was ironic that Connally would oppose Daniel since, as a Fort Worth lawyer in 1960, Connally had contributed $1,500 to Daniel's race for a third term—the largest contribution Daniel got that year.

Strauss says a December 1961 meeting at millionaire Dolph Briscoe's ranch near Uvalde was almost a formality. Connally had already made up his mind.[2] Strauss says he became a halftime lawyer in 1962, spending the other half on the Connally campaign. ''Growing out of the campaign, for the first time, was our relationship of intimacy,'' he says.

Connally chose Eugene Locke, a Dallas lawyer, as his state campaign manager, but since Locke had never managed a campaign before, Connally spent part of his time raising money and even writing his own campaign speeches. Connally's main headquarters were in Fort Worth, where he had made his home before he went to Washington. ''He had those [Fort Worth] contacts, and he had those friends, and he had the ability to move and go into a community and

1. In the final analysis, Daniel decided, according to Christian, that he didn't want to go out of office with the public thinking he had been run out of office. Daniel said, ''I'd rather be carried out of here feet first than be called a quitter.''

2. Among those at the meeting were Texas House member Ben Barnes; Lloyd Bentsen, who became a U.S. senator; Austin lawyer Frank Erwin Jr.; Killeen businessman Ted Connell; two college friends, San Antonio lawyer John Peace and Corpus Christi lawyer Cecil Burney; and State Highway Commissioner Herb Petry of Carrizo Springs.

talk and visit and inspire people," says Pickle.

After he announced for governor, Connally got his first chance to inspire a Texas audience in a speech at Hotel Brownwood[3] in Ben Barnes' stomping ground. Barnes, a first-term house member at the time, worked extra hard, he recalls, on his introduction of Connally. Harry Whitworth of the Texas Chemical Council often loaned members of his staff to Barnes *gratis* to help him with his speeches. Olan Brewer of the Council's staff helped Barnes prepare his remarks. Barnes says the late Charlie Woodson, publisher of the Brownwood *Bulletin*, had invited Connally earlier when he was secretary of the navy to speak at the luncheon honoring Brownwood's outstanding citizens. But Barnes says he had heard Connally probably would run for governor, so, in order to make a good impression, he started to work on his introduction even before Connally announced.

Connally's strongest pitch to the voters was that Texas was losing hundreds of millions of dollars because its second-rate system of higher education had not been able to attract scholars, who, in turn, would have attracted federal research money and new industries. It became such a well-known theme that three of Connally's brothers, Wayne, Merrill, and Golfrey, still repeat almost identical versions of it when asked why they thought John first ran for governor. Later Connally stated that he had first run in 1962 to "get extremists out of the Democratic Party in Texas."

Dick Cory of Victoria was a house member in Governor Daniel's inner circle when a constituent, Zac Lentz, took him to an Austin hotel reception to meet Connally. "I thought at once—here's another Shivers," recalls Cory, now a lobbyist for the Texas Brewers' Institute. "He had commanding presence, good looks and incredible vitality." Bob Bullock, former secretary of state under Governor Preston Smith, was lobbying for the Texas Automobile

---

3. Hotel Brownwood, in Brownwood, Texas, has since become Sid Richardson Hall, a downtown dormitory for Howard Payne College. The money to refurnish the hotel, Barnes says, was supplied by the Sid Richardson Foundation.

Dealers Association when he got a look at the new candidate at a breakfast meeting in the TADA board room at the Driskill Hotel. "In walked John Connally," Bullock recalls. "He walked around the table and everybody shook hands with him and looked at him. He stood up and made a speech, and it was the worst I ever heard. I never knew a man who knew less about state government. He left, and we all looked at one another and said we want to take another look at this fellow. We held another breakfast meeting for him about two months later, and I never heard a man who knew more about state government. He had polished himself up and could discuss the issues. What happened was, he started taking crash courses from people who knew about state government and listening to them. And John Connally was a listener then, not a talker."

And Connally was a fast learner. "You goddamn right," asserts Bullock. "He'd put on them old big rubber-soled shoes, and he'd get out and start walking and working. I'll never forget it. During the whole campaign, he wore an old cord suit. You know, the old wash-and-wear cord suits. And those old shoes—big, thick, louvered, rubber-soled shoes."

Attorney General Will Wilson, also running for governor, tried to make the LBJ brand stick even before Connally got his campaign underway. Wilson's charge that there appeared to be an attempt to "run Texas out of Washington" became more familiar as the campaign progressed. Wilson's sights were set on Connally and on Governor Daniel, who, he charged, might have made as much as $142,308 on land and mineral interests in Liberty County while he was in office. Connally concentrated on Daniel in the first primary, and he decided the best issue was that Daniel's bid for a fourth term would make Daniel a virtual "czar," with close friends controlling every state board and agency.

Connally started campaigning before the other candidates; at a time, in fact, when the only other announced candidates were Wilson and Marshall Formby of Plainview, former chairman of the Texas Highway Commission. Approximately nine hundred people paid $3 a ticket for hamburgers and catfish to hear Connally's first major address—a statewide telecast from the Rice Hotel ballroom in Houston.

The decision to run, Connally told the audience, was "mine and mine alone. I sought the advice of many. I asked the permission of none." Texas, he said, is one of the great states, "but we should make up our minds, as I have made up mine, that we should be the strong state of this nation. Together we can make Texas first in the nation in education, in industrial growth, in the broadening of job opportunities, in the exercise of state responsibility to all people." Three weeks later, on February 15, Connally stated in a television broadcast that no governor of the state should be awarded four terms, a speech which Preston Smith and others would remind him of numerous times when Connally was considering his own possible fourth term in 1967.

On March 4 Wayne Connally and Carroll Abbott, a long-time Democratic party worker, put together a barbecue at Connally's Floresville ranch, and Merrill Connally claims, "that's when John really took off. That meeting, attended by some ten thousand persons, made the difference." Connally's friendship with Lyndon Johnson and the candidacy of Edwin Walker of Dallas, a right-wing former major general who had crusaded against communism among his troops in Germany, attracted nationwide attention to the governor's race.

Another view of the race was that of Willie Morris, editor of the liberal *Texas Observer*, who wrote in the December 15, 1961, issue: "Great politicians appeal to a sense of crisis, enjoin the popular imagination for reform and change; Connally's candidacy gives us only a sense of monumental boredom. He offers the same mild remedies and pale nostrums undergirded by the same apathetic popular front, the same lackadaisical stance against a developing two-party system which threatens the well-springs of power and patronage and which have made of statecraft in Austin a miasma of meaningless jargon and expediency.''

On May 5 Connally led the first primary with 431,498 votes, and Don Yarborough, who had campaigned as a Kennedy Democrat with widespread liberal support, beat out Daniel for second place. Wilson was fourth, Formby fifth, and Walker last. The runoff between Connally and Yarborough began with numerous television stations offering the candidates free time for a televised debate, but Connally declined, deciding to play it safe with his 113,512-vote lead over Yarborough. Liberals claimed Yarborough was the most effective public speaker Texas had had since Governor Jimmy Allred in the late 1930s. Later in the general election, Republican Jack Cox made an issue of Connally's refusal to debate, asking, ''Why won't John debate Jack?''

Yarborough challenged whether Connally would support Kennedy's ''New Frontier'' and defined the runoff as being between ''small businessmen and farmers vs. huge Eastern monopolies.'' Connally assailed Yarborough for accepting support from the ''left-wing Americans for Democrat Action'' and ''Eastern labor organizers.'' Yarborough obviously got many Republican votes on the basis that he would be easier to beat than Connally in November, but Connally won the runoff by 26,250 votes out of a total of 1,104,098.

Connally outspent Yarborough $493,462 to $231,863, and he still had to face the general election against Cox, a Republican who had switched from the Democratic party. Connally's first move was to transfer his state headquarters from Fort Worth to Austin. Unlike previous Republican gubernatorial candidates, Cox was a *bona fide* contender. Connally got some labor support after he endorsed repealing the poll tax and said he would consider labor people for state appointments. Rumors that Cox, if elected, would appoint Edwin Walker to The University of Texas Board of Regents probably frightened some liberals over to Connally's side. It was also reported that Cox got ''fired up by a rebel yell in East Texas'' and said he hoped the federal government would be as forceful with Cuba as it had been with Mississippians over integration. Cox's remarks undoubtedly made Connally look better to black voters. To reporter Stuart Long the race became known as the "J.C." race for governor— John Connally, Jack Cox, and Jack Carswell, the Constitution party's candidate.

Connally claimed the Texas Republican platform devoted 112 lines to problems and 204 lines to "being against everything you can think of, including the advent of the 20th Century." It was the GOP platform which was partly responsible for the *Texas Observer*'s surprising endorsement of Connally, as the paper admittedly had been his "most dedicated and persistent critic." Editor Morris wrote that in the wake of the Cuban missile crisis "this nation . . . needs as much moderation, restraint, and understanding of the world power structure as it can get." Morris noted that the Republican state convention, which Cox's supporters had controlled, "set forth in irresponsible terms" that the United States should resign from the United Nations and must seek "complete and clearcut victory over communism."

Despite his liberal-conservative coalition, Connally found winning the election was no walkover. Jerry Hall, then a reporter for the Lubbock *Avalanche-Journal*, remembers how the crowd at the Texas-Texas Tech football game booed Connally when he was introduced on the field at halftime. "He was mad as hell," Hall recalls. "Connally turned to one guy who was heckling him and said, 'Why in the hell don't you go home?' " Strauss remembers his young daughter coming home one afternoon: ". . . she went to school with all those rich Republicans at Hockaday—and saying, 'Daddy, you and I are the only ones for Mr. Connally.' "

Connally was so pleased with a videotape recording of his appearance with Cox and Carswell before a luncheon meeting of the Dallas League of Women Voters that his headquarters sponsored a rerun of it on fifteen television stations. He had made a campaign train trip in the closing days of the runoff against Don Yarborough, but switched to a

LBJ-style airplane blitz for the general election. He made a forty-nine hour sweep of thirty-one cities, starting at San Antonio on the morning of November 1 and winding up at Corpus Christi. The day before the election, Connally toured Austin banks with his local campaign manager, Wallace Scott, a former Texas Longhorn football player and an oil and gas lawyer in the capital city. Connally talked to his campaign staff in Waco and shook hands with people leaving work in downtown Fort Worth. On election eve, he ate dinner in Fort Worth with his family for the first time in more than a month. On election day, he decided that he just might make a few more phone calls. But essentially, the campaigning was finished.

Connally polled 847,038 votes to win the election, although he ran behind the rest of the state Democratic ticket. Cox received 715,025 votes, by far the most ever received by a Texas Republican candidate for governor. Carswell received 7,135 votes. Connally's supporters claimed that Connally was the first to make a campaign train trip across Texas, and that it was the first time for a candidate's wife to travel thousand of miles on her own itinerary. Connally was "first" with morning coffees, and he was the first candidate to sponsor a television show on which his opponents appeared.

One anecdote illustrates what the election meant to Connally. Morgan Hall, a Democratic county chairman, met Connally's campaign train at Stanton and gave Connally a cotton sack, a symbol of how he might "harvest votes." But Connally missed the point. He took the incident seriously. One look at that sack, a spectator recalls, and he "launched forth in all earnestness about how 'Morgan Hall and I are striving to get away from that type of work.'" John Connally, governor of the Lone Star State of Texas, was on his way and had no intention of turning back.

"A Record Worth Fighting For"

Connally's election as governor in 1962 made a prophet of Sid Richardson, the Fort Worth oil man whose millions had shaped Connally's career. Ten years before, the Reverend Billy Graham was in Richardson's office, seeking another donation to spread the gospel. "Mr. Sid" told the Reverend Graham: "I want you to meet a fellow who's going to be governor of Texas some day." He picked up the telephone and said, "John, come in here." The campaign and election, however, were only part, and possibly the easiest part, of the process. Connally still had to face the legislature.

In 1969 Connally chose a passage from his first inaugural address as the keynote to a special hardcover book on his six years as governor: "We are all Americans. We are all Texans. Wearing these labels—and none other—let us be unified in our common purpose as we are united by our common heritage. . . . Let it be heard wherever there are men of purpose and goodwill, that here, on this day, Texas reaches for greatness." Connally's public relations man, Julian Read, who not only talks like Connally, but attempts to dress and look like him, wrote the words, but they were vintage Connally, typical of his public speeches—lofty and free of the thought of unenlightened men or petty political deals; the words of a visionary talking to people he feels he was born to lead.[4]

Connally's first inaugural had all the trimmings. The Reverend Graham prayed for the Connally administration at the traditional breakfast, and the new governor and his wife, Nellie, attractive and poised, but homey and folksy enough for Texans to love, paraded with floats, military groups, drill teams, and mounted posses around the capitol and down Congress Avenue. On inaugural night, shuttle buses brought Texas' elite from hotels to the capitol, where the Connallys shook hands for three hours. John Connally, private citizen, had become John Connally,

4. The book reflects Connally's style in other ways. There is a full-page color photograph of the governor taken by Gittings of Neiman-Marcus, the most prestigious photographic studio in Texas. In keeping with Connally's desire for "nothing but the best," the book is printed on slick and expensive paper. Connally rejected the first printing because he thought the paper was too cheap looking. The book was printed again at state expense and given to Texas legislators as a parting gift from Connally.

governor. "I had known him as John, and I addressed him that way once after he was elected, but his expression let me know it was to be 'governor' and it was," said a former employee. "It was 'governor' to everyone, top aides and all. Nobody just walked in his office, everybody was announced."

All the top state officials were new in 1963—Connally, Lieutenant Governor Preston Smith, Attorney General Waggoner Carr, and Speaker of the House Byron Tunnell—the first time since Texas became a state in 1846 that this had occurred. Connally's defeat of Price Daniel had dislodged Daniel from public office for the first time since 1947 when he became Texas' attorney general.

Crawford Martin, who had served in the Texas senate for fourteen years and had run an unsuccessful race for lieutenant governor in 1962, recalled briefing Connally—at his request—on two or three occasions during the campaign for governor. "He wanted to know about the personalities of different senators and representatives, how they felt and what they did," Martin remembered. "You can't brief John Connally too fast."

In taking the oath of office as Texas' 38th governor, Connally assumed a $25,000-a-year job as head of its biggest business—state government, with a budget of $3 billion and more than 200,000 employees. He appointed Martin as secretary of state and hired young lawyers Howard Rose of Midland, Scott Sayers of Fort Worth, and Larry Temple of Austin as aides. Also on the payroll were Bill Cobb, who had worked with the Industrial Commission and Legislative Budget Board, as budget director, and Frank Miskell, a bright, rotund man with a taste for good wine. "Connally's staff thought they were governor instead of him," says Bullock. "Connally's office was run by remote control. I think he had to look the world over to get the worst [staff] he could, and damned if he didn't hire them."

Connally hardly had time to establish an office routine before he was asked if he wanted to run in 1966 against United States Senator John Tower, Texas' first Republican senator since Reconstruction. "I just want to be the best governor Texas has ever had,'' he told the Texas Press Association. His first address to the legislature was staggering—fourteen legal-sized pages of specific proposals. ''I thought it was great,'' exclaimed Senator Franklin Spears of San Antonio, whose liberal political philosophy ran counter to Connally's conservatism. However, a former committee chairman and insider feels the Connally approach ''ruined the legislature, emasculated it. He did it by having huge, well-documented presentations on every proposal . . . they were well-written, the legal language was flawless, something a legislator with an inexperienced law student for an aide couldn't match. Even if Connally's proposals were bad, they were so well presented you could hardly oppose them. The slickness overwhelmed you.''

The ''vital issues,'' as Connally saw them, were to attract tourists and new industries to the state and to offer a better education to college students. Higher education had been his theme during the campaign, and he continued to plug it throughout his administration. While he was secretary of the navy, Connally said the choice defense contracts were parceled out to other states, even though they did not have the natural resources or other advantages of Texas. What he found, he said, were that the other states had more technicians and research centers which attracted scientists and scholars. ''In short,'' he said, ''a concentration of brainpower spelled the difference.''

Tourists also were shunning Texas. Few persons across the nation knew of Texas' excellent vacation areas and scenic wonders, for state law prohibited tourist advertising by the state. And many did not want to tour a state where alcoholic beverages could not be sold in bars or restaurants.

To Connally, more industry meant more jobs, and more business was good business. The boys in the business lobby could not have agreed more, and they lined up to support Connally's programs. He pointed out at the end of his first year in office that the Texas Industrial Commission had won a trophy, as 317 new plants and warehouses had been built in the state that year—second only to New York. A bill to establish the Texas Tourist Development Agency was signed into law, and more money was also poured into efforts to attract industry to Texas.

But it was not so much Connally's scorecard that was impressive, but the feeling that something was about to happen, could break loose at any moment. Proposals, ideas, and suggestions were fed in, sifted, and released so quickly that they were often submerged without being seriously considered. Connally's staff acted under two maxims which he stressed, "You ain't learning nothing when you're talking" and "It don't help to be smart, if you ain't loyal."

But Lieutenant Governor Smith and Speaker Tunnell felt no particular loyalty, and some members of the working lobby didn't like Connally. United States Representative Charles Wilson of Lufkin, a former member of the Texas House and Senate, says, "Unlike most governors, Connally dealt with their bosses, chairmen of the boards—his social friends. He didn't have time for the top-waters," an expression that means the small fish that swim on top of the water. "The lobbyists were afraid of him, and they resented his attitude. They thought it was arrogance."

Connally's proposal to repeal the poll tax was adopted by the legislature, but it was rejected by voters in November 1963. Another proposal removed the state attorney general from fourteen boards of which he was an ex-officio member, including the banking board. Connally replaced him with his friend, Robert Strauss. The governor's other appointments included Lyndon Johnson's business associate, A. W. Moursund of Johnson City, to the three-member Parks and Wildlife Commission, and Jack Valenti, a former Johnson aide, as a member of the University of Houston's Board of Regents. Connally called the hundreds of appointments a governor has to make "worrisome." He quoted a former governor as saying every appointment makes one person happy and ten mad.

The appointment of Austin lawyer W. St. John Garwood, a liberal and one of the foremost authorities on the United Nations, as a member of The University of Texas Board of Regents was turned down by the senate while Connally was in St. David's Hospital recovering from a hernia operation. Garwood's rejection apparently came as a complete surprise to Connally, whose inexperienced staff missed the signs of trouble in the senate. Connally replaced Garwood with Austin lawyer Frank C. Erwin Jr., chairman of Connally's inauguration and secretary of the State Democratic Executive Committee. Connally suffered another setback when his effort to establish a budget division in the governor's office failed. It would have given the governor control over departmental requests for state money and the first real power for the state's chief executive since Reconstruction. Connally, however, managed to put a supporter on the powerful Railroad Commission, which regulates Texas' oil and gas production. He named Judge Jim Langdon of the El Paso Court of Civil Appeals to replace William J. Murray, who resigned in the wake of publicized reports that he had profited from oil holdings while on the commission.

Higher education was clearly the focal point of Connally's budget proposals. It was, he said, his "most sincere ambition to be the catalyst in improving the quality of all education beyond the high school." His critics claimed it was "an elitest theory." In order to cover the cost of his education proposals and to make up for small tax breaks for sulphur companies and state banks, Connally presented a $32.9 million tax bill which, for the first time in recent memory, passed the legislature, without changes, before the appropriations bill.

Despite two days and nights of meetings, Smith and Tunnell refused to budge on Connally's request to meet him halfway on an extra $13 million for higher education. Connally gave up, and the spending bill was adopted in the house 117 to 30 and in the senate by a vote of 24 to 6. On statewide television, Connally summarized "accomplishments" of the legislature, which, he noted, had finished a 140-day session in 137 days, adjourning early for the first time since 1943. Then, he blamed a ten-member house-senate conference committee, which worked in private, for

98

slicing $13,249,055 million from his higher education budget.

Connally vetoed $12,439,924 from the spending bill "to provide a sort of layaway plan — a substantial down payment on excellence in education. I intend to let it accumulate as surplus to use for that purpose. . . . And you may rest assured that I plan to guard that nest egg like an old mother hen." For the first time since 1955, no special legislative session was required to finish the state's business. "I think we have written a record worth fighting for," Connally proudly noted.

"Connally's Quiet Spring"

In May 1963, just four months after he had begun his first term as governor, Connally told reporters it was a "safe assumption" that he would run again in 1964. It is a tradition in Texas politics that governors are assured of a second term, unless their administrations are marred by scandal or corruption. For Connally, the summer and the fall were merely seasons to mark political time, and he would pay his filing fee when it was convenient, after the first of the year. He could, however, count on strong competition, despite the second-term tradition. The liberals would almost certainly run a candidate to challenge Connally. It would be a scarring campaign, and the feeling around the capitol was that Connally could be beaten.

This feeling was erased with President John F. Kennedy's death, which saddened a nation and mangled Texas politics. Connally, wounded by the president's assassin, became untouchable. Only a fool or a zealot would test him in a public forum. But the realization that he had almost been snuffed out in his prime troubled Connally so much that he no longer wanted to run. Politics, he thought, is not all it's cracked up to be. It was, on his part, serious hesitation, no coy delay as a holdout for encouragement. Crawford Martin recalled a lengthy discussion over whether Connally should file again, and "when it was over, Connally said, 'I'm going to the mansion.' His wife, Nellie, could have vetoed it easily with one word, 'no.'"

On January 9, over a month and a half after he had been shot, Connally held his first full-scale news conference since Kennedy's assassination, in the Blue Room of the governor's mansion. Usually a skeptical breed, the reporters were awed and charmed by the governor. Connally was the handsome, smiling, and gracious textbook example of a wounded hero. Mannerisms that had been overlooked became significant, clues to his psyche. He had been shot; Lyndon had not. He was upstaging Johnson without even trying. Senator Ralph Yarborough almost became a suspicious character, as political cynics asked, "Where was Ralph when the shooting started? Fussing with Johnson over which car to ride in?"

Breaking the silence at the mansion, Bo Byers of the Houston *Chronicle*, whose tone to politicians always seems to imply, "We've both got jobs to do, how well are you doing yours?" asked Connally, "When are you going to announce?" Before the other reporters had a chance to suck in their breaths at Byers' audacity, Connally replied, smiling, "What's wrong with right now? I'll just announce now for reelection." The reporters had their story, thanks to Byers.

Nineteen days later, Connally, his arm still in a sling, appeared unannounced in the capitol pressroom. He said he had been taxing his strength by working as long as ten hours a day, and he would cut down to five or six hours. "Frankly, I don't think I will be up to a big campaign. For the next sixty days, I don't think I'll come close to having the physical stamina of 1962." However, it was not Connally's own race that was troubling him. It was the United States Senate race, and Connally wanted one of his supporters to run against the incumbent, Ralph Yarborough. Insisting on peace and harmony, President Johnson twisted Congressman Joe Kilgore's arm until he gave up. He would not run against Yarborough, and possibly Johnson's state would be spared an all-out political brawl.

Despite advice to the contrary, Don Yarborough filed again for governor. He talked of getting that one extra vote in each precinct this time. Even labor leaders tried to convince him the cause was hopeless. A sure tipoff of their attitude came when the AFL-CIO's powerful Committee on Political Education (COPE) voted not to endorse any candidate for state office. "It is my feeling that I have compromised everything but my wife and my soul in the governor's race," lamented Corpus Christi oilworker Homer Moore.

The *Texas Observer* referred to the Democratic primary matching Connally against Don Yarborough and two ministers as "Connally's Quiet Spring." Tending to his official duties, Connally stated, "Now I have a record and they can judge me by it." Don Yarborough made a half dozen speeches a day and called Connally "the worst governor in the history of this state." Yarborough criticized state shell dredging policies, a loan bill which Yarborough said legalized interest rates of 320 percent and Connally's tax proposals, but few listened. It was hopeless. Franklin Roosevelt and Dwight Eisenhower rolled into one couldn't have beaten John Connally in Texas in 1964.

Connally swamped Yarborough in the large presidential election-year turnout—1,125,884 to 471,411. Connally got a majority vote in 249 of 254 counties, with only Hardin and Trinity Counties going for Yarborough— more votes than any Texas candidate had ever received in a primary election.

The Republicans got the message and put up a sacrificial lamb, Jack Crichton of Dallas, against Connally in the general election. Connally conducted only a token campaign, but overwhelmed Crichton 1,877,793 votes to 661,675—still the record for most votes gained by a candidate for the Texas governor's office.

"I Am Obsessed with the Subject of Education"

By 1965, when Connally next appeared before the legislature, he was the master of Texas politics. He had survived the Kennedy assassination to become a folk hero. The September 1964 convention to write the state Democratic platform took only three hours and ten minutes and was a model of control and organization. Two years before, Texas Democrats had laid out seventy-one specific proposals. In 1964 the platform had 313 words. "When you like a dull convention is when you have the responsibility of running one," Connally said. "This is the type I like and think we ought to have—no shouting and whooping."

Bo Byers labeled the 1965 session a "Connally legislature" and claimed that no Texas governor since Jim Hogg in the 1890s had had such a "strong influence" over the legislature. A sudden shift in legislative control had made life easier for Connally. The ailing Ernest O. Thompson had resigned from the Texas Railroad Commission, and House Speaker Tunnell accepted Connally's offer to take the job. Excited and a bit scared, young Ben Barnes, a Connally supporter, latched on to Tunnell's old job, and Connally, through Barnes, took control of the 150-member House of Representatives. "You might say," recalls former Representative Randy Pendleton, smiling, "that Ben Barnes was one of John Connally's biggest admirers." Because Connally did not like to "sit down and talk to members of the legislature," Barnes says, "I guess, as Speaker of the house, I probably sold Connally's programs more than he sold them." If Barnes was his ally, one who could deliver votes in blocs, Senator Dorsey Hardeman of San Angelo, a legal scholar who could quote Texas history by day, month, and year, was Connally's nemesis. Reporter Stuart Long said they had an "undeclared war." Barnes recalls Connally was "furious" with Hardeman when the senate rejected W. St. John Garwood as a University of Texas regent in 1963, and their relationship deteriorated. A truce meeting finally was arranged by newspaper publisher Houston Harte at the Jim Hogg suite in the Driskill Hotel, and Barnes, who was there, remembers Hardeman was "charming . . . and he and Connally got along great. The next day, Hardeman not only opposed another of Connally's proposals on the senate floor, but called the governor 'arrogant' and 'mad for power.' Connally immediately called Harte and told him he never wanted to see that 'son-of-a-bitch' Hardeman again." Barnes also recalls getting Connally out of bed at three o'clock one morning during the 1965 session to work on redistricting bills. Connally, Barnes, and Senator Ralph Hall of Rockwall wrote the bills "in one night in John's office." The resulting legislative redistricting bill put Hardeman in a district with former house member W. E. "Pete" Snelson of Midland, who ended Hardeman's thirty-one-year legislative career in 1968 by defeating him in the race for the senate.

Personal problems were not evident in January 1965, when Connally magnified the moment in his inaugural address. "At no point in the 130 years of Texas history," he said, "have we faced a sterner test of our integrity as a people. In one generation we have seen a new Texas imposed on the face of the old. It is a Texas which bursts with vitality—growing, exploring, seeking its place in the sun." And the quickest way to that warm spot in the sun, Connally said, again, was through education. ". . . all that we seek to do for Texas must rest upon a base of excellence in education." That base had not been built, he illustrated, with statistics: Thirteen out of every one hundred Texans could neither read nor write; four out of every ten children who started the first grade would not graduate from high school. "Some of my friends have said I am obsessed with the subject of education," Connally said. "I will admit to my obsession."

Connally made the proposal which would become the highlight of his administration—a central board appointed by the governor to oversee college education in Texas, the Coordinating Board. Connally also proposed a Fine Arts Commission, tougher traffic safety laws, repeal of the poll tax, and a program to allow college students to borrow money for their education and to pay back the loan after they had gone to work. He suggested realigning state water and mental health agencies, and reminded legislators that the federal courts had given them until August 1965 to revise Texas' congressional and legislative districts to reflect population changes shown in the 1960 federal census.

Connally recommended a two-year budget totaling $3.5 billion, or an increase of $254 million from 1963, and it included significantly higher appropriations for two of Connally's favorite agencies—the Texas Industrial Commission and the Texas Tourist Development Agency. Connally said he planned at state expense to meet the "challenge of change" by educating or training Texans, taking care of their ailments, insuring them enough water to drink, protecting them with more police and better traffic laws, and adding more jobs and places to relax. "He covered the vast and complex field of our state's relationship to the people in a truly breathtaking manner," stated the Waco *Tribune-Herald*.

Speaking about Connally's attitude toward the legislators, former legislator Charles Wilson says, "Connally didn't know who I was until I got in the senate. On the other hand, Price Daniel had me over to the mansion the third week I was here as a snotty nose kid." Former Representative Dick Cory remembers Daniel inviting ten to twelve legislators to breakfast at the mansion every day, and, after he had invited all of them, he would start all over again; but Cory says, "You saw Connally at his pleasure, which was not too often, and not at all if you disagreed with him."

Connally's staff gradually dropped by the wayside, realizing that Connally was tiring of the job. His executive assistant, Howard Rose, resigned to practice law, and Connally made him the oil and gas representative on the Texas Water Pollution and Control Board. Connally reappointed his old friend Strauss to the State Banking Board.

The state sales tax, passed against Governor Daniel's opposition, had paid off more than had been predicted. After two years in office, there was a $98 million surplus in the state treasury, the first surplus since 1949, according to Connally.

Connally failed in his attempt to abolish the state property tax, and a proposal by Senator Hardeman was approved that would raise that levy from forty-two cents to forty-seven cents per hundred-dollar valuation to finance the construction of college buildings from 1966 to 1978. Five colleges were added to the list of those eligible for the money, including Angelo State College in Hardeman's hometown. Perhaps in retaliation for Hardeman's opposition to his program, Connally vetoed $1,158,941 for an administration and science building at Angelo State. He also rejected Hardeman bills to create Permian State College and to put the lieutenant governor on the building commission in place of a Connally appointee. Pendleton recalls when Connally called Representatives Ace Pickens of Odessa and Dick Slack of Pecos into his office to tell them he was vetoing the Odessa College bill. ''He pitched the veto message on the desk and said, 'Change it any way you want except for the veto. If you have any problems back home, just tell them to blame it on that son-of-a-bitch in the governor's office.' Slack said, 'That's just what I'm going to do'—Connally snapped his head around, and Slack added, 'But I'm going to tell 'em you're our son-of-a-bitch.' ''

Despite reported pressure from bankers, Connally vetoed a bill to allow banks, savings and loan institutions, and others supervised by the banking department to charge more than the legal interest of 10 percent on loans of up to $5,000. In a closing-day address Connally told the 1965 legislature that the session had been ''the most productive of any session in this century.''

"We Might as Well Abolish the Legislature"

House Speaker Barnes was doing his best, but he couldn't make any headway with the governor's brother. Representative Wayne Connally was typical of the Connally brothers in that after he had made up his mind, he ignored detours and obstacles and went straight ahead. In the spring of 1965, Wayne stubbornly pursued the issue of four-year terms, which had caused bitter controversy during most of the legislative session. Wayne agreed with John that governors should have four-year terms instead of two. However, he also wanted house members to be awarded four-year terms. And he was willing to go down to the wire on the issue. Barnes pleaded with Wayne that his doggedness was just calling more attention to Governor Connally's proposal

105

to give chief executives two extra years in office, which already had been approved for the November ballot. "Goddamnit, Wayne, you've got to back off," Barnes told him. "John ain't running the house," Wayne replied.

In the debate on four-year terms for house members, Representative Cory declared, "If the people give the governor four years and the house stays with two-year terms, the governor in an off-year election would be in position to exert tremendous political pressure on those who had not conformed to his wishes." Wayne agreed—"Cory presented the real issue. The house can be forever free . . . without the undue influence of the executive office in this state. Put it on the ballot, let the people decide."

Connally called Cory and Wayne into his office and berated Cory for "feeding this dumb son-of-a-bitch information." An observer says Connally then turned to Wayne and "chewed him up one side and down the other, chewed him until Wayne turned red, white, and blue—called him 'stupid'—he was always calling him stupid. Oh, if you scratched one, the other would come running, but did they ever have some arguments!"

In supporting four-year terms for governors, Connally strained his enormous popularity. Three years before, a Joe Belden poll showed that 62 percent of Texas' voters were against four-year terms. Seven weeks of parliamentary infighting in Representative John Allen's Constitutional Amendments Committee had kept the issue simmering in full public view. Committee members who were against four-year terms referred to themselves as a "kamikaze squad" because, they said, they were sacrificing passage of their own bills to oppose the measure.

Connally was accused of instigating a telephone and telegraph campaign to put pressure on legislators. One legislator said, "I was called out three times during the last committee hearing" on the proposal. In a personal privilege speech, a maneuver occasionally used by legislators to attract special attention to a topic, Representative Howard Green of Fort Worth said he had been contacted by "wealthy and . . . powerful" race track lobbyists asking him to support the measure. He also said that lobbyists supported four-year terms because it would save them money—they would only have to make campaign donations every four years. "The governor would become so great that we might as well abolish the legislature, because it would become merely a superfluous rubber stamp," Green added.

Democratic Representative Henry Grover from Houston, who switched parties and became the Republican nominee for governor in 1972, said Connally was "furious" over the committee delay on the four-year term proposal. Grover said an officer of Brown and Root Construction Company in Houston called him and "indicated" he should support the proposed constitutional amendment.

Supporters finally shook the proposal loose from the committee on a 12 to 7 vote, and Representative Bill Hollowell of Grand Saline said at least five members had changed their votes to gain passage of their own local bills. He called the four-year plan "an insidious plot to perpetuate one man in office." One who changed his vote was Representative Charles Whitfield of Houston, "dean" of the Harris County delegation. When reporters asked him about the switch, he pulled from his pocket a typed statement from Connally that stated that the governor was still "openminded" about Whitfield's proposal to abolish capital punishment.

Opposing the measure on the final committee vote were Green, Hollowell, and Grover, and Representatives Travis Peeler of Corpus Christi, Maude Isaacks of El Paso, Bob Vale of San Antonio, and Bob Eckhardt of Houston. The four-year term proposal was adopted by the house by a vote of 117 to 26. The senate had approved the measure early in the session by a vote of 29 to 2, and it was scheduled to go on the ballot in a special November 1965 election.

Connally stated that he was "strong" for four-year terms, noting a "very substantial increase" in his workload as governor. He said one-third of his time was being spent on programs which had not existed when he was elected in 1962. His friends stressed that the governors of most large states were serving four years and ran when there was no presidential election, leaving them free to campaign for presidential candidates without putting their own jobs in jeopardy.

The four-year proposal was so important to Connally that he canceled a two-week State Department trip to Japan, scheduled to begin October 19, 1965. Reporter Stuart Long said Connally put out thousands of letters in favor of the amendment, and he asked businessmen to help spread the word. An anonymous "Connally for King" circular appeared in opposition to the amendment.[5]

According to the *Texas Observer*, Senator Yarborough sent personal letters to two hundred "key Yarborough leaders in as many counties," enclosing suggested radio spots against the proposal and asking that they be run twenty times in each area, with local Yarborough leaders paying for the radio advertisements. A Yarborough aide, Chuck Caldwell, took a brief leave of absence to work against the amendment, the *Observer* also reported. United States Senator John Tower, a Republican, endorsed the four-year term, but several big city GOP leaders opposed it.

To encourage voting on the measure, Connally made the November 2 election a half-holiday for state employees, but the four-year proposal was rejected by a vote of 273,586, to 225,215. Connally's first reaction was that he was "delighted to have the opportunity to submit myself and my program to the people every two years."

Allen Duckworth, political editor of the Dallas *Morning News*, said the defeat of the amendment was Connally's "first major political loss" since he had taken office. Representative Wayne Connally fared even worse. The proposal to let house members serve four years was overwhelmed by a vote of 340,307 to 139,539, or 71 to 29 percent, and not even his brother, the governor, liked Wayne's idea.

5. A four-year term for Connally in 1966 would have extended his administration to eight years, longer than the record of seven and one-half years that Governor Allan Shivers served from July 11, 1949 to January 15, 1957.

Connally miscalculated when he announced for a third term before Texans had voted on the proposal to let him, and those who followed him as governor, serve four-year terms instead of two. It could have been that Connally thought his popularity would carry the issue. His early announcement, he admitted later, might have been the reason the proposal was defeated. Too many people, he said, apparently thought his support of four-year terms was selfish. He insisted it was not.

Two weeks after the voters rejected four-year terms, Connally made his second major mistake, putting his prestige on the line in Attorney General Waggoner Carr's race against Republican Senator John Tower. Men who had worked closely with Connally—Julian Read, Will Davis, and Howard Rose—pitched in on Carr's 1966 campaign. Dick Cory was Carr's campaign manager, but Randy Pendleton, who was doing advance work on Carr's campaign, says, "Connally was calling the shots" in the closing days. Tower easily won his first full six-year term, and Republicans quipped, "There's one Carr Big John's used car lot can't sell."

GOVERNOR OF TEXAS 1966-1968

8

"The Steam That Blows the Whistle"

John Connally said he never worried about anything so much in his life as he did over whether to run for a third term as governor. As a gubernatorial candidate in 1962, one of his first proposals was to cut down on the number of terms a governor could serve. Allan Shivers and Price Daniel had both been elected three times, controlling the chief executive's office from July 1949 to January 1963. Connally told a statewide television audience he wanted it written into the constitution that a governor could not serve more than two consecutive two-year terms. Now, in 1965, it seemed that everyone in Texas, except diehard liberals, was trying to pull him into the race again.

The State Democratic Executive Committee met on September 18 at the Holiday Inn in Amarillo, bedrock-conservative Connally country. There had been rumors for weeks that Connally would finally say "yea" or "nay." Seven hundred supporters waited in expectation as Connally sat on the bed in his room at the motel, mulling over what to do. With him were his wife, Nellie; Secretary of State Crawford Martin, a man Connally said had his "complete trust and confidence"; and press secretary George Christian, whose quiet manner and solid advice had made him indispensable. Connally had a written statement announcing he would run, but the group talked it over once more, and Connally motioned for Nellie to follow him. They went into the bathroom and closed the door, and it was there that the governor and his wife agreed on the most important political decision of the year in Texas—that Connally would seek another two years in office.

Blinking back tears, Connally made it public that he would run again, and the SDEC members and onlookers cheered wildly. "Nothing I've ever done has caused me so much concern," he said. It was the decision Attorney General Carr had been waiting for. When he had flown to Amarillo, he had two statements—one announcing his candidacy for governor; the other for United States Senator. It had to be the Senate for Carr. To challenge Connally was still political suicide in Texas. Carr knew it, and so did Lieutenant Governor Preston Smith, who would have to wait his turn. The Connally-Carr-Smith alignment was exactly as the Houston *Chronicle* had predicted in June 1964, almost a year and a half before the decisions were made.

What swayed Connally? "He obviously didn't want Preston to be governor," says Ben Barnes. "I think he [Connally] was interested in holding the party together and there wasn't anybody . . . around to fill the leadership void. I think that had a lot to do with it. Connally feels very strong about leadership and developing leadership. This is an old school that he grew up in."

It was four months before Connally knew who his opponent would be in the Democratic primary, and the feeling was that it took that long for the liberal-labor coalition to talk someone into squaring off against Connally. His opponent was Stanley Woods, a forty-three-year-old

Houston oil man.[1] A token candidate was Johnnie Mae Hackworthe, a Bible-carrying grandmother from Brenham who had been married three times but had been a widow since 1957. She filed under her maiden name to make her second race against Connally. Representative Bill Hollowell of Grand Saline, who had a reputation in the house for honesty and obstinancy, announced for lieutenant governor against Smith, and Woods and Hollowell formed a political team, the first in Texas in modern recollection, according to capitol reporter Stuart Long. The odds were all in Connally's favor;[2] and the campaign became one of unanswered questions. Woods referred to Connally as ''King John'' and alleged that he was ''profiteering'' as governor. For the most part, his allegations were so much whistling in the wind. Connally dismissed a Woods-Hollowell television show with a rhyme:

> To those who talk and talk;
> This motto should appeal.
> The steam that blows the whistle,
> Never turns the wheel.

The candidates' performance, he said, was similar to a tag team in wrestling, ''a great deal of sound but no substance.''

Why, Woods asked, was Julian Read, a Connally campaign director in 1962 and 1964, getting $12,000 to handle public relations at the Camp Gary Job Corps Center in San Marcos? Was the law firm of Joe Kilgore's, a close friend and former college classmate of Connally's, guaranteed $6,000 in legal fees by the Job Corps Center? Was there any connection, he asked, between Connally allegedly borrowing $300,000 from Travelers Insurance Company to buy 14,270 acres of land in Dimmit and Zavala

1. Woods had a law degree from The University of Texas and had practiced law before founding his own business, Woods Exploration and Producing Company. He said he had supported Connally in 1962 against Republican Jack Cox, ''because I thought he understood the oil and gas industry and its problems.'' That choice ''was a mistake,'' Woods said.

2. A Joe Belden poll in January 1966 showed 73 percent of the voters approved of the way Connally was doing his job.

113

counties and the subsequent raise in car insurance rates ordered by the State Board of Insurance? What about game wardens being forced to resign for speaking to sportsmen's groups that had criticized Connally's proposal creating the Parks and Wildlife Commission? Of Connally's tourist promotion, Woods commented, "As far as I'm concerned this is some more of Connally's political patronage."

All Woods' charges could not beat Connally's slick, well-organized campaign. Connally polled 932,641 votes, gaining 74 percent of the total. Woods received 291,651; and Johnnie Mae Hackworthe 31,105. Connally's percentage was even higher than it had been in 1964 when he ran with his arm in a sling, a reminder that the man who had assassinated John Kennedy also had shot the governor.

Another Houston lawyer, sixty-two-year-old T. E. Kennerly, ran on the Republican ticket against Connally in November. Kennerly had received 523,116 votes in the 1962 race for attorney general and 677,100 votes in the 1964 race for the Texas Supreme Court. But he only received 368,025 against Connally, as the governor scored another victory with 1,037,517 votes, or 72 percent of the total vote.[3] It appeared that Connally could be governor for life.

"Progress Unequaled in This Century"

With the legislature scheduled to meet in regular session in January 1967, the governor found that his job bored him. Connally learned in two terms what Crawford Martin had said was true—Texas governors really don't have any power. Even fancier trimmings—a remodeled office, a new $86,000 airplane, and a $10,000 limousine—had not revived his initial burst of enthusiasm, the desire to prove he was the best governor Texans had ever seen.

Too many performances and too many niggling chores had dulled his expectations. He got as many as fifty speaking invitations a week. He was making one hundred

3. Tommye Gillespie of the Constitution Party received 10,454 votes, and Bard Logan of the Conservative Party received 9,810 votes.

114

major speeches a year and attending countless smaller functions. He often relaxed at his Floresville ranch, and he regretted not having more time with his family. His relationship with Lyndon Johnson was uneven, as the president's proposals for a ''Great Society'' were pounding against statehouses like storm waves. Trying to wedge federal programs into the rigid framework of state government and scouting missions for new tax sources were the themes of the 1967 legislative session.

It would have been easier, Connally often thought, if someone besides Smith, who irritated him, were lieutenant governor. Connally's mere recognition of Texas' growing population guaranteed higher budgets, and he was not hesitant to propose taxes. Smith preached about the ''good ol' days'' and no tax increases. Senator Dorsey Hardeman made life so difficult for Connally, however, that the governor's speechwriters put together an address in 1967 which singled out Hardeman by name as an ''obstructionist,'' but Connally deleted the reference. Former press secretary Bill Carter recalls, ''It was still the meanest son-of-a-bitch speech I had ever seen.''

Smith, as presiding officer of the senate, and a handful of senators, including Hardeman and the late George Parkhouse of Dallas, seemed to thwart the governor daily. Carrying a fancy new gift rifle, Connally was waiting for a capitol elevator one day when an aide, John Mobley, saw him. ''Where you headed, Governor—the senate?'' Mobley asked. Connally went out the front door and two newsmen encountered him. They asked about the rifle, and Connally replied, ''I just hope I can get Dorsey Hardeman in my sights.''

When he was bored or discouraged, Connally could refuel by turning to the large segment of Texans who thought he looked and acted like a governor should, or to his inner circle, the ''palace guard,'' as they were sometimes called. Richard Morehead of the Dallas *Morning News* wrote, ''Connally's public image seems to grow brighter the longer he remains in office. . . . An almost-mystic Connally Cult has grown up among his closest followers, who sometimes bestow praise to an embarrassing degree." "Connally had a tremendous ego," a close Connally watcher says, "and his top aides thought he had a lot to be egotistical about. They put him on a pedestal. The other thing they all had in common was they didn't trust the press."

Connally's aides remained on all-out alert to insure his tranquility. One day the Tigua Indians were in the governor's reception room to make Connally an honorary "Cacique" (high priest) of the West Texas tribe after he had signed a bill clearing the way for state aid to the tribe. As part of the ceremony, Connally squatted while an Indian thumped an ancient drum. He was impatient and uncomfortable, an aide says, and "started getting mad—you could tell because his bottom teeth were showing." To avoid a twentieth-century attack by a white man on Indians, the aide whispered to the drummer to knock it off. Without expression, the drummer grunted, "Ummf, not through!" The Indians had dabbed paint on Connally's cheeks, and, after they finally finished with the ceremony and left the office, Connally yelled, "Get this goddamn stuff off!" Six highly paid assistants scattered in six directions to get facial tissue to clean the governor's cheeks.

It became almost impossible to keep Connally happy during the public sessions for signing proclamations in the large reception room. He even forgot one ceremony and drove out to play golf as Stanley Marcus of Neiman-Marcus and others waited at the capitol. A ceremony remembered vividly by those present was a particularly crowded one, where the list of proclamations seemed endless. A man, whose identity was not known to Connally or to his aides, rushed over several times to use a nearby desk telephone. Connally shook hands and posed for pictures, and finally the last visitors were ushered out. "Don't" Connally said, "ever get me involved in a three-ring circus like that again. And who in the hell was that goddamn guy using my telephone?" Connally seethed. "He could have been a goddamn communist."

116

Another function of the executive office, autographing photographs, also stirred the governor's ire. To autograph a glossy photo required a special pen, and the staff was continually searching for the best kind. They settled on a pen which had to be dipped in white ink, but Connally was always breaking the points. Nick Johnson, who was in the press secretary's office from 1965 to 1968, recalls that Connally "would ignore requests even from personal friends and $5,000 campaign contributors. People would send in expensively matted pictures of themselves and Connally at a dinner, for example, and they would just be tossed in a box. A form letter would be sent out occasionally apologizing for the delay. Some requests were three years old." Even Christian, one of Connally's closest advisers, brags about getting Connally to autograph a picture for him when Christian left to work for President Johnson.

During his third term, it was not any easier to see Connally. Nick Johnson says he had "to turn down fairly important guys" who wanted an audience with the governor. "About the only way to contact him would be through a mutual friend who had contributed to his campaign." To get Connally to approve speeches, Carter and Johnson would lay them on the desk of Connally's secretary, Maurine Ray, and "she'd try to slip them in with other material." Off the cuff, they say, "He had a tendency to ramble. An outline helped him to come to a logical end. He was a hell of a lot better with an outline than with a fully written speech which he might read." The routine letters from Connally's office were signed by the mail boys, Nick Johnson says. "One was Joe Longley.⁴ He got pretty good at imitating Connally's signature."

A late arrival in the Connally camp, a smart, successful, Houston plaintiffs lawyer, John Hill,⁵ ran into the protective wall Connally's jealous aides had built. Hill was appointed secretary of state in 1966, and a friend says he was "eager to please and anxious to be on the inside." One

4. Longley now heads the Texas attorney general's consumer protection division.

5. Hill was elected attorney general of Texas in 1972.

day Connally asked Hill to ride to the airport with him and Frank Erwin. "There was Hill, all bright-eyed and excited," the friend remembers. "But before he could get in, Erwin reached over and pulled the door shut in Hill's face, and told the driver to go." They left.

If you worked for Connally, it helped to be able to pick up danger signals. Just prior to the 1967 session at a meeting in the Commodore Perry Hotel, Connally asked first one aide and then another about proposals to the legislature. After a few hours, Connally stalked around the room emptying ashtrays. A newcomer sensed that "it was a red flag, and I kept my mouth shut." He asked about it later and was told it was one of Connally's idiosyncrasies—"and you had better never try to help him clean up."

On January 18, 1967, Connally presented his program to a joint session of the legislature. "I can conceive," he said, "of no other project which equals or even approaches in importance the proposal for constitutional revision through a Constitutional Convention. I truly believe that we are in one of the most pivotal periods in our history, and the future of our people will be influenced to a great degree by our decision in this matter." He asked the legislature to submit a proposal to the voters in November for a convention to rewrite the constitution, which had been amended more than two hundred times since its adoption in 1876. The convention would consist of three delegates from each of the 150 house districts, elected by majority vote. A twenty-five member committee, including ten appointed by the governor, would serve as staff. Connally also proposed that Texas switch from biennial to annual legislative sessions.

The long-range impact of federal laws eventually influenced several measures adopted by the legislature, including a highway safety act, a water quality act, and legislation enabling Texas to take part in the federal "Medicaid" program for welfare recipients. A 116 to 29 vote in the house in support of Connally's position that a state-employee pay-raise was not an emergency indicated Connally might get

118

anything he wanted in 1967, including liquor-by-the-drink for the first time since Prohibition. A 21 to 8 senate vote defeating Parkhouse's attempt to slice Connally's $5.5 million request for HemisFair '68 was also a victory.

However, Connally's top priority, to move ahead on rewriting the constitution, failed, and Jon Ford of the San Antonio *Express-News* reported that the "lobby headed off" Connally's $143 million tax program "in the Senate before it could get started in the House." In reaction to defeat, Connally, in an unprecedented request, proposed a one-year appropriations bill, requiring no new taxes. The governor stated that he would call the legislature into special session in 1968 to adopt another one-year spending bill and would suggest taxes to cover the cost of the second year at that time.

The legislature accepted Connally's abbreviated budget, and Bo Byers of the Houston *Chronicle* quoted Connally as saying the $2,386,038,269 appropriations bill was the best spending bill of his years in office. However, Lieutenant Governor Smith was so upset over the idea of a one-year bill that, when he learned Connally had nine senators in his office to discuss the plan, he abruptly adjourned the senate just seconds before they arrived to make a quorum.

In addition to the setbacks on constitutional revision and taxes, Connally could muster only 62 votes in the house for his liquor proposal, and it was never brought to the floor. Connally was amazed at the 7,000 letters he received on the issue. The legislature rejected four-year terms for governors even though Representative Ed Harris of Galveston claimed Connally had threatened to block another member's college bill unless the member voted for four-year terms.

In 1967, despite Connally's legislative problems, he was voted Texas "Man of the Year" by United Press International editors. House Speaker Barnes and Houston promoter Roy Hofheinz, who brought the Astrodome to Houston, tied for second place. One editor cited Connally's work during Hurricane Beulah, which caused damage to twenty-seven counties; "his acquiescence on the city sales tax, which cleared the way for passage; and his efforts on 'liquor

119

by the jigger' which will pave the way for final adoption before the end of this decade."

The editor's prediction was off by a year, although Connally, in a move that angered Texas Baptists, tried again during the June 1968 special session to legalize whiskey drinking at public places. His mini-bottle proposal would have permitted the sale of bottles of liquor of two ounces or less at restaurants, hotels, and motels in wet areas, on a local option basis. "The only question," Connally said, "is whether we are going to have it sold in smaller quantities than a fifth, and it is my opinion that it should be sold in small enough quantities to induce temperance and moderation." The bill cleared the house by a 78 to 67 vote, but was defeated in the senate 17 to 14.

His tax package of $120 million was also scrapped during the special session, which enacted a $153 million revenue-raising bill. Both bills included a hike of from 2 to 3 percent in the state sales tax. Connally vetoed $1,362,500 from the budget. During the special session in 1968, Connally watchers claimed he only spent six of the thirty days in the office. It was the last time he would do business with the full legislature, and nobody was happier about that than John Connally.

"The Flickering of the Spirit"

"It's a question," said Preston Smith, "of where do you stop?" Speculation over whether Connally would run for a fourth term started before he had been elected the third time.

Connally told hundreds of campaign coordinators that he might run again if an escalating conflict between Smith and Barnes jeopardized the 1967 legislative session. It also appeared that Connally would want to retain his job to guarantee solid support for President Johnson's expected bid for a second term in 1968. In February 1967 Connally hinted that he would become a candidate by reminding reporters of the unfinished matters of the state constitution and public education. In May, the last month of the legislative

120

session, newspaper columnists, among them Sam Kinch Sr. of the Fort Worth *Star-Telegram*, predicted the governor would seek a fourth consecutive term. However, Bill Carter thinks Connally decided midway through the 1967 session not to run again. "I think he got sick of people, fed up with trying to help people and have them fight him . . . particularly in the senate." Smith had been nourishing a dream to be governor since he was nine years old, and he had climbed to the next-to-last rung with his election as lieutenant governor over the favorite, House Speaker James Turman, in 1962. A cautious man, Smith had been waiting for Connally to move on. But no more. "How do I know," Smith said, "he won't run for a fifth term?"

On August 31, 1967, after Connally returned from an African safari, he told reporters he was not "dying for a fourth term." But a week later, he said he was leaning that way and his wife was "more amenable" this time than she had been at their motel room conference in Amarillo in September 1965. "Before the African trip, signs pointed almost 100 percent toward Connally seeking a fourth term," wrote Richard Morehead of the Dallas *News*. But Connally's friends say the trip changed him. He became more introspective, more philosophical. "He said it was the first time he had had a chance to think," recalls Mike Myers. "I didn't take him seriously at first, but his change in attitude began to show up in little things. It's hard to be specific, but, I think, he became more moralistic. It seemed he had gotten off that unbelievable treadmill of politics." Others say he simply no longer cared.

Barnes claims he announced early that he was running for lieutenant governor in an effort to force Connally into the 1968 governor's race. Barnes reasoned that Connally would do anything to block Smith. Despite Barnes' manuever, Connally startled forty-four of his closest advisers at a four-hour "hush-hush" meeting held at the governor's mansion on the night of October 3, by telling them he seriously doubted if he would try for another term.

Published reports of the secret meeting, quoting unnamed sources, drew immediate reaction from numerous

121

Texas newspapers, urging Connally to run. ". . . we self-ishly ask that he go the extra mile," editorialized the Dallas *Times Herald.* "The office is yours for the asking," stated the Wichita Falls *Times. Times Herald* capitol reporter Ernest Stromberger wrote, "It must be particularly galling to Lt. Gov. Preston Smith, an announced candidate for Connally's job, who is seeing his best issue —built-in resentment against a fourth term—being trampled in the rush of politicians pleading with Connally to run for reelection." Stromberger added, "All the hullaballoo was . . . Connally . . . reminding the politicians who is boss, and that the boss is ready for a long vacation. He was very convincing on both counts, but it's still hard to find anyone willing to bet he won't run." It seemed so certain that Connally would seek reelection that 27 of 28 capitol reporters felt Connally would run for a fourth term. Only Stuart Long said he would not.

While Connally wavered, Smith campaigned non-stop, reminding Texans of a speech Connally had made on statewide television in 1962, when he was opposing Governor Price Daniel, a candidate for a fourth term. Connally stated that if a governor

> serves four terms for eight years, which no man in history has ever done in this state, he will completely dominate every board, commission and authority in this state—dominate it in the sense that he will have appointed at least once every single member of that board. I am unalterably opposed to that in principle, because the last thing that Texas needs is one-man rule. The last thing we need is this type of control of the educational processes of this state and of the economic processes that reach into every facet of our lives. . . . I'm the only man in this race who had advocated a constitutional amendment limiting the term of the governor's office effective with my own election. I advocated it solely because I feel very strongly and very keenly that no man, or no one group of men, or no one clique of people should dominate the political life and political thinking of this state. And you are going to get that any time you have a four-term governor.

122

On October 9 Connally attended a two-hour, closed-door meeting in the Jim Hogg suite of the Driskill Hotel at which thirty-two supporters, many of them members of the business and oil and gas lobby, urged him to run one more time. Lloyd Bentsen,[6] a Houston insurance executive and former congressman from McAllen, and Houston *Chronicle* editor Everett Collier talked to reporters after the meeting. "There is a general demand that this man continue in office," said Bentsen, whose wife had served a term as Democratic national committeewoman during Connally's administration. "This man is the most highly qualified person who could fill the highest office in Texas. . . . It was the consensus of this group that the governor has started a progressive program, and we unanimously felt he is the best man to see it through to fulfillment."

One member of the business lobby recalled Connally's vacilliating at the meeting. The governor was at his best amid the antique furniture and the sense of history that the suite embodied, and he sat back in an old rosewood rocking chair and allowed his supporters to try to convince him to run again. "One minute Connally was telling everyone how sorry he was that he couldn't make the race. Then he'd rock awhile and look around at all the men who had been part of his team. He'd get caught up in the political talk, and say, 'You bet we're gonna beat 'em again!'"

Connally decided to wait until after the National Governors' Conference in the Virgin Islands in late October to announce his decision. "I have reluctantly concluded," Connally finally told a capitol press conference, "that after the drain of what will have been eight years of vigorous public service I no longer can be assured in my own mind that I could bring to the office for another two years the enthusiasm, the resilience, the patience that my conscience would demand and the state would deserve. I therefore do not

6. Bentsen reportedly said he had urged Connally to run for governor in 1962, but Connally replied, "I can't run for governor. I wouldn't know where to get my first campaign contribution." Bentsen is said to have signed a check and handed it to Connally, saying, "Open your campaign."

intend to be a candidate for reelection as governor of Texas."

Connally's public relations adviser, Julian Read, hand-delivered his own summary of Connally's November 10 decision to the Associated Press in Austin. A shortened version was released by the AP to Texas newspapers and radio and television stations. To Read, Connally's statement was the "reflection of the flickering of the spirit of a great contemporary political leader." Read's personalized account said Connally had been sick with the flu several days before his Friday morning announcement. Read recalled Barnes' emerging from Connally's office on Thursday, after Connally had met twice on Wednesday with supporters urging him again to run for a fourth term, and saying, "That man is my friend, and he just can't bring himself to do it again. I don't want anybody pressing him to, either." Read also remembers Connally's joking to the manicurist at the barber shop that, "I'm about ready to turn in my suit." She thought it was funny, Read said. On Thursday Connally tipped off "key newspaper publishers and editors that he would not run again," Read said. "One call went to the White House." Friday morning, "still coughing from a sore throat but dapper in a dark charcoal suit with vest," Connally made his decision public.

After Connally's announcement, the *Texas Observer* reported that within two weeks thirty-two men had been mentioned as his possible successor. There was published speculation that Connally might even change his mind and run because he did not like any of the candidates. Barnes recalls that a group of businessmen met with him at the Adolphus Hotel in Dallas and tried to talk him into switching from the lieutenant governor's race. Barnes says he thought about it but decided, "It would make me look pretty immature—like I was shopping around and could have anything I wanted."

The so-called "Connally candidate" was Eugene Locke of Dallas, former Democratic national committeeman and Connally's 1962 campaign manager. But despite Connally's help, Locke ran fifth in the 1968 Democratic primary.

Roy Evans, former president of the Texas AFL-CIO, says that Connally would have been beaten if he had run. One of the reasons, says Evans, was that organized labor had collected a large amount of material on Connally's business dealings, and "he was afraid we would release it during the campaign." The Yarboroughs—Ralph and Don—also thought Connally would have lost. Ralph said he felt enough liberals would have defected in the November election to elect a Republican governor. Don said, "He had alienated many groups. . . . I think he was aware his chickens were coming home to roost." Preston Smith recalls, "I think there's no question but what he [Connally] probably would have made the race for a fourth term if I had not entered the race. I believe he feels, and he might have been right in his feeling, that he could have defeated me. But I'm sure that he knew it would be a tough race. . . . I was well known throughout the state and I do think we could have made a good showing. Whether or not we could have defeated Governor Connally, of course, no one will ever know, but I think it had a great deal to do with his decision not to run."[7]

Since early in his administration, Connally had felt he was the apocryphal man in the rowboat that was springing too many leaks to plug. For awhile, he had tried, using the methods he had learned in twenty years as Lyndon Johnson's man in Texas—organization, persuasion, and force. "Open controversy virtually disappeared under Gov. Connally's iron fist . . . [he] not only dictated to the legislature . . . Democratic conventions, once a great and long circus, became duller than chamber of commerce meetings under Connally's command," commented Allen Duckworth in the Dallas *Morning News*. Not even a governor with the executive power that Connally commanded, however, could tie up all the loose ends in Texas politics. It was a race

7. After Connally left office, he joined the law firm of Vinson, Elkins, Weems, and Searls, later renamed Vinson, Elkins, Searls and Connally. One of the largest in the nation, the law firm had about 130 lawyers and offices in Washington and in Mexico City, as well as in Houston.

against a population which had grown by 1.5 million in six years, and, after three terms as governor, Connally told Ronnie Dugger, of the *Texas Observer*, that he doubted if one man could change very much, very fast in the governor's office.

One staunch critic, Bob Bullock, sums up Connally's administration as one of flowery speeches, rather than constructive programs.

> Here's an extremely handsome man, a mysterious man, a behind-the-scenes man with Lyndon Johnson, who was hit with a silver bullet in Dallas with the president. And the result is he's a mysterious man from Siberia, you know, with a lot of charisma, who makes beautiful speeches and who uses such words as 'greatness for Texas' and 'I want brains instead of mortar' and 'I'm not just interested in bricks and mortar for higher education' and I want this, and that—and it all sounded good. He created the Texas Fine Arts Commission to make all us dummies realize the arts. But he never did anything with them. He created them and that's all. He wanted to reorganize the Parks and Wildlife—he got his bill passed to reorganize it—and then forgot about it.
>
> You know I look back and I can't think of anything he did that worked out good. The Parks and Wildlife is still torn up over what he did to it. Our water agencies in Texas are a mass of confusion and conflict. The Coordinating Board has been absolutely able to do nothing from what it should have done. It had the potential for really coordinating higher education aims for this state and putting our institutions to probably surpassing the educational institutions in California. And what's it done? Nothing except fuss and fight in the university system. And HemisFair! My god, it's the bricks and mortar you're talking about, sitting down there deteriorating under the sun. What did he do? Create and then leave—like building a city and deserting it.
>
> Connally was the kind that had these beautiful ideas and names for these committees and stuff and they would come into being and he would forget it. . . . All he was interested in was getting the bill passed and

126

the publicity to go with it. And then how it was accomplished once it was passed, put into being, carry out the objectives—that was below him. 'Let me look at the big picture. I don't want to see the little fine brush marks.' That was John Connally.

Most Connally supporters refer to the College Coordinating Board as his crowning achievement, but the board has never managed to purge itself of the selfish interests that Connally warned against. Nobody denies that, as governor, Connally steadfastly sought more money for Texas' universities and colleges, but his enemies say it was merely an attempt to woo the more liberal professors' campaign support. The melding of the Texas Parks Board and Texas Game and Fish Commission into the Parks and Wildlife Commission in 1963 was considered a "political coup," but the agency has had difficulty in shedding the troubles that have plagued it.

Industrial and tourist growth were central themes of Connally's administration, and he noted in his 1969 farewell speech, "It seems incredible that Texas wasn't really in the tourist business until a little more than five years ago." Connally claimed that since the creation of the Texas Tourist Development Agency on September 1, 1963, out-of-state visitors had increased from over fourteen million to over twenty-one million, and tourist dollars spent in Texas had increased from $680 million to nearly $1.5 billion. During his administration, Connally said, "More substantive and far-reaching legislation had been proposed and passed than during any similar period in our long history."

After Connally had settled down in his Houston law firm and a magnificent contemporary home in the exclusive River Oaks section, he summed up his opinion of the governor's office and the machinery of state politics for reporter Henry Holcomb of the Houston *Post*: "The state government is about as cumbersome a political subdivision as there is in the United States. The most frustrating part of being governor is the ponderous machinery through which you have to work to get something done. If business was as ponderous as government, it would go broke."

Preston Smith says, "I think Governor Connally did make some progress as governor. He brought our government forward in a 'progressive' way, but I don't believe that label would fit him quite as much, perhaps, as an 'idealist.' He had great visions of progress and a lot of them simply never came about."

At his farewell appearance before the legislature in January 1969, Connally was acclaimed by Barnes as "truly, a man for all seasons." But it was not as it had been: the galleries in the house were not packed for Connally's speech, and the only time the audience applauded during his thirty-five-minute address was when he mentioned Nellie's efforts to spruce up the mansion grounds.

"Today," says Bob Bullock, "I read in the newspapers like the Dallas *Morning News*, which . . . leave the impression that he's one of the greatest governors we ever had. If you were to go out and get one hundred businessmen in Texas and sit them down and say, 'Who was the best governor Texas ever had?' A lot of them would say John Connally. A whole lot of them would. And yet if you ask that same one hundred, 'What did he do?'—I doubt if they could tell you."

Illustrations

—*Texas State Archives*

Lela Wright Connally on the porch of her San Antonio house. Merrill, Golfrey, Blanche, and Wayne with the family dog.

Lela Wright Connally and John Bowden Connally Sr.

Lela Wright Connally and John Bowden Connally Sr. on their wedding day.

—*Merrill Connally*

John Bowden Connally Sr.

—*Texas State Archives*

—Blanche Connally Kline

—Blanche Connally Kline

John Connally with his eldest child, Kathleen (left). John B. Connally Sr. with his granddaughter Kathleen (right).

John Connally and a friend at the Connally home, 115 Bristol, San Antonio.

—Blanche Connally Kline

Lyndon Johnson and John Connally in San Francisco during World War II.

—Blanche Connally Kline

John Connally on horseback.

Navy officer John Connally (left) and brother Merrill, a Marine, during World War II.

—The Cactus (University of Texas yearbook)

—Blanche Connally Kline

—Department of Drama
University of Texas

University student John Connally in top hat and tails (opposite, above left). Bluebonnet Belle Idanell Brill (opposite, above right). John Connally center stage in his role in the Curtain Club production of *Call It a Day* (opposite, bottom). Idanell Brill in costume as Princess Kukachin in the Curtain Club production of Eugene O'Neill's *Marco Millions* (above).

Lyndon Johnson (left), John Connally (second left), and Walter Jenkins (far right) with Johnson's office staff at the Austin office of the National Youth Administration.

Organizers and Board of Directors of Austin radio station KVET, September 1946: (Front Row, left to right) Willard Deason, John Connally, Bob Phinney. (Back Row, left to right) Sherman Birdwell, Ed Clark, Ed Syers, Jesse Kellam, and Jake Pickle.

Caricature of John Connally as a young man by his former college classmate, Jack Guinn.

Connally hugs his mother on election night 1962 in Fort Worth.

Lela Wright Connally.

The Reverend Billy Graham (left) chats with
John Connally (right) and Preston Smith
(second right) at 1963 Prayer Breakfast pre-
ceding Connally's inauguration as governor.

The Connally clan, including (Front Row, left to right) D. W.
"Speedy" Hicks, Blanche Connally Kline, Mrs. Wayne Connally
(Kay), Mrs. D. W. Hicks (Carmen), Sharon, Nellie, Mark, Lela
Wright Connally, and Mrs. Merrill Connally (Mary). (Back Row, left
to right) Wayne, John, John III, and Merrill.

Kathleen Connally

Bobby Hale, Kathleen Connally's husband (above). Kathleen Connally as a Fort Worth teenager before her marriage (left).

—Wide World Photos

—Austin American-Statesman

The Connally brothers (left to right) John, Merrill, and Wayne, with aide Julian Read on election night 1962 in Fort Worth (above). Young Austin lawyer John Connally in the 1940s (below).

—*Institute of Texan Cultures*

"To Dream Bigger Dreams"

9

When John Connally left the governor's office, he was quick to cite the innovative changes he had brought to the state of Texas. Education, planning for additional water resources, industrial growth, tourist development, development in the arts, and an awakening among the people of the untapped potential of the state were among high points that Connally mentioned in summing up his years as governor. To author Jimmy Banks, Connally lapsed into high-flown rhetoric to point up the accomplishments of his administration. "We have to dream bigger dreams, and we must have the courage to make the changes that will enrich the lives of the people who live here."

"A Highly Unethical Abuse of Power"

Despite Connally's dreams, many legislators and public officials felt that Connally's years in office were lacking in effective leadership. Others believed that Connally's insatiable drive for power had set dangerous precedents for the future. Connally's immediate predecessors had set an ambiguous path for him to follow. Governor Allan Shivers had kept a tight rein on the legislature, pushing through laws in the 1950s that would have far-reaching effects into the 1970s. Democrat Shivers also set a precedent by carrying Texas into the Republican column for Dwight Eisenhower. Governor Price Daniel's indecisiveness and vacillation had caused him problems with the legislature, and his opposition to the sales tax plunged him into conflict with lawmakers. Connally's concept of the governorship was a close-knit hierarchy with all the strings controlled by the man at the top—John Connally. One of the most well-known critics of Texas government, former University of Texas government professor Dr. H. Clifton McCleskey, evaluated Connally's effectiveness as governor for the Austin *Statesman* in 1967. When asked if Connally had been a strong governor, McCleskey replied,

> If you mean by 'strong' a governor who charts a relatively new path and steers the legislature down that path without difficulty, then the answer is 'no.' On the other hand, if by 'strong' you mean a governor who can have pretty much his own way, even if that way is not earthshaking, then the answer is 'yes.'
> This much is certain, politically he's the strongest governor in that he's the most invulnerable. . . . Connally has closer connections with Washington than any Texas Governor . . . however, he hasn't made the most of the opportunity at hand, and he hasn't done the things he could and should have done.

Connally projected his own conservative and business-oriented ideas onto the state's programs, and his ideas of how things should be done often differed from those of members of the legislature. His concepts of how the state should be governed focused on the executive office, and he believed that power should begin and end there.

Connally had no experience in the legislature and had declined to run for legislative office when the idea was suggested to him. Power was Connally's goal, and his administration focused on strengthening the authority of the governor and on making the state executive office the originator of both programs and legislation.

The power of appointment to state boards and commissions rested with the governor, and, in 1963, Connally exercised his privilege when the Game and Fish Commission merged with the State Parks Board into the newly organized Texas Parks and Wildlife Commission. The Game and Fish Commission had functioned under nine commissioners, but Connally set up a three-man commission for the merged agency, and appointed A. W. Moursund, a longtime Lyndon Johnson supporter and financial consultant, Will Odom of Austin, and James Dellinger of Corpus Christi as commissioners.

Howard Dodgen had been employed by the Texas Game and Fish Commission for thirty-one years and had served as director of the agency for eighteen years. In an interview with the *Texas Observer* on May 1, 1964, Dodgen claimed that Connally had been responsible for his being fired by the new commission. Dodgen claimed that his firing was the direct result of an alleged bird-hunting violation involving Moursund and Lyndon Johnson and that Johnson had told Connally that Dodgen "had to go."

Dodgen stated that Moursund had called him and asked that the game warden dismiss the case. Dodgen refused and stated that he had told Moursund, "The best thing for you to do is to plead guilty and pay your fine." When Dodgen asked Moursund if Johnson were involved in the case, Moursund replied, "Well, that doesn't have anything to do with it. The case was filed against me." When the case came up for trial, it was dismissed on the grounds that the wardens failed to have a warrant to search the automobile.

Dodgen further stated that he had discussed the merger of the two agencies with Connally in January 1963 and had told the governor that if he abolished his commission that he was abolishing him. According to Dodgen's interview with the *Observer*, Connally "laughed and said, 'Well, don't you worry about that. I'll recommend to the new commission that you run it.'" After the dove-shooting

149

incident, Connally refused to answer any calls from Dodgen and refused to see him when he called at the governor's office.

When the three new commissioners were sworn into office on August 23, 1963, Dodgen was not notified of the ceremony. However, Dodgen attended anyway and was surprised to see that all the shell dredgers from the Texas gulf coast area were in the governor's reception room. Dodgen was aware of a rumor that Weldon Watson, the assistant commissioner of the State Department of Welfare, was to take over his job. That same afternoon, Dodgen received a telephone call from Odom, the new chairman of the commission, asking him to come to the office of Howard Rose, a Connally aide. When he arrived, the commissioners informed him that he had been replaced by Watson and asked him to accept a job as consultant with the agency until the end of the year. Odom offered Dodgen full retirement pay, which Dodgen refused, stating that he was not entitled to it.

Dodgen contended that he had long opposed the maneuvers of shell dredgers to infringe on live oyster reefs closer than 1,500 feet. He claimed that the dredgers had put up money for Connally's 1962 campaign and told the *Observer*, "I think it was purely a political situation. The consolidation was motivated by politics, and shell was the big end of the push. The shell people knew that they were never going to get within 1,500 feet of those shell reefs as long as I was in there. . . ."

Although state Representative Bob Eckhardt and numerous sportsmen and oyster fishermen opposed the infringement on live oyster reefs, the new commission approved a rule permitting dredgers to dredge within 300 feet of the shell reefs—contaminating many oyster beds off the Texas gulf coast. The new commissioners and the governor refused to discuss the issue of Dodgen's firing. Connally repeatedly denied published reports that he had made appointments to the Parks and Wildlife Commission with the stipulation that the appointees not hire Dodgen as the executive director. During Connally's tenure as governor, the Parks and Wildlife Commission was tainted with the charge of political influence.

The fall of 1964 again saw Connally embroiled in a controversy which he labeled "much ado about nothing," but which many regarded as a gross display of dictatorial power by the governor. The controversy centered around highly profitable architectural contracts awarded by state government. The firm of Nesmith-Lane and Associates of El Paso had been awarded a contract as architects for a project at Texas Western College at El Paso by University of Texas regents. The project was the proposed Physical-Science Mathematics Building, and the Nesmith firm had, prior to the awarding of the contract, successfully completed two projects for the college to the satisfaction of the regents.

B. Rea Nesmith, the principal partner in the firm, later stated that friends had advised him not to begin work on the project, as contracts had not been signed and Democratic politicians were trying to block his being awarded the contract.[1] He claimed that friends had told him that his contract would be blocked by Frank Erwin Jr., a Connally appointee as regent. Nesmith also stated that he was called by a Houston reporter on October 24, 1964, and informed that the regents had voted 4 to 3 to replace him as the architect on the building.

The contract was rescinded on the basis of a rider in the 1963 appropriations bill, which stated that, "None of the funds appropriated in this Act may be expended for architectural fees without the advance written approval of the Governor after obtaining the advice of the Legislative Budget Board." Connally told reporters, "I never at any time attempted to dictate to the board of regents whom they should pick or not pick. I never took any action on this particular recommendation." But Connally allowed the appointment of Nesmith's firm to remain on his desk for five months. He denied, however, that his actions were dicta-

1. Nesmith had served as a member of the executive committee of the Texas Republican Party, an alternate delegate to the 1964 national Republican convention in San Francisco, county finance chairman for El Paso, and a member of the board of advisors of the El Paso Republican Party.

torial, and he said that such claims were "untrue, unwarranted and unfair, both to me and the university and to education in this state."

Erwin told the press that Nesmith's firm was one of five El Paso architectural firms considered by the regents, and that Nesmith's name was "neither the first nor the second name." He stated that he opposed the appointment of Nesmith as "I did not think the Nesmith firm was the best qualified firm on the list that was submitted. . . . At the time that I voted against the award of this contract to the Nesmith firm, I did not have any personal acquaintance with Nesmith . . . and I did not know that Mr. Nesmith was a Republican."

Nesmith directed his wrath against Connally, branding him as an "unscrupulous politician" and telling reporters that, "This power-mad man not only wants to select the university architects, but the next thing he will do is tell us who will teach English and who will sweep the floor." He labeled the four regents who had voted to rescind the contract—Erwin, Wales Madden Jr. of Amarillo, Walter Brennan of San Antonio, and Dr. H. F. Connally Jr. of Waco—as "men without courage," and stated that the three board members who had not given in to the "governor's pressure" were men of "integrity and character." Rabbi Levi A. Olan had originally voted against awarding the contract to Nesmith. However, he voted against rescinding the contract. He said that Connally's action "threatens academic freedom" and added, "If we consent to this pressure, we can look forward to others."

Regent John Redditt of Lufkin resigned in protest over the Nesmith matter, and he made public a letter that Erwin had written to regents stating that Connally "wants the state architectural contracts awarded to competent architects who have been friendly to him and his administration." Erwin's letter also stated that Connally believed that "since architectural contracts are not let on a competitive bid basis, they simply constitute valuable gifts that are awarded by the state government."

152

Connally's appearance at a regents' meeting in Austin in December 1964 emphasized that the architects' contract was a crisis he wanted to squelch. He denied that he had labeled state architectural contracts as "valuable gifts," but stated he felt architectural work awarded by the state should be passed around among competent architects in Texas. Connally dismissed the matter as one that had been "blown completely out of proportion."

Forced to defend the letter that he had written to the regents, Erwin replied: "Despite whatever artlessness and impreciseness of which I may have been guilty, I said merely that in my opinion the governor would prefer to approve competent architects who are friendly to him than be faced with competent architects who were unfriendly to him. How anybody can make anything bad out of that statement is beyond my comprehension. Any public official in his right mind would have that view and no one else in his right mind would criticize him for it."

But Nesmith accused Connally of "government by crony. . . . John Connally is doing for Texas what LBJ does for the nation—using government money as awards for political friends, denying it to the opposition." In an interview in the Austin *Statesman*, Nesmith charged that, ". . . this doesn't have anything to do with architectural ability nor technical ability. I didn't know government agencies selected their architects from political rolls."

Texas Republican leaders were indignant over the incident. National Committeeman Albert B. Fay of Houston charged that Connally was guilty of a "highly unethical abuse of power." Fay laid the blame partly on Erwin and called for Erwin to resign from the board of regents. Fay added that Erwin had a long record of bending rules to fit Connally and President Johnson. He told reporters, "It's a shame that these ruthless politicians have seen fit to turn our outstanding tax-supported educational institutions into means of furthering their own power."

The Texas Republican Party issued a news release stating that Nesmith had confronted Connally at a meeting of the chamber of commerce in El Paso shortly after the first of the year in 1965. Nesmith accused Connally of depriving him of some $90,000 in professional fees and felt that he would like to meet a man who could do that to a stranger. According to Nesmith, he told Connally, "Any man who has done to me what you have done at least ought to know me in person when you see me." Connally reportedly replied, "Texas is a one-party state and I'll see to it that it stays that way, and you look like an intelligent enough man to see it."

The controversy between the governor and the regents, and the architects remained a bitter taste in the mouths of many even after Connally had left the governor's office and the method of choosing architects for state projects had been changed. Land Commissioner Bob Armstrong points out that, "The architects in some areas were very bitter about the way contracts were awarded. You know, Connally was very 'even on' about this. He just said, 'I don't know how you tell one architect from another. Let's just give the contracts to the guys who contribute the most to the campaign. What's wrong with that?' I think there's a lot of things wrong with that, but he doesn't. And some people say that's a very straightforward way to be."

"Connally Won the Battle, but TSTA Won the War"

Connally may never have expected that the keystone to his program as governor—public education—would cause controversy around the state. However, in the past Texans had been somewhat reticent to spend their tax money on education. Controversies had centered around establishing a state university, funding public school education, and raising teachers' salaries. Connally found that even in the 1960s there remained remnants of a Populist distrust of "higher learning" and a conservative bias against funding public school programs that many considered as "frills and fads."

Connally had not counted on the fact that most public school educators across the state looked on change as a change for the better only when salary raises for teachers and other personnel were involved. When Connally announced his budget in December 1964, two items were missing. One was an esimated $68 million, which teachers in public schools were asking to finance a $45-a-month-across-the-board salary increase. He also omitted a proposal to raise college tuition rates, one means suggested to gain more money for colleges.

The 1965 legislative session saw Connally embroiled with the Texas State Teachers Association in a battle over the controversial issue of a teacher pay raise. With the TSTA supporting the teachers' demands for a $45-a-month pay raise in 1965, Connally proposed a ten-year slow increase with greater increases for those teachers with experience and training. Connally stood firm on the issue, stating that local districts should assume more costs for their own teachers without putting so large a burden on the state government. He said, "All I ask now is that the teacher salary issue be kept in its proper perspective. . . . When this is continually painted as essentially a state problem—to be solved by some kind of bottomless well of state taxes—the people of Texas are being deluded. There are no bottomless wells, and no money trees on the Capitol lawn."

With teachers across the state applying pressure to their representatives and senators, the TSTA pay proposal garnered ninety-two co-signers in the house and the support of about one-third of the senate. Meeting after meeting was held between Connally's forces and TSTA lobbyists. After Connally proposed his plan and with conflicting reports circulating in the newspapers and around the capitol, the public relations director for the TSTA, L. P. Sturgeon, and some of the state's school superintendents met with Lieutenant Governor Preston Smith and House Speaker Ben Barnes and stated that they could not support the governor's program.

Although Connally had said early in the legislative session that he had no intention of yielding on the issue of a teacher pay raise, he met with his legislative leaders and the TSTA lobbyists and worked out a compromise program. Connally won the issue of giving more experienced teachers more pay, but the TSTA has continued to push the matter of raising the starting salaries of the state's teachers toward the national level. As one administrator said of the fight, "Connally won the battle, but TSTA won the war." Connally lost face with many of the state's teachers and failed to raise the level of teacher competency across the state. And Texas still remains in the lower half of the states in regard to state funding per pupil in the public schools.

In January 1966 Connally appointed fifteen members to the Governor's Committee on Public Education to study the organization, structure, and financing of public schools in the state. Although some educators were included on the committee, Connally appointed Leon Jaworski, partner in the Fulbright, Crooker, Freeman, Bates, and Jaworski law firm in Houston, as chairman. Others on the committee included Morgan Jones, who also served on the board of directors of Lone Star Gas Company; Wales Madden Jr., who had served as a loyal Connally member of the Board of Regents of The University of Texas; and Dick West, editorial director of the Dallas *Morning News* and a confirmed advocate of Connally's. The most controversial member of the committee proved to be Dr. James H. McCrocklin of San Marcos, who was on leave from his position as president of Southwest Texas State College[2] and was serving as undersecretary in the U.S. Department of Health, Education, and Welfare. The *Texas Observer* later revealed that McCrocklin had been accused of plagerizing his doctoral dissertation, and he resigned as president of Southwest Texas State College. His doctorate was later annulled by University of Texas regents.

On August 31, 1968, after three years of study, the committee submitted its recommendations to the governor. The recommendations covered school financing, the reorganization of school districts, establishment of boards and agencies, and the equalization of education opportunities across the state, and provisions for vocational and technical

2. Southwest Texas State College's most distinguished alumnus remains former President Lyndon B. Johnson.

education. Unfortunately, for the committee's recommendations, Connally chose not to run for a fourth term, costing the committee its main support. Most of the recommendations that would have reorganized school districts and provided additional financial aid for the schools failed to pass the legislature.

The goals of the committee proved to be too far-reaching for many of the state's educators, as well as for many legislators. If the recommendations of the committee had been implemented, in effect, the financial structure of public schools would have been reorganized and the inequities in Texas public school education would have been abolished. The recommendations were opposed by powerful oil and gas interests and business interests in the metropolitan areas who held the purse strings to property taxes. The committee found that in many areas banking interests controlled the assessment of school taxes. In many regions where industry flourished, the tax assessor accepted the evaluation of a plant manager or business manager of an industry as the taxable value of a property. Moves to enact those parts of the education program that dealt with reassessing property for tax purposes were defeated.[3]

The committee's recommendations for the reorganization of the state's education system also met with opposition from many administrators. In essence, the committee studied the 1,200 school districts across Texas and determined that many were too large and too cumbersome for effective administration. Some districts were also too small to be able to supply quality education to students. Where

---

3. The matter of low assessment for tax purposes of some land in the state remained a controversial question even in 1973. At the end of the 1973 legislative session, with Governor Dolph Briscoe refusing to call a special session to resolve the school finance issue, Coleman Bailey, superintendent of the Asherton School District, claimed that a ''large landowner in Dimmit County'' had rendered his land's evaluation at $7.11 per acre. Pressed by reporters, the superintendent of the state's poorest district revealed that the landowner was Briscoe. Briscoe claimed that his land has always been assessed and taxed as all the other land in the district, but admitted that his cattle business in the district had been a lucrative one. As reporters quizzed the governor over the extent of his land and other holdings in the district, Briscoe called a halt, saying that this would be revealed under the new financial disclosure law.

smaller districts could be effectively consolidated, the committee recommended that this change be made. Where districts were larger than could be managed effectively, the committee recommended that the districts be divided into smaller districts and be considered as a larger district for tax purposes only. If these recommendations had been put into effect, hundreds of superintendents' jobs and assistant superintendents' jobs would have been abolished. The administrators balked at the recommendations, and Texas schools are still hampered by many districts that are either too large or too small. The organization and the financing of the Texas public school system remained behind the times.

"Connally's Superboard"

Connally's big push in his program for education came with the establishment of the Coordinating Board, Texas College and University System. The Governor's Committee on Education Beyond the High School had detailed the need for a unified system of higher education under a strong Coordinating Board that would work with institutions of higher learning. The prime concern of the Coordinating Board was to prepare a statewide master plan, mapping what should be the future course of Texas higher education.

As early as December 1964, Connally proposed an increase of $151,582,611 from various funds to be devoted to meeting higher enrollments in the state colleges and universities. He told the 1965 legislature that he wished to make "indelibly clear" that any recommendations he would make pertaining to higher education were conditioned on the establishment of a Coordinating Board. Connally proposed an additional budget of $22 million to cover the costs of higher education, but explained to the legislature that if the Coordinating Board should not be created, he would ask only for revenue to provide for additional enrollment.

Connally chose Representative Dick Cory to guide his bill through the house. Although Cory told other house members that the board could only recommend changes, in effect, the board was given the power to implement changes. The language of the bill stated, "The board shall represent the highest authority in the state in matters of public higher education," and, in regard to funding, one item of the bill stated that, "No funds appropriated to any institution of higher education shall be expended for any program which has been disapproved by the board."

Cory recalls that Connally called him into his office and discussed the bill with him. He says that Connally was so forceful and described proposals in such a persuasive way that after he had finished, his recommendations seemed best.

The bill also gave the board power to determine the best use of buildings, some on a year-round basis, and to conduct research into teaching methods. The board was given the power to "consider plans for selective standards of admission when capacity enrollment was reached and to approve or disapprove new construction, repair, and rehabilitation of facilities." Besides the far-reaching powers that the board was granted, it could recommend salaries, faculty standards, promotion and advancement policies, policies on teaching loads and teaching time, administrative assignments, and tuition policies. The board also had the power to "develop and recommend minimum standards for academic freedom and tenure"—a point of heated argument among the members of the legislature.

Cory whisked the bill through the House State Affairs Committee, although he met opposition over the fact that the bill had not reached the members' desks until one o'clock on Thursday, after the members had begun their customary three-day weekend. Debate began fifteen minutes after the house went into session on Monday. When questioned, Cory said that the bill had been printed in the newspapers and that he had over a hundred copies in his office, if any house member had wanted to come by and pick up one. Suggested amendments to add educators to the board were shouted down, with Cory stating, "If a man is engaged in full-time teaching, he cannot put in enough time to serve on this board."

When minimum standards of tenure and academic freedom were discussed by the house members, Representative Bill Hollowell indignantly declared, "We should not give some board appointed by the governor the power to establish tenure in this state. I think this government belongs to the people of the state, and we don't need six hearings and three appellate hearings to get rid of a rotten egg. What do you mean by academic freedom? Is this the power to riot, or what? They've had some academic freedom out in California. Do we want that?"

The bill establishing the Coordinating Board passed the house by a vote of 141 to 4. One house member stated, "I think we're creating a monster, don't you? If my best friend were the governor of the state of Texas, I think I'd vote against this bill."

Senator Bill Moore of Bryan, aptly called the "Bull of the Brazos" by his colleagues, was chosen to sponsor the bill in the senate. Moore joked before the state affairs committee about his unfamiliarity with the specific proposals of the bill. Controversy arose over the fact that a tape recorder had been placed on the committee table, and Moore, when questioned by members of the comittee, grinned and stated that he had requested the tape recorder. However, a Houston *Post* reporter later revealed that the instrument had been placed in the room by Julian Read, Connally's public relations man. The tape recorder was unplugged before the committee began discussion on the bill.

The senators questioned the concentration of so much power in one bureaucratic agency. Connally's longtime foe Senator Dorsey Hardeman had vowed that there would be no "super-duper board," and the Coordinating Board gained the name of "Connally's Superboard." When the bill passed the legislature, Connally stated, "This legislature did itself proud in the passage of this act. I don't know that I've ever signed one that gave me such greater personal pleasure than this."

The speed with which the Coordinating Board bill was swept through the house and the senate with little opposition was commented on by Representative Bob Eckhardt in the closing days of the legislature. In a personal privilege speech, Eckhardt stated, ''I think the house and the legislature have in large measure become the rubber stamp of the executive branch in this session. When H. B. No. 1, the higher education Coordinating Board bill, was acted on, we did not materially change it in its entire course through the house and the senate. Because of some strange fascination with the governor's power we acted as though we could not change it.''

Connally immediately named his committee members, and he chose five members of his Committee on Education Beyond the High School. The chairman of the new ''Superboard'' was John E. Gray.[4] Connally's other appointments to the Coordinating Board received wide acclaim across the state, even among members of the academic community. University of Texas Chancellor Harry Ransom stated, ''The establishment of the Coordinating Board alone is the most encouraging possible development for higher education in Texas, and the governor certainly has chosen a distinguished group of Texans to direct it.''[5]

Connally warned the members of the Coordinating Board at their first official meeting in Austin on September 20, 1965, ''I can imagine that you will be cultivated, ca-

4. Gray had served both on Connally's committee and on the Commission on Higher Education, where he had gained a reputation as an accomplished mediator and a champion of the broad view of state education. Gray had also been president of Lamar State College of Technology until he resigned to enter the banking business. At the time of his appointment to the Coordinating Board, he was president of the First Security National Bank of Beaumont and was a director of the Houston branch of the Federal Reserve Bank of Dallas.

5. The Connally appointees included six members of the former Texas Commission on Higher Education. Connally also named Mrs. John T. Jones Jr. of Houston, who had served as a regent of Texas Women's University and had been the first woman to head a governing board of a state school; a black former college president, Dr. J. J. Seabrook, who had served as president of Huston-Tillotson College; and a Mexican American, Dr. Joaquin Cigarroa. However, among the new members were some longtime Connally political friends and members of Texas' conservative business establishment, including Eugene McDermott, executive committee chairman of Texas Instruments.

joled, coddled, even brainwashed by those who would wish
you to take an institutional, regional, or partisan view.
Alumni and institutions will attempt to classify each of you
as 'my representative on the Coordinating Board.''' On
September 26 he cautioned the board members "to leave
politics to politicians."

As soon as the Coordinating Board began its work, it
was obvious that the same dissensions that had hampered
the Texas Commission on Higher Education would hamper
the Coordinating Board. Legislators still worked toward
establishing schools and obtaining funds for colleges in their
own districts. Also, colleges and universities ignored the
guidelines of the Coordinating Board and instituted new
course offerings and new degree programs.

The legislature approved a salary of $22,000 for a
commissioner of higher education, and on March 22,
1966, the Coordinating Board hired Dr. Jack Kenny
Williams of South Carolina at a salary of $40,000, making
him the highest paid public educator in the state. The difference in Williams' salary was made up by private funds. The
board also provided the new commissioner with a residence
in Austin. Williams accepted the post amid much fanfare and
met voiced opposition to the Coordinating Board with the
statement that, "They [those who criticize] believe that
coordinating means control. I think it means cooperation."

Obviously cooperation was not forthcoming, and
Williams had not anticipated the reactions of legislators and
the alumni of various Texas colleges to his broad plans for
limiting courses and degree plans. The legislature cut his
budget by $264,529 for the 1968 fiscal year. The largest
item cut from the budget was funding for continuing the
master plan. Williams' successors fared no better at the
hands of the legislature, and the Coordinating Board remains stymied by regional factions among the legislators and
hampered by lack of funds.

The unkindest cut of all to the Coordinating Board's
authority came from Connally himself. In 1967 the governor, responding in part to pressure from the legislature, reduced the board's recommendations for public

senior colleges by 16.7 percent in the all-important area of faculty salaries and departmental operating expenses. He cut the board's proposals for public junior colleges by 20.5 percent. In February 1967 Connally, in his tax message to the legislature, also stated that he did not approve of a tuition hike for the state schools, the main recommendation of the board to gain additional revenue. Connally stated, "Some would increase tuition to our college and university students. I do not recommend such action." Connally underscored the word "not" in copies of the tax message distributed to the legislators and the members of the press. Connally's critics were quick to point out that Connally had dealt a death blow to the Coordinating Board, and that while he advocated excellence in education he gave only lip service to the cause.

In June 1968 Williams suddenly announced he was leaving his post as education commissioner. He gave no reason for his decision, but his idea of a master plan had been eliminated by the board. Williams failed to understand the prime purpose of additional courses and degree offerings— to get more money from the legislature. He failed to realize that many alumni, college presidents, and administrators checked their representative's scorecard according to how much money was obtained from the legislature for their colleges.

Connally's supporters still claim that the concept of the Coordinating Board was his master stroke and his greatest gift to the state's educational system. Bo Byers of the Houston *Chronicle* lauded Connally as "the most aggressive promoter of Texas education since Mirabeau B. Lamar."[6] One of Connally's strongest advocates in the field of education is Austin lawyer and lobbyist Will Davis, who also serves as president of the school board for the Austin Independent School District. Davis believes that the Coordinating Board would never have been established had

6. Lamar served as president of the Republic of Texas from 1838 to 1841. He called for the legislature to set aside lands for educational institutions and stated in his message to Congress that "[a] cultivated mind is the guardian genius of democracy."

Connally not exerted his influence. According to Davis, Texas was divided into ''all those little principalities—some of them not so little, like The University of Texas and the Texas A&M system . . . having their own legislators, their own senators, their own chamber of commerce approach to education in Texas.''

Davis believes that Connally bucked some of his own appointees, such as Frank Erwin, the controversial University of Texas regent, in establishing the Coordinating Board. Davis feels that, ''It was absolutely through his [Connally's] personality—the sheer force of his personality—or his strength, that the bill ever passed.''

Davis says that as Texas moves from a small-town orientation to a more urban one—a twentieth-century emphasis that has been slow to develop in Texas—that the effect of major metropolitan growth will lessen the influence of The University of Texas. According to Davis, as the Coordinating Board develops or ''if it is allowed to develop, it will become a more effective device. But I think that the Coordinating Board has met the purposes which were sought. It can be more or less effective depending on how much authority the legislature is willing to let it have and willing to let it exercise.'' So far the legislature has been unwilling to grant the Coordinating Board the powers that the members of the legislature jealously guard. The board remains split by factional elements, and the legislature continues to battle over the administration and the establishment of colleges and universities across the state.

''The Personal Property of One Man''

Much controversy concerning The University of Texas centered around Connally's appointment of his outspoken political crony Frank C. Erwin Jr. to the university board of regents. Erwin's highhanded tactics, designed to purge the university's administration of critics and to repress student dissent on the campus, earned him the titles of ''Chairman Frank'' and ''Czar Erwin.'' The chairman, who once drove a Cadillac painted burnt orange and white, the football colors of the university, retains the position of the university's number one alumnus and has undoubtedly helped the university maintain a position of fiscal solidarity.

Erwin's attempts, however, to handle the academic functions of the university and his purge of top level administrators earned him the ire of educators and students alike and resulted in a rush of resignations and dismissals, including those of the chancellor and vice chancellor for academic affairs of the entire University of Texas system, the president and vice president for academic affairs of The University of Texas at Austin, the dean of the Austin campus' College of Arts and Sciences, and three of the five "university professors" at Austin.

On January 18, 1969, Connally stated that his friend Erwin had contributed significantly to the "high degree of order and stability on the [Austin] campus" and that he was due much credit for the university's recent advancement in academic circles.[7] It was true that at a time when many major universities across the nation were rocked by militant student protest, The University of Texas remained relatively orderly.

Erwin telephoned other regents, most of them Connally appointees, and got them to agree that classes would be held at the university during the nationwide protest against the 1970 Cambodian invasion, despite the fact that the faculty senate had voted to suspend classes. Norman Hackerman, president of The University of Texas at Austin, suddenly resigned that spring to accept the post of president of Rice University. Many people believed that Hackerman's resignation and his job offer at Rice were engineered by Connally, then practicing law in Houston. Hackerman had opposed many of Erwin's power thrusts and had managed to avoid confrontation with student dissenters

7. By 1971 The University of Texas was ranked among the top fifteen universities in the nation by the American Council on Education in its report on graduate education. Its libraries are rated among the "great libraries" of the world by the council.

during the campus May peace march. Erwin advocated engaging in verbal battles with student protestors.

At the end of the 1970 spring semester, the prestigious chancellor of the university, Harry Ransom, resigned in the wake of harrassment by Erwin. In effect, Erwin had taken over Ransom's job himself and had left Ransom in the position of a puppet. Erwin next came in conflict with the university's popular and independent dean of the College of Arts and Sciences, Dr. John Silber. Silber, whose reputation as an administrator and as a philosopher was without peer at the university, took a hard line with many dissenters, but he had upheld the right of dissent by peaceful means.

Erwin and Silber clashed over the issue of university enrollment, Erwin advocating unlimited enrollment and Silber favoring limited enrollment and striving for excellence. Silber also maintained the right of the faculty to control the academic affairs of the university. When the faculty committee that was appointed to recommend a permanent president for The University of Texas at Austin considered Silber and Page Keeton, dean of the law school, Silber again met Erwin's fire.

According to the *Texas Observer*, ''Silber was invited to resign, but not in writing. He was given no reason for his firing. He was simply canned. The *coup de grace* was given so suddenly, he had to work through the weekend to get out of his offices by . . . Monday morning.'' Erwin reportedly told Silber, ''John, you're the most intelligent, articulate, and hard-working man at this university. Because of these qualities, you make some people in the higher echelons nervous.''

Silber's firing stirred rumors of mass faculty resignations. Erwin huffed, ''If any person employed by the university wishes to resign, all he need do is quit playing games in the newspapers and submit his written resignation to the president of UT-Austin and I am sure his resignation will be promptly accepted.''

166

In response to the firing of Silber, William Arrowsmith, university professor in Arts and Letters, professor of classics, chairman of comparative studies, and one of the most outspoken critics of higher education in the country, promptly wired the university's new chancellor, Charles LeMaistre: "Your administration as chancellor has begun with an action that has earned you the just contempt of all intelligent members of the Texas faculty. . . . Many of us are now doubtful that the University of Texas is a desirable place to teach. Once it could be said of the university that it had the courage to appoint first-class men like Silber to positions of power." He also stated that the LeMaistre administration "is interested only in mediocrities and nonentities who can be counted on to carry out the megalomaniac wishes of Chairman Erwin."

When Erwin began a stringent campaign to investigate teacher effectiveness and faculty work load, Arrowsmith resigned. In a letter to president *ad interim* Bryce Jordan, Arrowsmith claimed, "Through political muscle and chicanery, a university of 40,000 students has become the personal property of one man." Erwin retorted that Arrowsmith had been paid $3,600 a month during the preceding academic year, had taught only one three-hour undergraduate course, and had produced only one Ph.D. graduate in ten years. "Apparently when Arrowsmith learned that his lucrative playhouse had been exposed, he chose to find another job rather than assume his fair share of the teaching load," Erwin said.

Erwin's tactics led to other resignations and recriminations. By 1972 the school of architecture's dean Alan Taniguchi, also an object of Erwin's displeasure, had resigned to follow Hackerman to Rice University. Erwin's longtime critic, law school dean Page Keeton, remains at the university, along with many disgruntled professors and administrators. But Erwin's influence on the regents remains firm, and many university faculty members and administrators feel that Erwin's power is merely a projection of the Connally power in Texas.

167

The high point of the 1967 legislative session was the funding of HemisFair '68, John Connally's "big show," directed by the governor and planned to bring the world to Texas. Former state Representative Randy Pendleton, who often disagreed with Connally over the funding of the San Antonio World's Fair, remembers that Hemis-Fair '68 "was one of the few things Connally was emotionally involved in." The battle over HemisFair pitted Connally against his longtime adversaries U.S. Senator Ralph Yarborough and San Antonio's Albert Pena. And the selection of San Antonio as the HemisFair city also brought blasts from business leaders in other urban areas who thought that the fair should come to their city.

Connally worked energetically in the initial conception and funding of the proposed fair, which many business leaders in San Antonio referred to as "this great excitement." He cajoled legislators into backing the proposal and seeing that appropriations were made for the extravaganza. During the 1967 legislative session, Representative Delwin Jones of Lubbock introduced a resolution to investigate the governor's request for more appropriations for the San Antonio fair and to determine whether the funds were being well spent. Jones was sitting at his desk on the house floor, when Mike Myers, a Connally aide, appeared at his side. According to Jones, Myers told him, "Delwin, the governor is very unhappy about the resolution to investigate HemisFair. You know, he could line item veto a number of your projects at Texas Tech." Jones told Myers, "You'd better go back and tell the governor that I can't be threatened. And I'm going to put out a news release saying just what you told me."

Shortly afterward the governor appeared in Jones' office and asked him, "Delwin, what in the shit is this about a resolution to investigate HemisFair? Goddammit! That's my project." Jones says that he told the governor that if he were really interested in the fair, he should welcome an investigation into how the money was being spent.

Later Jones managed to get into the appropriations bill a department for textile study at Texas Tech. But he heard that the governor planned to veto the department, and he caught a plane to see him. Jones says he explained to the governor how beneficial the department would be to the college. He also casually mentioned that he had never gotten a hearing on his resolution to investigate HemisFair. Connally told Jones, "I think we understand each other. I like to see a legislator with spunk. I'm not going to veto one red cent that goes to Texas Tech." Jones recalls that he was utterly amazed, as he had never had such success with his request for Texas Tech.

The complex history of the San Antonio fair reveals not only Connally's personal interest in the venture, but also charges against legislators and San Antonio businessmen that they had personally benefitted from the fair. Many believe that Jerome Harris, executive vice president of Frank Brothers, a San Antonio haberdashery, had the original idea of an international exposition in San Antonio. In an article in the San Antonio *News* in 1959, Harris advocated a "Hemis-Fair" that would incorporate "an interchange of the cultural, scientific, religious, industrial developments" that had taken place between the United States and Latin American countries. In 1962 San Antonio Congressman Henry B. Gonzalez again brought up the concept of a fair to William Sinkin, president of N. Sinkin Department Stores. Sinkin brought together eighteen businessmen to help plan the San Antonio fair.

The publicity reports for HemisFair depicted the exposition as "a people's fair," the concept of the original planners. It was to feature painting, sculpture, folk art, music, plays, and crafts of North and South America. Talent from all over the Western hemisphere was to bring the best of their music, dancing, and plays to the fair, and gondolas would float on the downtown river while mariachis strolled the banks.

San Antonio architect O'Neil Ford was hired to present the first design for HemisFair. He recalls, "I thought a fair should be like a park. The pattern of flow ought to be absolutely different from a street pattern. It was to be rhythmic, soft circles, so that the public flowed around things.'' Ford's concept was a ''fair of participation'' that would bring people from the Latin American countries and allow them to demonstrate their arts and crafts and to build their own type of houses on the HemisFair grounds.

Ford remembers, however, that very early in the planning stages of HemisFair, it became apparent that the creative planning of the fair was being turned over to elements that Ford identifies as ''General Motors, General Electric, and East Texas Bolt and Screw.'' It became increasingly a big show, rather than a ''people's fair,'' according to Ford, and his role in designing the fair diminished.

Ford and other conservationists were incensed over the fact that 122 old houses on the site were being destroyed. Preserving them, according to Ford, would have been ''the most unique thing that any fair had ever done.'' Instead, the fair ended up with buildings that Ford calls ''sheetrock modern.'' Ford remembers that he had been in contact with officials in Mexico and Central America who were anxious to come to HemisFair, not as ''chamber of commercers'' but to show what their countries were really like ''historically and artistically. It would have cost them far less than building a building . . . and many countries failed to participate because they couldn't afford it.''

Ford recalls that his firm was far long on the planning for a ''people-oriented fair,'' but ''we were gradually chopped down. It was a very insidious sort of process. First of all, they got frantic about making money. Anybody who assumes the fair is going to make any money has the wrong premise and purpose. The main premise is not to make money. It's to tell a story or it's to be a great exuberance of the people . . . in celebration.''

Obviously, the business-oriented directors of the fair differed with Ford's interpretation. As the planning progressed toward a ''big show'' and away from the concept of a "people's fair," Ford's firm was gradually usurped. Boone Powell, one of Ford's associates, was fired, and finally Marshall Steves, a member of the executive board of the fair, fired Ford himself. Ford remembers that the only part of the fair that he actually designed was the Tower of the Americas, and he did not even get to finish the landscaping at the bottom of the tower. Ford says that Jack Shelly told him, "Well, we're out of money," and Ford found out that they had $240,000 left in the budget. "We could have had wonderful gardens and trees around it." Ford also designed the San Antonio Paseo del Rio, which was Ford's original concept for adding to the beauty of the area near the HemisFair site. The river walk remains perhaps the only permanent lasting contribution of the 1968 fair to San Antonio.

Connally's main interest in the fair was the Institute of Texan Cultures, a gigantic exposition designed to show Texas' twenty-six cultural groups in a historic hodgepodge designated as "Texans and Texians." Connally first mentioned his concept of the Institute in a speech in San Antonio in 1966. The San Antonio *Light* reported that Connally envisioned an Institute of Living Cultures that would cost some $10 million. Connally ambitiously noted that the scope of the Institute would cover from "thirteen centuries before Christ to beyond the space age."

R. Henderson Shuffler, who became the Institute's director, says that Connally had seen the anthropological museum in Mexico City, and the museum had marked his thinking of what the Institute should be. He had discussed the idea with his aide George Christian and Christian's brother-in-law, Dr. Ed Jelks, an anthropologist. Both Connally and Christian envisioned the Institute as another cowboy and Indian show. They were impressed by the major pictographs on massive rock walls that illustrated early Indian life in Texas, and they wanted to move the boulders to the Institute—an impossible task that the Institute planners persisted in pursuing for many months.

Sue Flanagan, newspaperwoman and author who aided Connally in preparing his final report to the legisla-

171

ture, "Texas Reaches for Greatness," helped Connally in the initial stages of planning for the Institute, along with Christian and Julian Read. Ms. Flanagan brought ideas from Connally to Shuffler. Shuffler's initial reaction was, "For God's sake, don't do cowboys and Indians again." He suggested an honest study of the many ethnic groups of Texas.

Connally took his ideas to the Board of Regents of The University of Texas where Shuffler headed the Texana program. The regents granted Shuffler a leave of absence to direct the Institute. But Shuffler accepted the leave and his appointment as director with some hesitation, feeling that assembling the artifacts and the material for the show was impossible in such a short time. As Shuffler points out, however, "You don't always win your arguments with Mr. Connally." When Shuffler stated his hesitancy, Connally asked him, "What is your objection? You name it, and I'll fix it."

Shuffler told the governor that it was ridiculous to undertake a historical study of the type that he wanted in the length of time allowed. Connally responded, "Just put on a good show." Shuffler and his staff spent a year on the basic research. Shuffler soon realized that it was foolish to spend $10 million for a six-month fair and to have nothing to show when HemisFair was over. He sent a memo to the governor stating that the Institute shouldn't be just a show for Hemis-Fair. He felt that the legislature should determine a permanent use for the building and for the exhibits and that the permanent use should be established through law.

Opposition to HemisFair '68 and to the Institute of Texan Cultures cropped up early in the 1967 legislature. However, the governor had resolved to have his way. "He stepped on a lot of toes," Shuffler says, "and many of the legislators resented being forced to back Connally's plans." Connally's arch foe in the senate, Dorsey Hardeman, opposed the plan, although he tended to support most historic projects in the state. Hardeman still addresses letters to Shuffler at the Institute of Texan Cultures in care of "Connally's Carnival."

172

Many legislators resented that $10 million in state funds were being spent to showcase Texas to the world. Many of the state's liberals thought the money would be better spent on antipoverty and educational programs for the state's neglected minorities. San Antonio political leader and former president of the Political Association of Spanish-Speaking Organizations (PASO), Albert Pena, opposed HemisFair. Connally felt that Pena's opposition was personal, but O'Neil Ford believes that Pena "really believed that it was not a fair for the people. He saw the light, the way they were going to do it. It was going to cost too much for the poor people to go. It wasn't going to be a fair for the Mexican people. And, of course, sadly enough, he was proven right about many things."

Shuffler had an understanding with Connally that the Institute was to be completely free of politics. Shuffler says that to Connally's credit, "He lived up to his bargain 100 percent. He got red tape cut without interfering in the work of the Institute. I haven't known many men in public office who could have kept their hands off." Although both the governor and Shuffler agreed that it was impossible to put on the kind of show that the governor wanted, Connally knew that the Institute would reflect on him. Shuffler told Connally, "It can be one of the best shows or one of the silliest." Connally replied, "It had better be one of the best. My neck is out."

On "Connally Day" at HemisFair, Shuffler presented the governor with the history of the land that Connally's Picosa ranch stands on. Research for the book was done by the Institute staff, one copy was printed, and the type was destroyed. One Connally critic observed that the governor's personal history book was the "most expensive book ever printed in Texas."

Although Shuffler says that Connally allowed the Institute to run free of political interference, the governor was quite explicit about who was to design and to build his show. He stipulated that the Institute building be designed by the Houston architectural firm, Caudill, Rowlett, and Scott, with the San Antonio firm of Callins and Wagner

173

acting as associate architects. Warrior Constructors of Houston, a subsidiary of Brown and Root, was chosen to build the Institute. Caudill, Rowlett, and Scott found their design team on the West Coast—Gordon Ashby of San Francisco and Usher-Follis of Los Angeles. Immediately Connally, often in the company of Julian Read, began flying to the West Coast to confer with designers. The governor's personal touch was everywhere, and often researchers were startled to see Connally with a train of aides and HemisFair officials parading the Institute floor, pointing out exhibits and explaining the entire concept of the show.

Although Connally pushed through the original funding for the Institute, he went after renewed appropriations so often that even legislative supporters of state historical projects turned thumbs down on funding requests. In February 1967 Senator George Parkhouse of Dallas introduced an amendment to reduce drastically the $5.5 million request for Institute funding, but his motion failed by a vote of 21 to 8. Both liberal and conservative senators mumbled ''boondoggle.''

As time grew near for the opening of HemisFair, Institute researchers noted strange changes in the design of the show. While Connally continued to stress the importance of an ''historical and cultural'' approach to the show, exhibits of an entirely different sort were going up. The designers had planned the entrance to the Institute to establish an historical perspective by creating an atmosphere of Ice Age through tropical rain forest. But when the Institute opened, the main entrance displayed the artifacts not of the state's history, but of Texas industry. A giant airplane and an oil field ''Christmas tree'' painted purple were prominent. However, the object of the most awe was a wall-sized Texas flag in glaring neon and a huge color portrait of Governor John B. Connally.

Connally further dazzled legislators and other state dignitaries by throwing a gigantic dinner and dance for them at the Institute to preview his ''show of shows'' the night before HemisFair opened. Amid threats of picketing

174

by Mexican Americans, Connally greeted his guests attired in a striking blue tuxedo and circulated among them explaining the exhibits and accepting congraulations. To emphasize the fact that the Institute was the governor's show, members of the Institute's research staff were cordially invited not to attend the opening.

Connally's role as commissioner general of the fair was challenged. As early as 1965, when word got out that Connally would be designated to the post, the San Antonio *Express* editorialized, "If Connally seeks and wins re-election as governor, the question of conflict of duties may be raised." And the question was raised by Connally's old foe, Senator Ralph Yarborough on July 13, 1966, when the senator received an invitation to honor the new commissioner general at a reception in Washington.

Yarborough extended his regrets to HemisFair officials, stating that his presence at the reception for Connally might "be interpreted as approving the unconstitutional occupancy of the office of commissioner general by the current governor of Texas. . . . The collaboration of HemisFair and the governor to accomplish his investiture of the office of commissioner general of HemisFair 1968 is a flagrant violation of the Constitution the governor has sworn to uphold."

Connally's executive assistant Larry Temple answered Yarborough's charges with a statement that, "Obviously, the post of HemisFair commissioner general is an honorary position and not a compensatory office." Connally found Yarborough's charges "a little amusing" and said he regretted that Yarborough had not attended the reception. Connally then flew to South America to encourage other countires to participate in HemisFair. Yarborough hammered away at Connally's holding the dual position, stating that the Constitution clearly stated that the governor is required to devote full time to his public office and prohibited him from holding any other office.

Although Yarborough's was a voice crying in the wilderness, HemisFair continued to be plagued by divisiveness. In September 1966 the fair's chief of staff James Gaines resigned over a dispute with Senator Yarborough's attempts to save historic buildings on the HemisFair site. Militant right-wing San Antonio citizens protested invitations to communist nations such as Czechoslovakia to attend the fair. Even HemisFair supporters grumbled over paying the South American expenses of Governor and Mrs. Connally and Connally's aide Mike Myers. Many thought that a letter of invitation signed by the governor might have saved the fair some money.

Mexican American citizens protested being ousted from their homes in the wake of urban renewal around the HemisFair site. Even the Tower of the Americas became controversial. The bidding for the construction of the tower was not open to the public, but was bid by only one firm, D. J. Rheiner Construction Company of San Antonio, whose president was vice president of architecture and design and a member of HemisFair's executive committee. Congressman Gonzalez, who was one of the instigators of the plans for a fair for San Antonio, protested the unfair bidding practices, and it was subsequently revealed that four of the five trustees for the supposedly non-profit San Antonio Tower Corporation were members of the HemisFair executive committee.

To prevent the destruction of historic buildings on the HemisFair site, Yarborough tacked an amendment onto the federal HemisFair bill declaring that the historic homes were to be moved and restored with urban renewal funds if possible. Yarborough also proposed another amendment that stated that the secretary of commerce should be satisfied that ''there is and all time will be full participation of all segments of the San Antonio community. . . . This should be a fair for all, for the disadvantaged as well as the wealthy, for the working man and for the small businessman as well as for the big businessman, for Latino as well as for Anglo . . . and not just a show with a public relations facade.''

But HemisFair fell far short of being a show for all the people. Prices were so prohibitive that few of San Antonio's Mexican American families could afford to attend. On the day the admission price was lowered to one dollar, there was a larger crowd than usual. Food prices were high for many, and much of the food was of inferior quality. As one critic of HemisFair pointed out, the fair was planned "by big business for big business and to profit big business." Connally set the tone in his praise of Ford Motor Company for its decision to take part in HemisFair. He declared that the decision was a "major milestone" and praised Ford as a "distinguished and responsible corporate citizen of our state." One member of the state's business lobby said, after HemisFair had closed, that "The prime purpose of the fair was not to make money for the city of San Antonio. It was to make money for the boys up and down the roads. And that it did."

Although the San Antonio Chamber of Commerce published a glowing report of the economic benefits of the fair—including additional hotel and motel rooms, increased employment, and increased bank deposits—when the fair was over, all that remained was a tower jutting above San Antonio's skyline, a civic center, the river walk, and the shambles of a group of concrete buildings. The minirail stands unused and ugly over the HemisFair site. The historic houses are gone, but the Pearl and Lone Star buildings still stand. The Institute of Texan Cultures now uses the site for an annual arts and crafts fair, which resembles a convention of taco sellers and barbecue cooks.

In October 1970 the *Texas Observer* discovered that some of the most distinguished sculpture that had decorated the HemisFair site had been stolen, destroyed, or defaced. Tony Smith's *Asterikos*, which had originally cost $35,000, had been hauled off by city maintenance men to the San Antonio junkyard. When John H. White, first vice president of HemisFair, casually remarked that Anthony Caro's *Barford*, an arrangement of stainless steel bars, should be junked, workmen took him at his word. The cupola of a 1918 synagogue was demolished while still on display, and a Robert Tiemann mural was defaced with air conditioning equipment. The beautiful fountains that decorated the grounds stand without water, defaced and destroyed. As one San Antonio art lover commented, "It

177

might be well to recognize that there is a certain hazard for art in San Antonio.''

After living through the stock fraud scandal during the administration of Connally's successor Preston Smith, the Connally advocates tend to look back on Connally's administration with the nostalgic view that it was all ''productive and progressive.'' With the forgetful hindsight of politicians, they tend to remember only that which they wish to remember and to eliminate all thought of the con-

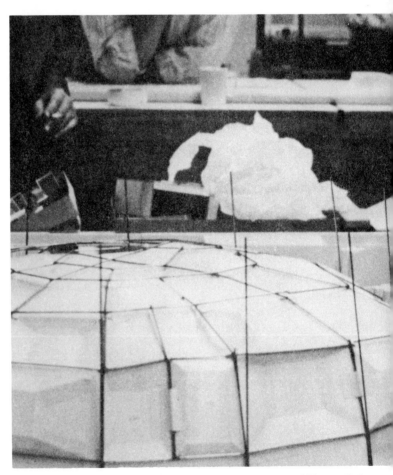

Governor Connally previews the dome of the Institute of Texan Cultures.

troversy of the Coordinating Board or the uselessness of HemisFair. Although Connally supporters see HemisFair as "the world's fair to end all world's fairs, the fair that put Texas on the map," many liberals see it as the state's biggest waste of funds. Some see the social and economic inequities produced during the years following Connally's administration as a direct result of one man's search for power. As one legislator has stated, "Nobody got $10 million worth out of the Institute of Texan Cultures—except John Connally."

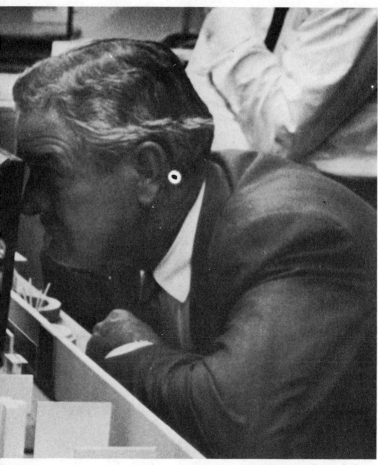

—*Institute of Texan Cultures*

Four Texas
Country Boys

10

Three Texas country boys—Ben Barnes, Ralph Yarborough, and Preston Smith—and, as the stories go, a
fourth country boy, John Connally, "made 'em, broke
'em, or tried to." Barnes and Yarborough and Smith were
of different generations, but it was their relationships with
Connally, in conjunction with Lyndon Johnson, that built
the framework of Texas politics in the 1960s. It was a
framework of uncertain tensions.

"Two Peas Out of the Same Pod"

Barnes was the most successful young man in Texas
political history; twice speaker and twice lieutenant
governor, at thirty-four he failed dismally in his bid for governor. Although he was Texas' senior U.S. senator in the
1960s, Yarborough, a liberal, was never a sure bet, always
the next election away from defeat if the conservatives
would just put their minds to it. Connally put his mind to it

and backed his chosen candidate, Lloyd Bentsen, in defeating Yarborough. Smith defied the odds and Connally's wishes, and was the only one of the trio to make a successful race for governor; but he, too, was voted out of office.

Connally was the driven stake, set and safe from swirling political currents. For Barnes, Yarborough, and Smith, Connally also was a common denominator, the largest fraction in a fractious political state. What he thought of each of them—whether they liked it or not—counted for plenty, among the "establishment" and at the polls.

There was never any question about how the two from the peanut patches of Floresville and De Leon would get along: a firm handshake and a few words in windy Brownwood in 1962, and Barnes was a Connally man. He admired and imitated him. "They was two peas out of the same pod," says Bob Bullock. As legal counsel for the Texas Automobile Dealers Association, Bullock had met Connally during his first campaign for governor. Bullock knew Barnes through House Speaker Byron Tunnell. Tunnell liked the energetic young house member, and Tunnell was so close to Bullock, his former law partner in Tyler, that they called each other "brother."

Bullock seems personally committed to tearing down the barriers between public and private politics in Texas. He claims to be a Texana "buff," and he's known for his extensive files on major political figures, especially on John Connally. Some say Bullock wants to set the record straight. Others say he's a man with a grudge. His knowledge of Barnes' early career seems encyclopedic. Since Tunnell and Barnes were his friends and trusted him, Bullock had a ringside seat when Connally appointed Tunnell to the Texas Railroad Commission, an appointment that allowed Barnes to advance to the Speaker's job much more quickly than any Texas politician had anticipated. "Connally wanted Byron out of the way," says Bullock. "Byron was tough; he's a little aloof; he's a real strong conservative. John Connally never got an inch off him. When Byron was Speaker, and John Connally wanted something out of Byron, he came to Byron's office and lobbied him. He lobbied him in the mansion and in their homes. And his wife lobbied Byron's wife. It was a major project for Connally. When Connally wanted something out of Barnes, Barnes went to his office. Connally could make Barnes jump a split-rail fence."

Barnes had worked for Connally in the 1962 governor's race. He recalls sponsoring a legislative reception for Connally during the first month of Connally's campaign. "I never will forget how mad Price Daniel was." Barnes says he carried Connally's "suitcases and traveled with Wayne [Connally] . . . worked in the Fort Worth headquarters, helping Gene Locke on the statewide organization." During the 1963 legislative session, the twenty-four-year-old Barnes served as errand boy and liaison between Connally and Tunnell.

Barnes also was Tunnell's "compadre," and Tunnell appointed him chairman of the House Rules Committee in 1963. Barnes hustled votes when Tunnell wanted a bill passed during the session. It was a foregone conclusion that Tunnell would be Speaker again in 1965. He announced in the first month of the 1963 session that he already had ninety-three pledges for the 1965 race and that he would run again. Nobody questioned Tunnell's authority. Reporters remember that house members were so accustomed to getting orders from Tunnell that they were not even allowed to decide whether to adjourn or recess. Tunnell just announced the time under the guise of a motion and declared that the motion had carried. Speakers of the house, like other politicians, prize loyalty above all else. In Texas, the Speaker may have an inkling that one or the other members of the house may want his job. But if he hears of a member sounding for votes, courting pledge cards, without his approval, he can, in Bullock's words, "stomp him in the floor of the House of Representatives." The power started and stayed at the top.

In the fall, after the 1963 legislature had adjourned, Bullock says Barnes casually mentioned the Speaker's job. Bullock recalls, "One day I was sitting down in my office and I got to thinking—this was mercenary on my part, don't make any mistake—I was lobbying, and I was inter-

183

ested in who was gonna be the next Speaker. I sat there and I thought—'I'm gonna go see Barnes.'" Bullock says he went to Barnes' third-floor office in the capitol and told the young house member, "Ben, I think it's time for you to make your move for Speaker." Barnes was worried about Tunnell's reaction, Bullock says, but Bullock assured him he could handle Tunnell. Bullock's idea—and he claims it had never been done in Texas—was to put Barnes' name on a conditional pledge card, one that would allow members to pledge their votes to Barnes in the event Tunnell should not run. Bullock typed the first card himself, trying to fire Barnes up over the idea of getting even one name on a card. Barnes said, "Yeah, I can get a card," and Bullock asked, "Who you gonna get one from?" Barnes replied, "I can get Bob Landis Armstrong [former house member from Austin and now State Land Commissioner]. I can get Bob Landis Armstrong to sign one right now."

Bullock said, "My car's downstairs. Get out there and go get him." Bullock recalls, "He jumped up like a little puppy and he ran out of the office, and goddamn, he was back in a few minutes. He had phoned Bob Landis' law office here in town, and he [Armstrong] had signed it. He had the card there, that I had typed just a few moments before—this is the truth. It was funny at the time. I was just tickled to death. I was so proud of him I didn't know what to do. I nearly popped a button off my shirt. I knew we had a winner."

In his first two terms in the house, Barnes' voting record was conservative enough to keep him in good standing with both Connally and Tunnell.[1] The *Texas Observer* noted, "Barnes clearly had something these two rising powers liked: a capacity for long and hard work, an ability to get along with people, good looks, a commanding bearing." Bullock recalls, "Ben and Byron and I traveled all over, and we'd have a reception for Byron in Dallas. After it was over, people didn't remember me and they didn't remember Byron, but they remembered old 'Ben Baby.'"

1. The more liberal Texas AFL-CIO judged him voting "right" six times and "wrong" thirty-five times.

184

In September 1964, a year after Bullock had typed the first conditional pledge card, Barnes collected pledges at the state Democratic convention in Dallas. His enthusiasm for the Speaker's race never waned. His advance work paid off with sudden swiftness when Tunnell resigned on January 8, 1965, just four days before the session was to start, to accept Connally's offer to succeed the ailing Ernest O. Thompson on the Railroad Commission. Barnes had 102 pledges supporting his candidacy, on the condition that Tunnell would not run in 1967. As an additional advantage, Barnes knew of Tunnell's appointment before other potential Speaker candidates.

Numerous unattributed accounts have been published about those days so crucial to Connally's legislative program and Barnes' political career. Bullock recalls that he was in the Arlington offices of the Carling Black Label Company trying to arrange a beer distributorship for Austin and three or four nearby counties, when Frank Erwin called and asked him to return to Austin because "Byron Tunnell needs you. Connally has offered the Railroad Commission to Tunnell." Bullock says, "I was shocked. It really shook me." He flew in a private plane to Ragsdale Aviation Service in Austin, and Tunnell and Barnes were waiting for him. Tunnell told Bullock that no one knew about the commission offer except Connally, Erwin, and Attorney General Waggoner Carr. "Ben tried to eavesdrop, and I ran him off," says Bullock. "Byron had not made up his mind. I told him to take it."

A few legislators, including Tunnell and Barnes, and also Bullock, had scheduled a trip to the home of Representative W. S. "Bill" Heatly in Paducah to parcel out committee assignments for the 1965 session. After the airport conference, they flew to Paducah and went into seclusion. Tunnell called Connally from Heatly's house and told him that he'd take the job. "That night," Bullock says, "Erwin called Barnes and told him, and Barnes woke me up. He was absolutely scared to death. We stayed up late talking about it." Barnes recalls, "I didn't sleep a wink that night."

The next morning Tunnell told Heatly and the others, "Fellows, I'm not going to be your Speaker. Governor Connally has offered to make me a railroad commissioner, and I've agreed to take it. Connally is sending his plane to get us." Tunnell added, "Ben, this is your chance." "We were given a definite advantage over anybody else that wanted to run. We knew what was happening. We knew how it was gonna work," says Bullock. "We were gonna put 'Benjie Boy' in as Speaker. We's gonna make him Speaker, whether he wanted to or not. He wanted to be, though. Goddammit, don't you ever think about that. No question about it."

The group planned a telephone campaign from Austin's Driskill Hotel, where Bullock had his office. Connally met them at Ragsdale, and they drove to the hotel where, Bullock recalls, "We jumped out real quick and ran inside, all Dick Tracy-like, you know, and got on the elevators. They held an elevator for us, and we run it up to the suite. We went inside and locked the door and made a pact that none of us would make any outside phone calls" until after the announcement of Tunnell's appointment. The men registered at the hotel under assumed names. Connally was there, Bullock remembers, and they stayed in the hotel room and "reminisced and talked about politics and a lot of things until about eleven o'clock. Connally stayed the whole time. Ben was just elated, nervous as a cat, walking all over the place. I know I jumped on him a couple of times, saying 'Goddammit, you're making everybody nervous. Sit down and be still. We're gonna get this thing going.'"

That night and the next morning the men selected names to call. They were on the phones dialing as soon as Connally made Tunnell's appointment public. After a thirty-six-hour telephone campaign that lasted through Saturday, Barnes' victory was assured. Liberal representative Bob Eckhardt of Houston said the manner in which Barnes was elected was "something unique and dangerous in Texas politics. It means perpetual control of the house by the lobby.'' A former prominent legislator says Barnes never would have been elected without the sudden switch engineered by Connally, because Barnes had angered private utility companies by aligning with the Rural Electrification Administration. However, Bullock, now one of Barnes' severest critics, disagrees. ''It would have been much harder, but we would have made it, even without Connally. In a fair and open race, he would probably have made it anyhow. His age would have hurt him. But at this time, it wasn't a fair and open race because of the fact that Barnes had the edge of having the [pledge] cards already. Nobody else would have had a chance in two days to come in and get first pledges.'' Bullock says he paid an $800 bill for follow-up telegrams to members after the telephone calls. He says he and Erwin split the hotel bill, which was some ''$1,500 or $1,600.''

On January 12, 1965, after Barnes' overwhelming election as Speaker, Connally edged his way through a crowd of legislators, families, and lobbyists at the lunch recess to shake hands with the new Speaker and to offer him his congratulations. Speculators said that Connally ran for a third term as governor in 1966 as a ''holding action'' until Barnes was old enough to make the race in 1968. However, several of Connally's friends scoff at the idea, and Barnes did not run.

Barnes' friends wish that he had run in 1968; because, in waiting until 1972, Barnes' political reputation was damaged by the Texas stock scandal. Barnes feels now he could have beaten Preston Smith for governor in 1968. Barnes says, ''I think Connally and Preston's relationship is what caused Preston and me not to have the kind of relationship we should have had. . . . He took out some of his animosity that he had for Connally on me, after Connally was gone.'' Connally's friends were Barnes' friends; Connally's advisers were Barnes' advisers; and Connally's proposals, such as annual legislative sessions, four-year terms, and constitutional revisions—programs Smith was accused of blocking—became Barnes' proposals.

187

Robert Strauss of Dallas, chairman of the national Democratic party, once said of Barnes, ''He is the best I've ever seen in twenty years of Texas politics.'' That, of course, included Sam Rayburn, Lyndon Johnson, and John Connally. Close Connally supporters who adopted Barnes included Erwin, Julian Read, Larry Temple, and Fort Worth lawyer Dee J. Kelly. In addition, Nancy Sayers, the widow of Connally's former aide Scott Sayers, became Barnes' second wife after Barnes and his first wife, Martha, were divorced in April 1970. In fact, one of the few times in public that Barnes indicated he was not four-square with Connally was in August 1971, when Connally was being touted as a Republican vice-presidential candidate. Barnes said he could not support a Nixon-Connally ticket ''under any circumstances—I'm a Democrat.''

How much influence Connally had on Barnes' decision to run for governor in 1972, rather than for the United State Senate, is not known. Connally hasn't said. Barnes says, not much. But Barnes admits Connally wanted him to run for governor to keep Connally's ''power base'' intact and to avoid a possible confrontation between Barnes and Republican Senator John Tower. A race between Barnes and Tower would have put Connally in a bind, as Connally was actively supporting Republican President Richard Nixon for reelection. Bullock says, ''Connally knew he could manipulate him [Barnes] like dough, mold him into the man he wanted. I don't think you'll ever find a single thing that John Connally was for that Ben Barnes didn't go right along with, straight down the line, and never asked questions. That's the way he [Connally] wanted it. So would I.''

''We've Never Been on the Same Side''

Ralph Yarborough was an Austin district judge when he first saw John Connally. A brilliant law student at The University of Texas from 1923 to 1927, Yarborough had Sunday dinner at Connally's law fraternity house in the late 1930s and met the young student. ''He was one of the

188

leaders of that meeting," Yarborough recalls, "and the impression I had was that he was . . . a handsome, young, articulate student." Afterward, Yarborough says he would see Connally at an occasional political rally, and there was little to indicate they would become Texas' most publicized "spittin' enemies." Yarborough admits that, "I haven't had but two or three conversations with him [Connally] in my life."

The Connally-Yarborough feud began after Connally broke out of Lyndon Johnson's shadow and, despite polls that indicated nobody knew him, ran for governor of Texas. "We've never been on the same side," Yarborough says of Connally, "but we've voted for the same people. I recall a campaign or two of Johnson's when we were both supporting Lyndon Johnson." In a model of summation, Yarborough adds, "Connally got out of the university and joined up with LBJ, and that gang has tried to get me all my political life." They finally got him in 1970 when Lloyd Bentsen upset the liberal leader.

Yarborough lost three races for governor in the 1950s. The third race was against U.S. Senator Price Daniel, who gave up his U.S. Senate seat to run for governor. His successor as senator was Yarborough, who was elected on April 2, 1957, with 364,605 votes, or 38 percent of the vote. Yarborough beat William A. Blakley, Dallas millionaire and the principal stockholder in Braniff Airways, for a full six-year term in 1958.

Obscured by the layers of controversy between Connally and Yarborough is the fact that Connally almost became Yarborough's colleague in the Senate. When Johnson was elected vice president in November 1960, he had to relinquish his spot in the Senate and Governor Daniel had to appoint a replacement to serve until the special election.

George Christian was Daniel's assistant in 1960 and remembers Daniel telling Connally he would appoint him to the Senate. Connally wanted the job, Christian says, to give him a head start toward winning the special election. As a matter of courtesy, however, Daniel told Connally he was going to check first with Blakley because he had once promised him he would appoint him to the Senate if he ever had the chance. To Daniel's astonishment, Blakley said he wanted to serve. Daniel broke the news to Connally and, deprived of the appointment he thought was to be his, Connally ignored the 1961 special election. "Going to the United States Senate was not something I was just dying to do," he said. Republican John Tower, a political science professor at Midwestern University in Wichita Falls, won in a runoff over Blakley after the two men had survived a field of seventy-one candidates.

Connally's refusal to run for the Senate left him free to accept President Kennedy's appointment as secretary of the navy. Daniel also had planned to name Connally to The University of Texas Board of Regents, but Connally's Washington appointment forced Daniel to make another choice. When Connally resigned the navy post to campaign for governor, Yarborough hinted that he, too, might run, but he backed off. The governor's office appeared to have become an almost mystical goal for Yarborough.

It was during Connally's first race for governor, after he had already won the Democratic primary over Daniel and a Kennedy-liberal, Don Yarborough (no kin to Ralph), that, according to Christian, the spark was ignited that touched off the Connally-Yarborough brush fire. Connally was struggling during his first campaign in 1962, and he needed all the support he could get. Twenty-one Texas congressmen signed a letter endorsing Connally, but the Dallas *News* noted Yarborough did not sign. He was quoted as saying he would support all Democrats, so why should one be singled out. "Except for that," Christian theorizes, "the barrier might never have been there. From then on, Yarborough usually made noises until Connally got his craw full." The tempo of their arguments picked up after the 1963 legislature, when Yarborough claimed a bill to regulate interest rates on small loans was "written by the loan sharks." Connally countered, "Any citizen has a right to criticize his government regardless of the ignorance of knowledge he displays in speaking on the subject."

190

Yarborough says of Connally, "I can't tell you anything that hasn't been in the newspapers. It's all there." The New York *Times* reported that if the 1964 presidential situation in Texas looked bad for Kennedy-Johnson, Johnson might run against Yarborough for the Senate. It was Bentsen, however, who was urged by conservative Democrats in 1963 to run against Yarborough. At Barnes' appreciation dinner in Brownwood, a month after the assassination of President Kennedy, Bentsen denied he would oppose Yarborough. But reporters noted that Bentsen was making a list of all the legislators at Barnes' party. Six years later Bentsen decided to make the race, with the support of Connally.[2]

The appearance of President Kennedy in Texas in November 1963 dramatized the Yarborough versus Connally-Johnson conflict. Three years after Kennedy's assassination, Connally remarked to a Dallas audience he had heard Yarborough refuse to ride in the same car with Johnson on that trip. In that same 1966 speech to the 500 Committee for Responsible Government, Connally said Yarborough was trying to "preach dissension and discord." In his book on Kennedy's assassination, William Manchester claimed the president visited Texas to patch up the Connally-Yarborough feud, but Connally wrote in an article for *Life* magazine that the main purposes of the trip were to raise money for the Democratic party and to allow Kennedy to woo Texans who had opposed him in 1960. Yarborough was not on the guest list for a reception at the governor's mansion, and he was quoted as saying, "I'm not surprised. Governor Connally is so terribly uneducated governmentally, how could you expect anything else?" Connally also planned to relegate Yarborough to a side table at the major Kennedy political dinner in Austin, Manchester said, but agreed to put him at the head table if Kennedy insisted. "Terrific," Kennedy said, "that makes the whole trip worthwhile." Within an hour, Kennedy was dead of an assassin's bullet. Manchester noted that Yarborough saw

2. Bentsen refuses to discuss his personal or political connections with John Connally.

191

blood on Connally's head and thought that he also had been assassinated. The governor was severely wounded, but his political *mano-a-mano* with Yarborough resumed before he had completely convalesced from his bullet wounds.

Connally felt that he should get the Democratic nomination for governor in 1964 without having to fight for it. But Don Yarborough entered the race also. To retaliate Connally invited Joe Kilgore to the mansion to talk to him about running against Ralph Yarborough. President Johnson, however, wanted the "Texas wrangling" kept low key, as he would be running for a full term himself in 1964.

An all-out Senate race involving Yarborough would make Johnson look like a man who couldn't achieve harmony in his own state, much less in the nation. In an obvious effort to reconcile the deep feelings that surfaced during Kennedy's visit, Johnson invited Yarborough to the White House three times in just over a week to talk over legislation.

A Joe Belden poll in December 1963 showed 63 percent of Texas Democrats in favor of Yarborough for senator, but Connally was not among that percentage. Christian insists that Connally did not urge Kilgore to oppose Yarborough but told him that if he ran, he would help. "He didn't beat the bushes for an opponent for Yarborough," Christian says. Crawford Martin remembered that Kilgore told Connally at the mansion that "he needed thirty minutes to think it over, and he went off in one of those downstairs rooms at the mansion. He came back and said he had decided against the race, and he and George (Christian) went upstairs to type out a statement." Kilgore couldn't buck the president.

Connally was so angry over Kilgore's refusal to run, in the face of Johnson's threats to block campaign contributions, that he considered quitting the governor's race and running for the Senate himself. But he chose not to. Although it has not been publicized, Connally's brother, Merrill, a former Wilson County commissioner and judge, wanted to run for the Senate against Yarborough. A third brother, Wayne, says, "Joe (Kilgore) decided not to run almost at the last minute and there simply wasn't enough time for Merrill to get anything organized. If he had just had some advance notice that Joe was not going to run, he (Merrill) would have become a candidate." Merrill says the story is true. A former "money man" in the Connally organization says, "That's just Merrill-Wayne talk."

Despite charges that Billie Sol Estes had personally given him $50,000, Ralph Yarborough captured the nomination with ease over Dallas radio executive Gordon McLendon. Connally defeated Don Yarborough in the Democratic primary by a vote of 1,125,884 to 471,411. At the June state Democratic convention, Connally strengthened his victory when Frank Erwin and Mrs. Eugene Locke, wife of Connally's 1962 campaign manager, were elected to the national committee at Connally's suggestion. The Connally-Yarborough rift was so wide that the Democrats had to hold two banquets. The liberals honored Ralph Yarborough, and the State Democratic Executive Committee sponsored a party for Connally. There were even two convention programs—one printed by the state committee and the other by Houston liberals.

Connally's election in November 1964 was assured, and he remained publicly aloof from Yarborough's Senate campaign against Republican George Bush, a handsome, articulate Houston oil millionaire. Yarborough won with 1,463,958 votes, giving him a lead in 220 counties. His campaign was aided by a last-minute boost from President Johnson, a landslide winner in Texas over Senator Barry Goldwater. Connally, embued with the Kennedy assassination mystique, beat Republican Jack Crichton by more than 1.2 million votes and commented privately, according to the *Texas Observer*, that he had regarded it as his role to help keep businessmen in line for Johnson, something he could not do by embracing Yarborough. The senator accused Connally of trying to throw the State Democratic Executive Committee's influence behind Bush, and Connally replied at a press conference, "I think it was a wild and irresponsible statement, and obviously untrue."

After Connally and Yarborough each won their second full terms in November 1964, their relationship went steadily downhill. Freed from the electorate for a time, they could concentrate on each other. Yarborough, who missed little of what was going on in Texas, called Connally "the worst, the most vindictive, the most reactionary governor in Texas history." His staunchest supporters wanted him to challenge Connally for governor in 1966, but even the *Texas Observer*, which had always admired Yarborough's "one-man-against-the-pack" stance, advised Yarborough supporters to think twice. Yarborough could lose, the *Observer* stated, branding him a loser for the remainder of his Senate term. Even if Yarborough should win a race for governor, Connally would be able to appoint his successor in the Senate. The feud was a war of a million words, charges, and countercharges. To Yarborough, it appeared that anything Connally did had a sinister motive. For example, the proposal to allow Texas governors four years in office, instead of two, was deemed a scheme to permit Connally a third term of four years, ending in 1970, when he would take on Yarborough. The Senate, Connally's friends say, was not Connally's cup of tea. Advancement was too slow and too risky.

President Johnson's "war on poverty" also spawned a skirmish between Connally and Yarborough. Yarborough accused Connally of trying to sabotage the anti-poverty program by quickly approving youth corps projects calling for $1 an hour in wages, but holding up $1.25 an hour proposals until the summer was almost over and the children were back in school. Washington columnist Leslie Carpenter stated that Yarborough was annoyed when Connally vetoed a $381,480 Neighborhood Youth Corps project in thirty-three school districts sponsored by the Farmers' Union, a "cornerstone of Yarborough's political support since he has been a candidate for office." Carpenter said Yarborough "masterminded" a closed-door Senate move to strip Connally—and all other governors—of their power to veto anti-poverty projects in their states. Connally stated that Yarborough's statements were "motivated by pettiness, directed by deliberate disregard for truth, and inspired by ignorance of the facts."

Although he had lost interest in being governor, Connally announced for a third term in September 1965, and Yarborough decided not to challenge him. But he kept up his relentless criticism of Connally's administration of state affairs. Advancing the state's educational programs had been Connally's public passion, but Yarborough complained that state support was declining and said Texans should "demand more leadership . . . before it is too late." The two-week voter registration period established by a special legislative session in 1966 became a state-federal issue between Connally and Yarborough. On the Senate floor Yarborough defended the use of FBI agents to monitor free registration of voters, the procedure enacted after a federal court declared the state's poll tax unconstitutional. "Whenever there is a dispute between the people of Texas and a federal official, you can always depend upon Senator Yarborough siding with federal bureaucracy—even if its actions have overtones of a police state," Connally protested. "And when he accuses me of 'fighting the basic right of people to vote,' he is making a falsehood for the sole purpose of creating and inflaming an issue when no issue exists."

A March 1966 meeting between Connally and Dallas businessmen to raise campaign money was described by Yarborough as a gathering of the "Main Street Gang." One businessman said, "The governor is concerned about party control in the county and the state and seeing that conservatives who support him, rather than liberals supporting Senator Yarborough, are elected." More than $100,000 was pledged. Connally's defender, the Dallas News, said in an editorial, "If the governor called a press conference tomorrow in the state capital and commented that it was a beautiful day, no doubt the senator would reply in Washington that the chief executive of Texas, not being a meteorologist, did not know a good day from a bad one."

Former Connally aide Mike Myers says Connally never hated Yarborough, and, in fact, had a grudging re-

195

spect for Yarborough's political success. Preston Smith recalls that after he was elected governor, he talked to Connally about inviting Yarborough to the inauguration, "'and Connally said he thought that I should. He told me he had nothing personal against Senator Yarborough." But several times Connally was heard in private to refer to Yarborough as a "paranoid son-of-a-bitch." In the fall of 1967, after Yarborough had charged that Connally had unnecessarily delayed a request for federal aid following Hurricane Beulah, Connally responded by saying Yarborough's statement was "the lowest form of demagoguery and the foulest distortion of facts and truth . . . he is a very despicable man."

Yarborough collects books about Texas and Texans, and he is often seen thumbing through sales at bookstores near The University of Texas. His love for printed words between hard covers and the realization that they are almost indelible seems to make him more cautious now when he is being interviewed. Knowing others will read what he has said, he is somewhat reluctant to comment on Connally. His outbursts usually come during the heat of political battle. He says, however, that "Connally is just one of many elected with the support of the 'big money.' 'Big money' controls politics in Texas, and 'big money' has controlled every governorship since Jimmy Allred [1935-1939] was elected governor. 'Big money' puts the money up, and they buy the governorship for the candidate. And naturally the people who got in the office, buy that system. He [Connally] is just one of many. He didn't create it; he's not the alter ego of it. It was there. He took advantage of it, and he used it. Money controls the government in Texas now, pure and simple."

After three terms of growing frustration at his limited powers as governor, Connally rejected another gubernatorial race in 1968 before he knew Yarborough's plans. But the senator also shied away from the governor's race although he claimed the desire for change was greater than at any time since Allred's administration. San Antonio "friends" of Yarborough's said that the senator wanted to run badly, and his mail was running ten to one in favor of his making the race. But organized labor, the core of his support, thought Yarborough was too important in the Senate, where his seniority would soon make him chairman of the committee on labor and public welfare. Connally bluffed that he might reconsider and run if a "campaign of personal villification or abuse or character assassination" should be waged against him or his administration, prior to the February 5, 1968 filing deadline. Yarborough was asked if his plans included "character assassination," and he snapped: "That's the governor's tactics, not mine."

Yarborough has always been sensitive about his failure to become governor, and he stated on numerous occasions while Connally was governor that his job as United States senator was a higher office. He lost the office in 1970, after thirteen years, to Lloyd Bentsen. Almost seventy years of age, Yarborough tried a comeback in 1972, but Barefoot Sanders beat him in the Democratic senatorial runoff by 76,699 votes, an amazing reversal after Yarborough had led the first primary by 245,102 votes. Connally and Yarborough would no longer have each other to kick around, at least for a while, except as private citizens.

"Much Less a Governor"

John Connally supposedly once said that Preston Smith "wouldn't even make a good county commissioner, much less a governor." Time apparently did not change Connally's opinion. An insider says that when Connally first heard of the 1971 Texas stock fraud scandal, which ruined Smith's chances for reelection,[3] he blurted, "Smith is a two-bit movie operator, and I hope they put him in jail."

3. Smith acknowledged that he and his friend, Dr. Elmer Baum, an Austin osteopath and state Democratic chairman, had made a quick $125,000 profit by investing in National Bankers Life insurance stock with unsecured loans from the Sharpstown State Bank in Houston, which went defunct. Smith denied, however, that he had a money-making motive in submitting to a special legislative session two banking bills which Frank Sharp, the owner of the bank, wanted. After the bills were approved by the special session in November 1969, Smith vetoed them on the advice

197

Mike Myers recalls Smith, when he was lieutenant governor, standing in Connally's private office at the capitol, nodding his bald head in agreement with something Connally was saying. "Preston Smith was a dunce," says Myers.

"The way Connally treated Preston was just horrible," Myers remembers. "Connally could 'con' him into anything. 'This is what I want you to do, Preston,' Connally would tell him. Then Preston would go back and call former Lieutenant Governor Ben Ramsey, and Ramsey would ask, 'Preston, you agreed to all that?' With Connally and Preston, it was always the boss to the flunky. Preston would come rushing over with some idea—you know how you get excited about things sometimes—and Connally would treat him . . . well, he'd just sort of say, 'Oh . . . oh yeah . . .' and you could just see it drain out of Preston. Connally just didn't want to waste his time with Preston. If I were Preston Smith, I would have hated John Connally."

It seems incredible, eleven years later, that Republican politicians once tried to drag Connally and Smith under the canopy of a single issue, but they did in the 1962 campaign, when Jack Cox challenged Connally as an "LBJ puppet" and the GOP's lieutenant governor candidate Bill Hayes echoed the charge against Smith. After Connally and Smith were in office, Smith and a small group of senators, including Dorsey Hardeman, repeatedly led legislative opposition to many of Connally's proposals. Barnes says Smith was always lying to Connally, saying he would go along with a bill, then withdrawing his support. Asked what Connally would do, Barnes states, "He'd just say he's a no-good, lying son-of-a-bitch." Barnes remembers Smith's trying to talk back to Connally once—"It wasn't a fair fight between Preston and John Connally." When they both spoke to the same group, Barnes says, "Preston would always tell one or two of his silly jokes. Then

of Allan Shivers. He often noted that the federal Securities and Exchange Commission lawsuit which ripped open the stock fraud scandal was filed in Dallas on the same day Smith was inaugurated for his second term in office.

Connally would come on and he'd get twice or three or four times the ovation.''

Smith was biding his time to get Connally's job, and the two politicians hacked at each other constantly. Connally said in his 1965 inaugural speech, ''I did not seek this office to be the custodian of out-dated concepts.'' To many, the implication was obvious. Connally was progressive, a sophisticated ''man-on-the-go'' who wanted his administration to be judged on solid accomplishments, not ceremonial puff; Smith, as second-in-command, was a ''fuddy-duddy'' who might have made it in simpler times. One of Smith's former aides says, ''Preston thought the Connallys snubbed him and his wife. But others say that's not true, that the Smiths would go to a party at the mansion occasionally, couldn't find anyone to talk to, and would leave for Lubbock to play bridge.''

Smith was understandably upset in 1965 when Connally vetoed a bill to set up a state medical school at Texas Tech in Smith's hometown of Lubbock. But several months later, Smith recalls, he was speaking to the Rotary Club in Lubbock and ''some of his [Connally's] people sent me an announcement that they wanted me to inject into my speech that I was endorsing him and requesting that he run for a third [term as governor]. I did this, and I was glad to do it. Since then, of course, I have wished that he and his people had supported me for a third term [in 1972] as I did them.''

Smith was so isolated from Connally and Barnes that he did not learn of Connally's 1967 decision to ask the legislature to write a one-year budget instead of a two-year budget until he got a letter twenty-four hours before Connally made the announcement. Recalling those days, Smith concedes, ''Governor Connally did whatever he could to move the political image of Ben Barnes forward much faster than he did the political image of Preston Smith.''

It was during Connally's five-week African safari in 1967 that Smith got the feel of the governor's office. As acting governor, Smith screwed his heels into the ground and began building a campaign staff to take on Connally and

199

anyone else in 1968. The odds were against him, however. A June 1967 survey of one hundred persons in Harris County revealed that eighty-eight persons recognized a black-and-white photograph of Connally, but only seven recognized a photo of Smith. He was obscure, and his penchant for handshaking, Populist-style politics would be no match for the well-financed television blitz that Connally could put together. The two men almost met when Connally flew home to Austin on August 31, 1967, just a few minutes before Smith and his wife caught a 7:09 a.m. flight to Lubbock. Smith remarked wryly that he thought all the reporters were there to see him off.

Smith says his support of Connally's third term in 1966 "helped him [Connally] a great deal." But enough was enough! "I came into the governor's office after he had returned from this African safari that he went on," Smith recalls, "and sat down and I talked with him, I suppose perhaps thirty minutes. I told the governor that all of my life I had wanted to run for governor. I had been in the house of representatives for six years, and in the senate six years, and lieutenant governor six years. And I thought if ever I was to make a race for governor that then was the time for me to do it. And I said to him, 'I hope, Governor Connally, that you do not run because I know you would be difficult to beat. But if you do run, why, we'll just have a political race and may the best man win.'" Connally refused to tell a news conference if he would support Smith, but he said, "You're never very enthusiastic about supporting anyone who announces against you." Smith said Connally knew "he would get beat" if he ran.

After Connally announced that he would not run in 1968, he and some of his supporters began to search for a candidate to beat Smith. Other Connally men, such as state Democratic party chairman Will Davis and Wallace Scott, the Austin lawyer who was Connally's Travis County campaign manager in 1962, told Smith they would support him. Smith said he wrote letters to 350 Connally coordinators and county chairmen and about 65 to 70 percent agreed to support Smith. "I would say that Connally's with-

200

drawal made my campaign at least a third stronger than it was,'' Smith said.

Former Congressman Frank Ikard's name was mentioned for governor in early December, and Thomas Mann, assistant United States Secretary of State for Inter-American Affairs, said he had been asked by both parties to run. Houston mayor Louie Welch also thought about becoming a candidate but decided against it. Ernest Stromberger and Jim Lehrer of the Dallas *Times Herald* broke a story that Connally and forty of his top political advisers had met at Connally's Floresville ranch during the first week of January 1968, and had taken a secret-ballot poll on their choices for governor, with Connally out of the race. Eugene Locke led the poll by a substantial margin, John Hill was second, and Smith reportedly received only three votes.

But Smith and Don Yarborough gained the Democratic runoff. Locke was fifth, also trailing Uvalde rancher Dolph Briscoe. Although Connally still declined to endorse Smith, it made no difference. Smith defeated Yarborough in the runoff 767,490 to 621,226 and won the general election over Republican Paul Eggers of Wichita Falls by a vote of 1,662,019 to 1,254,333. Connally left office when Smith was inaugurated on January 21, 1969. Following a tradition established in 1925 by Governor Pat Neff, the outgoing governor marked a passage in Neff's old Bible for the incoming governor—''Where there is no vision, the people perish; but he that keepeth the law, happy is he'' (Proverbs 29:18).

Comparisons of Connally and Smith as the state's executive were inevitable. Nick Johnson, former press aide to Connally, remembers, ''Connally would call self-serving press conferences, turn the charm on for ten minutes, and the capitol press would almost forget they were 'pissed off.' Then Connally would sneak in what he really wanted to say. He would do it so well that it would almost always be the big story, not the answers to dozens of questions the reporters had saved up. Preston Smith couldn't get away with it if he tried.''

Smith admits, "Following in Governor Connally's footsteps was rather difficult, because of the fact that he was pictured by the press as having lots of charisma and tremendous leadership. Any person, if they have these kinds of press releases and this sort of a press image, can do a much better job than when the press continually hammers at the public official saying he has no leadership, that he has no charisma, that he is dull, and that he is colorless. We've been subjected to a great deal of this." Smith's criticism of Connally on national television was widely reported in Texas, especially an August 1971 comment on "Face the Nation." Smith told interviewers, "I never was too impressed with his [Connally's] abilities, to tell you the truth. I have tremendous respect for his personality. I've never been too impressed with his knowledge of state government."

After his embarrassing defeat in the May 1972 Democratic primary,[4] Smith seemed to relish the role of a solid Democrat, as Connally criss-crossed the country swinging the Democrat vote for President Nixon. Smith blasted Connally on statewide television as "disloyal" to the Democratic party and dug up a ten-year-old newspaper article in which Connally called his 1962 Republican opponent for governor, Jack Cox, a political "turncoat" for switching parties to run against Connally. In what must have been one of Smith's finer moments, the youths, liberals, intellectuals, and sophisticates who had laughed at him stood and cheered as he led Senator George McGovern into the house chamber for a presidential campaign speech to the Texas legislature. "You can rely on old Preston," he must have thought, and, in the future, he could console himself with this memory when someone mentioned Connally's winning record. Smith laughingly recalls, "I've seen articles written both by Washington correspondents and by Texas correspondents that say that Governor Connally is king. Whatever Governor Connally wants, Gover-

4. Smith finished fourth behind Dolph Briscoe, Representative Frances Farenthold, and Barnes, receiving only 190,709 votes, less than 10 percent of the total.

nor Connally will get. Well, I think he wanted Eugene
Locke pretty bad, but he didn't get him.''

The passing of power—Governor John Connally and his political
protege, House Speaker Ben Barnes.

—*Ann Fears Crawford Collection*

"We're not Going to Change the Rules in the Middle of the Game"

11

White-thatched Merrill Connally was working around the clock to get Eugene Locke elected governor, but it was taking a great deal of money, and the supply was dwindling in the last five to six weeks of the 1968 Democratic primary campaign.[1] It was time to make the big push or to drop by the wayside. Merrill's brother, Governor John Connally, had been the "magic fund finder," credited with raising a couple of hundred thousand dollars for Locke. The calls went out again to the governor, a campaign worker recalls, "but we just couldn't reach him. Connally had dropped Locke, and Locke ran out of money."

1. Locke, A Yale-educated lawyer and diplomat, quit as deputy United States ambassador to South Vietnam to make the governor's race. He was a senior partner in the Dallas law firm, Locke, Purnell, Boren, Laney and Neely, when he accepted President Johnson's appointments as ambassador to Pakistan and later as deputy ambassador under Ellsworth Bunker in Vietnam. He had directed Connally's first campaign for governor in 1962 and was state Democratic chairman from November 1962 until March 1964.

Despite an expensive campaign of $571,000 and a campaign jingle, "Yew-gene Locke should be governor of Texas . . .," Locke finished out of the running—fifth in a field of ten, and more than 200,000 votes behind the leader, Don Yarborough. Merrill's wife Mary "was so mad she wouldn't even go around John for weeks," the campaigner says. His theory, as one close to Connally's office in 1968, is that Connally forgot about Locke "because he was concerned with his own chances to be vice president. . . . With Connally, it's himself first, last, and always."

What started speculation and negotiations in the tumultuous political year of 1968, of course, was President Lyndon Johnson's announcement over national television that he would not seek nor accept the Democratic party's nomination for president. The president made his announcement on Sunday, March 31, and Connally met at midnight at the governor's mansion with Will Davis, Frank Erwin, Merrill, and others to discuss strategy. The sixty-two member State Democratic Executive Committee, which was controlled by Connally, immediately went on "red-alert." There had been published reports that Barnes might try to lead the Texas delegation to the national convention in Chicago, but an observer at the mansion meeting says, "Connally was so dominating that although everyone appeared to be offering advice, they really were just telling him what he wanted to hear. He made all the decisions."

Two days later, in an attempt to keep Senator Robert F. Kennedy of New York from winning the presidential nomination, the executive committee unanimously endorsed Connally as a favorite-son candidate for president. Davis and Erwin said the secondary purpose of Connally's candidacy was to hold Texas' 104 convention votes for Vice President Hubert Humphrey, if he should become a presidential candidate. Connally said he would not run as a "stand-in" for Humphrey or for anyone else. "I never thought I'd live to see the day when Hubert Humphrey would be the most conservative man seeking the Democratic presidential nomination," said committee member Tom Moore, a liberal state representative from Waco. There was talk of Connally as a serious contender for either president or vice president, but Davis said, "We are realistic enough to know that neither of those is a possibility." As an offshoot of the Connally candidacy, Locke, in an effort to bolster his sagging campaign, tried to organize "Connally for president, Locke for governor" clubs. The first was in Comanche, in Barnes' home district.

Connally reportedly got thirteen other Democratic governors to remain uncommitted to any presidential candidate and, on May 1, went on statewide television to talk about his own candidacy. He said he had "no personal ambitions or aspirations toward the presidential nomination." However, he said that in 1969, for the first time in nearly forty years, there would be "no more John Nance Garner, Sam Rayburn, or Lyndon B. Johnson to help Texans in our nation's capitol. . . . It is the political uncertainty facing us . . . including my deep concern for the loss of Texan leadership in Washington that caused me to agree to become a favorite son candidate."[2] He spoke of the possibility of a convention deadlock and also said he knew Texans wanted a candidate who would support Johnson "in his efforts to bring about an honorable end to the war in Vietnam." Connally referred to those who opposed the unit rule, which was to become a major emotional issue at the convention, as the "militant opposition."

Connally's candidacy was challenged by supporters of Senator Eugene McCarthy of Minnesota, but Connally supporters won most of the Texas precinct battles. The statewide McCarthy leader, Don Allford of Austin, made the political mistake of publicly criticizing Texas AFL-CIO president H. S. "Hank" Brown. "Allford, regarding himself as the leader of a movement essentially idealistic, wanted nothing pre-agreed with labor about how to proceed

2. The *Texas Observer* commented, "This is conservative-Democratese for saying that, since Sen. Ralph Yarborough is a liberal, Connally ought to be installed on the Washington scene to really protect the oil industry and other such 'Texas interests.'"

in the precincts," wrote *Texas Observer* editor Greg Olds. A motion at the June state convention to support Connally as a favorite son candidate prevailed by 2,834-3/4 to 498-1/4, and Texas liberals "contented themselves with pasting Eugene McCarthy bumper-stickers on their Connally placards," the *Observer* reported.

The possibility of a Kennedy-McCarthy coalition dissolved when Senator Robert Kennedy was slain in Los Angeles, following his victory in the California presidential primary. Barnes remembers the California delegation as "very pro-McCarthy" and recalls the "mean speech" Jesse Unruh of the California legislature made about Texas at the national convention. "He said there were a bunch of Texas oilmen trying to get the nomination," recalls Barnes.

At the National Governors' Conference in Cincinnati, prior to the August convention in Chicago, Connally repeated over and over that he was not running for vice president. But in Texas there was the feeling he would take a place on the ballot if it was offered to him. *Newsweek* magazine reported Humphrey was under "unbelievable" pressure to accept Connally as his running mate if, as expected, Humphrey won the Democratic nomination for president.

The signs pointed to a hard convention for Connally's Texans. Others would challenge the seating of his delegation, Texas' unit rule had become controversial, and Humphrey appeared to be listening too much to the Vietnam "doves." Something had to be done, and it would take a strong man to do it. Connally always viewed himself as Texas' prime "strong man."

On August 21, Connally flew to Chicago, arriving three days ahead of schedule. He was going early, he said, to defend Johnson's Vietnam policies before the platform committee. His presentation on Thursday was described by United Press International as the "strongest appeal for a tough Vietnam plank delivered this far." Connally accused McCarthy and other doves of advocating what he called a policy of appeasement and surrender. His remarks were considered broad enough to condemn the other two leading Democratic Senate doves, George McGovern and Edward Kennedy.

A plank affirming President Johnson's policies was adopted by the committee, and opponents began drafting a minority plank setting up a test vote on the convention floor. Texas' 104-member regular delegation was challenged at a meeting of the credentials committee as a bunch of "month of May Democrats" who vote Democrat in the May primary and Republican in November. The challengers, a coalition of blacks, Mexican Americans, anti-Connally liberals, and McCarthy supporters, also protested that the unit rule had stripped liberals of their voting privileges and had restricted the number of blacks and Mexican Americans in the delegation to a token few.

The *Texas Observer* reported that Committeeman Will Davis was asked a question about Senator Ralph Yarborough of Texas—who was not a member of the delegation. New Jersey Governor Richard Hughes, the committee chairman, broke in to say, "We could be here a very long time if we tried to settle the internal disputes of the Texas Democratic Party—until Christmas or a year from Christmas." The challengers were seeking fifty of the 104 votes, but the credentials committee, after hearing four hours of testimony, voted 128 to 23 to seat the regular delegation.

On the issue of the unit rule, Erwin told the rules committee, "If this convention abolishes the unit rule or refuses to support it, there is growing sentiment [in the Texas delegation] that John Connally should withdraw" as a favorite son to nominate President Johnson for reelection. Speaking the next day at his *alma mater*, Southwest Texas State College in San Marcos, Johnson said, "I am not a candidate for anything, except maybe the rocking chair."

The rules subcommittee ignored Erwin's threat and agreed 18 to 3 to permit each delegate to vote as he wished. A complaint by the Texas delegation forced the issue before the full convention. The liberals also had decided to appeal the seating of the Texas delegation to the convention, so there would be at least two all-out floor

209

fights touched off by feuding Texans. If the liberals could not beat Connally, they could at least embarrass him.

After the committee jousting was over, Connally, his mood sour, confronted Humphrey to find out what was going on. Theodore White says in his book on the 1968 presidential race that Humphrey's staff had been supporting abolition of the unit rule before Humphrey's arrival at the convention, "thereby breaking a pledge" he had made to Connally. Humphrey had the votes all along, and, according to Barnes, Connally "felt like Humphrey should have run a stronger, tougher convention. . . . He thought he [Humphrey] shouldn't run off and leave Johnson's position on Vietnam and that he shouldn't try to appease the McCarthy people. . . . Connally was very upset."

What Connally apparently did not know was that when Humphrey had visited San Antonio's HemisFair '68 in early August, at Connally's invitation, Hank Brown and Roy Evans of the Texas AFL-CIO had cornered Humphrey at a reception and told him of organized labor's "great concern" about his choice of a running mate. Evans claims, "Humphrey said obviously he had to have Texas votes and Connally had them pretty well in the palm of his hand. But he [Humphrey] said, 'Well, I'll tell you that you will like whomever we have as the vice-presidential nominee.'" To Brown and Evans, that promise automatically ruled out John Connally.

Whether or not Connally knew about Humphrey's pledge to Texas labor, he was ready to do all the talking when he and a few others met with Humphrey in the vice-president's suite at the Conrad Hilton Hotel. It was a one-hour-and-fifteen-minute session on Monday, the opening day of the convention. Davis and Barnes were there for the showdown between Connally and Humphrey, and Barnes says Lawrence O'Brien, Humphrey's convention manager, a member of John F. Kennedy's "Old Guard" and campaign director and postmaster general for Lyndon Johnson, also was in the room.

Barnes recalls: "Connally said, 'See, we'll abolish the unit rule after the convention. But we came into this convention under the unit rule, and we held our state conventions under the unit rule, and we're not going to change the rules in the middle of the game.' Connally was saying those kids out there in those streets are gonna defeat us. He said the news media coverage of this convention with people seeing on their television screens these riots and violence in connection with the Democratic convention is something that we'll never be able to get over. . . . There were some of Humphrey's associates that wanted him to get up and blast Daley and hand out the olive branch to McCarthy, and try to bring those kids in the party. But Connally said, 'If you don't get up and commend Mayor Daley for enforcing the law and get up and speak for law and order, we'll never get over this convention.' And I say he was right; he was reading the American people out there.''

Davis states that, ''The tonguelashing he gave [Humphrey] . . . was an epic. It ought to be written in every kid's journal—to read it, talk about it. . . . He taught him the first lesson in politics about loyalty. Connally taught him, by God, he wouldn't be in Chicago if it weren't for Lyndon Johnson. He orally spanked that man as hard as I've ever seen anyone chastised. He either strengthened Hubert's backbone, or gave him some, or scared him half to death. Hubert just listened. This man who was governor of Texas could and did have the power, prestige, and presence of personality to absolutely lecture the vice president, who was about to be the presidential nominee.''

What was Humphrey's reaction? Did he, as he had done on other occasions of stress or sorrow, cry? ''John said he might as well have. He wanted to,'' asserts Davis. ''That's the difference between big men and great big men. Connally was a great big man and Humphrey was a big man that day. Connally stood head and shoulders over a man who obviously was going to be nominated and might be elected President of the United States.''

If Connally's treatment of Humphrey seems startling, another preconvention episode appears to have taken shape in the political twilight zone. Robert Strauss tells the story. He and his wife Helen shared a suite with John and Nellie Connally at the convention. It was Sunday, the day before the convention started. Richard Goodwin, a McCarthy aide, called and said McCarthy would like to talk to Connally. "Connally told him [McCarthy] to come on down to his suite, but Goodwin came alone," says Strauss. Most McCarthy delegates were having no part of John Connally. McCarthy, the poetic professor, had been the first to challenge Johnson on the war. His supporters had contested Connally bitterly in Texas conventions and had brought that bitterness to the national convention for one last attempt at scuttling or scarring Connally in full view of a nationwide television audience. The mere presence of a McCarthy emissary in Connally's room, if detected by McCarthy's youth corps, was enough to ruin his image and destroy his designs on the presidency.

McCarthy appeared to have come full cycle. He had backed Senator Lyndon Johnson for president at the 1960 national Democratic convention, and was one of the top nine names tossed about for the vice-presidential nomination when Johnson was nominated for president in 1964. In 1968 he had become a symbol of opposition to Johnson, to "Johnson's war," and to the style of politics Johnson had mastered—the style commonly referred to as "professional politics." The McCarthy movement was so anti-Johnson that its leader in Texas, Don Allford, selected McCarthy as his man, after first distributing ABJ (Anybody But Johnson) bumper stickers.

Connally and McCarthy were clearly in separate camps, but there was Goodwin in Connally's suite. According to Theodore White, Goodwin had "free-wheeling rights to make contact with various delegate brokers." Goodwin, a 1958 honor graduate of the Harvard Law School, had been a new frontiersman and, White wrote, had been "conscripted for duty" by Lyndon Johnson. "As he joined the inner circle, the presidential speeches began to glow with a new polish. ('The president's concert pianist,' someone called him.)" It was Goodwin, said White, who first drafted the phrase "great society" for Johnson, in a

212

March 1964 speech that was never delivered. But on May 22, at the University of Michigan, "in a speech written by Goodwin, the Great Society was elevated to capital letters in the text and hoisted by Lyndon Johnson as the banner over his purpose," White stated. Goodwin began working with McCarthy and ended up with Connally on a mission he could not have enjoyed.

Strauss recalls: "Goodwin and McCarthy wanted to make a deal. Goodwin said McCarthy had authorized him to tell Connally he could have anything he wanted . . . half the ticket—the vice presidency—and half the patronage in the nation" in exchange for supporting McCarthy for president. "They talked four or five hours, and Goodwin presented the case very eloquently, starting with McCarthy running in the New Hampshire primary and the way youth had been attracted to him," Strauss says. "But Connally disapproved of McCarthy and couldn't be part of that. He never seriously considered it. After Connally had told Goodwin he would not accept the offer, I remember him walking out of the bedroom into the room where Nellie and my wife Helen were, and saying to Helen, 'Well, I hope you're not mad. I just gave away half the patronage in the country.' He was smiling."

"It had become," Strauss feels, "an anti-Johnson convention, and this was transmitted to the [Texas] delegation." Barnes recalls, "The McCarthy people hated Johnson and the war. I mean, you know, the war was a burning thing." Former Kennedy aides Ted Sorensen and Pierre Salinger made strong pleas for advocating the minority report against the war. But the majority plank, supporting President Johnson's handling of the war, was adopted 1,567-3/4 to 1,041-1/4, and Texas cast all of its 104 votes with the majority. Three delegates had wanted to hold out, the *Texas Observer* reported, but former Governor Price Daniel told them the President had personally requested that each Texas delegate vote for the majority report as an illustration of solidarity by his home state. "The president will appreciate it," Connally told the delegation. To the press, he said, the vote was a "clear message to Hanoi. It's a vote of confidence in the president."

In the convention hall, the reaction to Connally and the Texas delegation made several Texans wish they had stayed at home. Will Davis was booed when he advocated seating the regular Texas delegation, and Strauss called the challenge report a "vicious and unwarranted attack." The vote was considered the first test of sentiment for Humphrey at the convention. The Texas liberals' challenge to Connally was defeated 1,368 to 955, a victory for Humphrey, as well as for Connally. Erwin and Tom Gordon of Abilene were booed during their speeches on the unit rule, and it was abolished by a voice vote. Six Texas delegates said they voted for abolishment, including Texas AFL-CIO president Hank Brown and Texas' only black state senator, Barbara Jordan[3] of Houston. McCarthy told demonstrators outside the hall the vote had "set free the people of Texas."

But Humphrey was nominated, receiving 100-1/2 votes from Texas after Connally, tired of the boos and catcalls, released the delegates.[4] Connally advised Humphrey to choose a running mate "more moderate" than himself, but Theodore White stated that a group of southern governors led by Connally was allowed to block the selection of Governor Hughes of New Jersey as a "consolation" prize "for their defeats on unit rule and credentials." There were reports that Connally also opposed Sargent Shriver, who was married to a Kennedy.

Connally ignored Humphrey when he visited Texas during the campaign in mid-September, and Barnes declined an offer to direct Humphrey's campaign in the state. Humphrey obviously was getting the cold shoulder in

3. When Barbara Jordan was elected to the United States House of Representatives, former President Lyndon Johnson telephoned Representative Wilbur Mills of Arkansas and got the new congresswoman a position on the powerful House Judiciary Committee.

4. Syndicated columnist Charles Bartlett stated that Connally yielded his delegates to vote for Humphrey because of the threat that Senator Edward Kennedy might be drafted.

sunny Texas. Just how cold the shoulder was was not suspected until just before the election when the Dallas *Times Herald* reported in a copyrighted story that Connally had met privately with state Republican chairman Peter O'Donnell Jr. and Dallas oilman William P. Clements Jr. on October 14 and had told them the country would be "better off" if Richard Nixon were elected instead of Humphrey. It was later reported that Connally also had met with Clements on October 7, and that the October 14 meeting had included Ben Carpenter, chairman of "Texans for Nixon," a committee that included several of Connally's friends and campaign contributors.

There were conflicting reports over whether Connally had given the Republican leaders a list of Texans to contact for money for Nixon. Clements said, "We did discuss names. There would be no point in the meeting if we did not discuss names," but he said Connally had not turned over a list of contributors. Clements said, however, the meeting with Connally had been "extremely helpful" to Nixon but Clements would not elaborate. In response to the *Times Herald* story, the governor's press secretary, Kyle Thompson, said the governor had "refused to lend his support to Mr. Nixon and in every case has advised those with whom he talked that he would announce his support for vice president Hubert Humphrey."[5]

Strauss said that in his conversations with Connally the governor had never stated he thought Nixon was the better man. Connally's appearance with Humphrey and Ralph Yarborough in Fort Worth, Dallas, Waco, and Austin on October 22 was proof enough, Strauss feels, that Connally wanted Humphrey to be elected. "That Yarborough-Connally trip had more to do with carrying Texas [for Humphrey] than everything else put together," says Strauss. Strauss relied on his friendship with Connally and diplomacy with Yarborough to arrange the trip—no mean feat. A report by *Time* magazine that was never substanti-

5. Many liberals in Texas claimed that Connally was guilty of "foot dragging" in campaigning for Humphrey in Texas. Not until Senator Yarborough opened a separate campaign office for Humphrey did the Texas campaign pick up.

215

ated said Connally and former Governor Allan Shivers had planned to go on television to announce their support of Nixon.

Connally's role in the 1968 campaign was revived in 1970, when Jules Witcover of the Washington bureau of the Los Angeles *Times* wrote in his book on Nixon that Connally had been ''instrumental'' in recruiting ''money men and politicians'' for Nixon in 1968. Witcover said Connally ''came to understand . . . he had an excellent chance to be the Democrat in the Nixon Cabinet—as secretary of defense—if Nixon carried Texas.'' Witcover added that Connally ''caved in'' because he thought Humphrey would win without him and Connally ''might be

Political enemies John Connally (center) and Ralph Yarborough (right) join in Democratic harmony with Hubert Humphrey (left) 1968 presidential campaign.

left out in the cold.'' Connally said Witcover's version of
his activities in the 1968 presidential race in Texas were
''an out and out lie. . . . I made no commitment to anybody to support President Nixon, did not support him,
raised no money for him. . . . His [Witcover's] stories as far
as my activities in the campaign are concerned are wholly
inaccurate and I think I should brand them in stronger language.'' Humphrey said, ''There is not one iota of truth''
to the report that Connally worked behind the scenes for
Nixon in 1968. Witcover quoted a ''Nixon insider'' as
saying, ''If the fellow [Connally] had a few more guts, he'd
be secretary of defense today.''

—*Texas Observer*

"A Brief Meeting in the Sun"

12

Presidential politics in 1968 overshadowed Connally's final year as governor and also the extent to which his relations with blacks and Mexican Americans had deteriorated. Many detested Connally, and his private fury toward the more militant minority leaders was barely concealed; no quarter was given nor expected. Connally retaliated against their public criticism at most opportunities. As an illustration, when he was nursing HemisFair '68 to completion, he learned that a photograph of Albert Pena Jr. of San Antonio was to be displayed in the Institute of Texan Cultures, the governor's pet project.

The purpose of the Institute was to display the numerous ethnic groups who had immigrated to Texas during the eighteenth and nineteenth centuries, and the wall displays were designed to include a section that featured the photographs of prominent Mexican Americans in Texas. The photographs included Congressman Henry B.

Gonzalez of San Antonio, one of the prime organizers of HemisFair; Dr. Edward Ximenes, also of San Antonio, a public school classmate of Connally's and a Connally appointee to the Board of Regents of The University of Texas; and Congressman Eligio "Kika" de la Garza of Mission, known as the "white man's Mexican" to many of Texas' Mexican American citizens. No problems there.

It was the photograph of Pena, whom Connally referred to as "Boss Pena," that Connally resented hanging on the wall at "his Institute." Pena, the outspoken and volatile Bexar County commissioner, and Connally had attacked each other in speeches and newspaper articles since Connally's first term in office. Pena was considered one of the more militant liberal leaders among the Mexican Americans, and he looked upon Connally as a symbol of the Anglos he accused of forcing so many Mexican Americans into the mire of poverty and "second-class citizenship" across the state. On the day the Institute planned to preview its historical exhibits to the members of the legislature, Julian Read, in charge of public relations for the fair, called the Institute and gave Connally's order. Pena's picture had to come down. And down it came.

Although many of San Antonio's most civic-minded Mexican Americans helped with the research for the Institute's exhibits, they refused to appear at any of the HemisFair functions for fear of being photographed with Connally. San Antonio city councilman Pete Torres and John Alaniz, a liberal lawyer and Ralph Yarborough's "man in Texas," were among those who boycotted HemisFair.

Many Mexican Americans and blacks had joined with labor-liberals to form a push-button coalition against Connally. The mere mention of his name stirred their distrust. Although some Texas labor leaders viewed him as a spokesman for the "big insurance, oil and gas interests . . . the reactionaries," at first they were impressed with the way he handled Lyndon Johnson's business. Few members of minority groups had even known Connally until

1962, when he ran for governor. His credentials had looked good. John Kennedy had appointed him secretary of the navy, and Kennedy was extremely popular in Texas with labor, blacks, and Mexican Americans. PASO, the Political Association of Spanish-Speaking Organizations and a potent political force among Texas' Mexican Americans, was organized in Texas as an outgrowth of the 1960 "Viva Kennedy" clubs.

But the gap between Kennedy and Connally's basic political instincts was obvious in Connally's first campaign, and organized labor recommended liberal Don Yarborough. After the primary, however, the Texas AFL-CIO's Committee on Political Education endorsed Connally over Republican Jack Cox in spite of so-called "right-to-work" planks in both parties' platforms. "Some of the candidates are so bad that I'm going to have to put a clothespin on my nose in November," said Hank Brown, labor president in 1962. Roy Evans, who later took over Brown's position, asserts, "Connally's technique in dealing with people was . . . you had to give him your left nut if he gave you anything . . . you traded your soul for something he might do and then he might not do. For instance, we had an understanding when we endorsed him in the [1962] general election that he would not put 'right-to-work' in the platform." Evans says Connally "denied putting it in there," but he claims Connally crumbled because businessmen told him "if he didn't put it in there he wouldn't have their money and support."

Although Connally won the grudging endorsement of labor, Pena was instrumental in getting PASO to remain neutral in the Connally-Cox race. There was isolated support from Mexican Americans, however, as thirty-three Wilson County "friends"[1] signed a political circular stating that no candidate for governor "better understands our people than does John Connally. . . . He operates a South Texas ranch and farms along with his mother and two brothers, near Floresville. Through the years they have em-

1. Among those endorsing Connally were Dr. Edward Ximenes and Lino Cuellar, father-in-law of Congressman Henry Gonzalez.

ployed people solely on the basis of their ability, without any discrimination. As Governor of Texas, John Connally will be fair, impartial and considerate of ALL RACES, CREEDS AND NATIONALITIES." This was Connally's promise, too, in his first inaugural address—"To serve the people at all, we must serve all the people alike, making no distinctions among them, for the governments which the people have created are not wiser than the God who created the people free and equal in His sight."

At Connally's request, the 1963 legislature approved a proposed constitutional amendment to repeal the state poll tax as a prerequisite for voting, a top priority item for organized labor and leaders of ethnic minorities. But the AFL-CIO was so displeased with the way most of its proposals had been treated that it asked Connally to call a special session to enact a minimum wage law, plus anti-discrimination legislation. The governor said such proposals had been rejected by the regular session and he saw no reason to call lawmakers back to town.

Evans says Connally was able to reject pleas by labor and ethnic organizations because he had established his own beachheads and did not need to rely on others for political favors. "He would have his own organization inside the black community, and so the black community would work for him rather than for their interests," Evans says. "[He] did the same thing within organized labor; did the same thing inside the liberal groups, primarily with university professors who would tell you he was promoting . . . higher pay . . . thought he had an organization within the Chicano community. This is the way he moved and primarily it was to annihilate any kind of opposition inside the Democratic party."

In March 1963 Connally appointed a black Baptist minister from Fort Worth, the Reverend C. A. Holliday, to the Texas Board of Corrections, which oversees the state prison system. He was said to be the first black man appointed to a major state board in Texas in the twentieth century. More important to Connally's political future was the United Political Organization, formed in the spring of 1963 and consisting primarily of blacks who had supported Connally against Don Yarborough the previous year. Reporter Stuart Long described UPO as a group of "college-degree Negroes" who had enabled Connally to siphon off liberal votes and had "blunted the integration drive of NAACP in several major [Texas] cities by putting emphasis on employment rather than integration." The *Texas Observer* said Connally was the first "anti-discrimination governor Texas had had since Reconstruction," but there were "many things Connally has not done that he should." [2]

The first UPO convention was held in Austin on July 2, 1963. The meeting was arranged by M. J. Anderson, UPO state chairman and Austin real estate and insurance man, to honor the six blacks Connally had appointed to state agencies. In his banquet address to the group, Connally stated, "There is no reason on the face of this earth why members of the Negro race should not be permitted to carry a pipefitter's wrench or wear a carpenter's apron!" Roy Evans claimed that this was an attempt by Connally to prejudice the blacks against organized labor—the ages old divide-and-conquer technique. "They don't want labor to be strong for one reason, and that is, labor will be able to raise wages not only of Anglos, but also of Negroes and Latin Americans," he said.

Within three weeks, over statewide television, Connally lent his voice to "one of the most serious and perplexing domestic issues of this nation in almost a century—the churning issue of civil rights." Connally was on his way to the National Governors' Conference in Miami, Florida, and he said he wanted to talk about his personal convictions on civil rights before he left. He said it was "tremendous," for example, that sixteen of Texas' twenty-one public senior colleges were integrated and that approximately half of the Negro school children in Texas could go to desegregated schools.

The "churning issue," of course, was President Kennedy's civil rights proposals, and Connally said, "They

2. The Houston law firm that Connally joined after his gubernatorial administration was the only major Houston firm without a black lawyer on its staff.

would be laws which in my judgment would strike at the very foundation of one of our most cherished freedoms—the right to own and manage private property, a right as dear to a member of any minority group as to any other Texan. I speak specifically of the proposed federal law which would deprive the owners of private business of the right to decide whom they would serve, and of the accompanying proposal to give broad powers of enforcement to the Attorney General of the United States. . . . I respectfully oppose these proposals. . . . Basically, Texans are sound, reasonable people who can be counted on to do what is right. They can be led, but they don't like to be shoved.''

Among blacks, even the UPO said it was in ''disagreement'' with Connally about the public accommodations bill, but it added that the governor's speech was the ''most significant and positive statement on civil rights by a public official in the history of this state.'' Nevertheless, UPO went ''inactive'' for eight months or so following Connally's address. Albert Pena stated that the governor's attitude on civil rights was ''indeed sad.''

Booker T. Bonner, a black man who had conducted lonely vigils to integrate theaters near The University of Texas campus, staged a twenty-seven hour ''sit-in'' in an effort to see Connally. The governor agreed to a meeting but backed out when Bonner brought along several other black leaders. Approximately fifty to one hundred blacks demonstrated at the governor's mansion during the first week in August 1963, and handbills called Connally a ''Jim Crow governor of the worst kind'' and a ''segregationist . . . [whose] record is one of exploitation of the trust and hopes of Negroes . . .'' Singing ''Tell John Connally we shall not be moved,'' six hundred blacks hiked in 102-degree heat from Rosewood Park, in the heart of Austin's black section, to the capitol on August 28. The march was timed to coincide with the huge Washington demonstration for civil rights. Bonner had arranged the Austin march, and Connally said that Bonner ''apparently believes that progress on civil rights comes through demonstration. I do not.'' Connally's executive assistant, Howard Rose, put out a news release stating that Connally had been in his office during the afternoon and it was business as usual. Rose said the governor was glad there was no ''serious incident'' during the demonstration.

Connally was uncomfortable around such people as Bonner, poor people trying to string together insurgents to achieve an instant goal, and usually avoided them. It became a personal trademark of his administration. He slipped up in confronting Texas farm workers, and his friends say he never would have done that if he had had any idea the confrontation would become such a *cause celebre.*

In trying to explain Connally's reluctance to deal personally with the poor, a young politician who admires Connally says

> I think that some people are poor in their upbringing and I think they are very proud of this, but I think that he [Connally], for some reason, seems ashamed of it. He doesn't want to remember this. As somebody said, he's just never quite as comfortable around people with button cuffs as he is with people with French cuffs, people without vests as people with vests. He has always [felt]—and this translates itself into a lot of his thinking . . . politically—that 'By damn, I made it, anybody can.' And yet, you know, it's so obvious that he's so talented and yet he just expects anybody could or might have been as talented as he was. And he just presumes that anybody should have been born in south Texas and worked themselves up to do just exactly what he did and if they didn't, it's just their own tough luck. . . . It's just very difficult for him to be around, and comfortably around, people who don't think like he thinks. You put him in a one-to-one situation with a poor black, and I just don't know how he'd react. . . . It's sort of a patronistic—the old patron feeling—that some of them are destined to be patrons and some of them aren't. And it's just tough on those who aren't. It's kind of a lack of humanistic feeling at all, and maybe he doesn't need this. Maybe people expect people in leadership positions not to have it. I'm not condemning him.

The president of the National (Negro) Baptist Convention of America said he was so concerned about black opposition to Connally that he almost asked Connally to cancel a speech scheduled for September 4, 1963, to the convention in Dallas. It turned into a *tour de force* for Connally. He was applauded fifteen times during his speech; and, as he prepared to leave, the convention president, Dr. C. D. Tettaway of Little Rock, Arkansas, told the audience Connally had insisted on speaking despite Tettaway's fears of trouble. The governor felt a "few boos will make a better speech," said Tettaway, adding, "I found out that one has to have courage to be a governor." The convention's five thousand black preachers gave Connally a standing ovation.

Five days later Connally attacked Albert Pena in a speech to the League of Women Voters, which was opening a drive to repeal the poll tax, a proposition set for a vote on November 9. At that time, Texas was the largest of the five states that still required a poll tax of its voters, and Connally had asked the legislature to repeal it. But his speech accusing Pena of organizing a large Mexican American bloc of voters in Texas was credited by some with defeating the proposal.[3] Connally referred to Pena as a "would-be boss whose favorite term is 'political action' by a bloc vote as a means of solving all the ills of our times, whether in Crystal City or throughout Texas." Connally said, "Any drive to bind a segment of our people into a solid bloc of voters, ready to do the bidding of some political boss, is an unhealthy development in this free land. It is evil, it is undemocratic, it is un-American." Connally and Pena became implacable enemies. When Pena quit as chairman of PASO in July 1965, he declared PASO would never support anyone who had been against the 1964 Civil Rights Act, and his statement was translated without too much difficulty to mean Connally. In the 1966 governor's race, PASO endorsed Houston oilman Stanley Woods, a man without a chance for election, against Connally.

Connally apparently decided after his first race for governor to seek reelection by appealing to black and Mexi-

3. The poll tax was outlawed by a three-judge federal court in 1966.

can American voters through their middle-class leaders. His decision was relatively unimportant. After he was wounded at the time of President Kennedy's assassination, he became such an overpowering candidate that he did not have to cater to anyone. Organized labor got caught in a squeeze when Don Yarborough made a second run against Connally, in 1964, without labor's blessings. Evans says he sat in on a White House meeting where "there was an agreement made" to try to keep Don Yarborough out of the governor's race if "Lyndon would keep any serious opposition out for Ralph" Yarborough in the United States Senate race. "Well," Evans says, "Ralph resented it; Connally resented it; I thought it was stupid in a way, and my personal feeling was that after the shot in Dallas and since Connally was running for a second term, it was absolutely insane anyway for Don Yarborough to be running. . . ." When Don Yarborough filed against him, Connally thought he had been double-crossed by labor.

Learning that COPE, the political arm of the AFL-CIO, would not recommend any candidates in state races, Connally agreed to speak at COPE's meeting in Arlington in February 1964. Connally said that in 1962 "I did not make you any public promises. I made you no private deals . . . I want to emphasize that nothing has changed in two years. . . . Whether organized labor is for John Connally is relatively unimportant in the sands of time." This was not what labor leaders wanted to hear, especially when it was said where the rank-and-file could hear. It was a subtle method of destroying the union men's confidence in their officials—they must not be doing their job if the governor did not even care how they felt about him. But at least Connally talked to labor groups. He refused an invitation from PASO to speak.

Don Yarborough also spoke to COPE, saying no labor man could support Connally without helping lobbyist Preston Weatherred, a staunch conservative member of the Dallas business community, "destroy the labor movement. John Connally is nothing more than their tool." Drowning many of his remarks in applause, delegates yelled, "Pour it on" and "Lay it on, boy," but their enthusiasm for Yarborough did not change COPE's position. Although his victory seemed assured, Connally met in secret with UPO in March 1964, and was quoted as telling his black followers he was "physically unable" to conduct a major campaign and "It's up to you" to deliver black votes. Many black leaders had bolted UPO after Connally opposed the public accommodations section of the federal civil rights bill, and key Mexican American leaders in San Antonio also had switched to Yarborough. Connally insisted he had placed "more Latin American appointees in positions in the state government than any other governor." Labor became angry at him again when he named Charles King Jr., a Dallas union official, as state labor commissioner without consulting the Texas AFL-CIO.

Connally's was the voice of reason when he spoke to the Southern Newspaper Publishers Association in Boca Raton, Florida, in November 1964. He urged publishers to take the lead in adjusting to the inevitable changes which the Civil Rights Act would cause. "Like most of you," he said, "I took issue with certain parts of the Civil Rights Act. But I submit to you that it is now the law of the land. . . We could make no greater error than to devote our resources to a course leading up a blind alley, to the neglect of work in behalf of growth and development so essential to the South."

The following year, 1965, was the year Texas labor declared war on Connally. As an old joke about a preacher goes, Connally had "gone to meddlin'." Organized labor thought Connally had gone too far by sending telegrams to Texas congressmen on May 21 "strongly" urging them to fight a proposal that would abolish the "right-to-work" law. To illustrate how important repeal of Section 14B of the Taft-Hartley Act was to organized labor, Roy Evans estimated that repeal would force 130,000 workers to join unions—workers "who are getting the direct benefits of collective bargaining and service of local unions without being members of the unions—free riding on their fellow workers." Those extra union members would add money to the state organization, which then would pump more funds into political races. And that's a large part of what organized labor's all about.

Connally also accused an unnamed Labor Department spokesman "for whom I have nothing but contempt" of leaking false news stories that he had been slowing down the federal poverty program in Texas and was "unsympathetic toward it." Connally and the man he appointed to direct the federal anti-poverty program in Texas, Terrell Blodgett, both criticized the $1.25 an hour that was paid to young people in the Neighborhood Youth Corps. Connally said he thought the $1.25 wage would place local school districts in the program in the "awkward and unrealistic position of paying inexperienced" youths of underprivileged families more than their parents were making. Asked what Texas could do about its low per capita personal income, Connally said, "What we're going to do is give 'em education. Once they get that, they're going to be in a position to become productive tax-paying citizens of this state. . . . [which would be] a good investment."

If 1965 was the year labor declared war on Connally, 1966 was the year it chose to wage the campaign. Unfortunately for union men, they had no ammunition. "He [Connally] is definitely not doing a good job in our opinion," Hank Brown of the AFL-CIO stated. But Don Yarborough had been beaten three times in statewide races since 1960, and the only alternative to Connally was Stanley Woods, who won COPE's endorsement. It was no contest from the beginning.

If any single event overshadows all others in Connally's relations with workers and minority groups, it was his mid-morning confrontation on August 31, 1966, with Texas farm workers, just off Interstate 35, near New Braunfels and approximately forty-five miles from Austin. The march began July 4 as a four- or five-day walk from Rio Grande City, home of striking farm workers, through the Lower Rio Grande Valley; but a select group of marchers turned north, pacing themselves to arrive in Austin on Labor Day. Their march was a demonstration for the right to be included under a $1.25-an-hour state minimum wage law. That was their crusade—five quarters for an hour's work, some of it "stoop labor" under the blistering Texas summer sun.

The governor's hometown, Floresville, was one of the farm workers' main stops en route to the state capitol. They hoped to convince Connally to agree to call a special legislative session to enact the minimum wage. The chairman of the Floresville committee to greet the marchers, Peter Devora, a Mexican American barber,[4] invited the governor and his brother, Representative Wayne Connally, but neither replied to the invitation. While in Floresville, the marchers learned that the national AFL-CIO executive council had granted the farm workers an organizing charter. Phone calls quickly went out to the Associated Press and United Press International, and the coordinator of the march, Eugene Nelson, said, "I think it's pretty significant that we should receive this tremendous news in the governor's home town. I feel certain now that he'll meet us on Labor Day at the State Capitol now that we're part of the mainstream of the American labor movement."

Senator Ralph Yarborough joined the marchers briefly in San Antonio, and Father Antonio Gonzales said "all the bishops of Texas" had written Connally, urging him to meet with the marchers in Austin. The Archbishop, the Most Reverend Robert E. Lucey, said in a sermon to the marchers that a "wage of a dollar and a quarter an hour is ghastly recompense for exhausting labor under the burning sun of Texas." Texans of Mexican descent, he said, "must stand up and defend themselves against discrimination and oppression." Drawing a comparison to Connally's all-out effort to fund the World's Fair at San Antonio, Nelson asked, "Why are there millions for HemisFair, but not even a living wage of $1.25 for the farm worker?"

Many people were skeptical that the march could be sustained. Some believed that the demonstration would

4. Devora was one of the thirty-three Wilson County residents, almost all Mexican Americans, whose names appeared on the circular urging Connally's election as governor in 1962.

disintegrate in the open countryside after reporters had returned to the cities, or that the logistics of providing food and shelter would prove to be too great. But the workers pushed on, and on Friday, August 31, the hot, sweaty band led by Father Gonzales in his straw hat and the Reverend James Novarro in a pith helmet and sunglasses trooped past the north city limits of New Braunfels toward the state capitol.

It was outside New Braunfels, alongside a busy interstate highway, that Connally, riding from Austin in a Lincoln Continental executive limousine, met the marchers. Ben Barnes recalls he was thinking about a speech he was to give to a Labor Day breakfast in Dallas when Connally called and said "he wasn't gonna be there when those farm workers got down there [to Austin], but Connally said, 'I don't think it's right for them to just march up here and nobody be here. . . . Let's drive down and be on the highway.'" Barnes and Attorney General Waggoner Carr, a candidate for the United States Senate, rode with Connally, but Lieutenant Governor Preston Smith stayed home. Staying home turned out to be the smartest thing to do. "Oh, sure, it [going to meet the workers] was proved to be a mistake," says Barnes. "It looked like he [Connally] was trying to insult them, but that wasn't it. Man, he was in a very good mood going down there and didn't say anything bitter. Oh, he didn't like [San Antonio Senator] Joe Bernal. Bernal had made a speech about all the Anglos in Texas were a bunch of Mexican haters . . . Connally just said it's terrible that for political gain a demagogue will get up and make a statement like that. He [Connally] said that didn't do anything but just divide the browns and the whites in the state. He said, 'That's sad.'"

Evans of the AFL-CIO says he had tried to get Connally to meet with the farm workers in his office, but Connally would not. He had agreed to see Evans and another labor official. Every time the two labor men thought they were getting their point across, recalls Evans, Connally "would pick up a Laredo *Times* or some paper and read something about one of the Mexican Americans blasting him. . . . He never did do a damn thing.''

A few reporters outraced Connally to the marchers and told them he was coming. The governor's party arrived amid smiles and shouts of ''Viva la huelga!'' and Connally, Barnes, and Carr walked down the line of marchers shaking hands. Connally, Gonzales, and Novarro were squeezed into the center of the crowd, and the governor told the men that none of the top state officials would greet them in Austin on Labor Day. He also said that if he were going to be in town, ''I do not think I would have met with you simply because my door is open; it has been open since this march started July 4 . . .'' Connally expressed concern that ''things can get out of hand in marches,'' but Gonzales brought the subject back to Labor Day. ''If they don't get their reception,'' he asked, ''how would you answer that to them?'' Connally stated that he was ''answering it by my presence here today . . . we have not been sitting idly by unaware of your problems.'' Nelson, the march coordinator, showed up a few minutes later and told Connally that he hoped he would be in Austin Labor Day. The mood of the roadside meeting shifted with Nelson's arrival and also with the arrival of Brown, the AFL-CIO president.

Talking to clergymen was different from talking to labor men, whose presence reminded everyone of the cold, hard political aspects of the $1.25 minimum wage issue. Connally said, ''I do not feel that as governor of this state that I should lend the dignity, the prestige, of an office to dramatize any particular march, and so I would not have been with you even if I had not had a previous commitment. I want to make that clear.'' Nelson asked Connally to ''take the leadership'' by calling a special legislative session to enact a minimum wage, and Connally replied, ''I tell you categorically today that I will not call a special session for this purpose because I don't think the urgency of it is of such a character that it has a compelling nature to it, so the answer to that is no.'' The leaders of the march appeared desperate. After two months on the road, there they were, nearly at their destination, and the governor of the state was telling them "No—No—No" in increasingly tougher tones.

Reverend Novarro answered Connally's remarks: "I believe your position here will invoke far-reaching political consequences in the state for years to come . . ." After the governor left the marchers, Brown said, "A brief meeting in the sun between the governor and the Mexican American farm workers is not going to resolve their problems . . ." Both Novarro and Brown apparently were correct.

True to his word, Connally was absent on Labor Day, as his old political foe Senator Yarborough stepped to the front of 6,500 marchers streaming up Congress Avenue to the front of the state capitol. One of the sympathizers who had joined with the marchers on the last leg of their journey was the governor's brother, Golfrey Connally, an economics professor at San Antonio College. Asked if there were any hard feelings over his taking part in the march, Golfrey says, "Not that I know of. No comment or criticism was ever made by anyone in the family about it."

The march became a magnet for Connally's enemies. Booker T. Bonner led a group of forty blacks from Huntsville for the Labor Day demonstration. Senator Yarborough, Albert Pena, and labor leaders such as Brown and Henry Munoz from Texas, and Cesar Chavez from California were there. Senator Robert Kennedy sent a telegram commending the marchers. Pena told the group that Connally thought "he was still the Anglo foreman talking to those little Mexicans back on the ranch in Wilson County, telling the people to go back home. But we couldn't go back home, we are home."

After sixty-four days and 468 miles, the march was over. Two farm workers, Benito Trevino and Reyes Alaniz, were left behind to maintain a vigil at the capitol's main entrance. The Fort Worth *Star-Telegram* reported that the Tuesday after Labor Day, Connally avoided the sentinels by going in a side door. After two months to reflect on the incident, Connally was asked at a meeting of the Beaumont Rotary Club if he would handle the farm workers' march any differently if he had it to do over again. "I would handle the matter just as I did in September," he answered. Ronnie Dugger of the *Texas Observer* says Connally's refusal to meet the laborers offended the Mexican concept of "Mi casa es su casa" and he wrote, "He insulted them and thus insulted us all."

The marchers turned thumbs down as they passed Carr's Senate campaign headquarters on Labor Day. A campaign brochure published later and directed toward Mexican Americans showed Carr talking with Father Gonzales, Senator Kennedy, Senator Yarborough, and President Johnson—but not Connally. Carr's appearance with Connally at New Braunfels obviously worked against him in the Senate race, which he lost to the Republican incumbent John Tower.[5]

The 1967 legislature rejected the $1.25 minimum wage, and the Valley farm worker flags, flown at the capitol since Labor Day 1966, were pulled down in mid-March 1967. Representative Jake Johnson of San Antonio, an impish lawmaker, jokingly proposed a John B. Connally Institute for Mexican Marching Affairs at New Braunfels, with Waggoner Carr as dean.

Evans of the AFL-CIO was asked why he thought Connally refused to meet the marchers at the capitol, as a few minutes with them would have saved him numerous explanations, some repercussions, and possible his political future. Evans remarks, "He looked at it as a politician and as a rancher that had kept the Mexican Americans down for a long time. He just figured . . . he just didn't have to see them, and that they were way beneath him. He looked at their activities as a political plot against him. I think he knew with his record and his attitude they would never be for him. So he was against everything we did in trying to build up leadership in the south Texas community. And his people inside organized labor fought everything we tried to do, too."

5. Given a choice between Republican Tower and Democrat Carr, many Texas liberals voted for Tower or "went fishing" on election day.

To counter criticism from Mexican Americans, Connally claimed at an April 1967 conference in San Antonio that, "More than any other governor in the history of this state, I have provided Texans of Mexican descent with the opportunity to succeed and serve their state in positions of high responsibility in government." [6] In 1968 Connally appointed a San Antonio lawyer, Roy Barrera, as secretary of state. One Connally critic remarked that Barrera served as Connally's "token spic." However, Barrera was a man of great dignity, who proved an asset in greeting visitors from Mexico and Latin American nations at HemisFair. Like Connally, most of his Mexican American appointees were "self-made" men who had achieved a measure of affluence and high social standing.

Senator Bernal of San Antonio criticized Connally for not appointing a Mexican American to the Constitutional Revision Commission. It was "another New Braunfels," Bernal remarked. Connally replied heatedly: "You suggest that a Mexican American should be appointed to the Constitutional Revision Commission merely because of the fact that he has a Spanish surname without any regard whatsoever for his ability, background, and qualifications to serve on a commission which is undertaking the most important task of rewriting the basic document that guides the operation of our state government. That is not my view. I refuse to be a party to the type of reverse discrimination which you suggest."

As a candidate for a third term for governor, Connally once again was "out of the office" when Bonner appeared at the state capitol, this time as the leader of sixteen blacks trying to petition Connally to investigate the arrest of several black youths during civil rights demonstrations in Huntsville. Late in the campaign, Connally appeared at a political rally in South Dallas, a black community. Connally's appearance was described as "an attempt to break up

6. His appointments included Ximenes to The University of Texas Board of Regents, Dr. J. G. Rodarte to the State Board of Medical Examiners, and I. D. Flores to the State Board of Health. Flores' ancestors founded Connally's hometown of Floresville.

235

the bloc voting in the Negro community." The meeting was sponsored by the Reverend S. M. Wright, a Baptist minister who had become a center of controversy in the black community through his endorsement of the "downtown businessmen's slate" of legislative candidates. The Dallas *Morning News* quoted a source as saying, "The governor flew up here to save Wright . . ."

Former Representative Randy Pendleton remembers Connally and Houston mayor Louie Welch meeting at Connally's Lake McQueeney home during the 1968 riots at predominantly black Texas Southern University, and how quickly Connally made up his mind "on a decision most men would agonize over—to send in the Texas National Guard, if necessary." Pendleton says Connally told Welch he "would not tolerate any violence and would take any measure to see that it was not escalated." Congressman Charles Wilson recalls that Connally "completely ignored" Senator Barbara Jordan of Houston, the only black member of the senate, until "he needed her vote on a rules fight." It is not surprising that, at the 1968 national Democratic convention in Chicago, Senator Jordan was the first member of the Texas delegation to announce she would not vote for Connally as a favorite-son candidate for president.

Just as the New Braunfels meeting had alienated many Mexican Americans and cast Connally in a "great white father" role, an off-the-cuff remark in response to the assassination of Martin Luther King sketched an anti-black image for Connally. Connally was quoted by the Associated Press as stating to a Weslaco audience that King had "contributed much to the chaos, and the strife, and the confusion, and the uncertainty in this country, but whatever his actions, he deserved not the fate of assassination." There was swift and angry reaction. The Reverend C. Anderson Davis, national field representative for the NAACP, said Connally "owes the American people an apology for such a dastardly statement." Connally said he was "quoted out of context," but KGBT-TV in Harlingen had taped the governor's speech, and a replay showed Connally had been quoted correctly. Dallas *News* reporter Jimmy Banks referred to Connally's statement as a "slip of the lip" and said it would be difficult for any reasonable person to argue with its accuracy. When demonstrators for King arrived at the capitol, they learned that the governor was once again not at home. He had gone to HemisFair.

At the end of Connally's six-year administration, Ronnie Dugger made a special study of "nine problem areas" across the state, including labor, and noted that Texas was the last of the ten largest states without a minimum wage law.[7] Also, he said, the maximum weekly benefit in Texas for injured workers was $35, the lowest in the nation. Only sixteen states had lower unemployment benefits than Texas' $45 weekly benefits. In addition, Dugger noted that a law was passed in 1967 creating an occupational safety board, but after eighteen months not a single safety standard had been adopted. Texas, he said, is "basically a non-union state."

Evans of the AFL-CIO says, "I think Connally had complete disregard, complete disdain, for members of organized labor. He was a very pompous person. I think that anybody who worked for a living he considered way beneath his class."[8] With their antipathy to Connally openly stated, labor, blacks, and Mexican Americans felt that their opposition had influenced Connally's decision not to run for a fourth term in 1968. Senator Bernal said he thought Connally had decided not to run because "he wants to be every man's governor" and black and Mexican American groups were committed to his defeat.

An incident on one of his numerous trips to California to check on films and exhibits for the Institute of Texas Cultures may have influenced Connally to retire from

7. Senator Yarborough told the Texas legislature in 1967 that an investigation by his labor and public welfare committee showed that some laundries in Texas were paying women as little as 33 cents an hour.

8. Former press secretary Bill Carter recalls Connally's refusing to help settle the La Casita strike in 1967. "One [labor] guy pounded Connally's desk so hard the papers bounced up and down. It was like two dinosaurs clashing." Afterwards, Connally asked Carter, "How'd I do?" Carter says he replied, "It was a draw," and Connally got mad. "He wanted a clear-cut victory."

public life. Connally stopped at El Paso in late October 1967 for the ceremonial signing of the Chamizal treaty.[9] After the ceremony with President Gustavo Diaz Ordaz of Mexico, President Johnson made a sudden decision to visit a border relations conference sponsored by the Inter-Agency Committee on Mexican American Affairs. In introducing members of his party, Johnson turned to Connally. According to Garth Jones of the AP, when the president introduced the governor, a "blast of boos broke loose. There were catcalls, whistles, hisses, and shouts of 'Throw him out.' Connally had a stern look on his face but said nothing." Another reporter wrote, "His smile froze." Jones said, "Johnson appeared startled, then frowned and rushed on with other introductions as the outburst died down."

"It really surprised me," said Dr. Clark Knowlton, chairman of the Department of Sociology at The University of Texas at El Paso and an active worker for years in Mexican American affairs. "Most Mexican Americans are very courteous and seldom, if ever, do anything like that. It was very surprising. . . . I would say that Governor Connally is the one politician who is totally *persona non grata* to the Mexicans."

After Connally announced he would not seek a fourth term, Brown of the AFL-CIO said the state's ethnic minorities, especially blacks and Mexican Americans, wanted a governor who offered practical solutions to their grievances. In opposing a resolution to endorse Connally as a favorite-son candidate for president in 1968, Representative Tom Moore of Waco said Connally's candidacy might divide the state party. "Whether justly or not, the governor does not enjoy a great deal of popularity, to put it mildly,

9. The Chamizal treaty settled a boundary dispute between Mexico and Texas that was nearly one hundred years old. The flooded Rio Grande had changed its course in 1867, moving south and west, leaving a strip of land north of the river-bed between El Paso, Texas and Juarez, Mexico. Both the United States and Mexico claimed this area, called Chamizal, because of the *chamizo*, a shrub that grew there. According to the treaty, the course of the Rio Grande was to be relocated and lined with concrete. Mexico was to receive 437 acres of land.

238

with labor, or with Mexican Americans or with a large percentage of the Negro voters,'' Moore stated.

After he retired as governor, Connally managed to avoid much criticism in Texas by maintaining a relatively low profile throughout the state. However, when he became active in President Nixon's administration and with his prominent role in the 1972 presidential campaign, he became an open target. Organized labor, with Roy Evans moving up from secretary-treasurer to president, took as many shots as possible. In April 1971 Evans warned political candidates that, ''Any involvement with John Connally, given Connally's ties to the Republicans, would disqualify the candidates from labor support.''[10] COPE decided in July that its number one priority was to help statewide Democratic party candidates and to ''oppose Nixon, Agnew, and Connally.'' In a caucus called by Evans just prior to the Texas Democratic convention in September 1972, organized labor denounced Connally as a ''traitor'' and urged Democrats to advise Connally ''that he is no longer welcome in our reformed Texas party.'' Evans swears that the Texas AFL-CIO has an ''ongoing file'' on Connally, including ''almost every business deal he's made, and if he ever tries to run for public office again, we'll release it.''

10. Joseph C. Goulden in his biography of AFL-CIO President George Meany reported that the AFL-CIO lobbyist Andrew Biemiller discussed with Meany the possibility that Connally might run with Nixon on the 1972 Republican ticket. Another member of the group stated that Connally would wait until 1976 and then run for president on the Republican ticket. Meany puffed on his cigar and stated, ''Well, I guess that gives me the incentive to stick around another four years.''

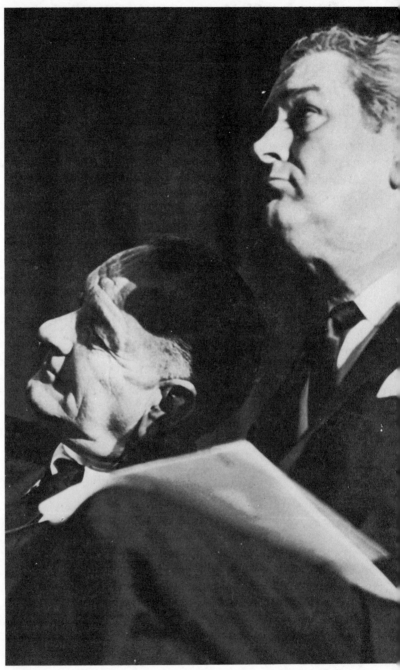

"The Shadow of Lyndon Johnson"

13

Sam Fore Jr. was putting out a weekly newspaper in Floresville when John Connally was growing up in the south Texas town. It meant something to be the editor of a small town weekly newspaper. It meant people listened when you talked, and politicians listened when you whispered. Before World War II and the metropolitan mushroom, the influence of the small town Texas editors extended far beyond the circle of their newspapers' circulation.

Connally's neighbors in Wilson County often asked, "What's the biggest thing in Floresville that goes up in the morning and down at night?" The answer: "Sam Fore's trousers." Everyone thought it was funny, but no one laughed where Sam Fore might hear. A big, fat man, Fore became the youngest president of the Texas Press Association, an organization of publishers of weekly newspapers from all over Texas. It was an organization which might deliver a substantial bloc of rural voters, one which Texas politicians could not afford to ignore. Luckily for John Connally and Lyndon Johnson, Sam Fore Jr. thought each of the men was "something special" and, according to Connally's sister Carmen, "When Lyndon was looking for someone to go to Washington with him, Mr. Fore was the one who suggested John."

In later years Connally told author Jimmy Banks that the organization built during Johnson's Senate races in 1941 and 1948 "basically was a Johnson-Connally organization, because I organized the young fellows who were my contemporaries, starting in 1941." National Democratic chairman Robert Strauss remembers that "even though we were the same age and had the same background—all ambitious and hungry—[Connally] had the unique quality of being able to assume the role of the leader without causing resentment. . . . Since he was at the university, he's always been 'chairman of the board.' " The youth corps Connally assembled for Johnson included former Congressman Joe Kilgore, Congressman Jake Pickle, and John Singleton. Connally and Pickle had both been student body presidents at The University of Texas and had supported a student candidate, Sidney Reagan, who beat Singleton, Strauss' candidate. Kilgore later lost a race for student body president. Campus politics had been their political training ground.

George Christian says, "I always had the impression that their [Connally and Johnson] relationship started out as sort of a little brother, big brother thing, that there was a great deal of affection between the two men; *simpatico*, whatever you want to call it. But . . . all through their careers, they had disputes over a variety of things. I've heard stories about Connally packing his suitcases and leaving the campaign, in 1941 even, when he [Johnson] was running for the Senate, and 1948."[1] There was a ten-day

1. Connally's former aide Mike Myers commented on the differences in the two men's temperament: "When Connally was mad he wouldn't say anything. You'd know it by the silence. I think it was an over-reaction to LBJ. He was silent—the other extreme—not the ass-chewings LBJ was known for. I'd rather he would have said what you had screwed up."

242

estrangement during the unsuccessful 1941 race against W. Lee "Pappy" O'Daniel after Johnson—according to Jimmy Banks—ordered Connally and Gordon Fulcher out of his house because they wanted to make public that he had laryngitis. Communication between Connally and Johnson again was shut off for two weeks in the 1948 Senate race against Coke Stevenson, Banks stated, because Connally had released against Johnson's wishes a story that he was going to the Mayo clinic to be examined for kidney stones.

Will Davis, state Democratic chairman under Connally, recalls, "Connally was always in the forefront or behind the scenes at any of Johnson's . . . and Mr. Rayburn's convention activity. . . . Whatever convention program they had, he would be participating in that program. . . . He was the organizer, always kinda the person in charge of operations."

In 1961 Connally decided to use the knowledge and the political influence he had gained while working for Johnson. He wanted to run his own show—as governor of Texas. In Connally's race for governor, Johnson's name often was a heavy cross to bear. The *Texas Observer* insisted that Johnson had shoved Connally into the race to prepare for Johnson's "inevitable effort for the presidential nomination in 1968." [2]

Will Wilson, who resigned as state attorney general to run for governor in 1962, reponded to Connally's candidacy by saying, "The shadow of Lyndon B. Johnson is cast over this event. Johnson is doing his job as vice president—and one office at a time is enough. . . . John Connally is so completely identified with LBJ, as campaign manager, secretary, and confidant, that the two are inseparable." Writing in the *Texas Observer*, a liberal lawyer from Silsbee, Texas, Houston Thompson asked, "Will Connally, if elected, still protect Lyndon's Achilles heel [Texas] and thereby give Lyndon an excellent chance to become the

2. Author Theodore White tells the story, however, of Johnson's musing aloud to a newspaper friend that "he never could see why John Connally left a good job like being secretary of the navy in Washington to go off down there to Texas and be governor."

next leader of the Democratic Party, and possibly (God, forbid) our President in 1968? Yes."

Aide George Reedy relayed the message that Johnson "does not take sides in primary races unless he is directly involved." Whether Johnson took sides or not, to many voters, Connally wore the LBJ brand, and it seemed impossible to erase. "The impact of a Connally victory," the wary *Observer* editor Willie Morris wrote, "would be far-reaching and disastrous. His present political power, a lesson from the Lyndon Johnson primer, comes from the top down, through the big law firms, the banks, Brown & Root. Johnson never had, as such, an extensive precinct organization. He has traditionally played the offsetting political groupings one against the other, using the liberal or the conservative organizations to his advantage as the times demanded. He thrived on the individual approach, the backroom manipulation which made him, in the United States Senate, one of America's greatest parliamentary geniuses. This, likewise, is the Connally technique."

Wilson sent Johnson a telegram, urging him to pull out completely from the Connally campaign "or bear the responsibility of splitting the Democratic Party of Texas." [3] Asked about the issue, Connally said, "I have not asked him [Johnson] to associate himself with it [the campaign] or to disassociate himself from it. I have not anticipated that he would take any part in it. And I presume that position will continue." As the rumors persisted that Connally was getting his orders from Johnson, Connally retorted, "I don't know anybody in the race—or potentially in it—who wasn't his [Johnson's] strong supporter." [4]

3. Wilson finished fourth behind Connally, Don Yarborough, and Price Daniel in the 1962 Democratic primary for governor and later switched to the Republican party.

4. In its April 14, 1962 issue, the *Texas Observer* mentioned that in 1960, three of the major candidates for governor—Governor Price Daniel, Connally, and Wilson—"went arm-in-arm to nominate Johnson at the Los Angeles convention."

Connally was able, however, to draw on Johnson's financial supporters, and former Texas AFL-CIO president Roy Evans says it was "through Johnson's contacts" that Connally was partially successful in getting labor to "take no position" in the Democratic governor's race. Don Yarborough was commended, but did not get labor's all-out support in the form of an endorsement. Connally's first speaking invitation as a candidate for governor was also a result of his connection with Johnson, according to former Lieutenant Governor Ben Barnes. Barnes says the late Charlie Woodson, publisher of the Brownwood *Bulletin*, had been "a strong Johnson supporter and supported the Kennedy-Johnson ticket. He locked Mr. Woodson in very strongly by coming out here [Brownwood]. Woodson had, I guess, six or seven newspapers then, and they all endorsed Connally." Woodson also gave the editor of the Brownwood paper a leave of absence, Barnes says, to travel "with Connally as one of his press men throughout the campaign."

"Lyndon's boy, John" was a common slogan across the state and often damaging to Connally. D. W. Hicks, a Bandera rancher married to Connally's older sister Carmen, was asked what kind of reaction he got in 1962 while campaigning for Connally in the rural west Texas areas. "Fair, I would say," Hicks says. "The people you knew and that knew you and believed in you, you could convince them that he [Connally] wasn't 'Lyndon Johnson's boy, John.' But so many of the people in west Texas believed he was a tool of Lyndon Johnson's. I would just tell it like it was . . . that he was his own man and he was running and he would stand up on his own feet."

Connally's runoff victory in the Democratic primary over Yarborough matched him against Jack Cox, a recent convert to the Republican party—so recent that in 1960 he had led to the state Democratic convention a Stephens County delegation pledged to support Johnson for president. Cox contended that Johnson wanted to run against Kennedy in 1964 and that Connally was sent to Texas as part of that master plan. Cox stressed that he was "independent of

Washington control'' and ran a full-page advertisement in the Dallas *Morning News* depicting Connally as a puppet on Johnson's lap. The *Texas Observer*, Connally's constant critic, endorsed him against Cox as the ''safer choice'' in a ''perilous period'' of global affairs. Even Texas author and folklorist J. Frank Dobie, a hero to word-conscious liberals, wrote the *Observer* that, ''Connally is of high enough caliber not to be a pawn of Lyndon Johnson or any other politician. . . . I think he'll make a better governor than any so-called Democrat that has been elected within the last two decades.''

Although Connally defeated Cox by 132,013 votes, a Belden poll indicated Cox was wise in stressing the Connally-Johnson alliance. Belden said Cox's anti-Johnson campaign got him 36 percent—or 257,409—of his votes against Connally.[5]

Richard Morehead of the Dallas *Morning News* stated that the year 1963 would be a ''critical year'' for Connally and Johnson. ''Should Connally stumble, or give his critics much cause to complain of Washington direction to the statehouse, the Democrats may emerge in internecine warfare. This would cloud Connally's future, and perhaps Lyndon B. Johnson's too.'' Two years later, Sam Wood wrote in the Austin *American-Statesman* that Connally's first inaugural speech in January 1963, had been ''surprisingly similar'' to Johnson's broad outline for the nation, the ''Great Society,'' which was delivered after the Connally address. In his inaugural address, Connally first stressed what would become a theme of his six years as governor. The mid-1960s, he said, ''is a time of trial and test for our federal system and for the role of states within that system. We will not accept the proposition that in a time when the central government must be strong, the state government must be weak. Power flows in when responsibility ebbs away. And I say to you that the strength of our system—and

5. Washington columnist Marianne Means claimed nine years later that Connally's 1962 victory had dissolved the ''teacher-protege relationship'' of Johnson and Connally, and said Connally had been ''independent of Johnson's dominance'' since then.

the order of our system—urgently demands a renaissance of responsibility among the states.'' In other words, so long as Connally was governor, Texas would have no soft spots for the federal government to move in on if he could help it.

Connally's first public disagreement with the Kennedy-Johnson administration was in 1963 and concerned civil rights. Connally stated that he wanted blacks to have the same voting and legal rights as whites, as well as access to public facilities; but he opposed President Kennedy's attempt to bar discrimination in private business. Connally's opposition focused attention in Texas on that provision of the civil rights proposals, and Clarence Laws, field secretary of the southwest region of the National Association for the Advancement of Colored People, said, ''Connally's pious, sugar-coated platitudes are unacceptable.''

The Dallas *Morning News*, a spontaneous Connally supporter, claimed that Kennedy had gone ''too far in sympathetic encouragement of the Negro's equality drive.'' Connally tried to convince the National Governors' Conference in Miami, Florida, that the governors were preoccupied with civil rights—there were other things to worry about. Texas liberals, however, believed that civil rights was the prime domestic issue in the nation, and the *Texas Observer* reported that Connally had refused to sign two civil rights petitions circulated at the governors' conference. Johnson, the *Observer* stated, had ''endorsed the public accommodations bill, saying that 'whatever the legalisms or traditions, it is wrong' that Negroes cannot find a bed or meals for their children along the highways, or wash up alongside fellow Americans, eat beside them, or go to school beside them.'' The *Observer* further stated that Connally would defend ''petty cruelties . . . in the name of private property'' but Johnson ''would forbid them in the name of democratic decency.''

Kennedy's death patched the Johnson-Connally split over civil rights for a while, and the two families sought strength in each other.[6] From his hospital bed in Dallas, the

6. Lynda Bird Johnson, a University of Texas coed, left her Zeta Tau

wounded governor described Johnson, the new president of the United States, as "a person of great charm and great poise." But he added, "At times he can be almost brusque and rude. . . . He is a person who will be viewed by some as being perhaps unlettered, and in some ways he is unlettered, but in other ways he is probably as literate a person as you will ever see in your life—literate in the understanding of the terms of human nature."

Connally was an old friend, but Johnson was also courting new friends. The president had personally invited Senator Yarborough to go to New York with him for Senator Herbert Lehman's funeral, and he visited with Yarborough on several occasions at the White House. A deal was in the making, but Senator Yarborough apparently did not know about it; nor did Connally. It was a horse trade between Johnson and national labor leaders —no serious competition for Yarborough; no serious competition for Connally in the 1964 elections. The Johnson-labor deal blocked Connally's friend Joe Kilgore from running against Yarborough, and Will Davis says, "This was a severe and difficult thing for Connally to accept. It would have severed any other type of relationship."

Connally felt he had been betrayed by Johnson. He did not want to run for governor again, but George Christian, his former press secretary, recalls, "Everybody was shoving him . . . Johnson was president and Johnson needed Connally to hold his political base in Texas. There were just all sorts of political reasons as to why he ought to run for reelection. Well, his argument was, 'I don't care what the political reasons are, I've got personal reasons for not wanting to. Why do I have to? Why can't somebody else do the same thing? Why does it have to be me?' It got pretty hairy from the standpoint of just indecision [as] to whether or not he was really going to do it. He finally filed. He filed very reluctantly. There wasn't anything phony about it. He felt pretty deeply about it."

Alpha sorority house and went to the governor's mansion to comfort the younger Connally children, Mark and Sharon. Author William Manchester said Lady Bird hugged Nellie Connally at Parkland Hospital in Dallas and assured her, "He [Connally] is going to get well . . . he's got to get well."

After making his "agonizing" decision to run for a second term, Connally discovered he would have to campaign against the liberal Don Yarborough who, despite labor's objections, had entered the race. To Connally, this meant that Johnson had failed. The president had managed to wipe out Senator Yarborough's strongest potential opponent, Kilgore, but he had not been able to guarantee Connally's victory. "He was mad, he was damn mad," says Davis. "Ralph Yarborough was his bad enemy and Joe Kilgore was his friend. He wanted Kilgore to run, and he [Kilgore] could have won."

Although the Connally-Johnson alliance had been frayed, the governor told a news conference at the Adolphus Hotel in Dallas, "I don't think it would be proper to say we had a spat. . . . The president and I haven't always seen eye-to-eye on political matters and, as time goes by, I'm sure other cases will come up in which our views differ. But we've always had a warm personal relationship and I'm sure we will continue to do so." Within a week, however, Connally turned down Johnson's invitation to visit the LBJ ranch, saying he had to go to his own ranch at Floresville. The Connallys and the Johnsons sat together at the funeral of Mrs. J. C. Kellam, the wife of Johnson's television station manager, but Connally's car pulled out of the motorcade after the services. They were public men, but Connally considered their friendship private, and he was offended if anyone questioned him about their troubles. In reply to questions, he stated, "As I recall, he [Johnson] said something to the effect that if you aren't busy, how about driving up to the ranch. I told him we had planned to go to our own ranch—and he apparently didn't have anything special to discuss with me anyway." He admitted to newsmen, however, that the stories he had read in Texas newspapers about the "rift" were "not unreasonable at all, and they didn't take any poetic license with the facts."

Their feeling about civil rights accentuated the different passions of the two men. Johnson seemed compelled by his own upbringing to make life better for those who had not done so well. Connally, on the other hand, had made it and seemed determined to erase all traces of the days when the Connally kids couldn't even play sports because they had to get home to their chores. It was Johnson, for example, not Connally, who broke the segregation rule at the Forty Acres Club, a private bar and restaurant near The University of Texas campus. A year after Connally became governor, Johnson took one of his black secretaries to a New Year's Eve party at the club. Four nights later, reporters at the Texas capitol gave a party for the White House press, and Andrew Hatcher, a black associate press secretary to Johnson, attended. [7]

No doubt Johnson's ideas had changed. The *Texas Observer* had quoted him in June 1960, before he was nominated for vice president, as saying, ''This civil rights program, about which you have heard so much, is a farce and a sham—an effort to set up a police state in the guise of liberty. I am opposed to that program.'' As Johnson had changed, he wanted Connally to change. The president sent his community relations man, Leroy Collins, Secretary of Commerce Luther Hodges, and former Tennessee Governor Buford Ellington to talk with Connally about civil rights. Connally told them that Texas had made ''excellent progress in human relations'' in the past few years, and he expected the state ''to continue its progress without the need for outside help.''

These temporal conflicts between Connally and Johnson deluded Texas liberals into thinking something good might come out of it for them. But it seldom worked that way. Connally and Johnson always mended their differences to take care of mutual interests or to do each other special favors. The year 1964 was really not a good one for liberals, as Johnson was repairing his political fences to run for president in his own name. Johnson allowed Connally to run the June state Democratic convention from start to finish, and Connally had himself named chairman of the Texas delegation to the national convention at Atlantic

7. Club directors voted to admit anyone—including blacks—in a private party, or anyone there on official business involving The University of Texas. This was ten years after the United States Supreme Court had outlawed segregation.

250

City, New Jersey. He also dictated the names of the dele-
gates-at-large and their alternates—all were Johnson's
friends, as well as Connally's. Connally said he had three
reasons for working for Johnson's election. ''One, I think
that in the interest of the country he will make a better
president than Barry Goldwater. Two, I don't think there's
any question but what the best interest of Texas will be
served by his election. . . . Three, I have, as you know, a
quarter of a century of personal and political association
with him that would lead me to try to be helpful in every
way I can.''

Connally and Governor Pat Brown of California
nominated Johnson for president at the national convention,
and Connally's nominating speech included a passage about
Johnson's helping Franklin Roosevelt fight for a ''two-
ocean Navy'' while ''less visionary men still slept
peacefully and dreamed of isolation.'' (This remark about
national defense is similar to Connally's attacks on Senator
McGovern during the 1972 presidential race.) Johnson,
said Connally, ''is an American first, a Democrat second.
. . . Never in our history has any man come to the
presidency better prepared or tested for the supreme task of
leadership.''

Johnson talked with Connally by telephone about his
selection of Senator Hubert Humphrey as the vice-presidential nominee. Some politicians say Connally advised
Johnson to pick Secretary of Defense Robert McNamara, a
Republican, as his running mate. Columnists Rowland
Evans and Robert Novak said Connally's convention role
established him ''as the most important new voice in the
national Democratic party.'' They further stated that Connally's advisers wanted him to campaign in places other
than the South to lay the framework for a national base. It
was more than a month, however, before Connally made his
first out-of-state speech on behalf of the Johnson-Humphrey
ticket, and that was on October 1 at Governor William
Guy's forty-fifth birthday party in Bismarck, North
Dakota.[8] In honoring Guy, Connally made no mention of

8. Three years later, Guy, the retiring chairman of the National

251

Goldwater, but he alluded to the Arizona senator in a comment about nuclear weapons—"When we talk about small, conventional [nuclear] weapons, let's remember they are neither small nor conventional."

On October 7 Connally spoke in Phoenix, Arizona, the first Democratic speaker to address a political rally in Goldwater's home state. Connally also met with Johnson in Washington to plan the closing days of the campaign, and the president took Connally to Herbert Hoover's funeral in New York and on a campaign swing through Ohio, Illinois, Missouri, and Tennessee. Apparently in an effort to compromise with Johnson, Connally abstained from voting at the Southern Governors' Conference on a proposal by George Wallace of Alabama to take away the federal courts' authority over public schools. [9]

There was also one minor incident during the campaign that was never explained, although Connally laughed about it at the time. The president sent a telegram of support to Senator Yarborough at a Dallas dinner on the eve of the September state Democratic convention. No telegram was received at Connally's "official" banquet, given the same night by the State Democratic Executive Committee. Connally denied there was any significance to this, and said, "I didn't ask nor anticipate" a telegram from the White House. In a regional telecast on the night of October 31, 1964, Connally appealed to Southerners to vote for Johnson, "a friend of the South—in every sense of the word. In the days and years ahead, the South needs a friend in the White House as we continue our drive for our economic growth and greater opportunity for our people."

Governors' Conference, made this suggestion as governors disembarked at New York following an eight-day cruise—"Why not run John Connally when President Johnson gives up the office? He would be an alternative to Humphrey and Senator Robert Kennedy, both liberals. . . . Connally [is] the party's best hope for a strong conservative presidential candidate to follow Lyndon Johnson."

9. There is a story involving Connally and Johnson, however, that illustrates their relationship and their division over the issue of civil rights. The tale, as best a number of persons can remember, goes like this: Johnson and Connally were flying from Washington to Texas with several stops en route, and the president was speaking on at each stop. Johnson asked Connally to look over his speech. Connally

The Connallys and Johnsons watched election returns at the Driskill Hotel and the governor's mansion, and later it was Connally, Johnson's friend of twenty-seven years, who told a "tumultuously happy" crowd waiting at Austin's Municipal Auditorium, "I am proud to introduce you to the President of the United States."

Connally postponed his own inauguration as governor for a week—an unprecedented move in modern times—so there would be no conflict with Johnson's inaugural ceremonies. The governor and his wife were special guests at the White House for Johnson's inauguration, occupying the historic Lincoln Room. They led the inaugural parade and watched the rest of the procession from the presidential box.

There was speculation that Connally might accept a cabinet appointment, but he told reporters in Austin, "I have not been offered one, I don't want one, I don't anticipate being offered one." He would, as he complained on numerous occasions, have his hands full just shuffling papers on burgeoning federal programs. According to Connally's brother Wayne, "back in 1962, 1963, 1964, many of the [federal programs] were in their infancy and I think he [Connally] wanted to have the opportunity to try to charter the course of the state in maintaining a responsible position of its own and yet establishing a permanent type of relationship with the federal government and not go giving up all the powers of the state. . . ." But beginning in 1965, the federal government's influence seemed to encompass the state, and Connally, a man accustomed to having his way, couldn't get a grip on the unwieldy federal bureaucracy. While he was governor, the number of federal programs grew from 45 to 400. He

did and made some suggestions, but Johnson ignored them in his speech at the first stop in Pittsburgh. Connally penciled in some changes before the president spoke again, but Johnson gave the full speech once more in St. Louis. Connally asked where he could catch a flight home. The presidential party was airborne before Johnson knew Connally had left, and he yelled to his aides to "get him." They finally located Connally by phone at Love Field in Dallas, urging him to meet Johnson at his final stop in Longview, Texas. Connally said he had better things to do than give advice that was ignored and he flew on to Austin. As columnists Evans and Novak wrote, "Though Mr. Johnson often enlists influential advisers for valet-like chores, such as carrying luggage or mixing highballs, not so with Connally. He is one adviser who can talk to—and talk back to—the president as a peer."

thought Johnson was stacking multi-million-dollar programs so fast that one couldn't find out what was in them.

The attitude of many Texans that the federal government was their "sworn enemy," author Theodore White said, is "thoroughly alien to a man like Johnson. For him the Federal Government is the greatest benefactor of Texas." Connally's criticism of the federal government, as well as his unwavering defense of Johnson's Vietnam war policy, was singled out by the media for special attention. George Christian notes that there were other politicians—such as Senator Harold Hughes of Iowa ("a pretty liberal fellow") and Governor Warren Hearnes of Missouri—who were also "upset by some of the [federal] attitudes." But not much was made of them in the news, as in Connally's case. So many Texans were paranoid about federal "intervention" that Connally, as the state's spokesman, was pressed to speak out on almost every federal issue, including the Supreme Court—so unpopular in some areas that billboards were erected decrying its influence.

Organized labor became a prickly topic between Connally and Johnson, although Roy Evans of the Texas AFL-CIO claims Connally "didn't understand labor and Lyndon Johnson really didn't until he got to be vice-president. The first speech that Lyndon Johnson made that was pro-labor was in 1963. . . . Their attitude was that if you said labor you said strikes and then violence—all of them were equal. And it was giving people voice and votes and influence that they shouldn't have. The basic attitude was a fear of any kind of organization that he [Johnson] didn't control, any kind of democratic operation." What set the two men apart publicly was Johnson's decision to ask Congress in 1965 to abolish the law which empowers states to enact "right-to-work" provisions. Such provisions outlaw union shops or shops in which everyone must belong to the union. Texas was one of eighteen states with a "right-to-work" law, and Connally wrote Texas congressmen to vote to protect the law. "It is only the latest in a series of positions the governor has assumed which put him squarely in agreement with the Goldwater wing of the Re-

254

publican Party," said Hank Brown, then president of the Texas AFL-CIO.

But of all the hundreds of presidential decisions and proposals and programs, the one that seemed to irk Connally the most was Johnson's attempt to achieve the monumental goal of erasing poverty in the United States. "After Johnson became president," Christian reflects, "there was a lot of opportunity for disagreement [and] . . . almost all of it revolved around the poverty program. Sarge Shriver's ideas on running the poverty program were contrary to Connally's ideas here in Texas. The OEO [Office of Economic Opportunity] was bypassing local officials and Connally was getting a lot of complaints from local officials."

When an unnamed labor department official was quoted in the Austin *American-Statesman* as saying Connally's opposition to a $1.25-an-hour wage for students in the poverty program threatened its success, Connally called a news conference to deny that he was obstructing the program. The Texas House of Representatives adopted a resolution deploring the labor department's action in setting the minimum wage of $1.25 and commending Connally for his statement. Connally vetoed a $381,480 federal anti-poverty grant to the Texas Farmers Union, designed to employ 790 high school students part-time in eight south central Texas counties, because, he said, the Farmers Union was a "quasi-political organization." And—in the language of Texas "pols"—it "weren't his quasi-political" organization. Connally's veto ignited a congressional effort to take that power away from governors,[10] and Leslie Carpenter wrote in his column from Washington that Connally's "foot-dragging" on the poverty programs was causing "some White House embarrassment." Connally said he had had dinner with President Johnson and was not lectured about it.

10. Senator Yarborough, who was trying to cut the veto out of the program, said, "On the outcome of that struggle depends the issue of whether we will have a war on poverty or a vetoed war on poverty that leaves the ragged still ragged and the hungry, hungry still. In no real war does a general allow a sergeant to revoke his orders."

In August 1965 Bo Byers of the Houston *Chronicle*'s Austin bureau quoted a close associate of Connally's as saying the governor wanted to quit because Johnson had become so liberal. "John thought that once Lyndon won the election, he would become more moderate," Byers' source said. "Instead, the president has been the most liberal president we've ever seen. He is pushing for repeal of 14-B, the Taft-Hartley provision that allows states to have 'right-to-work' laws. He is for a $1.75 minimum wage, which is going to tear up a lot of Texas farmers if it goes through. And apparently he is backing Ralph Yarborough in the move to eliminate the governor's power of veto in the anti-poverty program. What kind of position does that put Connally in, when he has to be defended in the Senate by the Republican senator from Texas, John Tower?"

Evans and Novak stated that Johnson surprised congressional leaders at a weekly breakfast by arguing that the best way to keep politics out of the poverty program was to repeal the veto, and "hot-line telephone calls" went out to several governors, assuring them that no vetoes were needed because their protests would be heard "in the highest quarters" in Washington. The columnists reported that Johnson had "decided the time had come to show all of Texas who was boss—the Governor or the President. Said a mutual friend: 'John pounded the table once too often.'" There were even reports in Washington newspapers that Connally had threatened to close the Camp Gary Job Corps Center at San Marcos, Texas, one of Johnson's showpieces, unless federal administrators would let him run it the way he wanted to. The governor initiated Opportunities, Inc., a program to allow private industry in Texas to assist the training center in what should be taught. The governor also appointed a three-member board of trustees to oversee the center. The board included San Marcos banker R. L. Thornton; Austin contractor Cecil Ruby; and Dr. Arleigh Templeton, a college president the governor liked.

Connally knew that federal government "bargains" often were more expensive than they first appeared. What irritated him most was the feeling that he was being pushed and shoved when he didn't want to be pushed and shoved by the massive motion of the federal government, by anonymous pencil pushers hiding behind pounds of paper and telephone extension numbers. A former aide recalls, "He really blew his cork over federal programs and the strings attached to them. Terrell Blodgett told the governor, 'The feds say we have to handle driver education this way,' But Connally interrupted, 'We don't have to do it any goddamn way, by God. We'll do it the way I want to.'"

The final straw was the Justice Department's decision to order the FBI to monitor a special two-week voter registration period in Texas in March 1966, during Connally's campaign for a third term. But this FBI supervision was no scatter shot. It was a direct aim at Texas and, by implication, at Connally, the president's old-and-good friend. Connally flew to Washington to confer with Johnson. When he returned on May 2, he was so mad he called capitol reporters into his office for an off-the-record briefing. A partial substance of the conference was reported three weeks later by the Los Angeles *Times*-Washington *Post* News Service to support the interpretation that Connally and Johnson "have had a falling out."

Some reporters typed notes on the briefing, and one recalls that the "basic theme" of the session was that the "highhanded tactics" of the OEO and the FBI surveillance of voter registration were part of a trend in the federal government to assume more power than the Constitution had reserved to the government. Connally stated that neither President Johnson nor any federal agency had cleared any appointment in Texas through him. Connally cited the case of a man that he said had a record as a communist, who was put on an advisory council for the poverty program. He was dropped, Connally said, after Connally informed Shriver about him. The governor also mentioned two federal grants which had received prompt federal approval, including the Farmers Union program, which he had vetoed once. He said the grant was even increased on the second attempt, but that he had contacted Secretary of Labor Willard Wirtz and threatened to release his five-page veto message, and Wirtz recalled the application. Connally told the reporters that he had warned two presidential aides from Texas, Jake Jacobsen and Marvin Watson, to remain calm if they heard Connally criticizing Johnson's administration because he [Connally] probably would be doing so. He said he felt compelled to speak out because other governors were remaining silent. Connally said that the previous fall he had told Johnson his feelings about "federal power plays," and Johnson agreed. But Johnson said he didn't have time to look into such matters.

Asked if he thought Connally's criticism of the programs spawned by the Johnson administration "bothered" Johnson, George Christian says, "No, I don't really think it did."

> President Johnson would have always liked for everyone to just say 'Amen,' you know, and march along with him. But he's realistic enough to know that he was force-feeding a lot of people besides Texans on certain programs, and Texas wasn't the only place he was having trouble. He had big disputes with the governors of a number of states, including pretty liberal governors—particularly over poverty programs—over what I always considered to be rather arrogant activities on the part of some of the federal agencies in shoving the states around. Connally used to resent very much the feeling on the part of a lot of people in the 'Great Society' that anybody involved with state and local government was a crook, or somebody's brother-in-law; that nothing would work if state and local agencies did it. And he just rejected that out of hand. He said, 'Heck, yes, we've got bad local officials in some places. Sure, we've got incompetence down here, but I'll match my incompetence against their incompetence any day.' You know, just because a guy's in an agency in Washington doesn't mean he knows how something ought to be done in Del Rio, Texas.

A traditional Democratic gathering, the Jackson Day dinner at Springfield, Missouri, in late March 1966, was the scene for what the Dallas *Morning News* stated was

258

an attempt by Connally "'to end speculation that a major rift had developed between him and President Johnson.'' If ending the ''rift'' was Connally's purpose, his speech there had a dual purpose of gathering support for the increasingly unpopular Vietnam war, a conflict Connally believed in. ''This is our struggle,'' he said, ''an American struggle, no different from any other struggle we have entered in the cause of freedom and security. Unity . . . does not require complete subjugation of personal opinion, but unity in time of war . . . support for the President, who must make these decisions of life and death . . . this should not be too much to expect of a people committed to freedom.'' Connally was often asked for his opinion on Vietnam because he was accessible even when the war was going badly, and Johnson was hard to reach. It was a subject Connally, whose ''patriotism'' impressed even his enemies, thought worth preaching about. He told a training class of Texas policemen that criminals should be treated the same way as the Navy had handled the North Vietnamese gunboats in the Gulf of Tonkin. He quoted Adlai Stevenson to the American Chamber of Commerce in Mexico City[11] to describe the United States' role in world events.

At the 1966 Jefferson-Jackson Day dinner in Louisville, Kentucky, another prestigious parley of the party faithful, Connally said, ''Every American, every Kentuckian, every Democrat should thank God we have a president in the White House with the determination to stand firm for freedom. A president who is concerned more about the future of this nation than he is about his own personal political popularity.'' This was about the time, says author David Halberstam, that Johnson began to feel that the war critics were his critics: ''Since he was patriotic, clearly they were not. He had FBI dossiers on war critics, congressmen, and

11. Connally cited Stevenson's words: ''It has fallen America's lot to organize and lead that portion of the world which adheres to the principle of consent in the ordering of human affairs. It is an assignment we undertook not by choice but by necessity. . . . The burden is without historical parallel and so is the danger, and so is our response. . . . The outward thrust of aggression in Europe has been arrested. Now we shall have to address ourselves to Asia, to perpetual siege and to the unending tasks of greatness. For the quest for peace and security is not a day's or a decade's work. For us it may be everlasting.''

journalists, and he would launch into long, irrational tirades against them; he knew what was behind their doubts, the Communists were behind them—yes, the *Communists,* the Russians. . . .'' This is a war, Connally told Rotarians in Beaumont, Texas, ''we simply cannot afford to lose. We have to let the Communist aggressors know we'll take any steps necessary to prevent their takeover in South Vietnam.''

Connally, too, was vehement about critics of the war, especially those who protested in the streets. ''It is difficult,'' he told Chicago businessmen, ''to hold anything but contempt for the vociferous herds of beatniks and peaceniks who have no faith in their own country and seek to undermine public confidence in everything it does.'' At an ''Americanism Day'' rally in San Angelo, Texas, he spoke out against ''beatniks, peaceniks, and draftniks'' and asserted that any non-Communist student ''who waves a placard saying 'Get out of Vietnam' is the front man, whether he believes it or not, for a Communist organizer or sympathizer somewhere up the line.''

Besides absorbing some of the public flack on Johnson's Vietnam policies, Connally was still in a position to do favors for the president in Texas, where some reporter was always trying to make a national reputation by uncovering Johnson tidbits. A bill quietly passed the 1965 legislature, for example, which granted University of Texas regents the power of eminent domain to add certain tracts of land to the Austin campus. But its significance was not made public until three months later, when it was announced that Johnson had accepted the regents' offer to set aside as much as fourteen acres of a residential section for Johnson's presidential library.

Although Connally was suspicious of the growing power of the federal government, he would often turn to it, on his terms, for large and small matters. In an address to the 1967 legislature, Connally proposed a federal revenue sharing plan with the federal government kicking back 5 percent of taxes to the fifty states. ''I personally am not ready to 'write off' the states as a dying member of our

260

federal-state-local team," he said. He sought federal money to repair hurricane damage, to eradicate screwworms, to establish parks and seashores; and, in 1968, he even went to the federal government with a request to preserve the one-hundred-year-old convent of Incarnate Word in Brownsville, Texas, which was scheduled to be torn down.

In 1965 Connally suggested to Texas' congressional delegation that the state needed a fulltime office in Washington to keep tabs on legislation and other federal matters affecting Texas. And, in January 1966, a three-term Texas House member from Breckenridge, Wayne Gibbens,[12] was named administrative assistant to Connally and assigned to Washington as Texas' first liaison man with the national government. Gibbens became the director of the Division of State-Federal Relations, created as part of the governor's office. It has never received high-priority funding. The standing joke when the office was set up was that Connally "just wanted someone in Washington to meet him at the airport."

In November 1967 Connally announced to the surprise of many that he was going to pack his nameplate and not run for a fourth term the following spring. Connally knew when he made his announcement that Johnson was also considering stepping down as president. Connally later said Johnson had talked of quitting as early as the spring of 1967, and in October 1967, Connally and Christian spent an hour and a half going over the type of statement Johnson might issue. Johnson wrote in *The Vantage Point*, his account of his administration, that Connally had told him in early 1967 he did not want to run again for governor, but would "if I wanted him on the ticket with me in Texas. I told him that I felt certain I would not run and suggested he base his decision on that assumption."

12. Gibbens was one of the most conservative, business-oriented members of the Texas House of Representatives. One clue to his leanings was a statement attributed to the chief lobbyist of the conservative Texas Manufacturers Association, Jim Yancy, who told other lobbyists in 1963 that any bill Gibbens introduced "you can assume is a reasonable bill."

After Connally's announcement, there was immediate speculation in the press that "strained" relations between the two men had nudged Connally into retirement. There were also numerous reports speculating about whether Connally's pulling out would hurt Johnson in Texas in 1968. The liberals contended Connally's retirement would consolidate support for the president, since Connally was so unpopular with Texas liberals. The conservatives thought, as a "lame duck governor," Connally's support would be sorely missed. Johnson wrote: "I was surprised and relieved, I told Bob McNamara, that there was so little speculation in the press connecting Connally's political plans with mine." During Christmas 1967, Connally said, he and Nellie, the president and Lady Bird, and Johnson's daughter and son-in-law, Luci and Pat Nugent, spent hours at the LBJ ranch talking about Johnson's future. Connally said Johnson had tried to dissuade him from quitting, and the governor did the same to Johnson.

In January 1968 a story by UPI's Kyle Thompson stated that prior to the previous fall Connally "had about 90 percent made up his mind" to run for a fourth term, and that his decision not to run "resulted partly from a political break" with Johnson. The "political schism" between the two men, Thompson said, began in October 1967, when Mexican Americans booed Connally at the meeting he attended in El Paso with the president. Thompson wrote: "One report said Johnson made some half-joking remark to Connally after the meeting to the effect that, 'It's hardly safe to be seen in public with you any more.'"

Ben Barnes, often mentioned as a protege of the two politicians, says, "Johnson needed Connally. . . . When Johnson got in trouble in the dark hours or when he needed some strength or support, he always wanted Connally there because he knew Connally was strong. Johnson liked strong people."

Although Barnes was friendly with both men, a friend of Johnson's was not necessarily a friend of Connally's. The best case in point seems to be Edward Clark, whose deprecatory humor as a lobbyist masked a cool, calculating, and critical mind. Writer Selig Harrison referred to Clark as the ''jolly Austin lobbyist who acts as Johnson's principal wheeler-dealer at the state capitol.'' Anyone who missed Clark ''in his prime'' is told repeatedly he has missed the master, and only the pupils, pale imitations, are left. Clark was one of Johnson's ''personal confidants,'' and news reports stated that he was so close to the president that he swam in the White House pool.

Bob Bullock tells a story of Connally's hearing that Clark was to get a lobbying fee for guiding a screwworm eradication appropriation through the legislature. Bullock says Connally called future Texas governor Dolph Briscoe, who was ramrodding the screwworm eradication program, and ''chewed on him, saying, 'Goddamn it, Dolph, I'm for it, the Speaker [Barnes] is for it, you don't need a lobbyist.' '' Connally didn't want Clark pulling in money on a cinch, Bullock says. It is the opinion of a former state legislator, Congressman Charles Wilson, and others who were aware of the unpublicized ''feud,'' that it was the result of ''jealousy over who had LBJ's ear.''

Another associate, close to Connally in the 1960s, says, ''I think if you interpret that Ed Clark was a very close ally of Johnson's, you're wrong. He appointed him ambassador (to Australia), but Clark's the kind of fellow that Johnson never did really love. But he rewarded him for being a loyal friend.'' Also, says one of Connally's former associates, Clark ''didn't think Connally had a chance to win, and he went strong with Price Daniel'' in the 1962 governor's race. ''. . . but I think it probably goes back to one time when Connally was trying to get in business and buy that radio station [KVET in Austin] . . . and Ed Clark gave him a bad credit reference. I think I've heard this discussed with Connally that Clark tried to cut Connally's throat financially—you know, when he was just getting started and didn't have any money and Clark wouldn't help him—kept a bank from loaning him some money.''[13]

13. Clark refuses to talk about Connally for publication. ''He has given interviews regarding dead governors, but he doesn't talk about living governors,'' his

Johnson wrote that Connally wanted him to tell the nation at the end of his state-of-the-union message that he would not accept the presidential nomination in 1968, but the president held off. In early March, at Connally's birthday party in Gregory Gymnasium at The University of Texas, heavily guarded because of anti-war protestors, Johnson assured the assemblage that Connally's ''greatest gifts to Democratic government are yet to come.'' Connally demurred. ''It [Johnson's remark] disturbed me. I don't have any more idea what he meant than you do. I have no plans whatsoever beyond returning to private life [for] a number of years.'' Johnson's decision to quit, Connally later said, was a ''noble act. . . . I don't think the president ever really expressed a doubt, certainly no fear, of his chances for renomination or for that matter for reelection.''

After Johnson had abdicated, Connally, too, could have relaxed. What was there to fight for? The war? The president recalled his older daughter, Lynda, crying and asking him, ''Why her husband [a Marine officer] might die for 'people who did not even want to be protected?' '' But Connally carried on, through the 1968 national Democratic convention—a hell of a spot to be in if you were from Texas. Some say he went through all the preliminaries and took all the abuse in Chicago only because of the outside chance Humphrey might put a check by his name, on a list concocted from knowledge and hunches, and proclaim— ''John Connally's it, he's my choice for vice president.''

Jules Witcover of the Washington Bureau of the Los Angeles *Times* claims, in his book on Nixon, that Johnson ''applied heat'' through Connally at the Democratic convention to hold Vice President Hubert Humphrey to the LBJ policy on Vietnam. After the antiwar plank failed, Witcover said, ''Humphrey was hooked. Connally won that one for Johnson.''

It may have been Connally's last victory for LBJ. Johnson retired from office on January 20, 1969, replaced

secretary stated. One writer claims Clark was the principal source for an unflattering article about Connally, but that Clark refused to be quoted by name. ''He hates Connally,'' the writer states.

by a Republican who had been considered a political mortality for years. Connally's term as governor of Texas ended the following day. His successor was a man Connally didn't like, didn't respect, and one whom he didn't think could do the job—at least, not the way John Connally had done it. Two weeks later, comfortable in his home in the fashionable Houston River Oaks section and firmly ensconced as the most prestigious member of a prestigious Houston law firm, Connally said, "There's no doubt but that nationally, politically speaking, we're in the weakest position we've been in since 1933."

Two men, Connally and Johnson, remained political friends for over thirty years, and both were talented, ambitious, and political; one moving, sometimes imperceptibly, when the other tugged, but neither in command. Christian thinks "their political differences were pretty well masked during the Johnson presidential years. I know after I got to Washington I saw it from the other end, and Johnson still had a great respect for Connally and still wanted his advice on certain things. But he would say, 'John's more conservative than I am on that. John won't agree with me on that because he's too conservative.' That type of comment showed that there were some philosophical differences that were the background of some of their problems."

In recent years, some Washington reporters, watching Connally closely for the first time, have written of the amazing resemblance between Connally and Johnson. Physically, except for their height, they don't look alike, and even the aging, graying process has shaped their contours differently. Johnson, a benevolent and Populist-oriented Senator Foghorn, white hair curling on his neck; a true unpolished product of the land; taking care of "his" people; and, as he grew older, gaining admiration and love, the sort of admiration and love many Texans express in a single almost emotionless phrase—"You gotta hand it to him . . ." Connally, the prosperous executive; cosmopolitan; conscious of his actions; a man whose appreciation of the finer, richer things in life is obvious at a glance; a man whose unyielding personality refuses to accept old enemies as friends and who drives the wedge deeper as the years go by; but a man so admired by his friends that they weigh his slightest motions for historical significance.

In commenting on his relationship with Johnson, Connally stated, ''Happily, our relationship is one that permits differences of opinion which must be a part of any association of thinking individuals. He would expect my evaluation to be fair, honest and, hopefully, objective; he would not always expect it to accord with his own.'' To the Commonwealth Club of California, Connally said Johnson is neither a ''doctrinaire liberal nor a doctrinaire conservative. Political labels have seldom adhered to Mr. Johnson. Some students of government have called him a 'consensus politician'—a man who seeks the majority view of the people by the process of reason and discussion. Certainly, if this is true it is not inconsistent with the American system.''

When informed of Johnson's death in January 1973, Connally was playing golf at the Tryall Golf Club in Jamaica, where he has a plush new residence. Connally's first statement was, ''Nellie and I are heartsick. The country has lost a great leader and president, but we have also lost a beloved friend. All of our adult lives have been intertwined with those of President Johnson, Mrs. Johnson and their family. We grieve with his family now in this time of great sorrow.'' In delivering an eulogy at Johnson's graveside, Connally commented that no one who knew Johnson could ''speak dispassionately of him.'' He spoke of the plain people that loved Johnson and that Johnson loved and stated that, ''. . . the silent people . . . mourn him the most. He gave them all he had for forty years.''

In citing Johnson's rise from his humble beginnings, Connally noted that Johnson often commented ''with a mixture of awe and pride, 'I guess I've come a long way for a boy from Johnson City, Texas.''' Connally said that one could never view Johnson as a ''man above men, a mythical hero conquering all before him . . . his life was one of opposites—of conflicting forces within him trying to emerge supreme. . . . He dealt with basic human qualities and basic human reactions. He was uninhibited by hypocrisy or false pride. He was not afraid to let his feelings show. . . . The same insecurities existed in Lyndon Johnson that exist in all of us. His strengths and his weaknesses were universally human qualities, shared by people everywhere who have also dreamed of the mountaintop, each in his own way.''

Shortly before his death, Johnson wrote to the authors of this book: ''Aside from physical attributes, which are certainly important, John Connally has learned to separate his private life from his political ambitions—a real achievement for any public figure. . . . He has patience, humor and a sense of loyalty. He returns loyalty with loyalty, which some politicians forget to do. From the philosophical standpoint, he's more conservative than I wish he was but he's always willing to listen to various viewpoints. . . . On the other hand, I've never looked upon John Connally as a man with a closed mind.''

The Connally-Johnson relationship invites comparisons, and Johnson's comment about Connally being ''willing to listen'' brings to mind a remark by President Nixon in Theodore White's book on the 1968 presidential race: ''One of the troubles with Johnson is that Johnson just doesn't listen to anybody. When you go in to see him, he does all the talking from the moment you get in; he doesn't ask questions.'' White said of Johnson: ''. . . his ego outran his own great achievements.'' The same has been said of Connally, but all politicians have large egos. In a 1965 article for The *New Republic*, Andrew Kopkind quoted an unnamed Texas Democrat's comparison of the two men: ''They weren't raised in the same political environment . . . although they had similar backgrounds. Connally grew up in the boom of the 'forties. Johnson grew up in the worst part of the depression. Johnson had to fight the business interests and the conservatives. Connally played them for all they were worth.''

Both men valued and demanded absolute loyalty. At a Texas political rally in the 1930s, Johnson volunteered from the crowd to speak on behalf of former Governor Pat Neff's candidacy for the Texas Railroad Commission. When he was asked why he volunteered, he answered, ''I couldn't let it go by default. Pat Neff once gave my daddy a job and I couldn't let him down.'' Connally's former aide, Mike Myers, recalls how Connally ''wouldn't let anybody get close'' until he was certain he could trust him. ''Once you had his confidence,'' says Myers, ''he was pretty free.''

Politicians deal in debts, many of them long-standing ones. Political debts in Texas have a reputation for being paid—or else. Both Johnson and Connally kept a close count on political debts outstanding, and they expected them to be paid. Friends were rewarded; enemies were punished. Theodore White wrote that one of Johnson's friends ''has said there might well be inscribed on his tombstone the epitaph which, according to legend, the Roman Sulla caused to be inscribed on his: 'No man ever gave me favor or did me ill but what I have repaid him in full.' '' Connally is a man who inspires both loyalty and fear, and those close to him often comment, ''He is a vindictive son of a bitch.'' Congressman Donald Riegle wrote in a diary, later published as a book, that, ''I never criticized Johnson personally or suggested that his motives were evil, but I did make speeches critical of his policies. And LBJ was the kind of man who took criticism personally. He got very angry about me.'' It was the same with Connally, says Ben Barnes. ''John Connally took people voting against him personally. I think that was probably Connally's greatest weakness.''

Both Connally and Johnson shared a passion for education, an issue that was often a political football in Texas. And both were past masters at raising money for political purposes. Writer Selig Harrison told of a business friend watching while Johnson ''must have raised $50,000'' over the telephone one night. Texas Land Commissioner Bob Armstrong recalls a report of a meeting in Corpus Christi, where Connally

> got a bunch of people together and just pointed out to them in terms of basic dollars that if you had a non-business-oriented governor, in terms of either a corporate profits tax [anathema in Texas business circles]

or in terms of anything that would strike at the heart of the major operators, that you were looking at a total tax bill or a total expenditure of 'X' hundreds of millions of dollars, which was gonna come out of their pocket, and he was very effective in tying this to . . . his . . . opponent. . . . What I think this is is just knowing where these people are tender and making them realize the monetary significance to them of what happens if you have a more progressive government or a more progressive tax structure. . . . He was very capable of rounding these people up. They had been people who were clients of his or friends of his clients. They were people who he knew socially. . . . He was just a master at knowing the territory and making it clear . . . how important it was for them to give [to his campaign].

An article on Johnson in *Time* in November 1966, noted that "far from giving him the ultimate power that goes with their assent, most Americans have withheld it because they vaguely fear that he already has too much power." This same vague feeling circulates among Texans concerning John Connally and apparently cost Connally a victory in 1965, when voters blocked his efforts to extend the governor's term from two to four years. Both men expected and accepted command jobs and handled them with ease; and, as politicians, one of their first priorities was to neutralize blocs of voters that might oppose them.

A similar story of lingering impact has been told about both men's aspirations and their taste in haberdashery. According to a report in White's book on the 1964 presidential race, after Johnson once left Speaker Sam Rayburn's office, Rayburn said, "Lyndon ain't been the same since he started buying two-hundred dollar suits." Johnson reportedly said in private that Connally only felt comfortable in three-hundred dollar suits and custom-made shoes and with other men who wore them.

Unlike Connally, a substantial portion of Johnson's support came from the minority groups. A liberal Texas banker, Walter Hall, wrote of Johnson's administration just before the president announced that he was stepping down—"It seems to me that Lyndon Johnson's greatest legacy to this nation has been to divert America's attention from affluence and pleasant living to the so-called 'invisible America' where a suffering minority—black and white—have lived neglected and forgotten lives for many generations.'' Connally has never shaken his image of a conservative, business-oriented governor, with an insatiable lust for power for the few. However, Connally has avoided the stigma of being only a politician, despite his long association with Johnson—who has ''politician, 100 percent'' stamped on him. Connally has maintained an image with many voters of being just a poor farm boy who got rich in business; and who wanted business, in turn, to get richer through his efforts.

In trying to erase the traces of his own upbringing, Connally, in contrast to Johnson, has created a public image with which many more modern Texans want to identify. Not all Texans want to be thought of as sophisticated city dwellers, nor do they want to destroy the characteristics of their Southwestern heritage. Many of them have wearied of the Texas stereotype, a brash or bashful cowboy who can't make complete sentences. The stereotype never fitted Lyndon Johnson, but his presence fostered the idea. Bob Armstrong, who blends an urbane manner with a love of things country 'n western, says ''whatever else'' Connally did while serving as secretary of treasury, ''he reflected a great deal of credit on Texas. He was much more articulate than most people thought Texans were. He dressed with a lot of flare and he caught the press' eye. And he sort of erased some impressions about Texans that I think were left over from the Johnson days, and it was just sort of a plus, I thought, in terms of general acceptance.'' John Connally always could go you one better, even if you were president of the United States.

Illustrations

271

—Jess Floyd

Connally, Nellie, and Johnson cut a cake in the form of the battleship *Essex*, on which Connally served during World War II, at a Fort Worth Chamber of Commerce banquet honoring Connally as Secretary of the Navy (above). Connally (center) accepts Lyndon Johnson's congratulations on his appointment as Secretary of the Navy. Speaker Sam Rayburn (left) looks on (below).

—Texas State Archives

—*Texas State Archives*

John Connally surrounded by young supporters during his 1962
campaign for governor.

—*Texas State Archives*

—*Texas State Archives*

John and Nellie Connally at their Picosa Ranch in Floresville during the 1962 campaign for governor (opposite above). The Connally family (left to right) Nellie, John, Sharon, John III, and Mark at the Picosa ranch in 1962 (opposite below). John and Nellie Connally in Fort Worth on election day 1962 (above).

—*Austin American-Statesman*   —*Wide World Photos*

John and Nellie campaign during his 1962 campaign for governor (above left). Connally puffs a cigarette, awaiting returns, on election night 1962 in Fort Worth (above right).

Texas' new governor, John B. Connally, and his happy first lady, election night 1962.

Nellie (left) and the Connally brothers, Merrill, Wayne, and John, relax after Connally's 1962 election as governor is assured.

—Fort Worth Star-Telegram

—Fort Worth Star-Telegram

—Austin American-Statesman

John Connally (far right) applauds President and Mrs. John Kennedy on their 1963 trip to Texas. United States Senator Ralph Yarborough applauds behind Mrs. Kennedy (above). The Connallys and the Kennedys in the Dallas motorcade, November 22, 1963 (below). A pensive Governor John Connally looks out the window of the Frito-Lay airplane (opposite).

—Austin American-Statesman

—*Blanche Connally Kline*

—*Austin American-Statesman*

—*Wide World Photos*

His arm in a sling following the Kennedy assassination, Governor John Connally chats with President Lyndon Johnson (above). Nellie Connally, President Lyndon Johnson, Connally, and Lady Bird Johnson talk outside the Governor's Mansion, on Christmas Day, 1963 (below).

Rancher John Connally at the wheel of a jeep .

The Connally family pose for their 1967 Christmas card.

President Richard Nixon and Vice President Spiro Agnew join the
in Austin. University of Texas regent Frank C. Erwin Jr. stands be-
William Rogers, Connally, and Texas Lieutenant Governor Ben

Johnsons at the dedication of the Lyndon Baines Johnson Library
tween Nixon and Johnson. In the back row stand Secretary of State
Barnes.

—*Courtesy of Time magazine*

Governor John Connally makes the cover of *Time* magazine following the Kennedy assassination. Connally signed the *Time* cover with his left hand, as his right hand was still in a sling.

Governor John Connally flashes ''Hook 'Em Horns'' sign at a Texas Longhorn football game.

Governor Connally ponders a reporter's question at an Austin news conference.

—*Austin American-Statesman*

—*Dick West*

—*Fort Worth Star-Telegram*

The Connallys laugh at one of Lyndon Johnson's anecdotes at a 1971 reception honoring Nellie Connally and others as distinguished alumni of The University of Texas (opposite above). Governor John Connally guffaws at a joke at the Fort Worth Gridiron Dinner, which traditionally roasts Texas politicians (opposite below).

Connally protege, Ben Barnes (left) greets his mentor at the opening of the Dallas-Fort Worth airport in 1973.

—*Shelly Katz*

COME ON IN, JOHN...THE WATER'S FINE!

—*Texas Republican Party*

John Connally (left) greets U.S. Senator Strom Thurmond at a 1973 Washington reception.

—*Texas Republican Party*

Connally shakes hands with deputy Treasury secretary William Simon as George Bush kisses Nellie.

—*Texas Republican Party*

Connally is solemn as U.S. Republican Senator John Tower of Texas introduces Nellie Connally at a Washington reception.

—*Mark Stinson*

—*Texas Republican Party*

National Republican George Bush listens to Connally.

—*Texas Republican Party*

Connally greets Congressman Gerald Ford of Michigan prior to Ford's appointment as vice president.

"I Have Memories Shared by No Other Man"

14

John Connally, male caucasian, age forty-six, was flat on his back, patched, stitched, and alive. The doctors had declared that he was going to live, when Texas Secretary of State Crawford Martin cocked his head around a hospital door and got his first glimpse of Connally since he had been shot by President John Kennedy's assassin. It was late November 1963, and not unusual that Martin, an elder in the Presbyterian church, would recall words of St. Paul's as he visited at the governor's bedside in Dallas' Parkland Hospital. "You've been elected, now you're one of the elect,"[1] said Martin, in hushed tones. "Your life has been spared for some purpose." Martin said Connally thought so too. "He's more religious than most people think." A

1. Martin's reference was to St. Paul's Epistle to the Romans 8:31-34, "If God is for us, who is against us? He who has not spared even his own son but has delivered him for us all, how can he fail to grant us also all things of him? Who shall make accusations against the elect of God? It is God who justifies! Who shall condemn?"

year after the assassination, one of the three letters Connally chose from thousands for an article in *Family Weekly* magazine was from a woman in Newport, Rhode Island, which said: "It is not up to us to question God, but He surely held you in the palm of his hand that day. You must be destined for something wonderful."

John Kennedy's destiny had been a brain-shattering bullet on a Dallas street, and his death shaped John Connally's life. It seemed that there would always be a Kennedy influencing John Connally's political destiny. Connally's first meeting with a member of the Kennedy family is not recorded, but Connally had nominated Senator Lyndon Johnson of Texas for president at the 1956 national Democratic convention in Chicago, the convention at which young Senator John Fitzgerald Kennedy burst the regional confines of Massachusetts by bidding for the vice-presidential nomination.

Connally served as Johnson's hatchet man at the 1960 national convention, and was one of the persons who announced to the press that Kennedy might be physically unfit for the presidency for reasons of health. Connally had advanced questions about Kennedy's father's alleged pro-Nazi views while Joe Kennedy was ambassador to the Court of St. James during the 1930s. During the 1960 convention, Connally also ran afoul of Kennedy's younger brother, Robert, who opposed Johnson as the vice-presidential candidate and suggested that he withdraw. Connally reportedly snarled at Robert Kennedy, "Who's the candidate, you or your brother?" Years later, in a private session in the governor's office, Connally told reporters that John Kennedy had taught Johnson and Connally a lesson in 1960 —that it was more important to get the governors behind you than Congress in a presidential convention. "We had all the senators [in 1960], every one of them," Connally said, "and they couldn't pee a drop."

Shortly after the 1960 convention, Connally was the main speaker at the opening rally in the Southwest for the Kennedy-Johnson ticket. He said Johnson had accepted the vice presidency out of a sense of duty and was not a "traitor" to his own cause. Connally said of Kennedy, "I think he's capable of being a great president. He has true courage and great independence. I don't think because a man is 43 years old is a good reason to vote against him— I'm 43 years old, and sometimes I think that's too old. . . . It would be a travesty [if Texas] . . . with a Texan on the ticket, did not vote for the Democratic ticket. If it doesn't, it'll be for one reason—religion. But I hope we won't . . . elect a man on the basis of his religion. Senator Kennedy said he believes in separation of church and state. He wouldn't be a good American if he didn't, and I know he's a good American."

Kennedy's appointment of Connally as secretary of the navy "projected [him] into some prominence; he gained at least a position from which to spring to some sort of statewide race," says Will Davis. "Now, obviously being secretary of navy doesn't make you a household word, but it made him more so than he had been a year before that, or a year and a half before that." The Connallys watched the 1961 inaugural parade from the presidential box—an excellent way to attract attention, also.

Back home in Texas in 1962, Connally shied away from any connection with Kennedy. His opponent in the Democratic primary runoff for governor, liberal Don Yarborough, asserted that Connally had "supped with the Democratic administration, then turned his back on President Kennedy and all he stands for." Kennedy declined to endorse a candidate in the runoff even though Yarborough had wholeheartedly endorsed his program and Connally had chipped away at it. But in the general election for governor, after Kennedy had drawn the line against Russian missiles in Cuba, Connally started mentioning the Kennedy administration. A hard line against communists was something Connally's constituents would appreciate.

Theodore White said that Johnson wrote Kennedy at Christmas in 1962—"Dear Jack, where you lead, I will follow—Yours loyally, Lyndon." Connally did not echo those sentiments. Connally "has no apparent perception of things that Kennedy, for instance, was aware of,'' says Bob Armstrong, part of the generation that thought of President Kennedy as someone special, someone who could attract and direct the fervor, goodness, and intelligence of American youth for the common benefit of the nation. "You know," he says, "there are some people who are really being held back by various things that start as early as whether they went to day care centers. And so let's do something about it, because these people drag us all down ultimately if we don't do something about it. Connally's theory is, by damn, they ought to be able to get out and do just like I did."

During the 1963 legislative session, Connally urged Congress to reject changes in mineral tax laws proposed by Kennedy, proposals which could add millions of dollars to oil and gas taxes. It was a natural reaction by Connally as oil and gas tax money was so important to Texas' economy. It was not the only way, however, in which Connally undercut Kennedy. He allowed a bill to go through the legislature which knocked out the "agency form," a method which made it easier to register large groups of voters. Kennedy's supporters claimed the additional voting strength might make the difference in Kennedy's winning or losing Texas in the 1964 presidential election.

Reporter Jimmy Banks stated that after six months in office some of Connally's "strongest supporters" had become "increasingly concerned over his future." Kennedy's proposal to give black men the same rights as white men was killing him in Texas, Banks said, and Connally "undoubtedly would find President Kennedy a heavy load to carry in the general election. [2]

But what few knew was that Kennedy, no matter how unpopular he might be in Texas, was coming to visit,

2. Bob Bullock says that Connally delighted in telling stories about John F. Kennedy's attraction for women. "Hell, he was human," Bullock states, "and he [Connally]used to tell some of the funniest stories about Kennedy you ever heard. He used to tell 'cock stories' on John Kennedy.... He used to tease and say, 'Barnes you're just like him!' . . . I've heard him tease Ben all the time about his woman chasing, and laugh about John Kennedy being the same way. And about John Kennedy's wife keeping such close tabs on him, and Kennedy getting mad because now that he was president he couldn't move and all that.''

and Connally would be his host. Kennedy, Connally, and Johnson made the decision in the president's suite at the Cortez Hotel in El Paso on June 5, 1963, and Connally said Kennedy was coming for two reasons: to raise money and to woo Texans. In a *Life* magazine article, Connally said he was "not anxious" for Kennedy to come to Texas, but he "counted him a friend" and he was "fully aware of the force of the White House" to get things moving. Connally said he was to be in Washington on October 4, 1963, and "with firm ideas on what the [Texas presidential] visit should be," he asked for an appointment with Kennedy. Just a few days before the Washington trip, however, Connally told Texas reporters, "I have no plans to invite him to Texas. But I'll tell him we'd be delighted to have him here." It was a political tightrope. Connally couldn't say "no," but when he said "yes" he had to make it appear his hand was being forced. In the *Life* article, Connally stated he knew "many of Mr. Kennedy's supporters would be fighting me" in the 1964 governor's race, but "on the other hand, if I couldn't rally support for my own party's President in my own state, it would be a political embarrassment that I would not be allowed to forget."

Connally went to Washington without a single aide, handling reporters' calls personally from his suite at the Mayflower Hotel, before he met with Kennedy in the Oval Office at the White House. It was there, Connally said, that Kennedy accepted his outline of the Texas trip, including the suggestion that the president's wife, Jackie, should accompany him. The suggestion that the "purpose of the President's trip was to settle" a "tiresome old feud" between Vice President Johnson and Senator Yarborough was "ridiculous," Connally said. "First," he stated, "both men operated in Washington, not in Texas. One was across the street from the President and one was less than a mile away, and Washington would have been the place to settle it. Second, Presidents never insert themselves into such quarrels, for they can only get hurt. Third, the

President couldn't have settled it anyway; the quarrel is implacable.''

After a forty-five-minute session with the president, Connally told reporters he had assured Kennedy that he thought he would win in 1964, and Connally cited a Belden poll showing Kennedy's leading Senator Barry Goldwater of Arizona by eight percentage points in Texas. More than $300,000 was raised for a $100-a-plate dinner for Kennedy in Austin on the night of November 22, and Connally claims he personally sold $50,000 worth in two nights of telephoning after "ticket sales lagged." Connally also stated that he wanted to skip a Dallas motorcade and go directly to a noon luncheon, but the president's "advance men . . . laid on the motorcade through the heart of downtown."[3] Ben Barnes says Connally had assigned him to

> work with all of Kennedy's staff people . . . [who] came down here with some animosity toward Connally already built in. . . . They'd listen to Ralph Yarborough, and Ralph, the real philosophical east Texas liberal, had told them that 'you're going down there and having a deal with Connally. He's an establishment type governor and he's not with the folks and he's gonna try to monopolize the president's time.' And they were convinced that Connally might be in bad political shape. Well, Connally was about ten points ahead of Jack Kennedy in the polls in Texas. Kennedy didn't come to Texas to heal the rift between Yarborough and Connally, or between Yarborough and Johnson. Jack Kennedy came to Texas on really his first campaign tour for 1964. He needed Texas bad. And the Democrats were going down in the polls. Connally had only about fifty-eight percent of the vote. Jack Kennedy only had about forty-eight percent, and he was legitimately concerned about the Democratic base in Texas.

It was the first time Governor Connally had been host to a president of the United States, and he met Kennedy in San Antonio and accompanied him to Houston,

3. Connally later told the Warren Commission investigating the assassination that he withdrew his objections to a motorcade after the decision was made to lengthen Kennedy's visit to two days.

Fort Worth, and Dallas. "I had been worried about Dallas," Connally stated in the *Life* article, "fearing not violence but embarrassment. An ugly advertisement had appeared the morning of the Kennedy visit in the Dallas *Morning News.*[4] A month before, United Nations Ambassador Adlai Stevenson had been hit on the head by a picket sign. There had been the 1960 attack on Senator [Lyndon] Johnson[5] in which he was jostled and spat at by Nixon supporters. I was afraid of rude signs or that the crowds might be hostile or, what is almost as bad, apathetic or sullen. I had objected to the parade route being announced well in advance because that lends itself to organized heckling." Organized heckling was not what the president had to fear— it was a $1.25-an-hour workman in a downtown book warehouse who had been brushing up on his ability to fire a high-powered rifle.

The night before the presidential party flew from Fort Worth to Dallas, Connally had gone down to the coffee

4. The Warren Report quoted Bernard Weissman, one of four men responsible for the black-bordered "Welcome Mr. Kennedy" ad in the November 22, 1963 Dallas *Morning News*, as saying: "... after the Stevenson incident, it was felt that a demonstration would be entirely out of order, because we didn't want anything to happen in the way of physical violence to President Kennedy when he came to Dallas. But we thought that the conservatives in Dallas—I was told—were a pretty down-trodden lot after that, because they were being oppressed by the local liberals, because of the [Adlai] Stevenson incident. We felt we had to do something to build up the morale of the conservative element in Dallas. So we hit upon the idea of the ad." The $1,465 to pay for the ad was raised from three wealthy Dallas businessmen, the report said—Nelson Bunker Hunt, Edgar Crissey, and H. R. Bright—and there was also some money collected from others. Weissman testified, the report stated, that the advertisement "drew 50 or 60 mailed responses. He took them from the post office box on Sunday morning, November 24. He said that those postmarked before the attack on President Kennedy were 'favorable' in tone; those of later postmark were violently unfavorable, nasty, and threatening; and, according to a report from [Larrie H.] Schmidt, those postmarked some weeks later were again of favorable tone."

5. The demonstration against Lyndon and Lady Bird Johnson on November 4, 1960, at Dallas's Adolphus Hotel is credited by some as swinging Texas' votes to Kennedy. Johnson, Kennedy's running mate, said he and Mrs. Johnson had been "hissed at and spit upon." The Johnsons were on their way to a political luncheon at the hotel when they found the sidewalk, lobby, and halls jammed with people. Most of the demonstrators wore straw hats with hatbands identifying them as Republicans. Reporters in Dallas said the Johnsons were never in any danger, but such a demonstration was so unusual at the time that it undoubtedly cost the Republicans votes. The Democrats won the 1960 election in Texas by 46,233 votes out of 2.28 million.

shop in the Texas Hotel for scrambled eggs and milk. Connally remembers that everyone was talking about Senator Yarborough's refusal to ride in the same car with Vice President Johnson. Bo Byers of the Houston *Chronicle* remembers something else—how interested Connally was in the political poll the *Chronicle* was publishing the next day. "He begged me to let him see the poll," Byers says, "and I laughed and told him to wait and read it in the paper. He kept saying, 'Come on, let me see it' and I had my original story [on the poll] in my pocket. As he was getting on the elevator, I gave it to him and he put it in his pocket. I never saw it again." The poll showed that if the presidential election were held on November 22, 1963, Senator Goldwater would carry Texas over Kennedy. "If a predictable 2.5 million votes were cast," Byers front-page story read, "Goldwater would roll up about 1.3 million to Kennedy's 1.2 milllion. That would mean a margin of 52 percent for Goldwater to 48 percent for Kennedy . . . General 'disenchantment' with the Kennedy administration and an adverse reaction to his civil rights program are the two most frequently mentioned reasons for the President's decline in popularity in Texas." Another story in the *Chronicle* indicated that Connally "would rate no better than a tossup" if he ran against Senator Yarborough in 1964 but "should defeat Don Yarborough handily" for governor.

In the article in *Life*, Connally stated that he and Kennedy had talked politics as the motorcade moved from Love Field toward downtown Dallas. The president asked how do "things look in Texas?" Connally replied, "There'll be a Houston *Chronicle* poll out tomorrow which should give us some ideas." Kennedy asked, "What's it going to show?" Connally said, "I think it will show that you can carry the state, but that it will be a close election." The president pursued the subject: "Oh? How will it show you running?" Connally said he answered, "Mr. President, I think it will show me running a little ahead of you."[6] That

6. Byers said he was told Connally was carrying his story on the Houston *Chronicle* poll in his pocket.

doesn't surprise me," the president responded, and Connally said that was the last time they talked.

Within minutes they had passed through downtown Dallas, and their limousine made an awkward and slow left turn toward the expressway, which would take them to the Trade Mart for Kennedy's luncheon address. The Trade Mart was only five minutes away. A final remark, etched in history, was not John Connally's but his wife Nellie's. She smiled and twisted in her jump seat to tell Kennedy, "You sure can't say Dallas doesn't love you, Mr. President." Author William Manchester says the president replied, "No, you can't." Connally said the president merely smiled and nodded. In a story in *McCall's* magazine, Mrs. Connally said, "He did not reply, or if he did, it was lost in the terror of what followed, for in that instant the first shot rang out." It was, she recalled, an "indescribably horrifying experience."

The Warren Commission report stated that two shots did all the damage, blowing the president's brains out and ripping through Connally's back and chest, breaking a rib (which was later removed), collapsing his right lung, and fracturing his right wrist, which had fine bits of Mohair from his expensive suit imbedded in it.[7] The bullet also dug into his left thigh, five inches above the knee, and doctors cleansed and sutured it, leaving a small piece of metal in the governor's leg. The governor almost bled to death, needing two and one-half quarts of blood, about one-third of the body's supply. Connally said he recognized the first noise as a rifle shot, and as he turned, the thought immediately crossed his mind that it was an attempted assassination.[8] If

7. Connally's bullet-torn suit, his necktie, and his shirt with French cuffs were displayed for a time at the state archives in Austin, and the clothing is still there. However, to see them, one must get Connally's personal permission.

8. The Connallys told *Life* magazine in 1966 that they were certain that one bullet caused the president's first wound, in the neck, and a separate shot struck Connally. This contradicts the "one-bullet theory" that the same shot that wounded Kennedy in the neck caused all of Connally's wounds. "No one will ever convince me otherwise," said Mrs. Connally. "I'll never change my mind," said Connally. Connally also told reporters in Austin that there was no need for another

he had not turned, said Dr. Tom Shires, chief of surgeons at The University of Texas Southwestern Medical School in Dallas, "there is a good chance he probably would have been shot right through the heart." [9]

The Warren Commission determined that the shots were fired from the sixth floor of the Texas School Book Depository. The commission report stated that all the shooting was done by one man, Oswald, [10] described by a phychiatrist as a youth as "seriously detached" and "withdrawn," an "emotionally starved, affectionless youngster." The commission concluded that Oswald "sought for himself a place in history—a role as the 'great man' who would be recognized as having been in advance of his times."

It was Mrs. Connally who told her husband the president was dead. "I knew," he replied, placing the oxygen mask back over his mouth and nose. Connally's welcoming message in the programs to be distributed that night at the Kennedy dinner in Austin was tragically prophetic. The message ended, "This is a day to be remembered in Texas." A terse news release from the governor's office that afternoon stated, "Frank C. Erwin, chairman of the Texas Welcome Dinner, has announced that the dinner has been cancelled." Walter Jetton, Fort Worth caterer and a favorite of Johnson's, took the half-baked potatoes and eight

investigation of the assassination although he disagreed with the Warren Commission's "one-bullet theory." But he said he was shocked by "journalistic scavengers such as Mark Lane" who had attempted to "impugn the motive" of the commission and tried to "cast doubts upon the commission as a whole and question the credibility of the government itself."

9. Texas Attorney General Crawford Martin stated that an intern kept his hand over Connally's chest, possibly saving his life. Years later, to repay him, Connally took two shotguns with him to Thailand, where the doctor was residing with his family, and presented them to the doctor's young sons.

10. The Warren Commission noted that Oswald had written Connally when he was secretary of the navy. The government had switched Oswald's honorable discharge to a dishonorable discharge after he defected to Russia, and Oswald was trying to get this reversed. He stated he would "employ all means to right this gross mistake or injustice." On January 30, 1962, Connally, who had already resigned to run for governor, advised Oswald he was forwarding his letter to his successor. Oswald's wife said in Russia "he spoke well" of Connally. "Lee said when he would return to the United States he would vote for him" for governor.

300

thousand steaks back to Fort Worth in seven trucks. The steaks were sold for seventy-five cents each, and the fruit, beans, and green salad were thrown away. Jetton knocked 40 percent, or $5,000, off his price because the dinner was never held, said Sam Wood of the *Austin American*. The Democrats who had bought tickets for the dinner got a memorial record album of Kennedy's speeches in Texas, a dinner program, and a copy of the speech the president was to have given in Austin.

In the article in *McCall's*, Mrs. Connally said, "I do not know why the President had to die—that vital, hard-working, young man—or why John was spared. Some things are beyond us; some things we must learn to live with." John Connally had to learn to live with worldwide fame. His life was never the same after the assassination. There had been two smart, tough politicians in the presidential convertible. One had been destroyed; the other lived. It was natural that the American people would probe the survivor, the wounded witness, for the same qualities that the dead man had. It became a frantic national effort, so intense that it seemed the nation was trying to bring Kennedy back to life. News stories constantly identified Connally as the man who was wounded during Kennedy's assassination. For a time, to the public, Connally had no personality of his own. He moved in the aura of a martyr. "You'd like to feel there's going to be an end to it," Connally said a couple of years later, "but I guess we'll have to live and re-live it forever."

As Connally recuperated, he was accorded the type of news coverage usually reserved for presidents. The fact that he spent a restful night, ate mush, juice, and coffee for breakfast, and dozed afterwards at Parkland Hospital was considered significant enough to be relayed on the news services' national wires. Of equal interest, UPI thought, was the fact that Connally watched part of Texas' 15 to 13 victory over Texas A&M on Thanksgiving, but that Nellie turned off the television while A&M was leading because Connally "was getting too worked up." Thousands of letters and flowers poured into his Dallas hospital room. After

301

thirteen days, he flew home to Austin on December 5. He chatted with reporters at the airport and scribbled his name with his left hand on a newsman's notepad. Then he drove with his family to the governor's mansion, closely guarded by state police.

Four days later Connally was taken to St. David's Hospital in Austin where an inflammed vein in his right calf was treated. A half dozen reporters were admitted to talk to Connally, and one said he resembled a ''caged, gray tiger.'' He removed his hospital gown and invited newsmen to inspect where the bullet had hit him in the back and the long scar on the right side of his chest where he said a wound ''as big as a baseball'' had been sewn. As he talked of the assassination, a newsman said, Connally's ''eyes widened with horror and a look of disbelief shadowed his face. . . .''

The assassination became a nightmare that wouldn't stop. Spectators saw Nellie Connally quiver and cry at the sound of cannon fire saluting West German Chancellor Ludwig Erhard's arrival at Bergstrom Air Force Base, near Austin, in late December 1963. Over a year later, at Connally's January 1965 inauguration, she flinched several times as the guns fired a salute. But privately it was worse for Connally than for his wife. He admitted in an article appearing in the November 22, 1964 issue of *Family Weekly* that after the assassination he had begun to wonder about public service—''Is it worth it? The constant demands, relentless criticisms, abusive attacks, these were part of the career, and I accept them. But is any endeavor worth that— *and* the risk of life? I knew John F. Kennedy as a selfless servant of his country, and yet his reward was death. I thought of Mrs. Kennedy, widowed now, with a young daughter and son fatherless. I saw Nellie and our children and again wondered: 'Is it worth it?' ''

George Christian says the shooting in Dallas was a ''traumatic experience, as we learned later—a good bit later.'' In January 1964 Connally ''had pretty much decided in his own mind, I think, not to run for a second term'' for governor, and no one could figure out why he was so hesitant—if not dead set—against making the race, an easy race by all indications. Christian says he learned later that Connally "was going through torment on just sheer nightmares. He had a recurring nightmare of being shot—just constantly, and he wasn't getting any sleep and he was in a state of real sorrow a good bit of the time over what happened, and just the shock of the whole thing. . . . And he was also at that time getting a lot of crackpot mail— people saying that you didn't get yours last time, but you'll get yours next time—stuff like that. . . . He had to have protection from the DPS [Department of Public Safety] which we'd never had before for any governor. They tracked him when he went anywhere and assigned plain-clothesmen to be with him. It bothered him and he didn't like it." Why me? Connally thought. Let someone else carry this cross.

Connally's fear of being shot did not subside quickly. In the summer of 1966 several men gathered at Connally's Lake McQueeney home to plan Waggoner Carr's race for the United States Senate. One of the men relates that they were outside when Connally spotted a man with a rifle some distance away. "He wouldn't even go back to the house, about 150 yards away," the observer says, "but hid behind a big tree, crouched down there and told someone to call the highway patrol." It turned out to be a man with a .22 rifle shooting turtles.

On January 28, 1964, more than two months after he had been wounded, Connally visited his offices at the capitol. Smiling, his right arm in a sling, Connally strode through the press room, and the reporters almost snapped to attention. Connally had become a celebrity, a charismatic man. Several reporters trailed in his wake, jockeying for positions with numerous aides, moving with Connally, occasionally breaking away to tell their colleagues what the governor was doing. For the news services, it was an almost breathless pace. Reporters stacked story on top of story as they reported Connally's whereabouts in the capitol. His departure was as if the air had been sucked out of the huge building, leaving a lull. Six days later, Connally made his first speech since the assassination—to the Associated Press

303

Managing Editors meeting in Austin. Those men, in charge of the news content of most of Texas' newspapers, listened in awe, soaking up the historical significance as Connally told them, ''It was as if someone had hit me a sharp jab in the back. I knew I was severely wounded. Frankly, I thought I was killed.'' Capitol reporters rushed from the Commodore Perry Hotel to their offices to file their stories.

Near the end of February 1964, Connally and his wife visited Kennedy's grave in Arlington national cemetery. ''We kind of relived the whole thing in our minds—all the sensations and feelings we experienced that day,'' he said. Before they left Washington, the Connallys called Jacqueline Kennedy. Within a week, Connally was able to discard the sling he had worn since he was shot, by mid-March his arm cast was gone, and on March 27, more than four months after the assassination, he was able to sign mail again with his right hand. A month later, however, after appearing at a ''long and difficult'' session before the Warren Commission, Connally carefully shook hands with his left hand.

Despite the assassination attempt, Connally's philosophy apparently had not changed. He said he still opposed the public accommodations section of the civil rights bill originally proposed by Kennedy. Manchester claimed that Connally urged Texas' congressional delegation to oppose Senator Thomas Dodd's bill to ban the mail-order sale of guns. Despite Kennedy's death in a Texas city, many Texas politicos felt little remorse. On May 29, one of the last days of the 1965 legislature, the Texas House rejected, by a vote of 75 to 70, a motion to consider changing the Richmond State School for the mentally retarded to the John F. Kennedy Memorial School.[11]

Another factor that broadened the gap between Connally and the Kennedy faction was Connally's adamant defense of the city of Dallas. Kennedy liberals blamed right-wing control of the high-rise, business-oriented city for the

11. Among those voting against the name change was the governor's brother Wayne.

president's death. To them, so much hate had been stirred and stored against Kennedy, that it had to break loose violently. Manchester stated that, "If the findings of poll takers are valid, over 27 million Americans had broadly indicted 'the people of Dallas' for the crime." Ten years later it is still a sensitive subject. As governor of Texas, Connally could hardly join a clamoring chorus against Dallas, which represented the second largest cluster of votes in the state. But his efforts to protect the city's reputation appeared to many to be excessive. Even Nellie took up the cause. In the *McCall*'s article, she stated that one of the main reasons she went on television shortly after the assassination "was the city of Dallas. It is wrong and foolish to blame a whole city for one sick mind that infiltrated it."

Every week in 1964, it seemed, Connally was in Dallas, or elsewhere in the state or nation, offering living proof to the nation that he thought "Big D" was not to blame—and that it was safe. A sampling of Connally's comments throughout that year show his defense of the Texas city.

> Dallas, February 4—'Any time a great tragedy occurs, there's a tendency to blame someone. There was an initial reaction against Texas, against Dallas particularly. But Dallas was no more to blame than New York, Dalhart or New Orleans.' . . . Connally predicted it would 'take a decade' for the outside world to place the blame where it belongs—on a man 'who's not even a Texan.'

> New York, February 25—'The other day a leading Boston newspaper prominently printed a letter from a reader alleging that Texas had banned the song "Dominique" because it was of Catholic origin. Of course, "Dominique" is on the radio in Texas 24 hours a day, and the Singing Nuns are probably more popular than the Beatles. It is a great temptation to try to dispel these stories and make a speech in New York about the magnificence of Texas. . . . If I were to yield to temptation I would tell you today that Texans are not all braggarts, not oil-rich nor dirt-poor, not dominated by fanatics, not inveterate pistol-toters, not isolationists who hate the rest of the world, espe-

cially the federal government. But then I am not going
to yield to temptation.'

Dallas, September 22—To the national convention of the American Legion—'As you know,
Dallas is a city which has been maligned and berated
in every conceivable way. Seldom in our history has a
community been abused with such venom by self-ap-
pointed critics, and with such utter disregard for the
facts. I am not here to defend Dallas. It is strong
enough and vigorous enough to stand on its own feet.
. . . Dallas is a capital of commerce—a capital of
insurance—a capital of technology—a capital of enterprise—and most certainly a capital of opportunity. We
sum it all up when we call this city Big D.'

Austin, Texas, September 28—In response to
the Warren Commission's criticism of the Dallas
police and district attorney—'Pandemonium existed;
chaos existed. People wanted to find someone to criticize and, with no facts, their reaction was to lash out
against Dallas. This man [Oswald], Marxist, de-
ranged man, was not a product of Dallas, of its
schools, of its environment or its culture. To
condemn a great city because a man like that chose the
city to do this thing does the city and state a great dis-
service.'

Asked if he thought Connally and Dallas had a
"special relationship," Robert Strauss says, "He
[Connally] lost Dallas badly to Jack Cox in 1962—he was
known here as 'Lyndon's boy, John.' But Connally is different than most politicians who would say, 'Let's punish
Dallas.' Instead, he said, 'Let's go and capture the town and
show it why they should have supported us.' "[12]

Throughout 1964 it was the same each time Connally appeared in public—crowds collecting, encircling,
eager for fresh insight into the bloody hour in Dallas. If they
had never known John Kennedy, Connally, who could say,
"I have memories shared by no other man," was next best.

12. There is a parallel to this situation. Connally never carried Houston's
exclusive River Oaks section in three successful campaigns for governor. But when
he left the governor's office, Connally made his home in River Oaks.

In mid-August Connally made a triumphant, exhilarating tour of four Mexican states bordering Texas. Blizzards of confetti greeted him. Crowds swirled about him as he bought cookies and had his shoes shined. The official receptions and security rivaled that of a president's visit. Connally told Governor Praxedis Balboa that his reception in Ciudad Victoria was "fantastic" and that he had seen only one visit to compare to it—"That was when Mrs. Connally and I were in Houston, San Antonio, Fort Worth, and Dallas with President Kennedy."

When a reporter mentioned a few months later that people all over the world associated him with Kennedy, Connally replied, "This was apparent on my trip to Mexico. I detected an emotional feeling on the part of the people that sprang from knowledge I was a part of this great tragedy. I sensed desire on their part to express warmth, a feeling of personal attachment to me for my association with President Kennedy on November 22."

Atlantic City, New Jersey, 1964, even during a national Democratic convention, was more subdued than the festive clamor in northern Mexico. But when Connally stopped to talk to newsmen after the convention had adjourned, hundreds of spectators flocked to glimpse him. He was questioned about the film memorial to Kennedy at the convention and was "visibly moved," one news story related. Columnists Evans and Novak noted that, "Strolling the boardwalk at Atlantic City . . . Connally, silver-haired and strikingly handsome at 46, was mobbed by autograph seekers."

There were numerous reminders of the assassination, of course, and the most bitter was William Manchester's controversial account of the assassination, *The Death of a President*. Connally reacted immediately to *Look* magazine's first installment in January, 1967, of a four-part, 60,000-word serialization of the book. To Margaret Mayer of the Dallas *Times Herald*'s Washington bureau, Connally described his associations with the Kennedys as "very pleasant" and, for the first time, he mentioned briefly what would become the theme of his own article on the trip to Texas—that the trip was of the President's own making.

In a hastily called news conference at the Texas capitol on January 10, 1967, Connally was grim as he read a statement that the first installment of Manchester's book was "an astonishing propaganda instrument clearly woven to reflect favorably on those who gave it birth, while rudely discrediting others involved. It is filled with editorial comment based on unfounded rumor, distortion, and inconsistency. This transparent attempt to dictate history through a captive voice is shocking. The privately commissioned author[13] has contrived a presentation which undoubtedly will achieve widespread readership. It cannot, however, qualify as factual history. It actually is a recitation of recollections and observations collected and reflected through the prisms of prejudice." Connally said that he and his wife had resisted repeated efforts to air more details of the tragedy because it "left deep emotional scars which we felt were best borne in silence. . . . However, in the interest of unmanaged history, I have reluctantly concluded that we have no choice but to assemble and present the facts and details as we know them relating to President Kennedy's visit."

What really rankled Connally, and hurt his wife, their friends say, was Manchester's account of a conversation between the Kennedys in their suite at the Rice Hotel in Houston:

> On a sudden impulse she [Jackie Kennedy] blurted out that she disliked Governor Connally.
> He [John Kennedy] asked, 'Why do you say that?'
> 'I can't stand him all day. He's just one of those men—oh, I don't know. I just can't bear him

13. Manchester noted in his foreword to the book that Mrs. Kennedy had suggested that he write an account of the assassination, and he said he recorded ten hours of interviews with her. But he said he received no financial assistance from the Kennedy family, and neither Mrs. Kennedy "nor anyone else is in any way answerable" for his research or for what he wrote. Mrs. Kennedy, in fact, filed a lawsuit to halt publication of the book.

sitting there saying all these great things about himself. And he seems to be needling *you* all day.'

Connally said it was at his suggestion that Mrs. Kennedy had made the trip with the president, and he told Margaret Mayer that, while the Kennedys were in Texas,
"Nellie and I were very solicitous of her [Mrs. Kennedy]. I
changed seats with her a couple of times so her hair
wouldn't blow." Nellie wrote in her article in *McCall*'s
that Mrs. Kennedy "in her gracious way" had told the
Connallys' oldest son at the president's graveside ceremonies, "John, the only good thing to come out of all of
this is that your father is going to be all right."

The Connallys seemed fond of Mrs. Kennedy. Yet,
in 1967, the whole world was suddenly aware—if they believed Manchester—that John Kennedy's widow couldn't
bear John Connally. Connally's friends and political associates, such as Ben Barnes and the late Crawford Martin, remember Mrs. Kennedy's comments as the unkindest cut of
all. And they say John Connally felt they were, too.

In March 1967 Connally was asked if he had been
contacted by book publishers, and he said, "Many of
them." The Associated Press tried to get Connally to let
Pulitzer-prize winning reporter Relman Morin present the
Connally version, but the governor refused. Connally's
reply was a 9,000-word article in the November 24, 1967,
issue of *Life* magazine, an article put together from recorded
interviews with Connally during the Virgin Islands cruise
of the National Governors' Conference in October of
that year. An autographed copy of the color picture of Connally used on the *Life* cover hangs in Robert Strauss' office
in Dallas, and Strauss says Connally taped interviews for
three hours a day over several days with a *Life* writer. In a
news conference after his article appeared, Connally said he
had dictated between 30,000 and 40,000 words of copy
"and I have more to go." The article, he said, "is not the
last thing I plan to do on this and other experiences. I don't
know when I will finish it—it may be done during the next
year or it may have to wait until I am out of office." Asked

if it would be a book,[14] Connally said, "not necessarily. I would rather refer to it as some type of document." He said it would cover the "whole relationship I had with President Kennedy and not just the assassination."

One Texas congressman says, "You have to swallow a lot to get along with the Kennedys." John Kennedy's death meant Connally had to swallow the younger brother, the new leader of the clan, Robert Kennedy, and that gagged him. "Connally and [Robert] Kennedy were two different types of personalities," says Jake Pickle. "Connally is turned on by a crowd, but Robert was kind of moody . . . unless it was a really big crowd . . . and, oh, he could excite the kids." Connally's brother, Wayne, says, "I think President Kennedy was just a slightly different stripe than the younger Kennedy brothers." The Connally-Robert Kennedy political relationship was not unusual: two strong men, commanding legions, poles apart philosophically, probing for advantages, both believing second best was the same as last. A former Connally aide claims, "He [Connally] hated Bobby Kennedy, and he disliked the entire Kennedy family." George Christian feels that, "Connally had a fairly good relationship with John Kennedy, as did [Lyndon] Johnson, but neither one of them could really approach Bobby in the sense that Bobby was a different type individual. He was a very tense, sometimes sharp, guy, and very political, and neither Johnson nor Connally were on the same wave length [with Kennedy]."

The animosity apparently started at the 1960 national Democratic convention in Los Angeles. Johnson was making his belated bid to become president, and Connally was in charge of the Johnson organization. That convention, says Pickle, "whetted his [Connally's] appetite for politics. He developed strong feelings about Bobby Kennedy and others." Christian recalls, "Bobby . . . was campaign manager for his brother. He was a tough one, he was an

14. In December 1968, about a month before he went out of office, Governor Connally was asked again about his "book" on the assassination of President Kennedy, and he replied, "I expect I will be age 89 before it is completed."

abrasive guy . . . hatchet man and everything else. And Connally was trying to run Johnson's operation and they had a lot of headon's, I think, during the 1960 nomination fight . . . mutual distrust, two strong men, just almost destined to run headon against each other.'' Their wives, however, seemed to enjoy each other's company. After Connally had decided to quit as secretary of the navy to run for governor, Mrs. Connally was asked about life in Washington. She said of the new friends she had made, she thought the most of Mrs. Robert [Ethel] Kennedy—''full of fun, a good friend of most anybody.''

At first there had been two main characters in the drama, John Kennedy and Johnson, supported by the bit players, Robert Kennedy and Connally. However, President Kennedy's death changed the cast, and the survivors became locked in a modern-day political passion play. Connally was aware of how Robert Kennedy felt about Johnson, the president by accident. Theodore White said that Robert Kennedy ''loathed'' Johnson, and both men knew Johnson was where he was, president of the United States, because the Kennedys had ''opened power to him.'' Congressman Donald Riegle of Michigan wrote of ''joint sessions when Lyndon Johnson had addressed us. Senator Robert Kennedy seldom clapped; he just seemed to smolder.'' The spotlight was set for Robert Kennedy, and Johnson and Connally seemed to wander into it by chance. Even at the 1964 national Democratic convention, by all standards a Johnson-Connally convention, it was the emotional gusher for President Kennedy, a fifteen-minute standing ovation, that loosened the delegates' tears and strengthened the Kennedy mystique. It completely overshadowed the nomination of President Johnson for reelection.

As president, it would have been unseemly for Johnson to trade political blows with the brother of a dead president, a man who had shown respect for Johnson and whom Johnson respected. Furthermore, Johnson seemed to have lost his desire for a confrontation with Robert Kennedy. But Connally felt no such compunction. He was convinced he was right and that Robert Kennedy was wrong.

George Christian states that the enmity between Connally and Robert Kennedy developed because

> Connally felt that the holdover Kennedy people, in general, and Robert Kennedy, in particular, were not the president's friends; and they were doing everything they could to hurt him, to sabotage him. They were looking toward their own futures, and not his [Johnson's], and Connally resented the fact that Johnson apparently didn't see this. Or if he saw it, he didn't do anything about it. I think he [Connally] thought that Bobby Kennedy, in the administration in '64, was there doing his own thing, all the way, with no loyalty at all to Johnson; and Johnson ought to have a 100 percent loyal attorney general. And that Johnson had made a bad mistake in not sweeping most of them out . . .

John Connally and Robert Kennedy shared a flare for speaking in lofty phrases. In his 1965 inaugural address, Governor Connally spoke of "faith that permits dreams of what might be, not what it is." Kennedy used the quotation many times that, "Some men see things as they are and ask why. I dream things that never were and say why not." Both politicians wondered how far they should reach,[15] and they were professional performers. But they performed best to different audiences—Kennedy to a frenzied street crowd; Connally to businessmen in a corporate board room.

The Vietnam War severed the lines of communication between Connally and Robert Kennedy.[16] Their feelings about that conflict were too passionate to be soothed by private words, and Connally minced few words in public. Con-

---

15. Author Theodore White quoted Kennedy as saying, "Should I run for president? I sit here reading my mail in the office, and it's about the sewage system in Dunkirk, New York, or upstate parks. Shouldn't I be doing something more than that?"

16. Connally, however, felt quite comfortable in quoting John Kennedy to make his point about the war. "As President Kennedy wrote in March 1963," Connally told the annual Democratic dinner at Des Moines, Iowa, in 1967, '. . . the Communist attempt to take over Vietnam is only a part of a larger plan for bringing the entire areas of Southwest Asia under their domination. Though it is only a small part of the area geographically, Vietnam is now the most crucial. If Vietnam should fall, it will indicate to the people of Southeast Asia that complete Communist domination of their part of the world is almost inevitable.'"

nally's strongest attack on the senator was in Kennedy's own backyard in a speech to the National Petroleum Council in Washington. He said the televised hearings of the Senate Foreign Relations Committee had deteriorated "into a public spectacle" in which President Johnson's

> top advisers were branded as warmongers for daring to say we were determined to defend South Vietnam from the aggression of Hanoi. . . . As strange as it seems, at a time when the communist world looks for every sign of weakness, every hint of discord, every shred of propaganda material, some Americans are recklessly willing to oblige.
>
> How especially strange that the brother of a man honored throughout the free world for his courage and his devotion to freedom should join in the public display. Knowing full well the power of his name, but isolated from the complete facts and information he once knew, Senator Robert Kennedy volunteers the opinion that we should offer the Viet Cong a share of governmental responsibility in South Vietnam as a means of ending the conflict.
>
> In effect, he proposes that we admit communists to the government we have been helping defend from those same communists. These are the people who last year murdered fourteen hundred village chieftains in South Vietnam, people who rule by terror reminiscent of the Nazi occupation in Europe, people who have already announced their intention to destroy the Saigon government in its entirety. Challenged by Vice President Humphrey and others, the Senator has tried to 'clarify' his statements, but his intention remains the same. . . .
>
> Senator Kennedy further says we must set an objective that will not humiliate Hanoi in seeking negotiations. He uses as an example the conflict over the Russian missiles in Cuba, and contends that President Kennedy secured their removal in a way that did not require the humiliation of Nikita Khrushchev. It is a poor example to use. John Kennedy's notice to Khrushchev was 'get out or be thrown out.' This was hardly an accommodation to the Russians—but they most certainly backed away.

313

These were mild words compared to Connally's off-the-record briefing in Austin the next day to political reporters at the capitol. They were surprised when Connally called them in; it was not like him. Given the ''not for publication'' guidelines, some reporters walked out. Others just listened, and then they went back to their offices and made notes. Connally feared that Robert Kennedy was financing gubernatorial candidates in fifteen states in an attempt to build a base for the presidential nomination in 1972. Connally told the reporters that Kennedy's ''power grab'' for the statehouses was an effort to weaken Connally and Johnson, and he claimed Kennedy was instrumental in lining up opposition to Connally for governor. Connally said he was even ''threatened'' with an investigation by the Internal Revenue Service, but he added that didn't worry him as he had been checked for the past twelve years. He said he had told Johnson aides, Marvin Watson and Jake Jacobsen, that Kennedy was going to keep chipping away until there was nothing left for Johnson to stand on. He also told Watson and Jacobsen that Kennedy had to be stopped, and that they were ''living dangerously'' by letting pro-Kennedy cabinet members, such as Attorney General Nicholas Katzenbach, stay on. He said he had told them, ''You haven't got anything more than what you left home with,'' implying that only a handful of Southern senators could be counted on to stand up for Johnson.

In particular, Connally said he did not trust presidential aide Bill Moyers. Moyers was as important to Johnson as Theodore Sorenson had been to John Kennedy. Formerly Sargent Shriver's deputy director of the Peace Corps, Moyers had been President Kennedy's advance man for Austin on his 1963 trip to Texas. He had double checked all of the preparations and, according to Manchester, was lunching with Connally's friend, Frank Erwin, at the Forty Acres Club near The University of Texas campus, when he heard of Kennedy's death. Moyers was ambitious, Connally said, and ''when I see an ambitious man, I watch out.'' Connally also said he had tried unsuccessfully to get Johnson to fire John Bailey of Massachusetts as chairman of

314

the Democratic National Committee. Connally even went so far as to say that it appeared to him that the Robert Kennedy forces were trying to foment civil disorder in the country.

By late 1967 Connally was so anti-Kennedy that he reportedly told close friends that, if Kennedy should win the Democratic presidential nomination in 1968, "I could not support him and would have to bolt the party." In an address to 1,300 Georgia Democrats at a February 1968 fund-raising dinner in Atlanta, Connally said Kennedy's critical words on the United States' role in Vietnam had been a "source of discord . . . The net effect of all he's said and done has been to hurt the course of the conduct of foreign affairs of this country."

For Connally, spring was open season on Kennedy. Robert Baskin of the Dallas *Morning News* wrote, "There is no love lost between Connally and Bobby Kennedy any more than there is love lost between Connally and [Ralph] Yarborough." In March 1968 Connally told guests at a Jefferson-Jackson Day dinner in Indianapolis that some presidential candidates had "come dangerously close to treason."

The Texas State Democratic Executive Committee hastily endorsed Connally as a favorite-son candidate for president to try to prevent Kennedy's winning the nomination. National committeeman Frank Erwin felt Kennedy was "unfit to hold any high office." Robert Baskin wrote that Connally's victories in state conventions in 1966 were regarded "by competent political observers here as having blocked efforts of the Kennedy faction of the Democratic party to get its foot in the door in Texas. . . . Perhaps he [Kennedy] did not reckon with the fact that while Connally and Mr. Johnson are growing wider apart ideologically they still have a political understanding that is intended, in part, to block the Kennedy faction from control of the party."

If so, the Johnson-Connally fears were allayed when Robert Kennedy, flushed with primary victories in California and South Dakota, chose to exit through the kitchen at

315

the Hotel Ambassador after acknowledging supporters' cheers in Los Angeles on June 4, 1968. His passage gave Sirhan Bishara Sirhan a clear field to aim a bullet at the senator's brain. "The senseless and untimely death of Senator Kennedy is an indescribable tragedy," Connally stated. "Words cannot describe the profound and heartfelt sympathy we have for Mrs. Ethel Kennedy, their children, and the entire Kennedy family. May God grant us guidance to seek out and put down this destructive tide of violence and lawlessness which is growing at such an alarming rate in our Country."

Then, there was one Kennedy left. Edward— "Teddy"—almost young enough to be Connally's son, but old enough to be a political threat. No one in Texas had paid much attention to Teddy, until Bobby's death. He was supposed to be friendly and easy going, not so intense as Bobby. More like Jack, only not so "political," really not a bad sort. He was good looking and his wife was smashing. Prettier than Jackie, even. He'd probably be a good senator, should make majority leader, and one day—oh, it was much too early to talk about yet—after all, he was the baby brother. But he just might run for president if he didn't get too excited about the poor and the black, and didn't think the federal government had to control everything.

It was amazing how fast Teddy Kennedy's image changed in Texas after the politicians and the papers made a quick study: Why this fella might even want to pick up where Bobby left off! Teddy Kennedy had praised Ramsey Clark when Clark was nominated for United States attorney general. And everyone in his right mind knew Texans were about to disown Ramsey because he had gone "soft" on crooks and spent more time talking about rehabilitating them than putting them into prison. That told you something about Ted Kennedy! And he might not be able to forgive John Connally either. John had been rawhide rough on Bobby, and those Kennedys had long memories—an eye for an eye, that's the way they played, mean. Then came the shocker. Some people, not in Texas, of course, but in other

316

states, were talking about Teddy Kennedy for vice president. You had to squash that kind of talk before it got out of hand. Even Mayor Richard Daley of Chicago said he hoped the Democratic convention, to be held in his hometown, would draft Kennedy for vice president. Connally's Texas supporters knew how those Kennedys were—rich enough that if the right moment came, they seized it. No waiting around to line up support and money. Besides, even if he had denied his interest, there was a feeling Connally might take that number two spot on the ticket. It might be the only way he'd ever get to be number one.

On July 23, 1968, Connally told a news conference in Cincinnati that he thought Vice President Hubert Humphrey would make a great president, and it was not essential for Humphrey to have a Southerner or a liberal on the ticket with him. He said he did not know Kennedy well enough to comment on what kind of backup man he might make, and he did not know if he would strengthen the ticket. According to an article in the Fort Worth *Star-Telegram*, Connally "candidly avoided joining the cascading boom for the vice-presidential spot for Kennedy . . . virtually turned thumbs down" on him. "Connally's counsel," the Dallas *Morning News* noted in almost record time, "is that Hubert Humphrey can find a better running mate" than Kennedy.

Within less than a year, it appeared Connally would not have to worry about Teddy Kennedy in politics again. Kennedy's political career seemed to be destroyed by the death of Mary Jo Kopechne, a former campaign worker for Bobby Kennedy, in what became known as the "Chappaquiddick incident." Few could pronounce the name of the Massachusetts island, and fewer could spell it. But after Miss Kopechne, a passenger in Kennedy's Oldsmobile, drowned when the car went off a narrow, wooden, humpbacked bridge, it became the most discussed locale in political circles. Kennedy's overnight delay in reporting the incident—he admitted on national television it was "indefensible"—and the public's concern over his "scrambled thoughts" even made the Kennedy diehards doubt they

317

would ever watch another Kennedy take the oath of office as president.[17] The July 18, 1969 incident had lasting impact. Two years later an important Texas politician, who apparently liked Kennedy, was asked how well he knew him. His reply was, ''I would not want you to ever mention Chappaquiddick, but let's just say I met him before Chappaquiddick.''

Kennedy was out of it, and he knew it—for 1972. Why get worked up over a losing cause when the odds would be better in 1976? George Christian claims Connally ''doesn't have any commitment at all'' to stop Kennedy, but another Connally associate, Will Davis, says Kennedy's candidacy ''would have a great deal to do with stimulating his interest and appetite'' in the 1976 presidential race. ''That's why you see so many in the Kennedy-McGovern wing of the Democratic party attacking Connally. They want to hurt him by criticizing him. They want to destroy his viability because they recognize the danger of the man as a candidate. . . . They recognize in him a danger to the things they represent . . . because he has the magnetism to capture the public's imagination and cause them to vote for him.'' Another close associate says, ''John Connally doesn't want Ted Kennedy . . . to be the president of the United States. He doesn't think Ted Kennedy has got the mental attributes to make a good president. He doesn't think he has good judgment. He thinks he has too many good times . . . he can go rather in length in pointing out a lot Teddy's weaknesses, which he will do in a private conversation.''

Shortly after President Nixon's victory over Senator McGovern in November 1972, Edward Kennedy was asked by reporters of the British Broadcasting Corporation if the

17. Kennedy pleaded guilty to the complaint that he did ''knowingly leave the scene of an accident causing injury, without making himself known.'' Kennedy's lawyer and the prosecutor asked for a suspended sentence, and state district court judge James Boyle ordered the minimum sentence of two months in jail and suspended it. He also lost his license to drive in Massachusetts. ''It is my understanding he [Kennedy] already has been and will continue to be punished far beyond anything this court can impose,'' Boyle said. A grand jury looked at the case and reported it found no criminal action was indicated. An autopsy was never conducted.

presidency appealed to him. He replied, ''Certainly not at the present time.'' They prodded him about his future, and he said, ''I'm committed to public life. We'll let the chips fall where they may.'' Columnists Evans and Novak said Kennedy's ''agents'' put out the word that Robert Strauss was not acceptable as national Democratic chairman, a sign that for the first time since Chappaquiddick, Kennedy was ''exerting leadership in the party.'' It was to Kennedy that Texas Secretary of State Bob Bullock wrote to ''prevent the selection'' of Strauss . . . [it] would be tantamount to handing over the Democratic party to Republican John Connally.''[18]

A former newsman who has known Connally since 1962 and who thinks he is a ''great talent'' wrestled with the attempt to put the Connally-Kennedy family relationship in perspective. He had thought about it numerous times and had talked to Connally's closest friends about it. This, he says, is the way it is: ''Connally's whole philosophy is based on discipline—that's why he admires Nixon so much, because he's so disciplined. He doesn't like Ted Kennedy because he doesn't think he's disciplined. He [Kennedy] wants to do things too fast, move the blacks and the browns too fast, by taking shortcuts, just like Bobby and, to a lesser extent, Jack.

''With Connally, it's like with the vampires. You know how you need a silver cross or a wooden stake to hold 'em off, to kill 'em—that's how Connally sees himself in regard to the Kennedys. He's the talisman to stop the Kennedys, the only one who can do it, he thinks.''

18. Strauss won the job with support of organized labor and regular party leaders who had been cool to McGovern. He invited Connally, in an interview, ''to return to this party and bring with him his constituency.'' Three days later, Connally replied, ''I never take seriously invitations which I first read in the press.''

"A Decade of Defeat"

15

Most political analysts overlooked John Connally's personal ambition when he first became a candidate for governor of Texas in 1962. They pegged him as Lyndon Johnson's agent, sent home to Texas from Washington to make sure no one jumped Johnson's claim to Texas. The broader view was that Johnson wanted Connally to corral the Republicans, who were challenging the Democratic party in Texas for the first time since Reconstruction. It was not until ten years later that the theory was widely circulated that Connally might have had another reason for running for governor—that it was Connally's way of telling Johnson that he wanted to run his own show. And when Connally came home to Texas in the booming 1960s, he was determined that no Republicans would be in the cast.

Texas politicians marveled. Here was a younger Johnson, with just as much talent and as much political "savvy," throwing out a political net large enough to drag in conservative Democrats, a few liberals, and Republicans. What, for the Republicans, might have been a time of triumph, ended in a decade of defeat. Allan Otten of the *Wall Street Journal* set the scene: "In the 1950s and early '60s, the Lone Star State appeared on the way to breaking its one-party tradition. The Republicans were slowly drawing conservatives from the Democratic Party; they carried the state twice for Dwight Eisenhower, almost carried it for Richard Nixon, elected conservative John Tower to the U.S. Senate, and won a handful of local offices."

Enter John Connally.

"It seemed," says Ben Barnes, "the Democratic party had become weak in Texas. He [Connally] was interested, of course, and he had worked hard for the Kennedy-Johnson ticket and he was interested in Texas staying a Democrat state and he felt like he had . . . to attract a broad base into the party. He thought he could do that. He thought under Governor [Price] Daniel that the party had slipped in power and prestige in the state."

But first things first. Connally disposed of the liberals and the Republicans by following the classic Texas political script. He defeated the liberal Don Yarborough in the Democratic primary and changed a few lines to get enough liberal support to beat Republican Jack Cox in November. Yarborough had tried to paste a Republican tag on Connally: "An elephant just can't hide under a donkey skin. The Navy secretary is sure trying it, though. But some mighty big parts are exposed"—but it didn't stick. Finally, as governor, Connally did what he could to step on all Republican hands. At his first meeting with the State Democratic Executive Committee, he called for a "Democratic revival"—that meant converting everyone who wasn't a die-hard Republican regular into a Connally Democrat.

It was Connally's idea for the State Democratic Executive Committee to sponsor the inaugural program, the "Victory Dinner" in January, 1963. It became a popular fund-raising event every two years, lining up the party regulars and filling the Democratic coffers. Will

322

Davis, chairman of the state party during Connally's administration as governor, says,

> Connally wanted to build the party up and he wanted to give it an image and give it a structure of its own. He said one way to do that is raise money independently of candidates for public office and you get it into the party. The best way to do that, you have these hundreds of thousands of people who are going to be very interested in the inauguration activities. We'll make a big deal out of it. We'll dress up a whole lot, and we'll give the inauguration an image which it hadn't had heretofore; make the inauguration of the governor and lieutenant governor a really high style sort of event.

Despite his party-building and his enthusiasm for fund raising, Connally's Republican leanings were visible, even as he stomped on the vestiges of the party of Lincoln. In August 1963 the Dallas *Morning News* quoted Connally as saying it was conceivable, but not foreseeable, that he could support a presidential candidate other than a Democrat. Author William Manchester's unflattering portrayal of Connally told of his violating protocol by bolting ahead of President Kennedy to shake hands with "his hand-picked team" of twelve—nine of whom were Republicans—at Dallas' Love Field in November 1963. "They knew he wasn't a traitor to their values, and they were prepared to push a Goldwater-Connally ticket in '64," Manchester wrote.

In 1964, however, Connally's "Republicanism" was no more than Texas conservatism, and the two were often indistinguishable. At a time when his critics were decrying his Republican tendencies, Connally dined with nine Dallas Democratic legislative candidates at the governor's mansion and complained that during the 1963 legislature, "We frequently found Dallas Republican representatives opposing us at almost every turn. . . . Those [Republicans] who speak for Dallas in the legislature took the position of pure obstructionists, purely for political purposes." He made similar pitches at other places and other times for Democratic candidates.

The first open plea for Connally to come over to the Republicans may have been a telegram from Albert Fay to the governor in July 1965. Fay, a Houston millionaire and Republican national committeeman, told Connally, "You sounded like a Republican" in opposing on nationwide television President Johnson's proposals on poverty, Medicare, and repeal of the so-called right-to-work law. "[We] believe that your enlightened leadership today comes from an understandable disenchantment with the top leaders of your party," Fay added. "Since you apparently find the positions of the Republican Party so attractive, perhaps you should consider a change in party affiliation."

Others, light years apart from Fay politically, such as Texas AFL-CIO president Hank Brown, also thought a Connally switch might not be such a bad idea. The governor wasn't advancing any of Texas labor's programs. Brown conceded that a poll had shown 54 percent of Texas' union men would vote for Connally, but the delegates at the 1965 state labor convention in El Paso adopted a resolution that if Connally "continues to refuse to support the platform of the Democratic Party," he should "seek a political party more in line with his own views." Al Barkan, national director of the AFL-CIO's political organization (COPE), said Connally was "cheating the Republican Party out of dues." Brown, a former plumber whose public speech and manner contrasted sharply with Connally's polished and premeditated gestures, said Connally was labor's number one political target in 1966, although "there is also a U.S. senator named Tower to retire from public life."

No match for Connally in power, performance, or personality, John Tower—short and tongue-tied in small gatherings—endured. He became the Republican leader in Texas in the 1960s, paralleling Connally's role for Democrats in the state. For the most part, they were polite, neither saying much publicly about the other. It was acceptance at arm's length.

In January 1965 Connally told the State Democratic Executive Committee, "I hope we can take care of" Tower in 1966, and regulars in both parties conceded that

Connally could beat anyone, including Tower, in a state-wide race. The Republicans held their breaths for fear that "Big John" would bear down on "Little John." Uneasy over Connally and aware of his upcoming test at the polls in 1966, Tower was quick to defend Connally in August 1965, in Senate debate on Johnson's anti-poverty bill. The primary issue was whether to allow governors to veto anti-poverty projects, and Senator Russell Long of Louisiana, the majority whip who conferred frequently with President Johnson, said, "The president made his old friend, John B. Connally, governor of Texas. But as much as he admires John Connally he opposes his demand for the right of a veto in the poverty program and agrees with Sen. [Ralph] Yarborough, who is on the other side." Commenting on Long's assertion that Connally owed his job to Johnson, Tower said, "The polls show that in Texas the governor is more popular than the president. He is governor in his own right." Also, Tower said, "The governor of my state is not of my party. He is a Democrat. But he has not acted through politics. He has acted with dispatch. . . . He has drawn no criticism from either political party in our state for the way he has acted in administering the program."

"What kind of position does that put Connally in, when he has to be defended in the Senate by the Republican . . . Tower?" asked a man close to the governor. Roy Evans claimed "Connally's establishment . . . put pressure" on Congressman Jim Wright of Fort Worth to stay out of the 1966 Democratic primary for the United States Senate so that Attorney General Waggoner Carr would not have any opposition. Although Connally put some effort into getting Carr elected, Tower couldn't have chosen much better than Carr if he had hand picked his own opponent. Carr's unctuous appearance and his image of an opportunist on the make in politics, the anti-Johnson sentiment in Texas, and the liberal defections were too much for Carr to overcome. It didn't matter much to Connally. He and Carr had their separate ambitions, and neither would have hesitated to sacrifice the other. When Connally had state business in Washington, he usually went to Tower since Connally and Yarborough hardly spoke. Following Richard Nixon's election as president in 1968, Tower appeared solidly entrenched, the link between the Republican administration and Texas. He so consistently repeated the Nixon line that he became known as Nixon's ''errand-boy.''

Tower's place in the sun in the Nixon administration, painstakingly built with almost sycophantic loyalty to the party throughout nine years in office, was blown away by the sudden gust of Connally's appointment as secretary of the treasury in 1970. ''I had to sit and digest it for a minute when the president told me what he wanted to do,'' Tower said, but ''I don't think it will affect my [1972] race adversely. If Mr. Connally does a good job for the administration and contributes to the effective functioning of the administration, that will be a positive help to me.'' As a Cabinet member, Connally became the favorite, Tower a supernumerary. Ralph Nader's 1972 report on congressional members noted, ''When the president makes a major speech, selected members of Congress are usually briefed beforehand, then less-select members are conferred with after the fact. Since Connally's appointment, Tower has fallen into the second category with greater frequency.''

Even after he became a member of Nixon's Cabinet, Connally assured his young friend Ben Barnes that he would endorse him against Tower if Barnes should run for the Senate in 1972. Barnes' decision to run for governor instead of the Senate—his own decision he insists—cut a path around that potentially thorny conflict. Had Connally embraced Barnes against Tower, wrote columnists Evans and Novak, ''the fury of the Republican regulars would know no bounds.''

With Barnes out, and Dallas lawyer Barefoot Sanders in the race against Tower in 1972, Connally devoted most of his time to a nationwide effort lining up Democratic votes for Nixon. Connally's personal role in the Tower-Sanders campaign became one of semantics. Tower insisted that Connally had not endorsed Sanders. ''[He] didn't say that—specifically. He said he would vote for the Democratic ticket.'' Connally ''has to maintain his credibility as a

Democrat to influence Democrats," Tower said, "so I think that what he's doing is absolutely correct."

Newspaper stories prior to the November election spoke of strained relations and friction between Connally and Tower over the senator's "left-out" feeling in Nixon's scheme of things. Tower was not invited to either of Nixon's 1972 visits to Connally's Picosa ranch near Floresville, and Connally's friends were closely connected with the Sanders campaign. Former Congressman Joe Kilgore was in charge, and Larry Temple, state chairman of Democrats for Nixon, contributed money to Sanders' campaign. Karen Elliott of the Dallas *Morning News* quoted "reliable" White House sources as saying Tower—apparently being taken for granted—"even had trouble getting his picture made with the president" until Nixon's September 22-23 trip to Texas. After dining with approximately 350 Democrats at Connally's ranch and spending the night there, Nixon allotted Tower and the GOP candidate for governor of Texas, Henry Grover,[1] half an hour at San Antonio International Airport before flying back to Washington. An Associated Press photograph showed Nixon waving to the crowd and Tower, unnoticed by the president, reaching out his hand, poised indefinitely, waiting for Nixon to turn and shake it.

At the same time that Tower was declaring that he would welcome Connally "with open arms" into the Republican party, Tower was quietly polling Texans to see how much Connally's endorsement would mean to Tower's race. The poll, a Tower aide says, surprisingly showed 45 percent of the Texas voting public would be less inclined to vote for Tower if Connally endorsed him. Tower's supporters did not think the negative reaction would run that high, but, as the aide notes, in Texas "Connally can be a plus or a minus." Tower, says Ben Barnes, "would

1. Grover, who came close to upsetting Democratic candidate Dolph Briscoe, repeatedly got one of his best laughs during his 1972 campaign by telling audiences that when he switched to the Republican party in 1968 in winning a seat in the state senate, Connally "took a dim view of party switching. Connally came into Houston and worked for my opponent. I beat him two to one. Now, Connally has seen the light, and I welcome him aboard. That's the only way for him to go."

like to see John Connally dropped off a bridge."

In stifling the gradual flow of Texas toward a two-party state, with a liberal Democratic party and conservative Republican party as most large northern industrial states have, Connally set the GOP time schedule back at least a decade. Ironically, at the end of that decade, Connally switched his allegiance to the Republican party.

Lyndon Johnson had been considered a safekeeper of the Democratic party flag, no matter what, while Connally was more capricious, looking within himself for an allegiance that would justify what he wanted to do, regardless of party philosophy. Larry Temple, admittedly a "Connally man in every respect," feels Connally's "disenchantment" with the Democrats started at that volatile Chicago gathering, the 1968 national Democratic convention, wrenched by emotional issues that neither Connally nor anyone else there knew how to handle. In mid-October, after the convention, Connally and his aide, Mike Myers, met privately with state Republican chairman Peter O'Donnell, Dallas oilman William Clements Jr.,[2] and other Republicans at the Sheraton-Dallas Hotel. They had told Connally they "had to see him" and appealed to him that Nixon "is more your kind of guy." Ernest Stromberger of the Dallas *Times Herald* wrote that Clements "pushed Connally hard to switch parties but he refused, while consenting to let Clements and O'Donnell spread the word among Connally's money men that the governor was not adverse to their contributing to the Nixon campaign."

Another version was that Connally flatly said it would be better for the country if Nixon were elected.[3] Several who

2. Clements was not considered a stalwart of the Texas Republican party but had been rumored that year as a possible GOP candidate for governor. In 1972 Clements, a close friend of Connally's, was the Texas chairman of Nixon's reelection campaign. On Connally's recommendation, Nixon named Clements deputy secretary of defense in December 1972.

3. A published report from a "GOP source" quoted Connally as saying, "I think of the two men the country would be far better off with Nixon as president than Humphrey. I have seen Humphrey break down and cry."

know Connally well agree that the Republicans asked Connally who among Texas Democrats "might be inclined" to support Nixon, and Connally advised them. "But he didn't turn over his files, or anything like that," says Temple. "He ain't giving those files to anybody—not to Lloyd Bentsen, not to Ben Barnes, not to anybody." Even though the Republican contact with Connally was limited, they felt so sure of him that they considered his appearances for Humphrey a double cross. Not only did Humphrey rake in Texas' electoral votes; but, in 1970, Bentsen, relying on Connally's guidance and support, whipped Nixon's choice for the United States Senate, the best Republican candidate Texas had to offer—George Bush.

In late April 1971 Connally said he had bought a $500 ticket to a Democratic dinner the previous week but had not attended. "I'm a Democrat," he said. The prospects for his changing parties? "Very remote." On a national television show, CBS' "Sixty Minutes," several months later, Texas Democratic congressmen Bob Eckhardt and Jake Pickle, and Ronnie Dugger, editor-at-large of the *Texas Observer*, disagreed. They said Connally would be willing to switch to the Republican party to run for vice president in 1972 and for the GOP presidential nomination later. Eckhardt, who has a Shakespearean quote to fit almost any occasion, compared Connally to Coriolanus, a Roman military leader who lived 2,500 years ago: "You know Coriolanus fought for Rome and when they didn't give enough recognition, why he fought for the enemies of Rome."

The news media's obsession with Connally irritated prominent Republicans in Washington. Columnists and commentators continually referred to Connally as the "best show in town" or the "only dab of color in a drab, gray Nixon world." Possibly jealous of her husband's position in the administration, Martha Mitchell, wife of the attorney general, said of Connally, "They're thinking of running him for Pope." In a copyrighted story for Andrews Publications, Inc., Warren Rogers stated that Attorney General John Mitchell sent a lawyer to Texas in 1971 to see if a stock fraud case which was pushing some Texas politicians into early retirement might knock Connally out of the "vice-presidential picture." Texas Republican leaders recognized that the conversion of John Connally to the Republican party would be a fantastic coup, but they could not appear too anxious—he was the enemy, you know, and the rank and file might not understand. In August 1971 Texas Republican leader Anne Armstrong told an Austin news conference that, although Connally would make the GOP national ticket strong in Texas, "At this point, the Republican party of Texas would not be part of any move to ask the vice president to step down." She could read the polls, and so long as Nixon and Agnew were in no danger, why bother with another one of those intraparty bloodlettings that required years to patch up?

As convention time 1972 grew nearer, speculation persisted that Nixon was grooming Connally to replace Spiro Agnew, but Connally said, "I don't think that event will occur." Agnew commented, "I just don't understand how anybody could seriously believe that a man who is a registered Democrat in the middle of May . . . can suddenly turn Republican and be nominated . . . Connally is just not it." Agnew was standing on fairly solid ground. The man who author Theodore White claimed once was considered a "political eunuch" by Nixon's staff was the favorite of 43 percent of the Republicans for a second term, and Connally was favored by just 8 percent for vice president.

In May 1972 the Senate Democrats had voted 29 to 14 to condemn Nixon's Vietnam policy, and Connally, who had become a spokesman on more than just the state of the nation's financial affairs, said the vote "does raise serious doubts in my mind about the basic stability and essential commitment they have to act always in the best interests of the nation." Since he was obviously at odds with the Democratic-controlled Senate over Vietnam, Connally was asked again if he had thought of switching parties, and he said, "I have no present intention to do so but the possibility certainly exists that I could do so."

For Connally, it meant he had to fight or switch—but not so suddenly that it would look like a blatant presidential blastoff in the second party of his choice. First, he stepped down as secretary of the treasury, escaping the trivia that could steal his time and sap his energy. "He was more bored than fascinated with the president's White House staff and the ritual of official life," wrote columnists Evans and Novak. "He resented staff chief H. R. 'Bob' Haldeman's trying to manage the timing and frequency of his private chats with Mr. Nixon. He made no new friends in the administration, spending far more time with old Texas Democratic cronies—Senator Lloyd Bentsen and Robert Strauss."

In late July Connally said he was "vastly relieved" that Nixon had not chosen him as vice president, and he skipped both national political conventions—a powerful and independent force aiming for the greatest impact. Connally said he would remain a Democrat to "lead a revival of broad support to recapture the Democratic party machinery," but his revival became a political crusade for Richard Nixon, and that was no way to capture the hearts and souls of Democrats. Connally, said national Democratic chairman Lawrence O'Brien, is a "toothless tiger they have around to growl." Said economist John Kenneth Galbraith, "John Connally isn't the first to bug out. There was a similar defection of Alf Landon." Texas congressman Wright Patman referred to the Connally-led Democrats for Nixon as a "turncoat crew," and in Texas, Connally's traditional enemies—labor, liberals, and some minority group spokesmen—concentrated as much on Connally as on Nixon in the presidential campaign. Bob Bullock, who seems to take on a healthier glow in the heat of a political controversy, cranked out weekly news releases criticizing Connally's "political gypsies" and "groupies," adding—"It is funny that some people's political loyalty disintegrates when the control of the powerful few is and someone like Senator George McGovern stands up to return government control to the people."

Liz Carpenter, a Texan and former press secretary to Mrs. Lyndon Johnson, labeled the Connally organization as the "Benedict Arnold Society." She also referred to Connally as a "political transvestite." They don't even have the ethics of cannibals, she said. "At least cannibals only eat their enemies." Barbara Jordan, elected in 1972 as the first black woman from the South to Congress, was more forgiving toward Connally. "If he sees the error of his ways, if he wants to be restored to the church, we ought to work with him and get him his catechism. Let's see if we can reshape him, and if we can't, it's up to the people to decide what to do with him," the congresswoman stated. What they did in some places, such as Waco, was to boo the mention of Connally's name, and it was there that McGovern proposed a political amnesty for Connally after the November election.

Bob Armstrong, one of McGovern's co-chairmen in Texas, says he believes Connally would have campaigned for Nixon "no matter who the Democratic nominee was." Armstrong's theory, if correct, debunks Connally's claims that he was only trying to stop the McGovern-types, those who espoused "peace at any price." What made Connally so effective in the Republican campaign, says Armstrong, was that he was good at appealing to the "general [Republican] philosophy that you protect your money base, you take care of the people with the big money, tell them what government can mean to them"—that is, how much it can cost them.

But the GOP also blamed Connally—in one Washington reporter's words—for "keeping Nixon's coattails extraordinarily short." Nixon was such an overwhelming favorite, especially in the South, that the Republican attitude was why bother with Connally's organization which, as the AP's Peggy Simpson notes, was "essentially an anti-GOP device." It also let some conservative Democrats, who were thinking of changing parties, off the hook, Republicans complained, giving them another excuse to stay in the Democratic party.

In September, before the election, Connally said, "I am not a Republican—in fact, I am a lifelong, active Democrat. I am proud of my party . . . But a political party is either the beneficiary of its leadership or the victim. Throughout most of its history the Democratic party has benefitted from its leadership. In 1972 it has become the victim." By mid-October, in what appeared to be a gradual escalation of a carefully rehearsed war of words, Connally pushed himself a bit further from the Democratic party—"If the Democratic party continues under the leadership of Senator McGovern and those who espouse his cause for a rather long time, frankly, I'm going to have to reassess my own allegiance and loyalties." Jack Waugh of the *Christian Science Monitor* filed a story just before the election quoting a "prominent" Texas Democrat as saying, "Nine of 10 Democrats here in Texas don't even mention Connally. He's a dead duck. He's killed himself with the party. He'd love to have somebody call him a traitor and pay attention to him. He's lonesome out there."

On election night in 1972, in Houston, Texas, Connally said, "Lightning did not strike me because I voted Republican for the first time—just as I said it wouldn't. I am a Democrat but my first responsibility is to my country. I just believe Nixon is the best man for the job."

In making a decision, Connally has always listened to the opinions of others, but even his closest friends are never sure if their views have had any influence on him. Nevertheless, he must have been aware of what his friends and foes thought about his support of Nixon, and what it might mean to his future. They consistently voiced their opinions in print and in interviews.

> He was cut off at the pass by the Democrats. He is philosophically more conservative, and his life style is more conservative.
> —Mike Myers, a former aide

> . . . loyal Democrats, of course, wouldn't support him, just as they wouldn't support former Governor

[Allan] Shivers. . . . Neither party is going to promote a man who helps defeat and tries to help destroy it.
—Former United States Senator
Ralph Yarborough, 1957-71

I don't think John Connally's really got a future in the Democratic Party . . . [but] the Agnew people are going to start cutting on him—they're already cutting on him. And the Republicans really don't like John Connally . . . the Republicans in Texas hate John Connally as nearly as bad as Ralph Yarborough hates him . . .
—Former Texas House speaker and
lieutenant governor, Ben Barnes

The most sophisticated politicians in the Democratic party say he has pretty well burned that bridge behind him; and the chances are, the odds are, he has. But as he has reduced his options in one direction, he has expanded them in others.
—Chairman of the national Democratic
party, Robert Strauss

I personally regret that he switched over and formed the Democrats for Nixon and became so active in that field. I think it would have been accepted and understood by his Democratic friends if he'd just voted and make a public statement about what he was gonna do. But he became an activist in it and I regret it, though I don't fault him on his feelings, because a lot of us had similar feelings and reservations, but we were in a little bit different position as an office holder in the party. I'm certainly going to support my party as long as I'm in it. No question about that.
—Democratic Congressman Jake Pickle

I think he has committed political suicide.
—United States Senator Lloyd Bentsen of Texas

I think he has made a tragic mistake . . . your loyal Democrats would not support Governor Connally . . . and I seriously doubt that the Republicans would trust him. . . . Some of our Republicans for many, many years have been loyal and faithful Republicans and they're sorta reluctant to take in someone who changed their colors overnight so to speak . . .
—Former Texas Governor Preston Smith,
Connally's successor in office

334

Both Connally's supporters and his foes, however, tend to forget that to John Connally second best is last, and Connally sees himself—and Texas Republicans agree—as the man who might possibly help steer a Republican to the governor's mansion.[4]

Peter O'Donnell, who resigned in February 1972 as Republican national committeeman, had a few remarks to make about his fight against a Democratic Connally. O'Donnell began with the GOP in 1956, served as Dallas County and state GOP chairman, recruited candidates, donated his time and poured in his own money to the state Republican party. As party spokesman on every political issue, he lived with defeat and dreamed of victory and was Mr. Texas Republican in the 1960s. He told Ron Calhoun of the Dallas *Times Herald*:

> It is really difficult to describe to anyone who is not thoroughly familiar with politics the handicaps that have been imposed on the Republican party by the acts of the [Texas] Legislature. We just had this terrible legal battle and political battle against the Connallys and the Johnsons and we could not defeat them. But they have not defeated us.

,When John Connally can't defeat a group, he's enough of a political animal to join it.

---

4. The Texas Republicans poured so much of their time and money into the Nixon and Tower campaigns in 1972 that they neglected Grover's campaign for governor, which with more effort and funding they possibly could have won.

"A Political Master Stroke"

16

Nellie Connally's friends say that she has always had a marvelous sense of knowing when she is needed in her husband's political world and when she is not. She always does the right thing, even when it means doing nothing. ''She provides an added dimension to his life that has meant a great deal to him,'' says Connally's close friend Robert Strauss. The Connallys have always talked out his major political decisions, but Nellie has always been careful to keep her voice low. She extracted one promise from him, however, when the couple left Washington in late 1962 for Connally to run for governor of Texas—that they would not go back to Washington until their children had all finished high school. Their youngest child, Mark, graduated from Lamar High School in Houston in May 1970, and on December, 14, 1970, President Nixon introduced his new friend, John Connally, to the White House press corps as David Kennedy's replacement as secretary of the treasury. The appointment was like mixing vinegar and Burgundy. *Newsweek* termed it an ''apparent misalliance.'' The president stated that he had selected Connally for several reasons:

> One, because of the confidence that I have developed in his judgment and his ability and his devotion to this country in these past 18 months working with him on the Ash Council;[1] two, because his experience as Governor of Texas for three terms, one of the major States, gives him special qualifications in the field of revenue sharing . . . three, because Governor Connally in the field of finance, while he is not a banker, has a great deal of experience.

> He is the head partner of one of the great law firms of the Nation. He is on the board of a number of financial institutions. He is familiar not only with the problems of finance in this country but also has traveled widely abroad . . . The problems that we face at home and abroad, whether it is a strong national defense, a strong foreign policy, or a strong economy are not Republican problems or Democratic problems. They are American problems.

> We need to approach those problems in a bipartisan spirit. John Connally brings into this Cabinet at the very highest level the viewpoint of a very great American, in my opinion, but also he brings the viewpoint of a leading member of the Democratic party. It means that we will be able to present our programs, both at home and abroad, not simply as partisan programs but as programs that both Democrats and Republicans, we believe, can support.

The president's announcement carried a Texas-size jolt even in Texas. Asked for their reactions, numerous state politicos asked reporters to repeat it; they couldn't believe it at first. The surprise was followed by speculation that the new job was a preliminary move to phase Connally on to the Republican ticket in 1972 as Nixon's running mate. John Connally has always been known for planning carefully and for using each opportunity wisely.

1. The President's Advisory Council on Executive Organization, under the chairmanship of Roy L. Ash, president of Litton Industries.

338

It had been almost two years since Connally, completing six years as governor, had moved to Houston to join the legal firm of Vinson, Elkins, Searls, and Smith. The life was secure and comfortable, but Connally seldom remains anywhere for very long. He has enormous resources and talent, and he is continually asked to use them. As a lawyer he told the Senate Finance Committee on September 29, 1969, about the tax plight of fifty Southwestern ranchers and farmers. The whole experience was frustrating. The week before, the committee had kept him waiting six hours, and he still didn't get to talk. On his way home, Connally told reporters in Dallas the tax-reform bill would make it virtually impossible for a man to "create great wealth."

In what would appear to be a portentous statement, Connally was asked about the Nixon administration's attitude toward the reform bill, and Connally said, "Nixon's position on the bill, as made public by his Treasury secretary, has created considerable confusion as to what his position really is." On October 9, 1972, a year later, Connally complained to a Democratic rally in Plano, near Dallas, "I don't think we need any more Republican prosperity. I know I've got all the 9 and 10 percent interest I want. I've got all the unemployment I want. I've got all the inflation I want, thank you just the same."

White House assistant John Ehrlichman said the president had considered Connally when he selected his original Cabinet, and a former Nixon speechwriter, Richard Whalen, claimed Nixon "had Connally in mind as a likely secretary of defense" during the 1968 presidential campaign. *Time* magazine reported that Connally actually turned the job down and later refused an offer to become secretary of the treasury.[2]

"He's always wanted to do all the things he felt he was capable of doing, really," says Connally's brother, Merrill. "Whether or not these were things he might

---

2. Margaret Mayer writing for the Dallas *Times Herald* mentioned an "unverified report" that Connally also had declined the position of secretary of interior.

choose to do at a given point in time, he felt compelled to do certain things, if he felt he had the equipment and if he were prepared to do them." Another brother, Wayne, says Connally "was perfectly happy where he was in Houston, and I think the president himself was the only man who could have gotten him to leave that position in Houston and go back to Washington."

Nixon's formal offer came on December 4, 1970, after Connally had dined at the White House. Robert Strauss recalls that he was with Connally at a Washington cocktail party the night before Nixon made his proposition, and Connally "didn't know he was to get the offer." It was a challenge. On the day Connally agreed to become the first Democrat in Nixon's Cabinet, the Labor Department announced unemployment had risen to 5.8 percent of the labor force in November, the highest rate in seven-and-a-half years. The Nixon economy was in trouble, and that meant Nixon was in trouble. "In the eyes of his admirers," commented Richard Whalen, "the Old Man had pulled off a beautiful triple play. He had repaired his relations with a hostile Congress; gained at least the appearance of bipartisan support for his economic policies, and an articulate advocate to promote their success; and—most important— put Texas within his grasp."

And Nixon and Connally set it all up just between the two of them. Not even Lyndon Johnson, who helped groom Connally, knew. Connally called Johnson just before the public announcement, according to Washington reporters, with Nixon listening in on an extension. It was one way of saying that Connally felt he was ready to go it alone, in anything he wanted to do. "The president had asked me not to talk about it with anyone. Johnson was miffed and I don't really blame him," [3] Whalen quoted Connally as saying.

The appointment was a "political master stroke," said Minnesota Senator Hubert Humphrey in Dallas.

---

3. Someone else who was not told in advance, or consulted later, was Connally's brother, Golfrey, a liberal and an economics professor in San Antonio. When asked if he offered Connally any advice while he was secretary of the treasury, Golfrey Connally replied, "No, nor did he solicit it."

340

Humphrey was en route to an appreciation dinner in Austin for a colleague, Ralph Yarborough, who had been defeated seven months earlier by Connally's chosen candidate, Lloyd Bentsen. Yarborough said the Treasury job was Connally's "reward" for working "to elect Republicans and to defeat loyal Democrats," and Roy Evans claimed that "reward" was special compensation for Yarborough's defeat. In an obvious effort to avoid any retaliation by Yarborough in his final days in the Senate, Nixon waited until the next Congress convened on January 20, 1971, to submit Connally's appointment to the Senate for confirmation. (If a senator objects that an appointee from his state is "personally obnoxious" to him, he can kill the appointment.) Bentsen couldn't have been happier and stated, "To have John Connally again in a role of effective leadership will prove to be of real value to the welfare of the country, its fiscal policies and its world monetary position."

Texas' Republican Senator John Tower hailed the appointment as a "wise step toward a bipartisan approach to the economic problems of our country." Political observers thought it destroyed Tower's chances of having any influence with Nixon, and the senator was visibly irritated when Texas reporters persisted in questioning him about whether he knew beforehand of the Connally appointment. He insisted he did. Margaret Mayer reported that Connally had assured Nixon that he would not oppose Tower's race for reelection in 1972. She also stated that Bentsen's victory over George Bush had convinced Republicans that Connally controlled Texas and they had to "neutralize" Connally for Nixon's sake.

A Texas Democrat and close friend of Connally's said the Treasury appointment was an effort to switch Texas "from the Democrats to the Republicans" in 1972 and "to have a spokesman in the South." Another Democratic party veteran complained that the appointment "practically destroys what is left of the conservative leadership." The *Texas Observer* stated that it obviously "hasn't helped Lt. Gov. Ben Barnes' bid for the Senate any," and the paper noted a rumor that when Barnes heard about the appoint-

341

ment, he muttered, "That son-of-a-bitch can't do this to me." [4]

The New York *Times*, a newspaper with little love for Connally, printed a story that stirred the hopes of a few liberal senators that it might be possible to block Connally's appointment. Martin Waldron, the *Times* correspondent in Texas, revealed that Connally had received $225,000 in executor's fees from the Sid Richardson estate in 1966-1969 while he was governor. Waldron's story, appearing on page one of the *Times* on February 1, 1971, was based on records filed by the Richardson foundation with the Internal Revenue Service, and Waldron noted that the records were sketchy until 1966, when the foundation listed the $225,000 debt it was paying to Connally at the rate of $75,000 a year. He raised the issue that the Texas Constitution prohibits a governor from receiving any "salary, reward or compensation or the promise thereof from any person or corporation for any service rendered or performed during the time he is governor."

Connally asked the Senate Finance Committee to reopen the hearing on his appointment so he could publicly refute the story, and his request was granted. At the second hearing, the day after the *Times* story, Connally said he had "no apologies to make" for accepting the fee as one of three executors of Richardson's will after the oilman died in 1959. He and his two co-executors agreed,[5] he told the committee, to pay him $750,000 for work, he said, was completed in the fifteen months prior to his 1962 election as governor. He said he received the money over a ten- or eleven-year period to cut down on taxes and that he actually lost $400,000 to $500,000 by waiving a portion of the fees he was entitled to when he accepted the 1961 appointment as secretary of the navy. "I don't go around, senators, bragging about it. I never said to anybody until this morning that I took

4. Others quipped, "Can he add?" and "The first thing Connally will do is print a three-dollar bill with Lyndon Johnson's picture on it."

5. They were Hal E. Smith, Richardson's brother-in-law who received $750,000 or less, Connally said, and Perry R. Bass, Richardson's nephew, who was paid "considerably more."

$400,000 to $500,000 less than I could have taken in order to serve my country," Connally testified. "I just did not go around telling the press all they wanted to know about my financial holdings." Chairman Russell Long, the Louisiana Democrat, commented, "I'm beginning to think someone, somewhere, is out to nail you." Connally replied, "It isn't the first time." The fact that Connally received fees from the estate while he was governor for work done before he took office meant nothing, said Utah's Republican Senator Wallace Bennett. The committee obviously agreed, voting 13 to 0 to recommend Connally's appointment.

His confirmation by the Senate on February 8 was routine, without debate, on voice vote; no one objected. He was sworn in three days later. Connally's first words after he was sworn in were, "Mr. President, you will permit me one big sigh? I finally made it. Today I go on the payroll." [6] The bipartisan approach was immediately in evidence as, after the ceremony, Connally was the guest of honor at a luncheon arranged by Robert Strauss, treasurer of the Democratic National Committee.

Chewing on unlit cigars and sipping a quart of coffee a day, Connally plowed through his first month in machine-like fashion,[7] testifying before congressional committees, mulling over Lockheed Aircraft Corporation's financial problems, socializing at the White House, and reading a briefcase full of books and papers from the Treasury department almost every night. He did his homework in a six-room suite at the Sheraton-Park Hotel on a small oval table borrowed from his conference room at the Treasury building. Margaret Mayer said even when he supposedly set aside a night for his wife's birthday, they

6. At an annual salary of $60,000. *Time* magazine stated in its October 18, 1971 issue that his earnings as a Houston lawyer ran as high as $800,000 a year. Asked about this figure, several Texas lawyers say it appeared far too high, that $200,000 is a better estimate, but that if any lawyer pulled down that kind of money, it probably would be Connally.

7. After he had had the job just over a year, Connally told Washington reporters that when he was governor a study had shown he worked an average of eighty-seven hours a week, but he said he believed he had worked harder than that as secretary of the treasury.

343

went to see a Jack Webb movie on law enforcement which needed Connally's approval.

An Associated Press reporter, a Texan, who watched Connally closely as he broke in on his new job says,

> I think every one of the senators was prepared to be able to laugh at him—a man with so-called Texas charm and suavity who obviously knew nothing about the Treasury or even about higher math. And some of the questions in the initial hearings . . . reflected this. The super-serious senators showing off all their 'know-how' and Connally answering with a laconic drawl about how he'd have to learn about that a little more, but he was sure it wouldn't be insurmountable. . . . He never was rattled; he gave a super-showman's performance each time; he almost defied them with his swaggering and his refusal even then to 'kowtow' to them by being what they'd have liked, a little more deferential. And he was livid at some of the criticism that was being leveled at him then. I remember asking about something that Ronnie Dugger of the *Texas Observer* had written, and he answered with an obscenity; and in a hearing the next day, he snapped something sarcastically that the *Texas Observer* wasn't exactly the best reputed rag in the state, and he'd welcome their opposition.

Even as he guided the controversial $250 million Lockheed loan through Congress, or worked out the guidelines of the wage-price freeze, or presided at an international monetary meeting in Rome, it was the Connally style, not the substance, that people wanted to read about. *Newsweek* magazine said European officials sputtered at the "arrogance" and "boorishness" of his balance-of-payments demands, and George Christian supports the notion that Nixon "used Connally to bruise some feelings on international economic matters. John could always see the core of the problem and charge ahead, for positive results, realizing it might unsettle some." An AP writer who occasionally covered Connally says, "He apparently offended almost everyone there was to offend in his foreign affairs dealings. . . . The financial columnists in the Washington *Post* refer even now [1973] to the "blunderbuss" tactics of Connally and how our affairs with other nations are still tender as a consequence. The general feeling around town seemed to be that he took great pride in dealing for big stakes, taking the great risks and more or less threatening countries as you would a poker partner or a competitor in a Texas business deal. . . ."

In Washington, the contrast with his predecessor, David Kennedy, also was clear. For example, Connally denounced the Chase Manhattan Bank for increasing its prime interest rate in the spring of 1971, and reporters recalled how Kennedy would never say anything for publication on prime rate increases. Connally "exudes dynamism and personality in an otherwise very dull Cabinet," wrote Hobart Rowen of the Washington *Post*, adding that Connally "has the knack of putting complicated questions into focus. Where economists suggest that consumers will soon have to start spending because of 'excessive liquidity,' Connally says, simply, 'People don't sit on money.'"

James Reston of the New York *Times* described Connally as, "the spunkiest character in Washington these days . . . He is tossing away those computerized Treasury speeches, and telling American business and American labor off-the-cuff to get off their duffs if they want more jobs, more profits and a larger share of the increasingly competitive world market."

It was also difficult to see him, just as it had been when he was governor. Richard Janssen of the *Wall Street Journal* quoted a Treasury man as saying, "He's sound-oriented like Lyndon. He doesn't like to read memos, and he's always talking to somebody, either on the phone or in person, so that you can't get through to him." Texas Governor Preston Smith stated on the national television program, "Face the Nation," that he resented not being able to contact Connally for clarification of the wage-price freeze. "Surely to goodness," Smith said, "if they have time for all those press conferences, they would have time to confer." A few days later, Nixon was asked what he planned to do about Smith's intention to defy the freeze to grant pay raises to 132,000 public school teachers and state employees. Nixon grinned and said, "Connally can handle it."

To avoid private interviews, Connally would invite a dozen or so reporters to lunch at the Treasury department's dining room and, after they had started on their first course —a soup, a salad, or hot bread—Connally would, one reporter says, "briskly move in, shake everyone's hand (usually remembering everyone's name), and then he'd sit down and plow right into the food himself, with vigor." A reporter who taped one of the sessions says, "Half of his answers were muffled or made grotesque because he was speaking around two mouthfuls of food. It reminded me of something out of 'Tom Jones,' the movie. . . . The questions weren't always that sharp, but, on the other hand, everyone usually came out of there with one or two good stories. The wire services [AP and UPI] usually got an 'urgent' story or so in his good days." Connally was so determined to cast the Treasury department in his own image that, according to *Newsweek*, "he bluntly told some of his higher Treasury colleagues, who had a tendency to baggy academic suits and rundown heels, to sharpen up."

A Texas politician who thinks Connally should have done more as Treasury secretary to "even out the efforts between all the various segments of the economy" says he cannot help but feel "very proud of the image he [Connally] created when he went to Washington." Ben Barnes says, "His ability to articulate the Nixon administration's economic policies is one of the masterpieces of this era. If you polled people on the secretary of treasury, I doubt if people could name more than one—Connally. John Connally on television talking about the wage and price freeze explained it better than Nixon could have. . . . The great people in the history of the country are people who come along in times of crisis and instill confidence in the American people in their system of government. That's what Connally did."

Overriding Connally's performance on the job, however, was his political personality and the fascinating possibility that Richard Nixon, the nation's number one Republican, and John Connally, a Democrat who had almost single-handedly destroyed the Republican party in Texas, had made a deal—a deal for the vice presidency, the stepping stone, for Connally, to the presidency. The concept of such a deal was both practical and preposterous; no political columnist worth his expense account could resist commenting on it. Carl Rowan claimed Connally "had intimates chortling over what he called the overactive imaginations of newsmen. The Texas Democrat left friends convinced that there was absolutely no political significance in his joining the Nixon administration." Rowan appeared to be a minority of one. James Reston wrote, Connally "is shouting out what he thinks, loud and clear, and this could in the end have political implications of the vice-presidency next November, even though Spiro Agnew is almost the only other character in Washington who speaks his mind." Flora Rheta Schrieber and Stuart Long quoted a longtime Connally political associate as saying Connally would consider the vice presidency "only if he were the hero, and only if lots of people were saying what they said when the Franklin Roosevelt-John Nance Garner ticket was announced in 1932 —that it was a kangaroo ticket, stronger in the hind leg than in the front."

As early as August 1971, just seven months after Connally's confirmation, Joe Belden polled Texans to see if they thought Connally should accept the vice presidency. Twenty-nine percent of the Democrats said "yes" and 50 percent said he should not go with the Republican president; 51 percent of the Republicans liked the idea and only 34 percent said "no." The others were not sure. That same month *Newsweek* quoted a Democratic senator from the Southwest as saying, "If Nixon offers Connally that second spot, he'll take it so fast Nixon's arm will come off."

But by early March 1972, Connally was telling friends and reporters he was anxious to get back to private life. At that time he would not speculate in public over whether he could take the number two spot if Nixon offered it. In one of his luncheon sessions with reporters, Connally said, "I've done my part. I've spent a lot of my mature life in public service and I've gotten a lot of satisfaction out of it. But now I'm tired and I want to do some of these other things.'' He mentioned learning to fly, more hunting and fishing, traveling, and the possibility of a new home in southern Europe—probably Italy—where he and Nellie could relax a few months each year. He had never been really happy as secretary of the treasury, a friend said, and he was bored and anxious to get back to Texas to make more money. And Nellie was itching to get home, too.

Although he had publicly laid the groundwork for quitting, Connally's decision to pull out of the Cabinet, announced by Nixon on May 16, was still a shock. *Business Week* commented that ''perhaps the most surprising thing'' about Connally's resignation was that it was announced ''barely a week before he was to have gone to Paris for what promised to be a crucial meeting of the Organization for Economic Cooperation & Development— the body he hoped would play a major role in forging a new international monetary system.'' The magazine added that many foreign officials were glad to hear he was leaving. ''I must say that there are people abroad who may have objections to the Secretary because he stands up so strongly for America, but they respect him,'' Nixon said. The president said Connally had agreed to take the post for one year, but had extended his term for six months because of the ''very, very sensitive monetary negotiations that were taking place''—presumably the international meetings over new values for the dollar and other currencies, as well as phase two of the wage-price freeze. Nixon said Connally was the ''architect'' of that policy and had ''led the fight against inflation, a fight which we are now winning. . . . I think even the most skeptical critics agree that perhaps no Secretary of the Treasury, as a matter of fact, no member of the Cabinet in an eighteen-month period has contributed more to this country than has Secretary Connally.'' Not only as secretary, but as a member of the National Security Council, Connally ''has been a tower of strength for the President,'' Nixon said. ''I have found that when the going is the hardest, when the going is the toughest, that Secretary Connally is at his best.''

Margaret Mayer wrote, ''At the peak of his performance and influence he walks away.'' She added that he had been protesting to his friends that ''he would not be happy in the yoke of the vice-presidency.'' But Connally's resignation reminded some of the earlier speculation that Connally would stay on as long as he thought he had a chance to be vice president. ''As soon as he knows he is out of the running, he'll leave,'' said one top Democrat.

A few days after announcing that he planned to leave office, Connally told reporters that ''further government service is not my objective, my hope or my aim.''[8] In what sounded like a ''politicians-are-no-damn-good'' statement, he said that politicians are afraid to tell the public the truth, preferring instead to ''pander to the prejudices, desires and disappointments'' of the people. Since he had a choice, however, he said he would vote for Nixon for reelection. What he did not say had been stated in a prophecy eighteen months before by a Washington Democrat, quoted by *Time* magazine, after he had learned of the Connally appointment, ''To my dirty mind, this appointment means one thing: the start of 'Democrats for Nixon' in 1972.''

8. Connally rejoined his Houston law firm as a full partner on July 1. The name was changed from Vinson, Elkins, Searls and Smith, to Vinson, Elkins, Searls, Connally, and Smith. He had worked with the firm from January 1969 to December 1970, when he was appointed secretary of the treasury.

"A Republican at Heart"

17

One glimpse of the crowd in the East Room of the White House let you know that someone from Texas, someone important, was there. A closer look told you it had to be John Connally, because in the crowd were Ben Barnes, Larry Temple, Warren Woodward, the Eugene Lockes, Robert Strauss and his brother, Ted, the Mike Myers—all Texans, comfortable, expansive, treating the White House like home. It had to be Connally. He was the one the Texans had flown to Washington to see, even though Richard Milhous Nixon, president of the United States, happened to be there, too.

The date was February 11, 1971. Connally, at Nixon's insistence, was taking the oath of office as secretary of the treasury. One of Nixon's Supreme Court justices, Harry Blackmun, swore in the new secretary as Connally rested his hand on a leather Bible, a personally inscribed gift from the president. It was a Connally crowd, of course. But what was amazing was how Nixon became just another face in the crowd. "Nixon let Connally completely take over center stage; you forgot Nixon was there," says Temple. "Lyndon Johnson would never have allowed that." Glancing at Nixon as Connally spoke, one Texan noted, "He [Nixon] looked almost infatuated." One might expect a Texan to portray Connally as a political "superstar" and Nixon as his admirer, but that doesn't account for the comments of national columnists and magazines. Connally, wrote Stewart Alsop of *Newsweek*, "has a downright hypnotic effect on the President." *Time* quoted a White House aide as saying, "The President is simply in awe of him."

At least one reporter traces the Nixon-Connally "friendship" back to Washington in 1949 when Nixon, full of the post-World War II anti-communist zeal, was a Republican congressman from California, and Connally was Johnson's administrative assistant. But a close friend claims it was the Reverend Billy Graham who told Nixon in 1952 he should get to know a fellow named Connally from Texas. Although Connally knew Vice President Nixon, there was no particular contact between the two, and Connally campaigned against him when he ran for president in 1960.

"Connally's respect for him was gained late," says George Christian, "because they were foes most of their careers." However, Connally's opponent for governor in 1962, Don Yarborough, had tried to link the two men. Yarborough said Connally "has adopted the attitude of Richard Nixon in saying that some things cannot be achieved because it would cost money."

It took Nixon eight years to become a household name again, and his emergence as the Republican presidential candidate in 1968 coincided with an upheaval in the Democratic party that destroyed the solid, familiar ground Connally had known for thirty years. Connally retreated from the Chicago convention to his Texas sanctuary, wondering about this man Nixon and that man Humphrey. "I think he was not overly imbued with the spirit of the Humphrey campaign," says Connally's brother Wayne, "and yet I don't think he knew—personally knew—Richard Nixon, at the time, well enough to feel like he wanted to actively support him and his programs." John Connally said stories that he had helped Nixon, as part of a deal to become secretary of defense, were lies. "I made no commitment to anybody to support Richard Nixon, and I did not support him. I did not raise money for Richard Nixon."

What he did, claims Richard Whalen, the former Nixon speechwriter, was to make "himself inconspicuously useful to the Nixon forces, giving advice, encouraging contributions from individuals . . . When Connally visited Washington early in 1969 and told White House political operatives that he had done 'all he could' for Nixon, the friendly signal brought a response in kind." The response was Nixon's decision to appoint Connally to the Advisory Council on Executive Organization. Nixon aide John Ehrlichman referred to it as an "out-of-town tryout." Wayne Connally comments, "John had several very intimate conversations with the president at that time as to what the president had in mind, what he wished to accomplish by him serving on this, and I think from that point forward the relationship continued to develop." Nixon recognized, says George Christian, that, "Here's a fella that's going to waste. He recognized him [Connally] for what he is —a very effective operator, a very effective man."

There were other, more subtle, indications that Connally would accept Nixon and his policies. A few days after the 1968 presidential election, Connally told the Texas Research League, a business-oriented organization which the state legislature often relies on for recommendations, that he believed Nixon would shift "responsibilities and authority from the federal government to the states and localities across this land." Connally endorsed such a transfer of power in a book summarizing his six years as governor. (The book was devoted to Connally, so much so that no one—not even state officials—was mentioned, unless it was in commemoration of a death.)

Connally's appointment as secretary of the treasury dramatized the Republican president's confidence in the former Democratic governor, but it was not so surprising to Connally's Texas friends. The late Crawford Martin, former Texas attorney general, had often visited Connally on state business in 1969-1970 in Connally's law office in Houston. "Nixon had been calling John for advice for a year or so," Martin said, "and if he called when I was there—as he did several times—I would always offer to leave the room. But John would motion me to keep my seat, and he would go on and talk to the president. It was obvious they liked each other."

As Treasury secretary, Connally was on what Jack Waugh of the *Christian Science Monitor* called a "feet-up basis" with Nixon. "It is limited to men he feels most at ease with. In all the country there are maybe 10 . . . John Connally is pre-eminent among them and the only Cabinet member with that kind of presidential access." Connally knew he would be able to see Nixon when he wanted to and about what he wanted to, or he would not have accepted the job. "I'm at the White House more than I ever was when LBJ was president," Connally said. Nixon aides were impressed by Connally's willingness to set aside his own problems to focus on whatever was troubling Nixon. They thought it unselfish and, coming from a life-time Democrat, almost incredible.

"We remember his leadership in the fight on inflation," Nixon told Connally's friends in Texas, "but I also recall those times when clearly out of his special capacity as secretary of the treasury, his capacity as head of the Cost of Living Council, as an advisor, as a friend, as a counsellor in all areas, I remember how much he has contributed to this Administration." Margaret Mayer of the Dallas *Times Herald* recalled how after just two weeks—two long weeks— on the job, the Connallys were invited to rest over the weekend in presidential seclusion at Camp David, Maryland. It was Connally's birthday, and he dined privately with the president and slept for eleven and one-half hours.

Connally said he told Nixon he had never had an employment contract. "That is the way I wanted it. I wanted to be free to leave at any time. And I wanted my employer free to ask me to leave at any time.'' There was never any danger that Nixon, who referred to himself as the ''coach'' and Connally as the ''quarterback,'' would tell John Connally to go packing. Whalen wrote, ''For the round-shouldered, palm-rubbing President to hear his views echoed and his courage praised by this strapping Texan is like standing on tip-toe and seeing an unexpectedly flattering image in the mirror.''

Connally's political stock soared in late June 1971, when Nixon designated him as his chief economic spokesman, a title no one had held in the Nixon administration. ''If I were you, when the secretary speaks, I would accept what he says as the word from the administration,'' White House press secretary Ronald Ziegler advised the press. Perhaps, thought reporters, it was significant that the new title was bestowed on Connally when Vice President Spiro Agnew was on a month-long trip to Asia, Africa, and Europe. Ben Barnes was at a conference in Sun Valley, Idaho, the next month, and Barnes' aides asked twenty-four Republican lieutenant governors how they would react to a Nixon-Connally ticket in 1972. Barnes claimed it was to satisfy his own curiosity—but, of course, what objection could there be to passing the word on to Connally?

Political weather forecasters checked the Nixon-Connally temperature at regular intervals, and they thought they detected a sudden cooling after January 2, 1972, when Nixon told CBS-TV newsman Dan Rather, ''My view is that one should not break up a winning combination.'' The implication was clear: Agnew was in, Connally out, and until mid-February nothing happened to change that conclusion. Then Connally went with Nixon and his constant social companion, C. G. ''Bebe'' Rebozo, to Grand Cay in the Bahamas, an island owned by another of Nixon's friends, Robert Ablanalp. It appeared to be more than a casual invitation, since Secretary of State William Rogers was the only other Cabinet member known to have been invited to the secluded island. Whatever Nixon's reason, it gave a boost to Connally's rating on the presidential thermometer. Nor did Connally's resignation from the Cabinet in May seem to squelch his chances at the number two spot. Texas friends maintained that it just gave Connally more elbow room. Connally's enemies, such as Roy Evans of the Texas AFL-CIO, snorted, "He's a Republican at heart. He likes deep rugs and rich people. He wants to be on the ticket this year and to be the GOP presidential nominee in 1976. The oil money wants him there, too."

Evans and other Texas liberal Democrats were incensed over the Connallys' party at their ranch for the Nixons on April 30, 1972. Columnists Evans and Novak said the party had been arranged for months "to kill speculation of a Nixon-Connally rift." It not only killed speculation, it buried it. Approximately two hundred of Texas' elite witnessed the burial, which was handled with amazing grace by the nation's best-known Quaker and a Texas Methodist of some note.[1]

The fare was barbecued beef tenderloin, corn on the cob, black-eyed peas, tossed salad and hard rolls, but it was the company, not the meal, that counted. The wind was so stiff it flattened Connally's thigh-high bermuda grass, and the Connallys and Nixons stayed inside the ranch house during the cocktail hour. Equally as stiff, the *Texas Observer* reported, was the president. He "is lousy at chit-chat. He looks like Ed Sullivan, is shy, and prone to comment on the weather."

A Texan right out of *Giant*, the owner of hundreds of thousands of oil-rich acres, tried his darndest to make conversation with Nixon—presidents, you know, don't come to Texas every day. He had tried everything he knew to engage Nixon in conversation, but was about ready to admit "this fella just don't know how to be sociable" when the Texan happened to mention he was building a ranch house incorporating some of the features of Nixon's home

---

1. Nellie Connally did her share, too, working for ten days to get ready for the Nixon visit. She helped the hired hands in washing lettuce and shucking corn and tramped the fields to gather a bouquet of wildflowers for Mrs. Nixon. She arranged bluebonnets, Indian pinks, firewheels, and tiny white and yellow daisies in an antique glass basket, put them in a room to stay cool—and, in the excitement, forgot to give them to Mrs. Nixon.

in San Clemente, California. "Nixon brightened," the Texan recalls, obviously a bit relieved at fanning a dead spark to life, "and talked steadily and enthusiastically" about the West Coast White House "because, he said, he had had a lot to do with its design." Nixon was so taken with the Texan's efforts to copy his own architectural suggestions that he invited him, right there in Connally's front yard, to take a look around the San Clemente place, and followed it up with a letter, repeating the invitation.

After the small talk, Nixon and Connally, at the head table of the rich assemblage,[2] got down to serious political business. They toasted each other with Moet Chandon champagne,[3] and Nixon's flattering remarks appealed to Texans accustomed to contributing large sums for political purposes—draw a line in the dirt, they'd step across. Or just ask, they'd make a check out of four figures and sign it.

> Nixon—"I am just glad he [Connally] is not seeking the Democratic nomination." (*Laughter*)

> Nixon—"I can assure you, if I don't know the answers, John will."

> Nixon—". . . I have the major expert on tax reform reight here in front of me. And it is no accident he is on my right, incidentally, in this respect."

> Texan—"Mr. President, leave it to John. He will work it out." (*Laughter*)

Nixon told the audience he would try to answer any questions they might have. And the first question was a good indication of how the Connally crowd felt about the Republican president: "Mr. President, do you anticipate any developments in Vietnam other than those *courageous* statements we heard on the television the other night?"

2. Seated at the head table were the Connallys, the Nixons, former Dallas Mayor Eric Jonsson and his wife, and former San Antonio Mayor W. W. McAllister and his wife.

3. With his inimitable penchant for describing his historical "firsts," Nixon noted that he was the first president to propose a toast to Connally at Connally's ranch. Then the entire gathering drank to the Connallys.

Seizing on the favorable interrogation, Nixon responded at such length that the Texans—most of them Texas Democrats—could only, once again, toast Nixon's "courage." Knowing his guests, Connally interrupted to close out the session with a question on busing—"Do you have any comments on it?" Nixon's answer was almost as long as that on Vietnam—"The reason that I am against busing for the purpose of achieving racial balance in our schools is that it leads to inferior education." The guests, said Nellie Connally, were "just a good bunch of folks . . . I think everyone had a good time." After they left, the Nixons settled down for the night in the Connallys' master bedroom. Even Lyndon Johnson had never slept there.

The party, said Congressman Wright Patman, "was a great disappointment to many Texas Democrats." Connally was nothing more than "Mr. Money-bags of the GOP," sniffed former Democratic Senator Ralph Yarborough.

Connally had risked nothing by going to Washington, and he was not losing anything by leaving. His talents had been paraded in print in front of the nation and, in working with Nixon, he had shaken the notion that he could not get anything done without Lyndon Johnson at his side. Connally had moved into a stiff and strange Republican world and had shaped it until it was as comfortable as a pair of old walking boots. "All John has lost," said an associate, "is a chauffeured limousine and a hot summer in Washington." And so long as he had his hands on the steering wheel of a Mercedes-Benz, Connally didn't mind doing his own driving.

In addition to kind words, Nixon gave Connally his presidential blessing for a round-the-world trip to fifteen nations, which Connally began in Caracas, Venezuela on June 6. He reported back July 14, at a three-hour meeting with Nixon at San Clemente, but when he emerged, it was not to tell travel tales. "I will not support" the Democratic ticket, Connally announced, "for the first time in my life." He said he would do "everything in my power to try to see President Nixon reelected,'' and this included herding other Democrats to the polls for the president. The Democratic nominee, George McGovern, was ''all too isolationist in character and also too radical in character,'' Connally stated. According to Connally, McGovern's plan to cut the defense budget would ''gut it'' ; his economic policies were ''the height of fiscal irresponsibility'' ; his promise to grant amnesty to young men who left the country to avoid the draft was ''a glorification of men who refused to serve their nation'' ; and his promise to pull out all U.S. forces from Vietnam within ninety days after his election ''sabotages the efforts'' of Nixon to negotiate an end of the war. [4]

The ''problem'' of the vice-presidential nominee had been discussed at the San Clemente meeting, Nixon said, ''. . . not only from the standpoint of ability to hold the office of vice-president, but from the standpoint of ability to win the election, Secretary Connally, whose political judgement I respect very much, strongly urged that Vice President Agnew be continued on the ticket.'' [5]

Doubting Republicans, especially in Texas where Connally had long opposed Republican candidates, still were not convinced the former governor was playing for keeps, not even when Connally announced the formation of Democrats for Nixon.

George Christian came up with the name ''Democrats for Nixon,'' but Christian says the idea of ''having something—some organization—outside the Republican apparatus'' was Connally's. ''He felt there ought to be some other apparatus because it was such a real revolt against McGovern that it ought to be a separate thing from the Republicans.'' Connally, says Christian, thought the Democratic party ''was really gonna have spasms.'' But

4. Bob Bullock said during the 1972 campaign that Connally's decision to support Nixon had nothing to do with McGovern's candidacy, that Connally knew as early as October 1971 that he would support the president for reelection. As proof, Bullock noted an October 27, 1971 Fort Worth news conference at which Ben Barnes suggested Connally may well end up effectively ''heading Democrats for Nixon.''

5. Reporters noted that shortly after Nixon announced Agnew would be his running mate, Connally, without explanation, cancelled a speech that night to the National Legislative Conference in New Orleans.

Connally told Nixon he felt an "obligation" to encourage Democrats to vote for the president and "would like to do it." The president encouraged Connally and told him he "would welcome that kind of help."

Connally, Christian, and former Johnson aide Jake Jacobsen met in Washington after the Democratic convention to map out Democratic defections. "I'm a Democrat, just like Connally, and I want to remain one," Christian said, "but I want to work for the election of Nixon this year." In Texas, Larry Temple, who had worked both for Connally and Johnson, resigned his place on the policy committee of the Democratic National Committee to become state chairman of Democrats for Nixon. "It is impossible for me to support Senator McGovern [and his] attempt to force our party to the left," Temple said. He added that he would remain a Democrat and later told a panel of newsmen on television, "If Senator McGovern is beaten decisively, there will be an opportunity to recapture the Democratic party." He announced a Texas steering committee of sixty Democrats, including W. Hunter McLean of Fort Worth, who had managed Johnson's presidential campaign in Texas in 1964. But, says Christian, "There wasn't anybody on the [Democrats for Nixon] staff except me and two or three volunteers"—Mike Myers; Warren Woodward of Dallas, an American Airlines executive; Paul Howell of San Antonio; and Leonard Marks, former United States Information Agency director.

It seemed ironic to old-time Johnson supporters that his protege, Connally, would lead the Democrats for Nixon campaign. They remembered 1956 when Johnson, aided by Connally, had wrested control of the Texas Democratic party from Governor Allan Shivers, a Democrat who successfully led Texas Democrats-for-Eisenhower campaigns in 1952 and 1956. "It's interesting to note," says another former Texas governor, Preston Smith, that Shivers "has never offered himself for reelection since. Now whether or not he thought he could not be elected, or whether he thought there was too much controversy about his having gone over and supported President Eisenhower, I suppose only he knows. But I think that down the road Governor Connally will be faced with probably the same problems as have confronted Governor Shivers.''

Officially, the road started on August 9, 1972, when Connally, fresh from a chat with Nixon, told a Washington press conference of the formation of Democrats for Nixon. What he said he had told the president took many reporters aback: ''My greatest contribution to my country this year is to head such an organization.'' Connally is one of the few contemporary politicians who could get away with such a self-serving statement, and it is a measure of his apparent sincerity. He commented on the McGovernites— ''Rarely in our history has a group holding temporary control of a political party done so much to alienate rank-and-file members of that party whose only sin is to have differing views. Far from becoming a more open party, the Democratic party is becoming an ideological machine closed to millions of Americans who have been the party's most loyal and steadfast members.'' He said he had told the nation's best-known Democrat, Lyndon Johnson, of his plans during a two-hour visit to the LBJ Ranch the previous week, and Connally remarked that, ''He [Johnson] did not discourage me.'' What can you say to a son, even if he is a political son, when he says he doesn't like the family name and wants to change it?

''It was obvious from the very outset,'' says Christian, ''that we were plowing pretty firm ground.'' Although Christian says that Connally was reluctant to campaign openly, Nixon insisted that Connally ''be made extremely visible during the campaign.'' The president was happy to stay in John's shadow; and, in fact, the Republicans opened their broadcast campaign in mid-September not with Nixon, but with Connally. Christian says, ''They wanted him . . . to do more than he would do. There were always suggestions that he make press releases on various subjects and just really take on McGovern on two or three things . . . he just rejected them. He said, 'I won't be somebody put in here just to cut up the Democrats.'''

Connally invited the Democrats he knew he could count on to a party at his ranch. The guests of honor for the second time in four months were the Richard Nixons. Chrysanthemums floated in the Connally swimming pool; crystal and silver were set for more than four hundred diners beneath an orange-and-yellow-striped awning. Nixon, flushed with pleasure over cheering crowds in Laredo, Rio Grande City, and Harlingen, shook hands with "Connally Democrats" as they were ushered from chartered buses and limousines. Democrats from twenty-two states and the District of Columbia were there, and even Johnson's former Air Force One pilot, retired General James U. Cross, sported a "Nixon Now" button. Nixon hailed them as "Democrats for America," and he said, "I know the risk you have taken. I know the heat you are taking." But Connally, seldom, if ever, troubled by afterthoughts, declared, "I, like you, have no doubt about what we are doing. I have no regrets whatsoever about what we are doing. The interest of this country leaves no choice." "I can only assure you," replied Nixon, "that I am going to do everything I possibly can to make your votes and support look good for America."

A few miles away, on the courthouse lawn in Connally's hometown of Floresville, McGovern-Shriver Democrats were hustling votes in an entirely different type of atmosphere. Sargent Shriver was at Floresville, his sleeves rolled up, swallowed by the crowd of 1,000 to 1,500 cheering voters, including many Mexican Americans and long-haired youths. One of the Texas co-chairmen for McGovern-Shriver, state agriculture commissioner John White,[6] told the crowd, "We don't have steaks and bartenders and diamonds and all those fancy things to share with you. That's over somewhere else."[7] What the Democrats did have—free for anyone that came—were ten thousand tamales, three thousand pounds of beans, four thousand jalapeno peppers,

6. In 1952 White, running for the first time for agriculture commissioner, was the only Texas Democrat for statewide office who did not endorse Dwight Eisenhower, the Republican candidate, for president.

7. The fare at the Connally ranch included roast beef, black-eyed peas, and Spanish rice.

240 gallons of beer, and, the staple of that rural area, peanuts—peanuts by the thousands stuffed in trash cans.

Admittedly, it was a staged contest, and Mary Lenz of the Dallas *Morning News* had the best version of the *tamalada*: "Sargent Shriver and his McGovernites swept down on the Floresville courthouse Friday, determined to rob headlines from the rich and give them to the poor. While wicked King Connally and the sheriff of Washington dined with assorted wealthy Texans only a few miles away, Shriver and his band humbly partook of tamales, beans and free beer." [8]

Connally "knew he wasn't making a lot of people happy in the Democratic party," says Christian. Connally was drawing fire away from Nixon, and McGovern and Shriver and their supporters knew it, but the uplifted Connally profile was too good a target to resist. Connally has that effect on some people. The most memorable political punchline was that of Liz Carpenter, former press secretary for Lady Bird Johnson, who had Eleanor McGovern in tow at an Austin, Texas, rally when she said of Connally's Democrats for Nixon: "Thank goodness we didn't have to count on them at the Alamo. They would have been out organizing Texans for Santa Anna." But it was McGovern and Shriver, criss-crossing the country, who kept Connally's name in the national news.

> Shriver commented in Houston "Connally and his so-called Democrats will help us win. He'll separate the millionaires and make it clear it's nothing but millionaires for Connally and the people for us."

> In Milwaukee, McGovern called Connally: ". . . the stooge of the Texas oil billionaires. He doesn't have a heart for you [laborers] . . . not for the little guys. He's for the special interests."

8. Less than a week later, the Associated Press noted the difference in dinner tabs at McGovern and Nixon fund-raising events in Los Angeles. The difference in two dinners held at the same hotel one night apart, was $750 a plate. To eat with McGovern it cost $250; with Nixon $1,000. Nixon's diners wore black ties; McGovern's wore business suits. The Nixon centerpieces were flowered candelabra; at the McGovern affair, potted ferns decorated the table. The donors were invited to take them home—for $5 apiece.

In Galveston, Texas, Shriver commented: " 'Big John Connally' is one of the 'big front four' [Connally, Mitchell, Agnew, and Laird] and behind that front door they've got Tricky Dicky at quarterback dancing around out there.''

In Minneapolis, McGovern stated: ''A good Democrat doesn't run away from his party any more than a good soldier runs away from his country.''

And in Dallas, McGovern recalled: ''Johnson and Rayburn never ran away from the national Democratic ticket. . . . It doesn't surprise me at all that John Connally and his billionaire friends are more at home supporting Richard Nixon's brand of Republicanism than they are backing the national Democratic ticket. And I don't mind at all being called radical by that crowd. Besides, if they ever came out for me I'd really know I was off the track.''

One of Connally's major political forays was into California. The sojourn provided a good example of how Connally went about the president's business. Connally was in Los Angeles for a ''non-political appearance'' before the Council of World Affairs, just happening to mention that McGovern's proposal to reduce the defense budget could turn the Mediterranean into a ''Soviet lake.'' He and James Roosevelt visited with campaign volunteers for Nixon, and Connally appeared on ''talk shows'' and made himself available for other interviews. From Los Angeles, he went to Monterey for a rally to appoint three Democratic mayors as co-chairmen of Democrats for Nixon in that area. Then it was on to Fresno for another round with the media and a fund-raising dinner, and then to another fund raising in San Francisco. ''He didn't go to plants to greet people at the gates and things like that because he wasn't a candidate,'' says Christian.

In the early morning hours in Los Angeles, Connally, perched on a desk in a mock office at a television studio, taped the major foreign policy statement of the Nixon campaign. Christian says Connally was ''awfully reluctant'' to do the half-hour network show the Republicans insisted on. "He said, 'Five minutes, yes, but good lands, nobody's gonna watch a thirty-minute speech of me lambasting McGovern's defense policies.'" After the film was made, some of Nixon's campaign officials thought it was "too strong"—too sudden a departure from the prim presidential campaign the new Nixon was waging. But Connally discussed it with the president, and the film ran, as scheduled, October 20, on prime national television time.

Connally depicted McGovern as an isolationist who was so soft on communism that he would rely on short-sighted trust to keep the peace, allowing the armed forces built by six American presidents—Democrats and Republicans—to grow weak and flabby. "He [McGovern] is out of touch with the real world," Connally stated. "He is so far out of the mainstream of American politics he has no business being president of the United States." He described McGovern's proposal to slash defense spending as the "most dangerous document ever seriously put forth by a presidential candidate in this century," and in another burst of superlatives, Connally praised Nixon as the "preeminent foreign policy leader of our time." The old Nixon must have enjoyed the sight of one Democrat pounding on another. "Nobody who sees that film could possibly vote for George McGovern," one Nixon aide exclaimed.

The night the program was telecast, Connally was at the LBJ Library in Austin, Texas, at a reception honoring his wife, Nellie, selected as a distinguished alumnus of The University of Texas. Bob Armstrong, co-chairman of the McGovern campaign in Texas, complimented Connally, "You did an excellent job, dammit." Connally laughed, Armstrong recalls. Armstrong also remembers, a bit ruefully, that television sets had been brought in for those who wanted to watch the Connally broadcast, and there were quite a few alumni who did.

Connally's televised speech reportedly cost $109,800 and, by any Republican accounting standard, it had to be a bargain. "From the standpoint of political reaction," says Christian, "I think it was number one in the campaign in terms of the response we got to it from all over the country—not just we, but the whole campaign . . . particularly the repeated use of it. Every committee everywhere in the country wanted to get prints of it and run it again. We ran it on the networks twice, and it was reused and used and used. We tried to weave a pattern that things had been going a certain way for twenty-five years under all these presidents and now he [McGovern] was gonna take a sharp turn away from this. It had some impact because it kinda pinned down the fact that he was a deviate from the norm, and people weren't ready for any kind of drastic change in anything.''

Nixon won reelection overwhelmingly, and he carried Texas, one of Nixon's eight ''must win'' states, for the first time in three tries.[9] But how important were the Democrats for Nixon? William Shannon of the New York *Times* dismissed the defectors as a ''paper organization,'' and he said if Connally ''is the more natural, self-confident politician, his alliance with Nixon in this campaign does nothing for his image.'' Washington columnist Jack Anderson told a college audience in Beaumont, Texas, that Connally's ''endorsement of Nixon has not swayed me much.'' Anderson said most of the ''bright boys'' deserted Nixon when he was defeated for governor of California in 1962, and, ''Only the duds stayed with him. . . . This is the reason I feel we have the biggest bunch of duds in Washington I have ever seen.''

In campaigning for Nixon, Connally was not exactly riding side-by-side with an underdog, and his brother Golfrey indicated that Connally's defection was really not that dramatic. Democratic support of Nixon, Golfrey said—without specifically mentioning his brother—was ''another step in the development of a Republican party in the South that has been in the process for about a generation.'' Christian says Connally insisted on financing at least half the expenses of Democrats for Nixon by raising one dollar for every two dollars the organization spent, commenting ''that will be fair enough.'' But McGovern supporter Bob

9. Wilson County, Connally's home ground, the site of those rival dinners in late September, went for Nixon 2,953 to 2,072, still less than Nixon's statewide margin of 66 percent.

Bullock, when he was Texas secretary of state, checked the campaign expense reports in his office prior to the election and said of the $2.25 million raised or borrowed by Democrats for Nixon, $1,960,275—87 percent—had come directly from the Republican Committee to Re-elect the President.

Connally could not even take credit for the dry holes McGovern hit drilling for oil and gas money in Texas. McGovern's proposal to phase out the depletion allowance had shut down that financial source. "Their endorsement of the Nixon ticket means little," former Senator Ralph Yarborough commented in an interview during the homestretch of the presidential race. "I do not believe their organization is pulling Democrats over to that side [but] Texas voters . . . are pulled over with a vast amount of money those people can put in and hire slick PR firms and slick PR people to make attacks to try to convince the people that McGovern is a radical, to try to convince them that the Democratic convention was a radical convention, which isn't true, of course. . . . Nixon's just a household word; it's just like seeing Uncle Dick come on TV every day, practically, and he'll get many votes that way. I think the votes that Nixon gets in Texas is going to be determined by Nixon, not by who endorsed him."

"The whole Democrats for Nixon thing was the tail on the campaign. We weren't trying to wag the dog," says Christian. "And yet in the final analysis it became the most public part. . . . The fact that the Democrats were working against the candidate of the Democratic party did have a psychological effect. . . . They just came unglued over this thing; they couldn't pass a day without taking some shot at Connally. Well, this was great for the president. We would put on a TV spot on the welfare program or the defense program and it was signed off as Democrats for Nixon. This had an impact on the public that was more than if it had been just a partisan Republican campaign saying it. . . . I think it cut them good." McGovern, in Christian's words, "got thumped" because the voters did not like or trust him as much as they did Nixon. But in the last two months of the campaign, Christian says, Democrats for Nixon were as valuable as any other Republican strategy in the Nixon landslide—''We had a real little bonanza, being able to say things and do things and call up the ghosts of former Democratic presidents and leaders . . . credibly.''

Once again, playing his own special game of political poker, Connally had used Nixon's chips in a high-stake match. Fronting for the president, the man with the stacked deck, Connally was virtually assured a share of the winnings. And even if Nixon had dropped all his cards, how could Connally be blamed? Traveling at no personal expense, appearing where he wanted to appear, and talking only to people he wanted to talk to, Connally linked his name with the presidency all over the country. ''He had some tremendous media exposure in Minnesota, Ohio, Illinois, and California—places he normally hasn't gotten much,'' says Christian. ''That—surely that helped some—building up a relationship, or a closer relationship, with a good many people around the country.'' Connally also left his own calling card, making sure everyone knew he was *someone*—other than just Nixon's man.

Ben Barnes made a week-long business trip to Chicago, St. Paul, and other cities throughout the Midwest the week before the election. He says everywhere he went the business executives were exclaiming, ''I'll tell you, I really admire John Connally. I met him and I heard him speak and I've seen him on TV. Boy, I'll tell you Nixon ought to stay off TV and let Connally be seen on TV. He's so much better than Nixon.'' Connally was aware of this kind of reaction, and it had to be sweet music to his politically attuned ears.

On election night, November 7, 1972, the Nixon bandwagon, rooted in the ''New American Majority,'' rolled over the McGovern forces. ''It's obvious I'm pleased at the Texas returns, particularly because Senator McGovern and Mr. Shriver came to Texas twelve times and each time made personal attacks on me,'' said Connally. Succumbing to the temptation to gouge McGovern, Connally noted that the South Dakota senator had supported Progressive party candidate Henry Wallace for president in 1948; therefore, Connally's support of Nixon "ought to enhance my chances to be the presidential candidate of the Democratic party."

Connally had not been so jocular at a farewell staff party for the girls who worked in the Washington office of Democrats for Nixon. "During the campaign," he said, "sometimes I felt like a donkey and sometimes I felt like an elephant, and you know the problems with hybrids—they have no pride of ancestry and no hope of posterity." Despite his allegiance to the doctrine of self-reliance, Connally, at fifty-five—rich, handsome, and, some would say, famous— needed Richard Milhous Nixon to preserve his political posterity. "His only salvation is Nixon who, being entranced with him, will probably rescue him," commented a Washington reporter.

After the election Nixon met with Connally at Camp David on November 16. Columnists Evans and Novak reported that Nixon had asked Connally to become secretary of state when he resigned as secretary of treasury the previous June. But Connally declared, after the Camp David meeting, "I do not seek a Cabinet post and I hope that if it is offered I have the good sense to turn it down." Twelve days after his meeting with Connally, Nixon announced Connally "would prefer at this time not to take a full-time position." It is easy to imagine Nixon, the nation's highest ranking sports buff,[10] thinking of Connally this way: he's a great prospect, unsure of where he wants to go, but we hope to recruit him, for keeps. Connally had had an eighteen-month tryout in the Treasury department and had made the first presidential team. But, as Nixon might say, it was the big game that separated the all-Americans from the also-rans.

The United States of America kicked off in a big game on May 8, 1972, and Nixon and Connally were shoulder-to-

10. Nixon's election-night statement, a statement that could have been polished for months, came up short with this sports-minded phrasing: "The important thing in our process, however, is to play the *game*, and in the great *game* of life, and particularly the *game* of politics, what is important is that on either side more Americans voted this year than ever before, and the fact that you won or you lost must not keep you from keeping in the great *game* of politics...."

shoulder. It was, Nixon said, a "pretty hard one"—it was the decision to mine the harbors of North Vietnam to cut off the flow of imported war materials, the first time the United States and the Soviet Union had lined up, nose-to-nose, since the Cuban missile crisis. *Newsweek* magazine said Connally, who sat in on National Security Council meetings and was the only Cabinet member to have a regular weekly appointment with the president, was summoned to Nixon's side at least a half dozen times during the decision-making week. "I advised him but I won't say how," said Connally. But *Newsweek* commented that it was shortly afterwards that Connally "began calling the Republicans 'we' and the Democrats 'they.'" Four months later, on his second visit to Connally's ranch,[11] Nixon said Connally had "never wavered" in his support of the president's decision to mine the harbors.

It was a decision that might have been expected. Because it was a "tough" decision, Nixon and Connally made it, and that was that. "Toughness," "courage," "strength"—there are words they used to flatter each other because these are the qualities that mean the most to them. "We are close, but not intimate," said Connally. "Nixon has the courage to make the tough decisions . . . above all else, he has the courage to do what he believes to be right in the interest of this nation."

In turn, said Nixon, extending five fingers, "Connally is one of this many people who understand the role and use of U.S. power in the world." Nixon's ideas in foreign policy "reflect an unusual awareness of the uses of power in the broadest sense," Connally stated.

In a main compartment of their personalities is stored the hard nugget of discipline, and both men, in judging others, start by separating the disciplined from the undisciplined, and cast a wary eye on anyone who relaxes control at any time. Connally told his friends, in Nixon's presence at the ranch, that he respected Nixon "for the

---

11. In his first term, Nixon never favored another Cabinet member with even one visit to his home.

manner in which he conducts himself. . . . [He] is as disciplined a man as I have ever known, mentally and physically. . . . He disciplines his time" among many duties "without sacrificing the more responsible task that the president of the United States has." Ted Knap, writing for Scripps-Howard newspapers, stated that Nixon "lived it up" in Hawaii one morning by adding a slice of papaya to his usual breakfast of juice, dry cereal, and black coffee. Connally remembered Nixon's "amazing ability" to focus all day and past midnight on the reports that formed the basis of the wage-price freeze in August 1971.

Will Davis, who worked closely with Connally when he was governor, says he, too, is a "very deliberate and a very disciplined person in every sense of the word." Neither fools with "the nitty-gritty," says Christian. "They let others do it." Author Theodore White described Nixon, the presidential loser in 1960, as a "man of major talent—but a man of solitary, uncertain impulse." But Christian says it is, in fact, Nixon's "stability" that Connally admires so much. Connally's friends consider both men articulate, but they give the edge to Connally because "he is faster on his feet, and he says whatever he's saying with more confidence." Not only more confident, wrote James Reston, but "younger, more handsome, more passionate and eloquent." Christian says that, "Connally is a sprinter; Nixon is a long-distance runner." Will Davis adds that Connally "can do a week's thinking in two hours." And, they might have added, the crowds turn out to see the sprinters, not the cross-country runners.

"The worst thing you can do in this job," Nixon told Saul Pett of the AP, "is to relax, to let up," and that feeling carries over into Nixon's private life where, it is said, he is the type of man who wears a suit and tie even when he's alone. "I never allow myself to get emotional," he once stated, and an assistant added, "He doesn't invite affection because he is not at ease with people." Connally demands relaxation as an inalienable right. But he can be just as happy sweating out a work shirt as in a white tie at a glittering gala. "He wasn't warm many years ago," says Strauss. "People thought him cold, but he has learned to be [warm]. He doesn't take himself so seriously." When asked, "Was it something he worked out, consciously?", Strauss replied, "Oh no, it came with security. He didn't work on it. He probably never knew he had to." Part of that security came with wealth. Although he has never been required to file a financial statement, Connally is undoubtedly worth more than Nixon.

Unlike Nixon, Connally thinks anyone who is cutting on his policies is also carving a piece of his hide, and he won't put up with this. Although Nixon, when he was winning and knew it, could say, "I do not question the patriotism of any critics of this war"—Connally wondered aloud about whose side the protestors were on, anyway? Nixon, states Jack Anderson, "is animated by politics as by no other subject," and the same holds true for Connally, who has been known to refer to private life as "blah."

The similarities in the two men's formative years is amazing. They were both poor boys from the West, members of large families,[12] whose fathers held several types of jobs, including driving motor vehicles for a living. (Nixon's father was a Los Angeles street car motorman; Connally's drove an auto-bus.) They both excelled at debating, and they both started their political careers in college in the 1930s. Nixon was student body president at Whittier College, a small Quaker institution, and attended Duke University Law School. Connally was president of the student body at The University of Texas, and he also gradated from law school. At a little theater tryout in Whittier, California, Nixon met Thelma Catherine "Pat" Ryan, and they were married in 1940. Connally met Idanell "Nellie" Brill at a college Curtain Club rehearsal, and they were married the same year as the Nixons. Both men were naval officers during World War II, returning to private life to seek careers in politics.

12. The Nixons had five sons, two of whom died at early ages; the Connallys had six sons, one of whom died young, and two daughters.

Each man's political life depended on an older man. Nixon was a first-term senator when Dwight Eisenhower made him vice president at thirty-nine, the second youngest man ever to be elected to that office. Although Connally was living in Fort Worth and working for oil millionaire Sid Richardson, he was hooked onto Lyndon Johnson's political fortunes with rawhide-tough strings. (Outliving their older mentors, Nixon gave the eulogy at Eisenhower's funeral in March 1969; and Connally eulogized Johnson in January 1973.) Nixon was making a political name, and Connally was making money. From the power the two men inherited from Eisenhower and Johnson, they made their own way in the world of politics. Power or money guaranteed you could get in the door, and, if you had talent, too, you could make it to the top.

Nixon and Connally even had a similar campaign theory—the candidate must change pace, shift gears, deftly move in and out of the treacherous curves, saving the final surge for the right second. But if someone bumped Nixon off the road, he might, as Brock Bower stated in an article in *New York* magazine, do his "self-humbling bit better than Uriah Heep." Connally would be prone to run the culprit off the road. Jack Anderson spoke of Nixon as a "warm and decent" man. Nixon's aides told Pett of how thoughtful he was, and Connally mentioned he had "found in Nixon a surprising kindness toward individuals." Connally's friends speak of him as a gentleman, but in a formal sense.

Watching and waiting, Nixon and Connally knew, after they had made the "A" team, they could never go back. They would test their mettle only against others who had made it. Nixon's major public defeats in 1960 and 1962 are documented, part of the nation's history. By comparison, Connally is undefeated. In private, their victories are incalculable, their defeats hidden. It is said Connally rejected Nixon's offer to make him secretary of defense. Connally wanted to be secretary of state, and Washington reporter Leslie Carpenter said Connally "wouldn't take over the State Department unless Henry Kissinger was first removed from the White House."

Others claimed Kissinger, the president's adviser for security and foreign affairs, simply blocked Connally's appointment. Christian, who got a point-blank look at presidential power in action during Johnson's administration, admits, ''There would have been potential for conflict if Connally had become secretary of state and Kissinger was in the White House.'' Texas Congressman Jake Pickle made headlines with the comment that Nixon was ''using Connally'' as a stick to stir unrest so that no other Republican could siphon presidential power away from Nixon before 1976. Using people like Connally, says Christian, is a presidential game, and only the president can get away with it.

New Republicans John and Nellie Connally.

—*Dallas Morning News*

"A Hell of an Interesting Animal to Watch"

18

Since that November day in Dallas when John Connally was hit by the "silver bullet" fired by presidential assassin Lee Harvey Oswald, Connally has taken on an almost mystical aura among some. They often describe Connally in such lofty terms that it is difficult to imagine him as a mere human being. Washington reporters and insiders are not immune to the Connally charm and charisma. Connally-watching has become an avocation for many, and, since his term in Nixon's Cabinet and his role in organizing Democrats for Nixon, Connally's appearance, his manner of dress, his lifestyle, and his personal idiosyncracies have been reported and commented on *ad infinitum* and, as many believe, *ad nauseum.*

A former Connally associate put it succinctly when he stated that, "John is meaner than an alligator with abscessed teeth, but he's also a hell of an interesting animal to watch." While governor of Texas, he vacillated between an image of a larger-than-life Texan and a clean-cut conservative businessman. As early as 1948, the Austin *American-Statesman* noted, "Of late, he has become more standard in dress, a little Western on the businessman's side. Once he was just as likely to show up in a Homburg and banker's formal attire as khaki pants and shirt open at the neck. His tastes run to colorful ties and silk shirts." When Connally came to Texas in 1961 to discuss running for governor, he stepped off the airplane wearing a black pin-striped suit, a black ve: and a Homburg. Will Davis commented, "We can't elect a man in a Homburg hat governor of Texas." But they did—three times.

In the late 1960s and early 1970s, Connally represented the new Texan—the man on the go, the business-oriented Texan who still retained his love of the land while pursuing big money and big politics. The editorial director of the Dallas *Morning News*, Dick West, whose praise of Connally knows no bounds, wrote in 1969, "Connally is indigenously and thoroughly Texan. He looks, talks and walks like one. He loves the Texas air, its scenery, its sky, its people. 'In your work,' he once remarked, 'you must have a love that keeps your body and soul in harmony with the task.' That love is Texas, and always will be." Even Connally's enemies noted his adoption of the Texan image. Joe Bernal of San Antonio, at the time the only Mexican American member of the Texas Senate, remarked, "I'll always remember him as an immaculately dressed, handsome, Texas-type son of a bitch."

Connally was never more flamboyant than in February 1963, when he rode in the San Antonio Stock Show dressed in a whipcord cowboy suit, boots, silk shirt, and honorary sheriff's badge. He visited with French businessmen touring the United States after the show, and surprised the men by whipping off his coat and loosening his tie to show them the labels—Christian Dior—New York and Paris, and Neiman-Marcus. Connally's choices in haberdashery even caught the eye of Washington columnist Maxine Chesire, who commented in the Washington *Post*

> [Former] Texas Gov. John Connally's attire
> attracted a lot of attention at the [White House] party.
> He wore an outfit that can best be described as
> 'Midnight Blue Cowboy.'
>
> His Tex Ritter tuxedo was two-tones of azure
> and delphinium, with piping around the double-
> breasted jacket and four large mother-of-pearl buttons.
>
> His shirt was two different tones of blue and so
> was his large bowtie.
>
> His wavy white hair is shorter, but otherwise,
> he looked so much like his close friend, former Presi-
> dent Johnson, that some guests were startled. 'He
> found Lyndon's tailor,' someone whispered, 'Now if
> he just finds his barber, they'll be twins.'

Connally has always been letter-perfect in any role he plays, and since his college days he has been master at playing more than one role at a time. Richard Morehead of the Dallas *Morning News* commented in 1965 that Connally "fits just as easily into a governor's chair, an oil-man's office, a cowman's saddle, or a drawing room as do men who were born to those stations." Admittedly, Connally is a great believer in the accoutrements of office. On his ranch or on the golf course, he can be casual. But the panoply of office is important to him, and he always manages to "look the part." He remarked to a judicial conference in Brownsville, Texas, "I, for one, am a great believer in robes. You may disagree, but I think a robe sets a judge apart from the crowd, so to speak, and gives him that extra prestige his office should demand. I think the wearing of robes on the bench should be a standard procedure, as should the rules of decorum in the courtroom."

After the Kennedy assassination, reporters began to refer to Connally's "charisma." In March 1969, Houston *Post* political affairs editor William H. Gardner described Connally as "urbane, polished, and handsome. People used to say: He looks like a governor ought to look. He was a friend of one president and shot down at the side of another, a traveler to foreign lands, an inspiring political leader, a national figure, a man used to high levels and inner circles." As Connally moved through

379

foreign nations in his role as secretary of the treasury, his charismatic appeal increased. He was the Texas "wheeler dealer," putting the polished men of affairs of foreign nations in their place.

The German sociologist and political economist Max Weber used the word *charisma* to describe the authority of those who claim to be divinely inspired and endowed by Providence with a special mission. This sense of mission conveys itself to the public, and people begin to accept the charismatic leader as divinely inspired and destined to lead. Connally's friends would be the first to agree. Many feel that where Connally leads, they are destined to follow— even into the ranks of the Republican party. Will Davis says, "He's an individualist, and he's a leader of whatever ship he's on. . . . The whole time I've known him, I have never heard any person, except his wife, refer to him as other than 'Governor,' 'Mr. Secretary,' 'Mr. Connally'—with an air of respect . . . never, never intimately.''

Many legislators never got the chance to know Governor Connally. His staff formed an impenetrable wall that few dared to broach unless summoned. Texas' first black congresswoman, Barbara Jordan, served with distinction in the state senate while Connally was governor. She never had direct contact with Connally or any "acknowledgment that I was here." However, many legislators accepted Connally's word as law, and freshman senator Jim Wade of Dallas commented in reaction to one of Connally's policy speeches in 1965, "John Connally will be to Texas what Winston Churchill has been to England."

Connally used his memory for names and events and his appeal to good political advantage with legislators. Former state representative Delwin Jones of Lubbock tells an interesting anecdote of Connally's recall. Jones' wife, Reta, was well-known for her delicious homemade chocolate fudge. After Jones gave boxes of the fudge to Connally and other officials, the governor repeatedly reminded Jones of how delicious the fudge was and how much he and his family had enjoyed it. At a reception for the legislature at the governor's mansion, Connally greeted Reta

Jones by name, saying, "Reta, let's have some more of that good fudge!" Jones recalls that every time he met Connally afterwards, the governor mentioned his wife and her fudge.

If Connally could ingratiate himself with members of the legislature when it suited him, he could also be a tyrant in the office and around his aides. His reputation for a flaring temper and for fits of sulking dates back to his child-hood. The coffee his office staff prepared for him never quite suited the governor. One former employee recalls, "It was never right. We tried every type of pot, but couldn't satisfy him. I remember him screaming one day, 'This is the worst goddamn coffee I've ever tasted.' He thought the best was boiled in a pot. He liked Folger's coffee, and I remember the time he found out that a woman in the office had been buying whatever type of coffee was on sale and pouring it into a Folger's can. He was furious."

Connally's secretaries thought he was "stern and arrogant . . . but he could be so charming!" When one of the girls, who was young and attractive, modeled for an advertisement for an Austin health spa, Connally repri-manded her, "We do not advertise!"

John Connally—the man Lady Bird Johnson once referred to as "the handsomest man in the room"—has always had a fine sense of place, position, and presence. After Connally left the governor's office, his portrait remained in a storeroom. In 1972, when Connally led the Democrats for Nixon campaign, his portrait made news. When legis-lators were questioned about why the portrait did not grace the rotunda of the state capitol, they were perplexed. Someone was obviously holding off for a celebration. Repre-sentative Jim Cole of Greenville, chairman of the House Administration Committee, stated that, "Gov. Connally's portrait has been finished and kept in a storeroom for many years. I don't know why it had not been hung." However, Secretary of the Senate Charles Schnabel replied, "You just can't walk out there and hang a picture of a former gover-nor. Especially John Connally."

One of the legislature's most mischievous members is Representative Neil Caldwell of Alvin, who was appointed to the coveted chairmanship of the powerful House Appropriations Committee following Texas' 1972 election. During Connally's administration Caldwell found the governor "very inaccessible and very aloof." However, Caldwell, who lampoons fellow legislators and other political figures in cartoons and in writing, thought it might be a fine idea to use his artistic talent to catch the Connally image for all time.

Caldwell recalls that

> During the 1965 session I worked at The University of Texas art school at night. And I worked like crazy to sculpt this larger-than-life bust of Connally. It was of hydrostone with a good-looking wooden base. You know, having your bust done is a real 'ego trip' for a man. I mean, busts are usually sculpted of generals, heroes, and gods. And I knew that it would appeal to Connally, whose vanity is unlimited.
>
> Now, don't think I planned on sculpting 'ol' John' for political reasons, because he really has the features. But, it just so happened that I had a bill on industrial safety going through committee, and the governor had said that he favored an industrial safety bill. However, the Texas Manufacturers Association was blocking my bill with a bill that Representative Gene Fondren of Taylor was sponsoring in the house. And, of course, it was really a 'no safety' bill.
>
> Well, I finished the bust, and we planned a big presentation in the house chambers. I was head of the delegation to go to the governor and get him into the house. He thought the presentation would be made in his office, but I made the presentation before the entire house of representatives. Connally was genuinely touched by the gift, and he gave a long speech on art and beauty, and how we never give our Texas artists enough recognition. And I was pleased that he was pleased.
>
> A few weeks later a couple of my relatives were in Austin, and I was showing them around the capitol. When we entered the governor's reception room, I said to the governor's receptionist—sort of as a joke, as the governor was not in the habit of seeing legislators who were not on the Barnes team—'Well, I'm here to see the governor now.' She went into the

governor's office and returned quickly, saying, 'The governor will see you in five minutes.' And, sure enough, in five minutes out he came and ushered us into his office with much fanfare. He proudly displayed the bust which stood behind his desk to my relatives and raved about my great talent. Then he turned to me and said, 'You know, Neil, I think you could have moved my hairline back just a bit.' And you know, I think I could have.

Connally considered the Texas capitol and the governor's mansion his private domain when he was in office. When the daughter of one of his aides wanted to write an article about the mansion for a college class requirement, Connally refused permission. ''If anybody writes about the mansion, it will be us,'' Connally replied, referring to himself and Nellie. He continues to be wary of reporters and interviewers writing stories about him or his activities. He considers that everyone wants to make political capital out of him.

During his term as governor, Connally developed a common ailment of an executive under pressure—a stomach ulcer. To help him curb his smoking, his personal secretary Maurine Ray kept his Pall Mall cigarettes in her desk.[1] The governor would buzz the outer office and have her bring him one from time to time. Ms. Ray recalls that he made a ''big production of his ulcer. Even if someone were in the office when it was time to take his liquid medicine, I would carry it in on a tray. Then he changed to tablets and milk, and it seemed like every couple of hours I would take them to him. But he said the milk was too fattening, so he switched to skim milk.''

Connally's personal temperament and ability to appeal to people is much like that of the little girl with the curl right down the middle of her forehead. When he is good, ''he is very, very good, but when he is bad, he is horrid.'' White House staffers told *Time* that while Nixon's advisers would counsel moderation in dealing with adver-

---

1. When asked by one reporter if politics caused him to smoke, Connally replied, ''Politics aggravates it. You know I can go out to the ranch and I won't smoke six cigarettes all day long.''

saries, Connally would say, "Kick 'em in the ass!" John Connally practiced much of his ass-kicking while governor.

If Connally played the tyrant with his staff, legislators who were not on the "Connally team," and minor lobbyists, the establishment members of the lobby and legislature which formed the nucleus of the Connally power structure continue to worship him with almost god-like devotion. Walter Caven, general counsel of the Texas Railroad Association, is a lobbyist who supported Connally and believes that he is destined for greater political roles. Caven has great stature among Texas lobbyists and remains a personal friend of Connally's. He says

> . . . his traits of personality go beyond the term *charisma* in my view. He's a much more complex individual than comes through just in that sort of a term. I think his depth and his accomplishments and his stature go far beyond the theory of charisma. He certainly has that. He's a most dynamic and attractive individual to both sexes. . . . To men he treats himself in such a light that it is very easy to follow him because he is so articulate, so dynamic, and generally so correct in his judgment. As far as women are concerned, his looks, his stature, his physical bearing, his warmth . . . all come through to the opposite sex. They have naturally the same admiration for his character that men have.
>
> John Connally was a leader—a strong, articulate, charismatic leader. He was able to sway to his way of thinking most people, even though they may have been originally opposed to his ideas. . . . What he truly is, is a man of the nation and of the world.

Texas political leaders who are "strong" for Connally are "strong" for the man, the leader, who could sway the people's thinking to their [the establishment's] way of thinking. Few consider Connally's programs of great impact. As Walter Caven explains, "I think a general overall acceptance of his administration by the public was to me the high point. He provided what I call, just for a brief term, absolute leadership, and acceptable leadership to the vast majority of the people of the state."

After the Kennedy assassination, Connally became an international celebrity. Much of the charisma of John Kennedy rubbed off on the injured Connally. During the summer of 1964, Connally, accompanied by his wife, Nellie, visited the governors of the northern states of Mexico as part of the continuing Good Neighbor policy between Texas and Mexico.[2] He walked through the cities, greeting the Mexican crowds in Spanish. The Mexicans were so elated over Connally's appearance that they imported a band from Tampico to Ciudad Victoria to play luncheon music for the Connallys because the band could play "The Eyes of Texas."

Texas land commissioner Bob Armstrong cited Connally's forays into Mexico as one example of Connally's charismatic appeal. "I think you either have it or you don't, and he obviously does. I don't think you can watch John Connally walk through the Washington's birthday celebration in Laredo and not see the physical effect that the man has on people. And it's devastating in many ways. It's the kind of thing that people around him, who sought to emulate him—and I refer particularly to Barnes—wanted to have and were able to emulate to a degree." Many people have noted Ben Barnes' ability to work people in a receiving line and to devote his entire attention to the person to whom he is talking. "Connally, of course, has this ability," the land commissioner states, "but Connally's is due to a keen intellect. He also has a very commanding stature, and he knows he has it, and knows how to use it. It makes him a very compelling public figure, and I think it also makes him a very compelling advocate as far as his ability to move people. . . . He is one of the two or three most compelling 'stand-up-and-go' speak-

2. Before the twentieth century, antagonism between the rival state and country had been so strong that few governors met or visited. However, in 1915 Governor James Ferguson met with Venustiano Carranza in the middle of the International Bridge at Laredo. In the 1920s, Texas Governor William P. Hobby befriended Mexican president Alvaro Obregon and attended his inauguration. Governor James Allred visited Mexico in 1937 to promote good will, and Coke Stevenson in 1943 visited Mexico City and five state capitals. Governor Allan Shivers continued the policy of visiting Mexico and attending inaugurations, and Price Daniel, during his term as governor, entertained President Lopez Mateos in Austin and began the practice of attending Laredo's annual Washington's birthday celebration.

ers that I've ever heard. I don't care whether he's dedicating a plaque on the Driskill Hotel or whether he's talking to his troops after a campaign victory.''

At the Johnson inaugural in 1965, one of the major topics of conversation was speculation on Connally's future. The Waco *Tribune-Herald* reported that, ''the assumption being that he will rise higher, much higher, in the service of his country.'' Well-wishers mobbed the governor and his wife, and Texans had to form a human cordon to protect the Connallys. In 1967 the Fort Worth *Star-Telegram* reported, ''There isn't a single man, woman or child old enough to read in Texas who doesn't recognize Connally on sight and who hasn't in some manner been affected by the Connally image. Few if any chief executives of the past can match Connally's successes at the ballot box, in the legislative halls or around the Democratic party's council tables. Tall, handsome [and] prematurely gray, Connally looks like a governor, acts like a governor, and conducts himself as one.''

In July 1967 Connally departed on an African safari that lasted for forty days and received wide publicity. Other participants in the safari were Bing Crosby, Phil Harris, Clint Walker, and David Janssen. The trip was part of the hunting and fishing series ''The American Sportsman,'' produced by the American Broadcasting Company for television. Connally bagged a nine-thousand pound elephant, a nine-foot nine-inch lion, a cape buffalo, a warthog, a Thompson's gazelle, an impala, a topi, an oribi, and a sable. However, the governor missed the prize he coveted most—a leopard, one of Africa's most elusive and dangerous game animals. ''Well, the big one got away,'' the governor sighed.

Connally was quite impressed with Africa and the hunting sites in northern Tanzania, including the movement of wild animals and the vastness of the wilderness. *Sportfolio* magazine quoted him as saying, ''You tend to acquire an almost abstract objectivity in relation to problems, and you realize just how minute, how inconsequential you are in the overall scheme of things. You are profoundly impressed, no matter how great your effort or how consuming your desire, with the fact that you can't solve all the world's problems.'' In December 1968 Connally once more made news with his wild-game adventures, when he left for Monaco to attend the convention of Game Conservation International, a strange place for a man who had just bagged one of the most publicized ''kills'' in Africa. Connally spoke on the exotic species of game in Texas and narrated the ABC film of the African safari.

Connally's name became more widely known as he appeared on such nationwide television programs as ''Meet the Press.'' In 1967 he was invited to speak to the New York Chamber of Commerce.[3] Aide Mike Myers accompanied the governor on his speaking assignment and states, ''Those guys are tough, and you could almost see them sitting on their hands thinking, 'Oh, another governor. What's he doing here?' But when he was through speaking, they gave him a standing ovation. And you know, that's not the Olney [Texas] Chamber of Commerce.'' Myers also defines his test of charisma in terms of Connally's impact on businessmen. ''Charisma is evident when you walk into a room filled with the chief executives of all the major corporations, and they come up to you, seeking you out, saying, 'John, John . . . governor.'''

Some members of the press were not quite so impressed with Connally's performance before the television screen or with his speech at the New York Chamber of Commerce. Murray Kempton, writing in the New York *Post*, stated

> Gov. Connally has cold eyes and a sulky, self-pitying mouth; one remembered a television program on which he, Sen. John Tower, and State Atty. Gen. Waggoner Carr appeared in succession, each fixing the same basilisk gaze upon the camera and the shattering impact of the recognition that, when the Eyes of Texas Are Upon You, you are in serious trouble. . . .

3. The New York Chamber of Commerce is the nation's oldest, and previous speakers included Alexander Hamilton, the nation's first secretary of the treasury; Grover Cleveland; Theodore Roosevelt; Herbert Hoover; Georges Clemenceau; Andrew Carnegie; Frank Lloyd Wright; and Dwight D. Eisenhower.

> Texas is not a state nor John Connally a governor to be trusted to house animals at my expense as a taxpayer without stringent precaution and regulation. . . . He is Texas in parody, at once pitied and overweening.

Much of Connally's appeal to the Nixon administration was his tremendous charm, his good looks, and his sense of presence. A Texan attending an artistic function in Washington commented on Connally's appearance in contrast to the other men around Nixon:

> I saw Mr. Connally standing head and shoulders above everybody and far more handsome than all those little grey people. Mr. Nixon's got a bunch of people around him who are very nice, like Leonard Garment, who's in charge of cultural affairs, and a great many men like that. And all of them are about five-feet seven-inches tall, and they're sorta grey colored. I mean, I guess they're inside all the time or something. But John Connally looked so magnificent, and so handsome, and so full of health. . . . And the confidence of the guy, you know, is just amazing.

Even Washington's experienced reporters, who have watched politicians come and go over the years, waxed eloquent when Connally was appointed secretary of the treasury. James J. Kilpatrick touted Connally under the headline, ''Connally Comes on Like West Texas Sunshine,'' and praised ''the explosive emergence of John B. Connally as secretary of the treasury. Zowie! What a guy! . . . Connally has arrived on stage like Engelbert Humperdinck at a Pi Phi convention.'' Kilpatrick cited other Texans who had made names for themselves as colorful personalities in Washington, among them W. Lee O'Daniel, Maury Maverick, and Sam Rayburn, but said of Connally

> John B. Connally seems to have something special.
> Part of his appeal doubtless arises from the contrast he brings to his drab surroundings. The Nixon administration has its merits, but pizzazz it has not. . . .

Now comes Connally, six-feet-two, silver man, with a handsome phiz and a he-man tan. He stands straight as the shaft of a six-iron. In private conversation—even in a press conference—he looks you straight in the eye, but it is not like it was with Lyndon. Mr. Johnson had the flinty eye of a faro dealer. Connally has the friendly gaze of a good coach or a parish priest. Want to buy a used car? This guy could sell an old Toyota to Henry Ford.

... here in Credibility Gulch, he possesses one attribute more precious than nuggets of gold—the appearance of absolute candor. . . . Connally, at 54, has the look of eagles; and he is flying high to somewhere.

San Antonio architect O'Neil Ford, who is a member of the National Council on the Arts, recalls an incident in Washington when Connally's ability to handle himself with anyone he meets shone forth. The occasion was the National Ballet's performance of Duke Ellington's ballet, "The River," choreographed by Alvin Ailey. The performance was at the Kennedy Center, and Connally attended with the Nixons and other Cabinet members.

Nixon invited members of the National Council on the Arts to his box during intermission, and Ford went with actor Gregory Peck and his wife Veronique. Ford spotted Connally in the president's entourage and took the choreographer, Ailey, over to meet him. Ailey is one of the most lauded choreographers in the nation and is a native Texan, a fact that Ford counted on Connally being unaware of. Ford, a wit and raconteur, tells the story:

Ford: Mr. Secretary, this is Alvin Ailey. [*Ailey is a black man, you know, and I knew Connally had no notion who he was.*] You will no doubt recognize that he is the choreographer of this beautiful show tonight.
Connally: Oh, yes indeed!
Ford: Mr. Ailey is from Rogers, Texas.
Connally: Oh, from Rogers, Texas.
Ford: [*You know, typical Connally and people like him. They know somebody in every*

town. Men like Connally, and Connally particularly—and I guess Lyndon Johnson and old Bill Kittrell—they knew somebody in every town. Doesn't make any difference where you're going. A lot of people in Texas know everybody in Texas, and I'm sure John Connally does. He mentioned a name, and I'm not sure exactly who it was, so I'll just call him Joe Smith.)

Connally: Oh, Mr. Ailey, I wonder if you know Joe Smith from Rogers?

Ailey: Not really. You know, my family wasn't in a financial position or a social position to know Mr. Smith. We were just poor farmers.

Ford: *[Connally answered him quickly, and it just shows how bright the man is.]*

Connally: And I bet if you ever borrowed any money from him, he'd charge you 20 percent.

Ailey: *[Laughing.]* You know, I think he did.

Ford: *[John Connally caught that, and quick as a flash turned it right around, which I thought was pretty clever. You know, he could have gotten himself into a trap. Alvin Ailey is vastly more important than this Joe Smith. So I brought another man up to Connally.]* Mr. Secretary, I have another man I'd like you to meet. I believe you remember this gentleman conducted the orchestra tonight, Mr. Maurice Peress, and he's the conductor of the Corpus Christi Symphony Orchestra. And sometimes of the Austin Symphony Orchestra, I believe.

Connally: Oh, yes, Mr. Peress. As a matter of fact, I've been to one of your concerts in Corpus Christi.

Ford: Now, here's one more man, who's president of the National Ballet, and he wants very much to meet you. His name is Scherwin Goodman.

Connally: *[By that time he was getting wise to my joke.]* Mr. Goodman, where are you from?

Goodman: Muleshoe, Texas.
Connally: [*He turned to me with a grin.*] Is he from
           Muleshoe?
Ford: Yes, sir. He's from Muleshoe. [*And we
           all laughed. You know, it was really sort
           of wonderful. I could have been playing
           the big trick on the big man. But he was
           very gracious and very nice. And as we
           were getting ready to go, John and Nellie
           Connally were speaking to Gregory Peck
           and his wife. I had come with the Pecks,
           but Connally had no way of knowing that.
           I just casually strolled over and wasn't
           saying anything, really wasn't even lis-
           tening. I was just waiting to go back in.
           And John turned and saw me. He quickly
           brought me into the group.*]
Connally: Oh, O'Neil. I'm very sorry. I'd like you
           to meet Mr. Gregory Peck and Mrs.
           Peck.
Peck: I don't think I want to meet any damned
           architect.
Ford: And I don't care much about meeting any
           cowboy actor, either.

Ford remembers the occasion with amusement and comments, "There was John Connally, who would like to have
been Gregory Peck. And there was Gregory Peck, who
would have loved to have been John Connally."

If they had to describe Connally with one word, his
friends say, it would be "student." "He has never stopped
learning," says George Christian. "He travels a lot, so he
became interested in airplanes and read everything he could
get his hands on. He hardly drinks, but he became a wine
expert."

Connally has often complained of being hemmed in
by public office, weighted down by built-in bureaucracy
encrusted with form and tradition, and "denied the opportunity to give play to any creative interests you might
have." His obsession with a bondless life could be a psychological rebellion to the early years when, as his brother
Merrill recalls, their parents instilled in the children the
"byword of the time, that you must work hard—in fact

391

to the point, really, to where I think there's a . . . sense of guilt on the part of some members of the family if you own a swimming pool. It's a little bit hard for us to take the time out and enjoy some of what we would call luxuries today without some twinge or some pangs of conscience.''

However, says Christian, ''Connally doesn't want to be a drudge . . . he hunts, plays cards, cuts tree limbs—just other things. We used to pack up boxes of appointments when he was governor and go to the ranch for the weekend. Then we'd lug 'em back. Last September we had a thousand things to do on the Nixon campaign, but we just sat around watching the Olympics on television.''

Relaxing in style is important to Connally; the office is for work, his home for relaxation. At Tryall, a three-thousand-acre private Jamaican resort owned by his friend, Dallas millionaire Pollard Simons, Connally rests in his ''under $100,000'' house on a high hill that catches Caribbean breezes. He stretches his legs by whacking eighteen holes in the nineties every day on the golf course.

Roy Evans, former Texas labor president who has never had a good word to say about Connally, insists, ''The only thing I ever saw him work at was party politics, and I'll admit he did a hell of a job of creating a one-party system by absorbing the Republicans into the Democratic party. . . . He was probably a greater absentee governor than [John] Tower was an absentee senator. . . . I guess he didn't like the responsibility that goes with power.''

Evans has it all wrong, according to Merrill Connally. ''It's nothing for him [John] to put in fourteen to eighteen hours a day at most any chore. He's had the physical stamina which would permit this.'' Connally's greatest supporters say it is just a matter of matching the challenge to the man. Will Davis says he expended no more than ''30 percent of his capacity'' as governor. ''He was much bigger, and much more talented, than the job demanded.''

Says Larry Temple, ''He comes out of the chute like at a rodeo on big problems.'' Once out of the chute, says Robert Strauss, he would not dawdle, pawing at the ground with the toe of his boot. ''He has the capacity to be president, and he would like to fulfill and satisfy his ultimate capacity. He has the ability to communicate with people. He has a high IQ. He can absorb tremendous amounts of information and retain that which is important and throw off the minutiae. And he can recall it when he needs it. He learns quickly, and he knows how to make decisions. And he has courage. . . . He doesn't force people to accept his opinion. But he's so goddamn good that, after he has expressed himself, everyone realizes what he says is best. And they just sort of adopt it as their own view.'' He's one of the few men, says former Texas house member Randy Pendleton, whom ''you can sit down with and give him your right arm, if necessary.''

Part of Connally's charismatic appeal to his aides and the other people around him comes from Connally's insistence on doing everything in exactly the way he feels is best for him. He accepts the speaking engagements he wants to, he retires to a life of privacy when he wants to, and he never waits in line. Myers recalls how Connally loved to climb into bed at night with ''a big dish of ice cream and read [4] until midnight or one in the morning, then he'd get a late start. He didn't like to get up early—that's why I was so surprised when I learned that the McGovern speech [Connally's criticism of McGovern's defense proposals]—I think it's the finest thing he's done—was taped at about two o'clock in the morning.''

To exit from any social occasion when he pleases has always been important to Connally, because he doesn't drink hard liquor[5]—and he cannot tolerate drunks—too much booze is a sign of weakness. Myers says that for years Connally sipped cokes at parties, but even his close friends, seeing him with a glass in his hand, thought it was whiskey. ''I think one reason he didn't drink was because he never

4. Unlike his mentor, Lyndon Johnson, Connally has always liked to read fiction, and to discuss it. Two of his favorites during the 1972 presidential campaign were Frederick Forsyth's *The Day of the Jackal* and *The Odessa File.*

5. Connally sips wine and prefers white Burgundy, such as Montrachet and Corton-Charlemagne. His wife prefers Dubonnet, an aperitif made of sweetened wine, bitter bark, and quinine.

wanted to be at less than full capacity. He didn't make a point of not drinking, he didn't preach about it, but he was upset by those who lost control. Connally thinks things should be proper, your desk, your conduct . . . everything should be proper, should be done properly. You should never make an ass of yourself. . . . I know, some great men may have made asses of themselves, but you are never going to catch John Connally making an ass out of himself.''

The man Jake Pickle calls a ''softie at heart'' had a hard enough hide as Navy secretary, the congressman re- calls, to make admirals feel ''they were Mr. Seaman first class.'' To some, Connally is a bullying range boss, nurs- ing grudges in hope of retaliating. ''All I want,'' he once said, ''is a fair advantage.'' In contrast, he is an instinctive gentleman. One observer tells of Connally's reaching to help Senator Ralph Yarborough to don an academic robe at ceremonies honoring the Johnsons and complimenting him on how well he looked, even though he disliked Yarborough as a politician.

This was an instance of the boy showing through the gloss of the man, a boy who developed his moral code during the hard times of the 1920s and 1930s, a moral code based on what was important to the parents and passed on to the child—work, sobriety, education, and the church. The Connally children all went to church unless, as they remember, there was a ''real emergency''; and years later, when Connally was a fifty-year-old man, his mother insisted that the church had been the strongest single influence on his life. It was that same year, 1965, according to the Dallas *Morning News*, that Dr. Billy Graham, the evangelist, suggested Connally was the best qualified person for the Democratic nomination for president in 1968.

Connally told the 1964 meeting of the Associated Press managing editors that he had been ''fortunate enough to have stern, God-fearing parents who didn't abide with foolishness.''[6] It was his first speech since he had been

6. His older sister, Carmen, recalls their father ''just could look at us or raise his voice a little bit and we scampered to do what was necessary. . . . He would

394

wounded by Kennedy's assassin, and he said the assassination had delayed his plans to call a statement conference on morals and ethics.

Although a "white paper" on morals and ethics seems a bit ludicrous, if not impossible and meaningless, Connally spoke with fervor about the conference, and said he would set a date. "In fact," he said, "I will admit that the thought has crossed my mind that Lee Harvey Oswald was the end product, in an extreme way, of many of our own failures in our dealings with young people." He suggested it would be "very easy to devise simple courses in kindergarten or first grade to teach children not to lie, not to cheat, not to steal, not to covet." Although Connally uses some curse words in his everyday speech, his friends say the words are merely punctuation in his conversation, to emphasize a point. "He's not profane, and he doesn't like others to be," says Myers. As governor, he once commended general manager P. Bert Haney Jr. of KNEL radio in Brady, Texas, who had banned, in Connally's words, "the use of recordings whose lyrics are not only suggestive and incident, but outright profane."

Former ambassador to Australia Ed Clark used to say a politician should always hire aides in whom he had confidence and trust and who—added Clark, grinning before he delivered the punch line—were "reasonably honest." Connally did this, and his six-year administration as governor was free of scandal—a noteworthy accomplishment in Texas. The late Crawford Martin said, "Connally doesn't practice cronyism, he doesn't select a friend for a job just because he's a friend," the implication being that a friend not qualified to do an appointed job might reflect badly on Connally, and that's enough to end a friendship.

Although Connally has always been able to comprehend quickly facts and figures on papers stacked in front of him, even predicting with accuracy how well a program might work, he seldom envisions programs in terms of the people involved. "There's a difference in a feeler and a

sit you down and talk to you, and believe me, you'd rather have had a spanking, maybe a beating."

planner—he's a planner," said Crawford Martin. "He has a plan and he sticks with it like a football coach, if he feels like it is a winning deal."

It is difficult to distinguish between Connally's own sense of importance and his attitude toward public office. Both, in his mind, appear to merit special treatment. Richard Nixon's "trust and favor satisfies Connally's own estimate of himself," Richard Whalen wrote in *Harper*'s, and various news magazines have published anecdotes to illustrate the Connally ego. *Newsweek* reported that, "Aides once allowed him to be scheduled as the second speaker at some campaign dinner long ago. 'I don't speak second to anybody but the president,' Connally railed, "and you all better get that goddamn clear right now.'" *Time* related that when a Nixon aide bounced back to Connally a memo he had sent to Nixon, "Connally exploded: 'That's my memorandum. I don't want that son-of-a-bitch to get into the act.' He sent an acid note right to the offending aide, and soon afterward the memo went through unquestioned."

Molly Ivins of the *Texas Observer* wrote gags for the Headliner Club's annual luncheon. One gag spoofed Connally in 1973: "He couldn't be here. He's busy building his birthplace. They're putting in the hay today." Quipped Frances "Sissy" Farenthold, unsuccessful candidate for Texas governor and the Democratic vice-presidential nomination in 1972, now chairman of the National Women's Political Caucus, "I believe he [Connally] may be looking to celebrate the bicentennial with a dual nomination (from both the Republican and Democratic parties)."

It is not unusual for people to translate Connally's ego and arrogance into a dislike for the man. "I think," says a Washington reporter, "he's one of the more widely disliked people by politicians in both parties"—and this undoubtedly results partly from his unyielding insistence on formalities. He has a grand ceremonial style, a mixture of good looks, grooming, carriage, and an awareness of the impression he makes. It has been Connally, among others, says a prominent former student of The University of Texas, who has tried to make the school's ex-students' association an elite group. The former student says there was a clear division among "exes" over the presentation of awards to the distinguished alumni chosen each year.

> One side argued that if we get people out of the tux and into street clothes you'd get a better crowd—that you'd have a better chance of the young ex-students coming and joining the organization. But they [officers of the association] said, 'Well—you know Connally thinks it ought to be almost an annointment in full.' Nobody ought to be required to wear tails as an example of their achievement . . . this is not the way the times are trending. And you're gonna have to make a decision whether you're gonna keep having twenty or thirty or forty or fifty or two hundred people in tails who are capable of financing the whole thing at $500 apiece, or whether you're gonna try to have an ex-students' association that will attract the person who gets out of school right now, and those kids just aren't buying tails.

Connally's sense of importance, his aristocratic manner, his upperclass values are not put-ons. After years of the rich life, they come naturally. In his speeches he projects the image of a down-home, next-door neighbor type with a sophisticated version of the "aw-shucks" speech. Connally talks as much about humility and about being humble as Nixon does about being "first." Introducing Connally to a small group of Nixon supporters during the 1972 campaign, Mayor Sam Madden of Monterey, California, said, "We could call the man 'governor,' we could call him 'Mr. Secretary' or as far as I'm concerned, we could call him 'Mr. President.'" Connally replied, "Thank you for that introduction, but I could be called 'Citizen Connally.'"

Connally's immediate family contributes a good deal to his public image, with Nellie Connally a particularly attractive asset. She has maintained the extreme good looks and smiling outlook of her college years. She is seldom seen looking anything but pert and well-groomed and travels extensively with her husband. She can laugh at the time her husband spends away from home, and commented once when he was secretary of the navy that, "If he were to get in trouble or disappear, we wouldn't realize it for two or three days. No one would think it unusual or think of hunting for him before that." She recalled that she had to call his office three times to tell his secretary to get word to him that she needed him to make the hospital trip with her for the birth of their first son.

Connally's three children have the good looks of their parents, and all have attended The University of Texas. John B. Connally III and his wife, the former Tracy Smith, graduated from the university and now live in Houston, where Connally's eldest son practices law with the firm of Baker and Botts. Connally's daughter, Sharon, and her husband, Robert Conrad Ammann III, reside in Austin, where Ammann works for the Texas Water Quality Board. The youngest Connally son, Mark Madison, is a senior at the university.

With his expanding horizons in business, Connally also is expanding his leisure image. Going "back home to the ranch" became rather commonplace after the Johnson years, and Connally began to look for newer, and more exotic, places to "take his ease." On retiring from Nixon's Cabinet, he sighed, "I've done my part. I've spent a lot of my mature life in public service and I've got a lot of satisfaction out of it. But now I'm tired and I want to do some other things." He mentioned he was contemplating buying a house in southern Europe, possibly in Italy. However, Montego Bay, Jamaica was the spa that Connally chose for his vacation hacienda.

At a White House dinner, Pollard Simons, a contributor to Nixon's campaign coffers through Connally, invited Connally to visit his newest venture in Jamaica, the Tryall Golf Club, located fourteen miles west of Montego Bay and near Round Hill, where Senator Edward Kennedy vacations. Connally fell in love with the lush and verdant scenery, and Simons generously donated the highest hill as the site for the Connallys to build on. With Connally's abundant enthusiasm for land and the products of the land, he exclaimed to Dallas *Morning News* correspondent Karen Elliot, "Isn't this land magnificent? . . . Anything will grow here—bananas, coconut, mangos. The place has tremendous potential." Part of the potential is establishing a multi-million-dollar beef and dairy cattle operation, involving 11,000 acres of grazing land, a $5 million packing plant, and a quarantine station. Simons, former Delaware lieutenant governor John Rollins, and Connally are cooperating in the venture.

Connally's Jamaican house has caused much comment. *Women's Wear Daily* and *Time* both list the price of the Connally residence as $250,000, but Connally states that it cost under $100,000. The house is constructed with a latticed roof and ceiling fans. Only the Connallys' bedroom is air-conditioned. Another aspect of the house led to some speculation. Off the kitchen of the house is a long, narrow room with a locked door. Rumors have circulated that Connally keeps papers from his days as secretary of the navy locked in the room. When Karen Elliott asked the Connally maid what lay behind the yellow-trimmed wooden door, the maid replied, "That is Mr. Connally's." To Ms. Elliott's repeated inquiries, the maid finally said that the room contained liquor.

Writers for *W*, a publication devoted to the best articles from *Women's Wear Daily*, enthused over the new Connally-in-Jamaica look, "John Connally . . . has put away his bronzer stick and is getting some real sol on his movie-star face." *W* further reports that the fifteen island laborers who constructed Connally's sprawling house refer to the former governor as "Boss Man," and that other residents refer to the Connally house as "the winter White House." The Connallys are decorating the house in a style Nellie refers to as "Nellie and John hodge-podge." Dallas Decorator Ray Barrett, however, describes the decor as "Oriental contemporary." Among the furnishings are a sunken marble bathtub, Japanese sliding-glass panels, and tropical wicker furniture.

The Connallys have entertained many of their friends, including former University of Texas regent

Jack Josey of Houston, American Airlines executive Warren Woodward of Dallas, and political supporter Dee Kelly of Fort Worth. Connally's neighbors give a proper political aura to "the winter White House," and include United States Senator Lloyd Bentsen from Texas, Oklahoma Congressman Jack Jarmon, and Vice President Gerald Ford of Michigan.

Connally's admiring public follows him even to the golf course, and Tryall pro Caleb Haye reported, "People come from all over the states and island and say, 'I want to play on John Connally's course.' They all want to get a closer look at him and they stare but no one bothers him until after the game." Haye also said that one golfer commented, "I guess he won't have much time to come and play when he gets to be president." And Connally undoubtedly puts on a good show for his ever-present audience. The man in the Homburg and the conservative business suit has changed his image to trim golf clothes and burnt orange-and-white patent leather golf shoes.

What he eats and drinks remains a constant source of fascination to social columnists, and *W* ranks him with Mick Jagger, Egon von Furstenberg, and Yves Montand as one of the "Juicy People." Identifying a "Juicy Person" might be difficult for the average, run-of-the-mill American, but *W* gives us all the guidelines:

> . . . First, and above all, they are sensuous, not just sensual.
>
> They are big livers, sometimes big lovers.
>
> JPs make the juices flow in others. And it has nothing to do with power.
>
> For instance, the Nixon administration has no juice. Not even Henry K, who certainly tries hard to be juicy.

If the lineup of "Juicy People" isn't enough to make the juices flow, try Suzy Knickerbocker's account of the dinner that the Algur Meadows honored the Connallys with in Palm Beach in March 1973. John and Nellie flew to Palm Beach in their private plane with Mary Mead and the Pollard Simons to dine on "salmon mousse with cucumber sauce, sliced veal with cream-and-white wine sauce, asparagus, endive with Brie, and strawberries Bavarian with petit fours. For spiritual accompaniment there was Montrachet Bassard, Chateau Lafite-Rothschild, and Dom Perignon." Even Suzy Knickerbocker feels that the Connallys "are eating higher on the hog" than the Nixons, "who are still messing around with cottage cheese and ketchup." And John Connally is certainly eating higher on the hog than he did in the depression days in Floresville when his father was hard pressed to "keep beans on the table."

Charisma is only part of the man. The other part is Connally's astute and cynical political nature, the part that weighs the chances and counts each vote before taking the "big step." It is difficult to establish where charisma ends and cynicism begins in Connally. Both are part and parcel of Connally's personality. Much of the charisma has been created by the press, his aides, and admirers. Much of the cynicism is part of the political animal, fed and nurtured in the maelstrom of Texas politics. However, to ignore or to underestimate either is to present a distorted picture of the man.

"Big John" will remain big news to the social and the political columnists, especially as he makes his decision whether to run for president. To many in Texas Connally remains virtually a "knight in shining armor." To many in Washington he represents a new look in presidential candidates—one who can draw support from both political parties and just might be able to "put it all together and win in '76." Many look at Connally and say, as Harry Daugherty once said of Warren G. Harding, "Gee, what a great-looking President he'd make!"

—*Dick West*
Dallas Morning News

"His Eye on a Star"

19

John Connally has never been a stargazer. He was, and is, a stargrabber, determined to clutch at all that glitters. His brother Merrill recalls, "John's always had his eye on a star, out beyond." By the time that John was a teenager and in college, making the friends and acquaintances that would shape his life, his parents were no longer poor. But the early years in south Texas made an indelible impression on John Connally. He refers constantly to the years when his parents were tenant farmers, the years of sweaty, dull labor which was the legacy of one tenant-farming generation to the next. Tenant farming is described by James Agee in a chapter, cut, perhaps because of space limitations, from his 1941 book, *Let Us Now Praise Famous Men:*[1]

1. The complete chapter, edited by Victor A. Kramer, was printed in the *Texas Quarterly* in the summer of 1972.

There is nothing of slave driving about any of this; there doesn't have to be. A child begins because he is imitative and interested, before he is ever told or taught; then he is taught; the work becomes more regular; it is more and more regularly and casually expected of him . . .

There is never any question about this work. It is the heart and centre of living . . . it is done to hold life together. Not relative comfort or discomfort or one of another degree of social standing, but life: food, and clothing, and shelter . . . for a man, and a woman, and their children: for just this life and nothing more: and with no possibility that the work will ever let up.

Money and politics have been the twin pillars of John Connally's life for nearly forty years, supporting his opulent lifestyle and his massive ego, setting out challenges and demanding his full attention. ''Frankly,'' Connally told a Los Angeles press conference in October 1972, ''I hope I never seek public office again. I'm not saying I won't. I hope I never do. I've been active in politics since 1935. It's a tough, hard grind. No man can do it without being pilloried. It takes the skin of a rhinoceros and the stubbornness of a cape buffalo.''

Lyndon Johnson reserved Connally's place in the political galaxy, and Connally has moved in and out of it like a shooting star. Undoubtedly, his most incredible feat as a politician is to appear not to be one.[2] Punctuating his public life with private interludes, Connally always emerges as a fresh face, a possibility. He turned down a congressional seat that was his for the asking in 1948 to stockpile money, and he has refused several times to run for the U.S. Senate when odds were decidedly in favor of his winning. Asked in 1968 if he would accept an appointment to the Senate, Connally replied, ''I doubt it.'' Says Will Davis, ''He'd

2. In 1963, during his first term as governor, Connally told the Texas Association of Broadcasters that a Gallup poll of ''several years ago . . . indicated that while all mothers want their sons to grow up to be president, 73 percent of them don't want them to be politicians in the process.''

rather be the leader of the state, or the leader of the treasury, or the leader of his law firm, or run his own ranch, than be one of the one hundred members of the U.S. Senate. [It's] not his cup of tea.''

Connally's theory is that one should start at the top and work as he pleases. He has been secretary of the navy under a Democratic president and secretary of the treasury under a Republican—holding neither position for more than a year and a half—and he reportedly has rejected at least two other Cabinet positions. ''He understands you don't need a long period of time to make a favorable impression and that the longer you are there the more you can get cut up,'' says Davis. Connally has been mentioned for vice president and president of both parties in recent years, linked with such diverse personalities as Barry Goldwater, Hubert Humphrey, Edward Brooke, Robert Finch, Eugene McCarthy, and Richard Nixon.[3]

Theories continually circulate concerning Connally's next move in the political world, and Connally, an unfettered force, seems to fit each theory, comfortably and naturally. Congressman Jake Pickle thinks of him as a ''third person,'' floating, hovering, drifting on political currents from one pocket of popularity to another.

''If there's a way to the top,'' said another Texas Congressman, Olin Teague, ''John will find it.'' However, Connally has never discussed running for president with anyone, not with Lyndon Johnson, not with Robert Strauss, not with anyone, with the possible exception of his wife. ''I don't think he had any friends that were close enough for him to ever divulge any such intentions or plans,'' says Wayne, who has never heard John even indicate he might like to be president. Hugh Sidey, chief of Time's Washington bureau, claims Connally is immersed in a ''bizarre search for fulfillment'' and ''only the highest rewards satisfy'' Texans' ''gnawing ambitions.'' But Connally's silence, the airtight bottling of his thoughts,

3. Goldwater-Connally 1964; Humphrey-Connally 1968; McCarthy-Connally 1968; Connally-? 1968; Nixon-Connally 1972; Connally-Finch 1972; Connally-? 1971; Connally-Brooke 1976.

forces his closest friends to speculate, and they disagree over whether his ambitions center on the presidency.[4]

The late Crawford Martin stated, "I definitely think he wants to be president, but only if the party leaders came to him. He would never go to them." Mike Myers says, "He's not willing to do what you have to do to be president. You know what I mean. He's not going to shake hands for four years and kiss every ass from here to Pocatello, Idaho. That's not his style."

Connally has been taking stock of other possible presidential candidates—their talent against his talent, their wealth against his wealth, their looks against his looks, their "patriotism" against his; and, says Davis, those measurements "would have to tell him that he is as capable, if not more capable, of running the affairs of this nation than most of the men he's come in contact with." Strauss recalls that a reporter for an Eastern newspaper "may have said it best when he told me that Connally had been close to four presidents—Eisenhower, Kennedy, LBJ, and Nixon and 'he knows he's better than any of the four.'"

In contrast to many presidential aspirants, Connally's moves are harder to detect than those of a magician. He seems to generate motion without moving, and all one sees is the *fait accompli*. Campaigning for Nixon in 1972, Connally said, "I have no aspirations or ambitions to be fulfilled, none at all. I do have a concern about this country and where it's going." One is reminded of Theodore White's comments on Nixon in 1968.—"He had all the money he needed now, $200,000 a year, and he lived in

4. The authors asked Connally's brother-in-law, D. W. "Speedy" Hicks, about Connally's aspirations in an interview at Hicks' ranch home in Bandera, Texas:

Q. Where do you think he's going?
H. Oh, I guess he'll go to the top.
Q. Anywhere he wants to go?
H. Anyplace he wants to go.
Q. Where do you think he's gonna get?
H. I don't know; I imagine he'll be president some day, if he wants to be.
Q. You think if he puts his mind to it that he can be?
H. I believe it. After he ran for governor, he can be anything he wants to be. If he makes up his mind.

this affluent apartment—with a wave of the hand, he displayed the affluent apartment. But it didn't excite him. He didn't need that much money . . . it was in his blood; he liked politics.''

Political animals find it difficult to shed their political skins and, as George Christian commented after the Nixon 1972 campaign, Connally's ''never going to be on the backseat looking at politics from a distance.'' Was Democrats for Nixon a preliminary run for Connally's own political race? ''It could be, I guess . . .,'' says Christian. ''But he very deliberately avoided making this a 'John Connally campaign-type thing.' He discouraged any efforts to do that. It would've been a mistake. He would've been transparent. We didn't even have a picture of him in our campaign office . . . Some of the girls wanted to put up a big old photograph of him and stuff, but hell, he wasn't a candidate. We discouraged all that stuff.''

Just before his death, in response to the authors' questions about Connally's ambitions, Lyndon Johnson wrote, ''John's decision to head Democrats for Nixon obviously wasn't made in the belief that it would help him run for national office as a Democrat. What will happen in the future is difficult to predict. John Connally is a man of great talent and we can't afford to discard men of talent.''

A friend who has known Connally since he was a teenager says, ''When he makes up his mind, he doesn't care who stands in his way—even the family.'' Standing in his way are Republican regulars; Ted Kennedy and other Democratic aspirants; and smoldering ethnic minorities and liberals, especially in Texas, who hate Connally so much, who want to beat him so much, that they reject blindly the fact that—with Johnson's death—Connally was the most popular figure in Texas.[5] ''I know that it would be difficult for him to get the support of the ethnic groups,'' says Connally's brother Wayne. ''I don't think they could probably ever accept him as their leader. I don't know that

5. A Texas AFL-CIO poll in 1972 showed LBJ with a popularity rating of 77 percent and Connally 72 percent.

he could get the labor support. . . . I would say there is pretty much of a dilemma if he has any aspirations of becoming a candidate for president on any ticket.''

Another brother, Golfrey, who campaigned in San Antonio for McGovern, relates a story that makes an ironic footnote to John Connally's political history. Golfrey's first recollection of the Connallys' talking politics around their dinner table was in 1928 when his father, whom all the children admired, spoke of Democrats defecting to Hoover. ''Dad never would leave the party,'' says Golfrey. ''He was for [Al] Smith.''

Despite his defection to the Republican camp in 1972, Connally must appear reluctant to seek the presidency—not so much for political purposes, as for his own sake. How would it look if John Connally went all out for political office and lost? It wouldn't look the way Connally would want it to look. John Connally never loses.

Connally's followers talk about 1973, an off-year in politics, like oenophilists talk about off-years in the Bordeaux vineyards—there are many leaders, but not very many outstanding leaders. Or, to carry the wine metaphor a bit further, it might have been a good year, but it certainly was not a great year. Those who attracted the most acclaim were Connally and Kennedy. Republican Senator Edward Brooke of Massachusetts knocked down the notion of a Connally candidacy: ''He [Connally] is a very able man, and very persuasive. But I doubt that a converted Democrat is going to get the Republican nomination, any more than I thought Mayor John Lindsay [New York] was going to get the Democratic nomination.''[6] For every Brooke, however, there seemed to be a John Wayne, a movie star-turned politician, who cradled a $50,000 gift rifle, inlaid with rubies and decorated with gold, from a Texas rifle designer and told a cheering Denton, Texas, fund-raising gala, ''We all want him [John Connally, right

6. After Connally was quoted in a news service dispatch from Turkey as saying he would seek the presidency as a Republican with Senator Brooke, a black man, as his running mate, he replied that the report was ''absolutely absurd. I never told anybody I'm running for anything.''

there with the Duke] in '76. I'm willing to help start it, anytime."

Texas Republicans, tromped under the Democratic heel for over one hundred years, are enthusiastic about Connally. He could well prove to be their silver-maned Moses, leading them out of the Democratic wilderness. Listening to Texas Senator John Tower or to presidential counselor Anne Armstrong talk—she said that Connally's conversion to the GOP would mean a "monumental break in the dike"—one could envision "twenty million Democrats who voted for Nixon in November" following Connally in a massive frontal assault to obliterate Democrats. Connally single-handedly has the power, they said, to speed up the realignment of the nation's political parties, making it a solid South for Republicans. Yet Tower has said, "I don't think he's coming in with the intention of taking over the party." He wouldn't have to; they'd give it to him.

It could all come down to Nixon's nod, and columnist Stewart Alsop judged in February 1973, that "the president has already pretty well made up his mind that he wants Connally." George Christian says that, "More than anything else, President Nixon wants a candidate who can win." A column by Marianne Means of King Features deserves special attention. It seemed so accurate to Texans who talk regularly with Connally that they kidded him about favoring her with inside information. Ms. Means said Nixon told William Ruckelshaus, then head of the Environmental Protection Agency, to let newsmen know Nixon thought Connally would make an excellent GOP presidential candidate in 1976. Then the president called a news conference to say he felt Connally "could handle any job I can think of," including the presidency. Connally said he was "extremely grateful" for the president's remarks. Nixon was looking out for the Republican party, more than he was Connally, Ms. Means stated. Nixon believed Connally could strengthen the party, but his "buildup of Connally does not necessarily mean he has made a decision in favor of Connally as his successor. . . . Nixon is indulging in presidential games. If Connally does not maintain his current popularity, Nixon may push someone else next year.''

More than just a candidate who can win, Nixon wants a candidate who also can do something extra for Nixon, and that something extra could be to help chip out a memorial to Nixon as a leader in achieving world peace. ''Above all, I want to complete the foundations for a world at peace,'' Nixon told nationwide radio and television audience a few days prior to his reelection. He recalled in a nationwide radio address two days later that in his 1969 inaugural speech, ''I said that the greatest honor history can bestow is the title of peacemaker.''

A Texas specialist in international affairs visiting in Washington said a common theory at diplomatic cocktail parties was that the end of the Vietnam War would allow Nixon to concentrate on the other major trouble area in foreign affairs, the Middle East. Connally, with his background in oil, would be perfect to deal with the oil-rich Arab nations. Connally met with King Feisal of Saudi Arabia, in December 1972, and the Los Angeles *Times* said political sources in Saudi Arabia ''regarded it as unlikely that such a close associate of President Nixon would meet the king and his advisers without some discussion of the Middle East crisis.''[7] Nixon stated that Connally had ''at my request, undertaken some informal discussions with leaders in various parts of the world.'' Pickle predicted Connally would maintain a relationship with Nixon similar to that Colonel Edward Mandell House, another Texan, had with President Woodrow Wilson.[8]

7. Connally flew to Saudi Arabia on a private jet with Dr. Armand Hammer, chairman of Occidental Petroleum Company. There was conflicting speculation over whether Connally was on private or political business, or a combination of both. There was no doubt, though, that his association with Nixon gave him greater prestige than a mere attorney would have had.

8. Although House consistently refused any political office, he acquired a reputation as a ''king-maker'' in Texas politics. Governor James S. Hogg awarded him with the honorary title of ''Colonel.'' House was instrumental in holding the votes of Texas' ''Immortal Forty'' for Wilson in 1912, and became President Wilson's closest adviser. Wilson appointed him a commissioner to the peace conference

Most of Connally's Texas friends—and they are his closest friends—take Nixon's support of Connally for granted, and they think other Republicans will come around by 1976. Connally may be the only person who can beat Ted Kennedy. And that's what Republican presidential politics is all about. If there were no Kennedy, what would be the need for Connally? Against a Kennedy, it's better, Republicans feel, not to gamble. Like the old two-gun Westerns, there's room enough in town for only one. And there wasn't a political party big enough for both John Connally and Ted Kennedy.

Even chairman Robert Strauss of the Democratic National Committee, who has been very close to Connally in recent years, couldn't stretch his "umbrella" far enough to cover Connally and Kennedy. Connally endorsed Strauss for chairman of the Democratic party at a Houston news conference five days before Strauss' election, and he admitted, "I haven't known whether to endorse him or denounce him. I don't know which will help him the most. I'm prepared to do either if it will help him." Strauss reportedly told friends it would have been better if Connally had kept quiet. Asked if he thought Connally should be the Democratic nominee for president in 1976, Strauss said, "I do not."

Supported by organized labor and party regulars who had been turned off by McGovern, Strauss was elected over Charles T. Manatt of California and George Mitchell of Maine, despite a last-minute mail campaign by Roy Evans and Bob Bullock, who protested Strauss' "association with a potential candidate [Connally] for the Republican presidential nomination in 1976." Another Texas liberal, former Senator Ralph Yarborough, also called Strauss a "henchman" of Connally's, and said it would be a "disaster" if he were elected. "I belong to no man," Strauss claimed, and he added, "I was told here today I could be elected unanimously if I would denounce John but I have

after World War I, and House helped obtain Britain and France's acceptance of Wilson's "Fourteen Points." Wilson also appointed House to represent him in drafting the Versailles Treaty.

411

gotten this far without denouncing my friends and I will not start now." But Strauss said, "If John Connally were a member of our policy commission, I'd say get him off." In an interview with Carl Leubsdorf of the Associated Press, Strauss described Connally as "my political mentor" and said, "What I intend to do is to ask John Connally to return to this party and bring with him his constituency" of fifteen million Democrats. "I never take seriously invitations which I first read in the public press," snapped Connally. Nor does he accept them, and, with or without Connally, Strauss now had his most important salvage job to do—"I'm trying," he said, "to put a political party back together."

Most certainly, in that party, his role still undefined, will be Ted Kennedy. Even Robert Baskin, the Dallas *Morning News'* senior political analyst, whose dislike for liberals runs deep, thought Kennedy's speech at the 1972 Democratic convention was "fairly electrifying" and wrote, "On the stump [he] has all of the appeal that his late two brothers, John and Robert, had. His speaking manner is in the familiar Kennedy style. He has the good looks, the easy assurance and the ability to arouse an audience with forceful language that the other Kennedys possessed." Kennedy, said his brother-in-law Sargent Shriver, is "probably the single most popular person in the Democratic party." Not a startling statement from a relative, unless one considers it was made two days before vice-presidential candidate Shriver and Senator McGovern were to be judged at the polls.

A Gallup poll said an October 1972, survey indicated that Kennedy could have run a much stronger race than McGovern. The same poll showed that more than three out of four people who voted for George Wallace of Alabama for president in 1968 preferred Nixon in 1972. And Texas politician Bob Bullock says that Connally put in a claim for those votes in 1976 by encouraging his brother Wayne to accept the chairmanship of a national drive to block the busing of school children to achieve racial balance, a cause which should please Wallace supporters.

412

"I can't see any Republican on the scene who is a traditional Republican that could beat Kennedy," says Will Davis, "but I sure could see John Connally beating him, because Connally has the TV image, magnetism, personality, all of the graces and charms that Kennedy can bring plus, I think, the same sort of energy, the same sort of dedication to the job. . . . He can match him [Kennedy] stride for stride, word for word." Texas Republican leader Dr. George Willeford of Austin affirms, "It would be one of the real battles of the century."

Not only would a Kennedy-Connally battle match rich, handsome men of conflicting political views—one going to the poor, into the streets for his backing; the other to the clubrooms and corporation boardrooms—it would also pit one section of the country against another in a civil-political war that could make the subsurface tensions between Robert Kennedy and Lyndon Johnson look like a mere skirmish.

Connally was incensed by the anti-Texas sentiment at the 1968 national Democratic convention, a convention that paid tribute to the slain Robert Kennedy but not to Lyndon Johnson, leader of the party, president of the nation.[9] Will Davis does not think the suspicion, the distrust, the anti-Texan feeling has burned itself out. The embers are there to be stoked again. Johnson, before his death, and now Connally have become symbols of the state of Texas and targets for any hostility toward the state. Johnson would anguish over it; Connally resents it. The hostility, says Davis, is related to the "population and economic development of this state. I do think that economic and political forces in the

---

9. A former aide tells an amusing anecdote about Johnson during the 1968 Democratic convention. Johnson had flown to the LBJ ranch in central Texas, but he was dying with curiosity about the convention. He had every television in the house on, but that was not enough. The networks, he thought, were not telling him what was really happening. At the same time he wanted to be able to tell the press that he had not talked to anyone at the convention, so he would not appear to be overly curious about it. He would have an aide call Connally, and Johnson would relay the questions through the aide. On occasion, he would even listen in on an extension, cupping his hand over the phone to whisper to the aide, "Now ask him" such and such. The questioning went on for hours.

East and other places just hate to give up the leadership of the country that they have enjoyed for two hundred years and turn it over to California, Texas, Florida, or the South generally. They fought a war to keep that from happening here at one time. . . . The antagonism toward Texas, whether it was through Connally or Johnson, or whomever, is tied into that.''

Responding to questions the authors posed for him about the difficulty of Connally's garnering support for the presidency, Lyndon Johnson said, ''Yes, it might be difficult for a Texan to achieve the presidency in the near future, but not impossible. I don't think we've come to the point that the American people would reject a qualified man or woman for high office just because they were born in some particular region.'' In a final burst, probably his last for publication against those he felt had maligned his presidency, poking fun at him and his Texas ways, Johnson added, ''The prejudice against Texans in public office is mostly concentrated in the hearts and pens of a few columnists and commentators who think the country begins and ends on the Eastern seaboard.''

If Connally were to be elected president, one of his first moves would be to dispel the ghost of Lyndon Johnson from the Oval Office. Many thought of Johnson and Connally as one might think of an elderly couple, so close for so long they began to look alike and to act alike. Their relationship of more than three decades was built on politics, and they often had to cling together to withstand shifting ground and treacherous winds.

Their obvious similarities are common knowledge. Texans by birth and politicians by choice, they left poor rural areas to make millions in the cities, often returning to manicured ranches near their birthplaces for rest and relaxation. Johnson openly sought public office, time after time after time. Politics was his life, so much so that many thought Johnson would go out like the legendary cowboy dying with his boots on—with a telephone in his hand, offering a political proposition. One of Johnson's former associates recounts how Johnson, when he first went to the

414

U.S. Senate, accompanied Senator Richard Russell of Georgia to the Washington Senators' baseball games in a blatant effort to pick up as many political pointers as he could from the veteran committee chairman. But after a few games, Russell complained that he wasn't going with Johnson anymore, because "he [Johnson] doesn't watch the game; all he wants to do is to talk politics, and I can't concentrate on what's going on."

Connally has always presented the image of one yielding to pressure from others who think he is the only one who can do the job. It appears that there are other things he would rather be doing, that he only submits to a relentless draft through a sense of duty and an offhand notion that he can handle the job—whatever it is. "I have an insatiable curiosity about everything. I try to learn something about everything I do," he said. Connally insists that politics must leave him time for a hundred other things. Four months before he resigned as secretary of the treasury, Connally cracked, "Hell, there's not even a good Mexican restaurant in this town. I just want to go home and enjoy life." At the end of his six years as governor, he talked of building a collection of books on Texas history and agriculture and said he and Nellie "are both interested in art, paintings, sculpture, books, in the outdoors and wildlife . . . we love to travel—not only to see the scenery but also the people—and there's a lot in this world to see."

Connally's view of the executive office seems textbookish and simplistic. "It is difficult for anyone to fully comprehend the burdens of the presidency," he told the Executives Club in Chicago. "The president expects criticism, so that when he faces the awesome decisions of war and peace he need not look over his shoulder in concern of who may be behind him." Most important, to Connally, is a smooth course. As governor, he once told a writer, he hoped, during his administration, to nudge Texas ten degrees for the better. His was a mountain climber's pace, slow and steady. People, he said, "want to see something straight . . . something secure."

415

Security, for Connally, is embedded in the American mass, not its fringes. He feels safest with the political core, locked to tradition, unquestioning and with few self doubts. In a March 1964 speech to his hand-picked State Democratic Executive Committee, Connally berated the "far right (breast-beating super-patriots who reduce all problems to slogans and name-calling)" and the "far left (dissenters who fail to see or appreciate the bountiful life that blesses so many of us)." But most often his criticism weighs heaviest on the left, or liberal, side of the scale. He told Texas Boy Scouts in February 1966 that the answer of "extremists on the left" to national and world problems is to "promote total socialism and destroy all vestiges of individual initiative and enterprise [at home]," and "in the world at large, retreat from every communist aggression and abandon our friends and allies."

At an April 1972 dinner honoring retiring Chief Justice Robert W. Calvert of the Texas Supreme Court, Connally complained that some liberal elements of society think they are endowed with a special power to see all that is wrong with society, while those more conservative cannot. His criticisms, many say, are not rooted in philosophy, but stem from personal encounters with liberals as arrogant as he is—resulting in a Texas standoff. "I don't think Connally has any philosophy," says former Texas labor leader Roy Evans. Everything he has done, says Evans, has been "for his own personal benefit—political and financial. I don't think he has any other motivation." Congressman Bob Eckhardt of Texas once described Connally on CBS-TV's "60 Minutes" as a "man who likes to exercise power. I don't know that John Connally has any particular political philosophy. He's a political pragmatist, I suppose."[10] Such a lack of philosophy makes Connally a

10. To Texas liberals, his severest critics, Connally has not changed over the years. When he was first a candidate for governor in 1962, a politician about which little was known publicly, *Texas Observer* editor Willie Morris, later editor of *Harper's* magazine, described Connally as, "A political manipulator with Madison Avenue style, a man with no deep political convictions of any kind, a Cowtown patrician who has never hesitated to subdue the less powerful with scorn and contempt."

juicy target for both columnists and historians as the man who doesn't care, loyal only to himself. He would say Nixon "has a sense of destiny for the nation that is an abiding light in him," but he would comment about himself, "If people knew me well, they'd realize that on many of the things they discuss about me so vividly, I haven't any views."

Although he is most at home with the very rich, Connally, like Nixon, feels he is in step with middle and poorer America, because he, too, wants to recapture the spirit of "making do" for yourself. He has always cautioned those who wanted to rocket to Washington for "magic money" to walk, instead, and to think twice before they make each step. So effective is Connally in a room with the rich that it is scary. If Connally could raise $100,000 at a private dinner for sixty in California, what could presidential candidate Connally do in oil-rich Texas or the financial centers in which he is a frequent and titled guest?

Connally is extra skillful with lawyers, businessmen, and wealthy people—his kind of folks. "He has never done anything yet except what the oil and gas and insurance industry want him to do," claims Roy Evans. The New York *Times* noted that in less than a year after Connally returned from the Treasury department in June 1972, he had been appointed to the boards of Texas Instruments, First City National Bank of Houston, Gibraltar Savings Association of Houston; Pan American World Airways; [11] the Haliburton Corporation, parent of the huge Brown and Root Construction Co.; and to the executive committee of the American General Insurance Company.

The rich and influential not only opened their doors to him, they begged him to come in. In one twenty-four hour period in New York, Connally met with Herbert Brownell, former attorney general in Eisenhower's cabinet, and Dr. Armand Hammer, the chairman of Occidental

11. The New York *Times* later reported that Pan American had hired Connally in January 1973 to "help plead its case" in Washington in an effort to reverse Pan American's economic decline. One of the benefits of the job is that Connally can fly free on Pan Am anywhere in the world.

Petroleum Company; ate breakfast with Charles Bluhdorn, president of Gulf and Western Industries, Inc.; and made two speeches, to the Calvin Bullock Forum, a group of Wall Street bankers, and to the Wharton Business Statesman award dinner, honoring one of Nixon's largest contributors, Donald Kendall, chairman of the board of PepsiCo., Inc. Introducing Connally, the president and chairman of Norton Simon, Inc., David Mahoney, said, "We are sure that rising star of yours will continue to rise. . . . Each of us needs your leadership."

One Texas politician remembers how "very capable" Connally was of rounding up the Texas rich, "people who were clients of his or friends of his clients . . . people who he knew socially. . . . He was just a master at knowing the territory and making it clear how important it was for them to give" money to keep his opponent—who might "strike at the heart" of big business—out of office.

In his private investment ventures, Connally lends his name, know-how, and contacts—and keeps his money. He has a farm boy frugality that he summed up for a Texas small-town audience in his first governor's race: "You shouldn't spend a penny unless you spend it wisely and well, nor a penny you haven't earned or surely will earn." A former aide says, "John and Nellie don't blow their money," and to prove his point, he recalls how their youngest son, Mark, sold programs to Texas Longhorn football games to make extra money while his father was governor. It's the classic poor boy-made rich philosophy: after years of nothing, you want it all, every dollar, half dollar, dime, penny, and paperclip. "I save everything," says Connally. "I'm like a packrat. I have whole boxes of pencils, pens, lighters—I never throw anything away."

Connally's staying power in any office has been notoriously short since his University of Texas days. After he quit as governor and later as secretary of the treasury, much was made of Connally's wanting challenges, finding quick solutions, and getting bored after he had solved them. It was the game, not the final score, that counted. Could the nation stand a bored president? A somewhat farcial question, but it is supported by enough history to make it appropriate. Larry Temple, an aide to Connally and to Johnson, says, "There are so many big problems [as president] . . . one crisis after another . . . he would be at his best"—and, presumably, not bored.

To concentrate on Connally's feelings about inept bureaucracies, sticky red tape, the paper crush, the boredom of government, and even other politicians, ignores the passion of his life: anti-communism. He is ever-alert, his ears cocked for the evil sounds of creeping communism, the system that became a major governmental force in the Soviet Union in 1917, the year of John Connally's birth. The mere thought of communism frightens him. "The totality of the struggle is staggering," he told Ohio lawyers in one of his first speeches after Kennedy had appointed him secretary of the navy. "It encompasses diplomacy-trade-economics-law-religion-ideology-subversions-war and peace-propaganda-science—in short, the entire spectrum of human understanding both of the nature and scope of the Communist menace and of our own principles and aspirations."

"The communist goal," Connally said, "is nothing less than the complete domination of the entire world, including of course the United States." He said he was impressed that Dallas lawyers had worked with the school board there on a teacher's guide, *The Principles of American Freedom in Contrast to the Tyranny of Communism,* but that lawyers should do more. "We lawyers must take the case of communism versus democracy to the people . . . the political differences between liberal and conservative in America are minute in contrast to the great gulf separating both from the philosophy of tyranny and enslavement which is Communism." Sounding the alarm was a ticklish situation, and Connally knew it: "We are in grave peril of having *all* programs designed to inform the public in the nature and extent of the Communist conspiracy identified in the public mind with right wing radicalism."[12] On the

12. Connally's speech was printed in the January 15, 1962 edition of *Vital Speeches of the Day,* a semi-monthly publication which states that it contains "The best thought of the best minds on current national questions."

campaign trail in 1962, and later as governor, Connally cried, "Watch out—the 'Commies' are coming" so often it was like a modern-day version of the boy and the wolf. Years later, the *Texas Observer* accused Connally of "Joe McCarthyism" in Connally's national television speech which warned of the consequences of electing George McGovern president.

His anti-communism stance was especially strong in 1964 and 1965, when he and Lyndon Johnson had just been elected to office. Connally's voice became an echo of Johnson's foreign policy, an important echo because of his friendship with Johnson. To Connally, everything became a race between the United States and the communist nations —education, economic development, everything. And he firmly believed that, if this country lost those races, the free world would be completely obliterated. During the bloody Vietnam years, Connally never wavered. It was them against us, good versus bad, and there was little reason to waste time pondering why the United States was in Vietnam. His philosophy was to settle the thing and to get out. It was Connally who urged Nixon to mine the harbors. It is doubtful Connally would ever have held up on the bombing unless the enemy had surrendered. Fight fire with fire, match strength against strength or, Connally believed, mankind would be covered with a communist blanket.

In probing for the nuances of Connally's personality, in trying to determine what kind of president he might be, one tends to go deep beneath the soil without picking up what's on the ground. There are many feelings that Connally keeps to himself, but his broad feelings about this country are plain and simple. He believes it is the best nation in the world. "We're the envy of every nation, large and small," Connally told 1,000 Dallas civic leaders late in 1972. "And what's wrong with that?" He believes the American people can do anything and can make any sacrifice if the reason is good enough. It was his theory that the country was divided over Vietnam because the average citizen felt guilty that young men were dying in combat while back home not even tires or gas were scarce—nothing was rationed and there were no women in defense plants. For the first time during wartime the American people felt "they had no personal stake" in the war, Connally stated. He believes it is naive to think the United States can make friends with other countries by passing out American dollars, and that another country's respect for the United States is as important as friendship, anyway. Connally's "get tough" policy on aid and credit to others was reiterated time and time again. "We can afford to get tough with Latin America," he stated, "because we don't have any friends left there anyway."

As secretary of the treasury he told the State Bar of Texas convention in Dallas, "We are not going to be the recipients of gratitude from the nations we have helped in the past. If you want to know who is going to look after the United States, no one is going to except the United States itself." In 1973, at another Dallas convention, members of the American Quarterhorse Association rose and applauded as Connally called on the United States to be "pragmatic enough to say to the rest of the world, 'We're your friends and we're compassionate, and we'll help you with your poverty, your sick and your natural disasters, but we're not going to be a patsy for you anymore!'" What Connally wants for the United States is the best bargain it can get. And "no question about it," he says, "the battle field of the future . . . certainly for the rest of this decade . . . is going to be in the economic field." Columnists Evans and Novak claim Connally has a "chauvinistic goal of a world dominated by the U.S., from trade to monetary relationships to military power." Connally refers to his goal as exercising "leadership with an eye to our own well being."

Leadership, to Connally, means making decisions, and no one doubts he has the self-confidence to make any decision—right or wrong. What worries many is not that Connally will not make decisions, but that his mind appears to have no "fail-safe" device. Once committed, even mistakenly, there is no turning back. Loss of face to Connally is no disaster; it is worse than disaster.

Many who know him feel he has proven to himself he is as smart as anybody and should be president. At fifty-seven—he would be nearly sixty when American voters choose their next president—1976 is almost certain to be his last chance. "He's always taken a strong stand, but now he's speaking his piece more than he ever has," says his friend, Mike Myers. "He knows he might not live much longer." Sitting around with friends at Frank Erwin's Austin home, on a Texas Longhorn football weekend, Connally chatted about national politics and about his own life. His friends left him that night, late, with this impression: "He believes he's right—more now than ever . . . down in his heart. He doesn't care so much what other people think."

Predicting how Connally might perform as president can at best be speculative. Would he follow the same type of hard-line policies that Johnson followed with the war in Vietnam? Connally has been known to wield executive power with such a heavy hand that strong men quivered. He bulldozed bills through the Texas legislature with little regard for legislators' feelings. Like Lyndon Johnson in Vietnam or Woodrow Wilson with the League of Nations, Connally could pursue one set policy down a collision course leading to defeat. As many presidents have been, Connally is an overly rigid personality, often determined to stick to a decision no matter what the consequences.

Connally takes his political defeats personally. He is much like Johnson, who felt that, when the Viet Cong attacked, they attacked him personally. The Vietnam war was Johnson's war, and each defeat was Johnson's defeat. "Just like the Alamo," he once responded. However, Johnson's saving grace was his belief in people, his paternalistic image of Lyndon Johnson's saving the world. Connally is much less a public-oriented man than Johnson. Connally remains completely out of touch with the downtrodden, completely engrossed in the world of those who have made it to the top of the business and social ranks.

James Barber, in his study of the presidential character, ranks both Johnson and Wilson as active-negative presidents and asserts that for this type of man in the president's role, "having experienced severe deprivations of self-esteem in childhood, . . . develops a deep attachment to achievement as a way to wring from his environment a sense that he is worthy; progressively, this driving force is translated into a search for independent power over others, pursued with intense dedication, and justified idealistically." Barber's central thesis is that a president's personality shapes his performance and that personality traits form his character, his world view, and his style.

Connally's brother Merrill refers to the fact that people in Floresville referred to the Connallys as "poor white trash," and Connally's numerous references in speeches to his boyhood picture a time of financial deprivation. As a boy, Connally struck back at his environment through temper tantrums and sulking; in manhood, through arrogance and a determination to have his own way. Colonel Edward M. House once commented about Woodrow Wilson that Wilson "finds great difficulty in conferring with men against whom, for some reason, he has a prejudice and in whom he can find nothing good." Connally has a similar prejudice, and he is inclined to ignore or to avoid people with whom he cannot work. Again and again key Texas legislators would find themselves unable to gain entrance to Connally's office, or they would be forced to communicate with the governor through his aides.

Connally first achieved success in the field of dramatics and public speaking, and he has been "onstage" ever since. A relevant and influential event in Connally's youth was losing a speech contest to a boy who was from "the right family." John Connally has lost few contests since that day, and he has always moved and surrounded himself with the "right people." Even his aides were considered exceptional young men. Frank Miskell, before his untimely death, was considered one of the most brilliant men in government. Both Howard Rose and Larry Temple, who remain loyal Connally supporters, graduated at the top of their law school classes. Connally aligns himself with the "movers and shakers," the members of the boards of corporations, the presidents of industries.

423

Some speculate that Nixon uses Connally as his "alter ego" letting Connally tell off the "big boys" while Nixon preserves his image as peacemaker. James Barber states that Nixon's motto might well be, "Don't Tread On Me!" He quotes Nixon's mother as saying, "I never knew a person to change so little. From the time he was first able to understand the world around him . . . he has reacted the same way to the same situations." Connally's temper is legendary, and when faced with a challenge and after meeting it to his own satisfaction—Connally quits, always on top, always ahead of the game. When Connally quits, he goes home, back to the plush life, the accoutrements of success, the world of moneymaking that is both familiar and secure to him.

Using Jung's description of extraverted, intuitive types, Harold D. Lasswell in his study, *Psychopathology and Politics,* categorizes the extraverted, intuitive by this general description: ". . . He seizes hold of new objects and ways of doing things with eager intensity, only to abandon them cold-bloodly, when their implications become obvious. . . . Here is the facile promoter, who senses the dawning future and speeds from project to project, bored with routine and detail after projects have been accepted and the blueprints finished." Connally conceptualized bold plans for legislation as governor and became bored with the legislative process, isolating himself from any contact with legislators who failed to "play his game."

On May 2, 1973, John Connally chose a room in the First City National Bank of Houston[13] for his announcement that he was switching from the Democratic to the Republican party. "This has to be the worst kept secret of the century," said Texas agriculture commissioner John White, a co-chairman for McGovern's presidential campaign in Texas. It had been common knowledge for months that Connally was changing his allegiance. Texas Republicans had a Connally cover prepared for the April issue of

13. The First City National Bank, site of Connally's law firm, was the largest in the state, controlling seventeen smaller state banks.

their official newsletter, the *Texas Republican Citizen*, but held up on it because Connally "kept waiting for the right moment."

The right moment, coincidentally, came four days after the birth of a grandson, John B. Connally IV, and Nellie Connally laughed, "I told John he should have gone into that press conference and told everybody he had called it to announce the birth of a grandson. They would have lynched him."

As early as mid-February 1973, a close associate who had talked to Connally indicated he expected Connally to join the Republican party at any moment. The widening Watergate scandal, however, made the GOP less and less inviting; and Connally postponed his announcement, despite reports that he was being pressured by the White House to speak out. Other reports said Connally had decided to wait several more months before switching parties, but changed his mind after hearing Nixon's April 30 television address on Watergate.[14] Connally's telephone call to Nixon that night must have been welcomed by the president, who was so upset that he cried when he concluded his television speech.

Connally, according to an associate, had been "up-tight" and "tense . . . over this Republican thing" for months. Prior to his announcement he was described as being "geared up, like an actor before opening night." At his news conference in Houston, Connally denied he had been pressured to change parties, and he said, "I don't think any future activites within this nation should be judged in its chronology either B.W. (before Watergate) or A.W. (after Watergate)." Connally insisted he was not a candidate for any office, and columnist James Reston said that was "malarky." Reston said Connally "has entered the presidential race by denying that he was doing anything of the sort."

14. The *Dallas Morning News* quoted a "well-informed source" as saying Connally helped Nixon write the speech.

The reaction in Texas to Connally's announcement was predictable. One of the first bumper stickers turned out by Texas Republicans read, "I'm Switching with Connally." They viewed him as an instant leader, capable of reversing more than 100 years of Republican defeats into victories. Said Robert Porter, Dallas County Republican chairman, "This is certainly one of the best things that could happen short of electing a Republican governor in our long battle to bring a viable two-party system to Texas politics." Congressman Jim Collins, also of Dallas, said Connally was the "ideal man to be our presidential nominee in 1976." "I think you have to assume I will vote for a straight Republican ticket although I don't want that to be irrevocable," said Connally.

"Good riddance" was the attitude of liberal Democrats, summed up in a statement by the Democratic Rebuilding Committee, which mentioned that it had tried as early as 1962, in Connally's first race for governor, to convince Texas voters that Connally was a Republican at heart. "I'm elated," said former Senator Ralph Yarborough. "This is just a public confession that that's where he's been in spirit all these years. . . . I think it is much better for the Democratic Party to have an open opponent in the Republican Party than to have a Trojan horse inside the Democratic Party. Connally doesn't go where the people are; he goes where the money is."

Former Secretary of State Bob Bullock said the only thing Connally had added to the Republican party "was his name." He said the only candidate Connally had supported in recent years who had won was Nixon. Bullock noted the defeats of Eugene Locke for governor in 1968, Ben Barnes for governor, Wayne Connally for lieutenant governor, and Crawford Martin for attorney general in 1972. Conservative Democrats were much more concerned over Connally's defection, but Texas governor Dolph Briscoe and Calvin Guest, chairman of the Texas Democratic party, said they were proud to be a member of the party that had produced such national leaders as John Nance Garner, Sam Rayburn, and Lyndon Johnson.

There was immediate speculation in Austin, where the state legislature was in session, that the 1976 presidential race would match Connally and Senator Edward Brooke of Massachusetts against Senators Edward Kennedy of Massachusetts and Lloyd Bentsen of Texas. Others predicted wholesale crossovers to the Republican party in Texas, if Kennedy were to be the Democratic nominee for president in 1976.

The Watergate scandal spread to the White House, and the jarring developments of what once had been considered merely a foolish political break-in absorbed most of the impact of the Connally announcement, pushing his switch to the Republican party off the front pages after one day. His switch was a calculated risk but endeared Connally even more to Nixon. Even ''Mr. Conservative,'' Senator Barry Goldwater, had sent back his ticket to a fund-raising affair at which the president was speaking, and Nixon told the depleted audience, ''The finest steel has to go through the hottest fire.'' And Watergate was the hottest fire. It was often compared to the 1920s scandal revolving around Teapot Dome, when President Warren Harding's Interior Secretary Albert Fall leased Wyoming and California oil fields to Edward F. Doheny and Harry F. Sinclair, oil tycoons who made $100 million each—and enriched Fall by $400,000.

Despite Watergate, Connally took an extra step: he accepted Nixon's appointment as ''special adviser,'' an unpaid job which would not require the Senate's approval. ''Connally has signed on as a cabin boy aboard the *Titanic*,'' was one of many witticisms circulated in Washington. The announcement of Connally's new job came on May 10, 1973, two days after he had been summoned by Nixon to Key Biscayne, Florida for a two-and-one-half hour conference in the president's study. ''Connally is a man whose judgment the president values,'' said press secretary Ronald Ziegler. ''He has agreed to assist and advise the president in any way that he can. The president appreciates that very much. He looks forward to sitting down and talking to him on a more frequent basis.'' Ziegler said Connally would be in his Executive Office Building offices across from the White House three times a week.

Newspapers the next morning questioned whether Connally wanted to have his cake and eat it, too. Since he had not resigned from his Houston law firm, which had numerous business clients, reporters raised the possibility of a conflict of interest[15] in Connally's advisory role and his job as a lawyer. "The luster of the firm will not be dimmed by having a partner who talks with the President in the seclusion of the Oval Office or the Executive Office Building several times a week," noted Norman Baxter of the Houston *Chronicle*'s Washington bureau, adding that Connally could become "the most influential private citizen in the United States." Fred Bonavita, a Houston *Post* reporter in Washington wrote, "In order for there to be no conflict of interest, Connally and the President will have to avoid discussion on any topic in which Connally has a direct, personal interest or in which his law firm has clients with such interests. This includes oil and gas exploration, development and pricing, electronics, insurance, shopping center and real estate development, cattle ranching, airlines, construction, banking and savings loan associations, and so on." Martin Schram of *Newsday* reported that Connally's law firm represented Gulf Resources and Chemical Corporation, whose president, Robert H. Allen, was being investigated by a federal grand jury in Houston in connection with Allen's $89,000 contribution to Nixon's 1972 campaign. Schram said the money "wound up in the Miami bank account of convicted Watergate conspirator Bernard Barker." "John Connally better look on the bottom of his boots. He may have just stepped in Watergate," wrote John Geddie of the Dallas *Morning News*' Washington bureau.

15. Among his law firm's corporate clients were Armco Steel, Dow Chemical, Olin Corporation, and Occidental Petroleum. The firm also represented Travelers Insurance Company, Hartford Insurance Company, American General Insurance Company, Pure Oil, United States Steel, and General Motors. Connally was instrumental in bringing a number of clients to the firm, among them Pan American Airlines and Haliburton.

Connally's law firm quickly denied it was representing Allen ''in the current inquest,'' and Connally was just as quick to say he had decided to take a leave of absence from the firm so long as he was an adviser to Nixon.[16] He also said he was resigning from all corporate boards on which he served. His brief stint as presidential adviser gave Connally unprecedented on-the-job training. ''It's not going to be a cakewalk for him because . . . there are other people that have been struggling in the vineyards of the Republican party for a long time,'' Spiro Agnew said of Connally in *U.S. News and World Report.*

The national ratings are what Connally's friends say he is really counting on to capture the Republican nomination in 1976. Nixon was so mad at the resolution by Senator Charles Percy, which urged Nixon to appoint an independent prosecutor to take charge of the Watergate investigation, that he told his Cabinet: ''Percy will become President over my dead body.'' Another influential factor is that in 1976, when they count delegates, Governor Nelson Rockefeller of New York will be sixty-seven years old and Governor Ronald Reagan of California will be sixty-five. National GOP chairman George Bush has long wanted to be president—some say even more than John Connally—but Bush is not a factor yet, and many unswerving conservatives have never trusted Bush's independent, intellectual stance on some issues. Considering the possible candidates in both parties, says James Reston, ''you have to give Connally a serious chance even with the burden of switching parties.''

In Kansas City, Missouri, part of America's heartland, Connally, inspired by a standing ovation from 800 members of the American Feed Manufacturers Association, reminded reporters of America's bicentennial, stating that 1976 ''is the year of our 200th birthday. It ought to be a great year, a vintage year.'' It could well be ''vintage Connally.''

16. Connally supposedly severed all connections with his law firm on Friday, May 11, but reportedly presided over a meeting of the firm on Monday, May 14.

—*Shelly Katz*

Epilogue

Feigning indifference, John Connally sits on the edge of the presidential arena. Prospects for a baronial private life pull him away, but his submerged fascination with the presidency pushes him toward it. In late 1973, he insisted that he had until 1975 to make up his mind—"1976 is eons away."

Connally ignored the discouraging polls—"I ranked about eighth when I ran for governor"—and piled up credits by shoring up Republican campaigns across the nation, delivering stemwinding speeches that wouldn't wind down. A young GOP fan heard one that had an especial evangelical ring and reluctantly admits, "He must have peaked four times. I thought he'd never stop." In Texas, aides circumspectly sounded out "liberal intellectuals" about meeting with Connally to see if they had any common ground.

Even as the circles of Connally's presidential interest widened, others wrote him off as a candidate. A New York publisher backed away from a contract on a Connally book, reasoning that Connally had tied himself too closely to the sinking rock of Richard Nixon and was dead politically.

Connally's apparent unstinting loyalty to the harried president trapped him in mistakes he normally would have sidestepped with ease. His acceptance of a special adviser's job again raised questions of conflict of interest, and he quit in disgust eleven weeks later, complaining of the ''screwed up mess'' at the White House. The Watergate cancer metastasized in a menacing manner, and, in defense of Nixon's desire to hold onto the White House tape recordings, Connally blurted—''There are times when the president of the United States would be right in not obeying a decision of the Supreme Court.'' His regal attitude suggested a dangerous precedent, and his impromptu statement could be used against him in a 1976 presidential race.

Connally again blundered in public when he told cheering Republicans at Los Angeles that he hoped Spiro Agnew would be ''completely exonerated'' and ''found guilty''' of federal kickback charges involving engineering contracts while Agnew was governor of Maryland. Connally was inspecting cattle at Gus Wortham's Nine Bar Ranch, near Houston, when he learned that the vice president had resigned and pleaded guilty to evading income taxes in 1967. It was, many thought, Connally's magic moment— the break for which he had been waiting.

But for the second time in eighteen months, Nixon dangled the vice-presidential bait in front of Connally and withdrew it—this time to avoid a congressional war over the appointment of Connally. Reporters canvassing Congress on Connally's chances said they thought he would have been rejected. Liberal Republicans were mad because they thought Connally was too eager for Agnew's job, and many Democrats were angered over Connally's insinuation that they were being unpatriotic by holding out for a ''caretaker'' vice president—one who would not run for the presidency in 1976—rather than one who would be the best man. Connally insisted that he would have been confirmed ''without a question,'' and he added, ''I am flattered by the apparent fear that some have of me and my prospects.''

Reporters and photographers who were clustered around Connally's ranch gate were invited to watch Nixon's vice-presidential announcement on television. Connally placed only one restriction on their visit—no photographs or TV film showing the interior of the expensive ranchhouse. "It was good to see that Connally's color-TV was no better than anyone else's,'' quipped one reporter. "Nixon looked green; but maybe he felt green.'' After Nixon announced that he had appointed Michigan congressman Gerald Ford as vice president, Connally slipped a prepared statement from his pocket praising Ford, whose name had been written in.

In post-mortems, Connally's aides tell others that he never really wanted the vice presidency, that the job would have made him an easy target for his enemies for three years. A close Connally aide, elated over widespread published opinions that Connally was the most qualified candidate for vice president, but that Nixon had sacrificed him as a gesture of peace toward Congress, reflects, "They [Connally's enemies] may have won the battle, but lost the war'' for the presidency in 1976.

Bibliography

Newspapers

Austin *American-Statesman*
Corpus Christi *Caller-Times*
Daily Texan
Dallas *Morning News*
Dallas *Times Herald*
Floresville *Chronicle-Journal*
Fort Worth *Star-Telegram*
Houston *Chronicle*
Houston *Post*
New York *Times*
San Antonio *Express-News*
San Antonio *Light*
W   A Publication of *Women's Wear Daily*
Waco *Tribune Herald*
Washington *Post*

Books

Associated Press. *Triumph and Tragedy: The Story of the Kennedys.* New York: Western Publishing Co., Inc., 1968.

———. *The Warren Report.* (Two volumes.) New York: Western Printing and Lithographing Company, n.d.

————. *The World in 1970.* New York: Western Publishing Company, Inc., 1971.

————. *The World in 1971.* New York: Western Publishing Company, Inc., 1972

Banks, Jimmy. *Money, Marbles, and Chalk. The Wondrous World of Texas Politics.* Austin: Texas Publishing Company, Inc., 1971.

Barber, James David. *The Presidential Character: Predicting Performance in the White House.* Englewood Cliffs: Prentice-Hall, Inc., 1972.

Bishop, Jim. *A Day in the Life of President Kennedy.* New York: Random House, 1964.

Bishop, Jim. *The Day Kennedy was Shot.* New York: Funk & Wagnalls, 1968.

Conn, Jerry Douglas. *Preston Smith: The Making of a Texas Governor.* Austin: Jenkins Publishing Company, 1972.

Christian, George. *The President Steps Down: A Personal Memoir of the Transfer of Power.* New York: Macmillan, 1970.

Domhoff, G. William. *Fat Cats and Democrats; The Role of the Big Rich in the Party of the Common Man.* Englewood Cliffs: Prentice-Hall, Inc., 1972.

Evans, Rowland, Jr., and Novak, Robert D. *Nixon in the White House: The Frustration of Power.* New York: Random House, 1971.

Frost, Gordon H., and Jenkins, John H. *I'm Frank Hamer: The Life of a Texas Peace Officer.* Austin: The Pemberton Press, 1968.

Gantt, Fred, Jr. *The Chief Executive in Texas: A Study in Gubernatorial Leadership.* Austin: University of Texas Press, 1963.

Gantt, Fred, Jr.; Dawson, Irving Owen; and Hagard, Luther G., Jr. *Governing Texas: Documents and Readings.* (Second edition.) New York: Crowell, 1970.

Goldman, Eric F. *The Tragedy of Lyndon Johnson.* New York: Alfred A. Knopf, 1969.

Goulden, Joseph C. *Meany.* New York: Atheneum Publishers, 1972.

Haley, J. Evetts. *A Texan Looks at Lyndon: A Study in Illegitimate Power.* Canyon: The Palo Duro Press. 1964.

Hersh, Burton. *The Education of Edward Kennedy: A Family Biography.* New York: William Morrow and Company, Inc., 1972.

Jenkins, John H. *Neither the Fanatics nor the Faint-Hearted.* Austin: The Pemberton Press, 1963.

Johnson, Lady Bird. *White House Diary.* New York: Holt, Rinehart, and Winston, 1970.

Johnson, Lyndon Baines. *The Vantage Point: Perspectives of the Presidency 1960-1969.* New York: Holt, Rinehart, and Winston, 1971.

Katz, Harvey. *Shadow on the Alamo: New Heroes Fight Old Corruption in Texas Politics.* Garden City: Doubleday & Company, Inc., 1972.

Kinch, Sam, Jr., and Proctor, Ben. *Texas Under a Cloud: Story of the Texas Stock Fraud Scandal.* Austin: Jenkins Publishing Company, 1972.

Lasswell, Harold D. *Psychopathology and Politics.* (Revised edition.) New York: The Viking Press, Inc., 1960.

Lasky, Victor. *J.F.K.: The Man and the Myth.* New York: Macmillan Company, 1963.

Manchester, William. *The Death of a President.* New York: Harper & Row, Publishers, 1967.

McClesky, Clifton. *The Government and Politics of Texas.* (Second edition.) Boston: Little, Brown, & Company, 1963.

Mooney, Booth. *The Lyndon Johnson Story.* New York: Farrar, Straus and Company, 1956.

McGinnis, Joe. *The Selling of the President 1968.* New York: Trident Press, 1969.

Phillips, William G. *Yarborough of Texas.* Washington, D.C.: Acropolis Books, 1969.

Pool, William; Craddock, Emmie; and David E. Conrad. *Lyndon Baines Johnson: The Formative Years.* Southwest Texas State College Press, San Marcos, 1965.

Rainey, Homer P. *The Tower and the Dome: A Free University versus Political Control.* Boulder: Pruett Publishing Company, 1971.

Rickover, Jules. *The Resurrection of Richard Nixon.* New York: G. P. Putnam Sons, 1970.

Salinger, Pierre. *With Kennedy.* Garden City: Doubleday & Company, Inc., 1966.

Schlesinger, Arthur M., Jr. *A Thousand Days: John F. Kennedy in the White House.* Boston: Houghton Mifflin Company, 1965.

Sorensen, Theodore C. *Kennedy.* New York: Harper & Row Publishers, 1965.

Texas Legislative Council and Texas Highway Department: *The Texas Capitol: Building a Capitol and a Great State.* Austin, 1967.

Texas Almanac. Dallas: A. H. Belo Corporation, 1970.

Texas Reaches for Greatness. (Connally's Report to the Legislature.) Austin, 1969.

White, Theodore H. *The Making of the President 1960.* New York: Atheneum House, Inc., 1961.

_____. *The Making of the President 1964.* New York: Atheneum, 1965.

_____. *The Making of the President 1968.* New York: Atheneum, 1969.

_____. *The Making of the President 1972.* New York: Atheneum, 1973.

White, William S. *The Professional: Lyndon B. Johnson.* Boston: Houghton Mifflin, 1964.

Monographs

Committee on Public School Education. *Reaching for Excellence in Texas Public School Education.* n.p. n.d.

Coordinating Board, Texas College and University System. *Plurolism and Partnership: The Case for the Dual System of Higher Education.* Austin: Coordinating Board, Texas College and University System. n.d.

Governor's Committee on Public School Education. *The Challenge and the Change.* Austin: n.p., 1968.

House Education Committee Report. *Vocational and Technical Education: State of Texas/1968.* Austin: State of Texas, 1968.

Articles

Alsop, Stewart. "Facts Hard and Soft." *Newsweek* (December 18, 1972): 112.

_____. "The Connally Equation." *Newsweek* (February 12, 1973): 96.

"A Matter of Reasonable Doubt." *Life* 61 (November 25, 1966): 38-49.

Anderson, David. "Mrs. Connally: A Pleasant Perfectionist." Dallas *Morning News* (December 8, 1968).

Andrews, Brad. "Crazy, Mixed-up Melting Pot." *Texas Parade* XXVIII (November 1967): 10-12.

"Architect Nesmith Tells His Story." *Texas Observer* 57 (July 9, 1965): 14.

"As Others See Us." *Texas Observer* 58 (March 17, 1967): 3.

"Back to Dallas." *Time* (November 24, 1967).

Banks, Jimmy. "Nellie's Nightmare Fading." Dallas *Morning News.* (January 26, 1964).

Baskin, Robert E. "John B. Connally: Organizer." Dallas *Morning News* (May 27, 1956).

Byers, Bo. "Connally can brag . . . just a little." *Outlook.* Houston *Chronicle* (April 21, 1963): Section 7, 7.

_____. "Connally Urges Universities To Cope with Uprisings." Houston *Chronicle* (December 4, 1968).

"Campaign '72 Wallace, Rockefeller, Connally." *Nation* (May 29, 1971): 74-75.

"Connally and Group Plan Fort Worth Development." Dallas *Morning News* (April 15, 1969): 7B.

"Connally: AN EARFUL OF LATIN COMPLAINTS." *U.S. News and World Report* (June 19, 1972).

"Connally: 'Controls'." *Texas Observer* 54 (November 16, 1962): 1.

"Connally Contradicted by Some Videotape." *Texas Observer* LX (April 12, 1968): 8.

"Connally Fingers the Switch." *Newsweek* (April 2, 1973): 20-21.

Connally, John. "Civil Rights: The Integration Issue." *Vital Speeches* (September 1, 1963): 679.

_____. "My Spirit." *Family Weekly* (November 22, 1964).

_____. "Texas Educational Goals." Dallas *Morning News* (May 1, 1964).

_____. "Why Kennedy Went to Texas." *Life* 62 (November 24, 1967): 86A-104.

_____. "The Communist Conspiracy." *Vital Speeches XXVIII:* 7 (January 15, 1962): 212-214.

"Connally, Miss Brill Are Wed." Austin *Daily Tribune* (December 22, 1940).

Connally, Mrs. John B. "Texas' First Lady Relives the Day the President Died."—Houston *Chronicle* Texas magazine (November 22, 1964). (Reprinted from *McCall's*).

"Connally Plugs Hard to Reelect President: Is He Looking to 1976?" *Wall Street Journal* (September 15, 1972): 1; 12.

"Connally's Au Revoir." *Newsweek* (May 29, 1972)

"Connally's College Board Choices Widely Acclaimed." Houston *Post* (September 2, 1965): 1; 18.

"Connally's Debut." *Wall Street Journal* (March 22, 1971).

"Connally's New Toughness." *Time* 101 (June 11, 1973): 77.

"Connally's Texas." *New Republic* (November 20, 1965): 9-12.

"Connally's Victory: Democratic Governor Slows Trend in Texas to Two Party System." *Wall Street Journal* (September 20, 1966).

439

"Connally, Texas, and HemisFair." *Texas Observer* 58 (July 22, 1966): 6-7.

"Connally was bold but rough." *Business Week* (May 20, 1972): 28.

"Connally will talk a hard trade line." *Business Week* (June 10, 1972).

"Democrats Mellower Mood." *Time* (January 1, 1973).

Dreyer, Martin. "The Institute of Texan Cultures." *Texas.* Houston *Chronicle* (July 7, 1968): 4-9.

Dugger, Ronnie. "Connally and the Richardson Estate." *Texas Observer* 56 (May 1, 1964): 5-7.

————. "Curious Coincidences." *Texas Observer* 54 (November 16, 1962): 1.

————. "Howard Dodgen's Story." *Texas Observer* 56 (May 1, 1964): 1-4.

————. "John Connally: Nixon's New Quarterback." *Atlantic* 228 (July 1971): 8-16.

————. "Oil and Politics." *Atlantic* 224 (September 1969): 66-78.

————. "The Changing of the UT Guard." *Texas Observer* LXII (August 7, 1970): 1-5.

————. "The Politics of HemisFair—And of San Antonio." *Texas Observer* 58 (September 30, 1966): 1-7.

Elliott, Karen. "Connally Enjoys Jamaica Isle for Golfing, Politics." Dallas *Morning News* 124 (March 18, 1973): 1.

Ford, Jon. "Connally Will Join Houston Law Firm." San Antonio *Express-News* (October 17, 1968).

Galvin, Lois. "First Ladies Have Made Texas Governor's Mansion a Family Home." Austin *American-Statesman* (December 7, 1969): F20.

Gardner, William H. " 'He is, to the contrary, a most uncommon man'." Houston *Post* (March 16, 1969): 1.

"Governor John Connally." *Texas Parade* XXV (January 1965): 25-28.

"Governor John Connally." *Texas Parade* XXVII (January 1967): 25-28.

Halberstam, David. "Losing Big." *Esquire* (September, 1972).

Hamilton, Martha. "The governor as a ladies' man." *Texas Observer* LXII (August 21, 1970): 7-8.

Harrison, Selig S. "Lyndon Johnson's World." *New Republic*, 142:24 (June 13, 1960): 15-23.

"He Had to Spring to Attend Radio Station Dedication." Dallas *Morning News* (January 24, 1965): 8-11.

"Here Come the Rangers." *National Review* (December 29, 1970): n.p.

"Historical Notes: A Matter of Sides." *Time* (July 27, 1970).

Ivins, Molly. *"Asteriskos,* R.I.P." *Texas Observer* LXII (October 16, 1970): 3-5.

"Is Texas Oil Empire Up for Sale?" *Business Week* (December 21, 1957): 22-23.

"John Connally: Mr. Nixon's No. 2 Man?" *Newsweek* (August 9, 1971): 16-20.

"John Connally: Now Mr. Inside?" *Newsweek* (May 22, 1972): 25.

"Johnson's Texas Troubles." *Nation* (February 12, 1968): 196.

"Kennedy Choices for Top Posts in Government." *U.S. News and World Report* (January 9, 1961): 20.

Kilpatrick, James J. "Connally Come On Like West Texas Sunrise." Fort Worth *Star-Telegram* (August 23, 1971).

Kramer, Victor A., ed. "The Complete 'Work' Chapter for James Agee's *Let Us Now Praise Famous Men."* *Texas Quarterly* XV: 2 (Summer, 1972): 27-48.

"Lyndon Johnson's Successor." *New Republic* (February 13, 1961).

Maguire, Jack. "The New Navy Boss." *Alcalde* (March 1961): 16-17.

Mansell, Walter. "John Connally: Secretary of the Navy." *Texas.* Houston *Chronicle* (February 5, 1961): 10-11.

Menefee, Marjorie. "Five Outstanding Young Texans." *Texas Parade* XXVI (February 1966): 39-42.

Moorman, Travis. "'I knew John Connally when . . . ." Corpus Christi *Caller-Times* (April 2, 1961) 3B.

Morehead, Richard M. "'Connally Day' at HemisFair." Dallas *Morning News* (September 29, 1968).

"Mr. Nixon Enlists a Texas Democrat." *Newsweek* (December 28, 1970): 13-15.

"Mr. Nixon's Democrats." *Newsweek* (August 7, 1972): 9.

"Nixon and Kissinger: Triumph and Trial." *Time* (January 1, 1973): 13-16; 19-20.

"Non-Expose." *Time* (February 15, 1971): 52.

"Oil Folks at Home." *Holiday* (February 1957): 55-56.

"Oil Politics." *New Republic* (May 27, 1972): 9.

"Oil Slick on the Potomac" *Commonweal* XVIC: 18 (February 5, 1971): 436-38.

Olds, Greg. "HemisFair '68 and Legislature '67" *Texas Observer* 58 (February 3, 1967): 1-4.

Patrick, Carolyn. "Third Term Wasn't Mrs. Connally's Idea." Dallas *Morning News* (October 15, 1965).

"Political Intelligence." *Texas Observer* LXV (March 16, 1973): 11-12.

"President Nixon Takes a Democrat." *Time* (December 28, 1970).

"Proxmire on Connally." *Texas Observer* 52 (March 18, 1961): 7.

"Recreation Program Comes Alive." Dallas *Morning News* (January 24, 1965): 8-11.

"Remarks on Plans to Nominate Secretary Kennedy as Ambassador-at-Large and Governor Connally as Secretary of the Treasury," *Public Papers of the President* (December 14, 1971): 1129-31.

"Republicans: Cloth-Coat Convention." *Newsweek* (August 7, 1972).

Semple, Robert B., Jr. "Connally Watching." *New Republic* (July 1, 1972): 12-15.

Sidey, Hugh. "John Connally, 'There are no leaders in my own party. Nixon is a man of courage.'" *Life* (May 7, 1971): 39-41.

"Solving a Crisis: John Connally Superstar." *Newsweek* (December 13, 1971): 85.

Stilwell, Hart. "The Herman Brown Story" (Typed copy of shorter version that appeared in *Nation*, November 10, 1951).

Sussman, Robert. "John G. Tower." *Citizens Look at Congress* (Ralph Nader Congress Project.).

"Texas: Close to the Land." *Time* 83 (January 17, 1964): 16-20.

"Texas' New Junior Senator." *New Republic* (April 22, 1957).

"Texas Rebels." *New Republic* (May 21, 1962): 5.

"The battles that Connally will face." *Business Week* (December 19, 1970): 36-37.

"The Connally Appointment." *Nation* (December 28, 1970): 676.

"The Forthcoming Devaluation of the Dollar." *Time* (December 13, 1971): 18-19.

"The Institute of Texan Cultures." *Texas.* Houston *Chronicle* (July 14, 1968): 6-17.

"The Johnson-Connally Axis." *Nation* (May 23, 1966): 605.

"The Juicy People." *W* (February 23, 1973): 20-21.

"The Making of the GOP Candidate '76." *Newsweek* (September 4, 1972): 28-29.

"The Rising Star from Texas." *Time* (October 18, 1971): 18; 23-26.

"The Superboard Nears Reality." *Texas Observer* 57 (February 19, 1965): 1-4.

"The Valley Strikers Are Walking to Austin." *Texas Observer* 58 (July 22, 1966): 7-8.

"Well-Oiled." *New Republic* (February 13, 1971): 10-11.

West, Dick. "John Connally. He Kept His Word." Dallas *Morning News* (January 19, 1969).

_____ "LBJ: His Influences and Talents." Dallas *Morning News* (January 28, 1973).

Whalen, Richard J. "The Nixon-Connally Arrangement." *Harper's* (August 1971): 29-42.

"What Mr. Connally Is Saying." *Wall Street Journal* (May 3, 1972): 12.

"Who Are America's Ten Richest Men?" *Ladies' Home Journal* (April 1957): 72-73.

"Winner Resorts." *W* (January 26, 1973): 14.

Index

A

Brown and Root Construction Company: 47, 50, 57, 174, 244, 417
Brown, George: 49
Brown, Herman: 47, 49
Brown, H. S. (Hank): 207, 210, 214, 221, 229, 232, 233, 238, 255, 324
Brown, Pat: 251
Brownell, Herbert: 417
Brownsville: 261, 379
Brownwood: 182, 191, 245
Brownwood *Bulletin*: 245
Bryan: 160
Bullock, Bob: 88, 89, 95, 126, 128, 182, 183, 184, 185, 186, 187, 263, 294n, 319, 331, 359n, 367, 411, 412, 426
Burleson: 81
Burney, Cecil: 87n
Burns, James McGregor: 71n
Bush, George: 193, 329, 341, 429
Business Week: 348
Butler, Paul: 72
Byers, Bo: 100, 102, 119, 163, 256, 298, 298n

C

Caldwell, Chuck: 108
Caldwell, Neil: 381, 382, 383
Calhoun, Ron: 335
Callins and Wagner: 173
Calvin Bullock Forum: 418
Calvert, Robert W.: 57, 416
Camp David: 354, 369
Camp Gary Job Corps Center: 113, 256
Carling Black Label: 185
Caro, Anthony: 177
Carpenter, Ben: 215
Carpenter, Leslie: 194, 255, 373
Carpenter, Liz: 332, 363
Carr, Waggoner: 95, 109, 112, 185, 231, 232, 234, 234n, 303, 325, 387
Carranza, Venustiano: 385n
Carrizo Springs: 87n
Carswell, Jack: 92, 93
Carter, Bill: 115, 117, 121, 237n
Caruso, Enrico: 65
Case, Francis: 62
Caudill, Rowlett & Scott: 173, 174
Caven, Walter: 384
Chamizal Treaty: 238, 238n
Chappaquiddick: 317, 318, 319
Chase Manhattan Bank: 345

Chavez, Cesar: 233
Chesire, Maxine: 378
Chicago: 67, 206, 208, 236, 260, 264, 292, 328, 368, 415
Christian Dior: 378
Christian, George: 69, 87, 87n, 111, 117, 171, 172, 189, 190, 192, 242, 248, 254, 255, 258, 261, 302, 303, 310, 312, 318, 344, 352, 353, 359, 360, 361, 363, 364, 365, 367, 368, 371, 374, 391, 392, 407, 409
Christian Science Monitor: 333, 354
Churchill, Winston: 380
Cibolo River: 2
Cigarroa, Joaquin: 161n
Ciudad Victoria: 307, 385
Civil Rights Act (1964): 226, 228, 304
Clark, Edward: 47n, 48, 262, 263, 263n, 264n, 395, 396
Clark, Ramsey: 316
Clemenceau, Georges: 387n
Clements, William P. Jr.: 215, 328, 328n
Cleveland, Grover: 387n
Cobb, Bill: 95
Cofer, John D.: 57
Cole, Jim: 381
Collier, Everett: 123
Collins, Jim: 426
Collins, Leroy: 250
Columbia University: 61
Comanche: 207
Commodore Perry Hotel: 118, 304
Connally, Charles P.: 2
Connally, Golfrey Michael: 3, 12, 14, 15, 19, 88, 233, 340n, 366, 408
Connally, H. F.: 152
Connally, Idanell Brill: 7, 23, 24, 24n, 25, 27, 37, 38, 43, 44, 45, 48, 59, 79, 86, 94, 99, 112, 128, 176, 212, 213, 262, 266, 299, 299n, 300, 302, 303, 305, 307, 311, 337, 348, 356, 356n, 357n, 358, 365, 372, 383, 385, 391, 393n, 397, 398, 399, 401, 415, 418, 425
Connally, John Bowden Sr.: 4, 11, 12, 14, 15, 16, 17, 19, 20, 21, 45
Connally, John Bowden III: 309, 398
Connally, John Bowden IV: 425

447

448

Democratic National Committee:
71, 315, 343, 411
Democratic Rebuilding Committee:
426
Democrats for Eisenhower: 62, 360
Democrats for Nixon: 331, 332,
334, 349, 359, 359n, 360, 361,
363, 364, 366, 367, 368, 369,
377, 381, 407
Denton: 408
De Rivera, Pedro: 1
De Rubi, Marquis: 1
De Sapio, Carmen: 72n
Devora, Pete: 230, 230n
Diaz Ordaz, Gustavo: 238
Dibrell, Kellis: 56
Dimmit County: 6, 113
Division of State—Federal Rela-
tions: 261
Dobie, J. Frank: 61n, 246
Dodd, Thomas: 304
Dodgen, Howard: 149, 150
Doheny, Edward F.: 427
Dorbandt, Mrs. Seth W.: 57
Driskill Hotel: 89, 102, 123, 186,
253, 386
Duckworth, Allen: 72, 108, 125
Duffner, Lucille Long: 17
Dugger, Ronnie: 67, 68, 126, 234,
236, 237, 329, 344
Duke University Law School: 372
Duval County: 55

E

Eckhardt, Robert: 32, 107, 150,
160, 186, 329, 416
Edwards, India: 71
Eggers, Paul: 201
Eisenhower, Dwight D.: 46, 61,
62, 63n, 64, 100, 148, 322,
360, 362n, 373, 387n, 406, 417
Ellington, Buford: 250
Ellington, Duke: 389
Elliott, Karen: 327, 399
El Paso: 98, 107, 151, 151n, 152,
153, 238, 262, 295, 324
Environmental Protection Agency:
409
Epworth League: 13, 14
Erhard, Ludwig: 302
Erlichman, John: 339, 353
Erwin, Frank Jr.: 87n, 98, 118,
151, 152, 153, 164, 165, 166,
167, 185, 187, 188, 193, 206,
209, 214, 300, 314, 315, 422

Espiritu Santo Bay: 1
Essex: 46
Estes, Billie Sol: 193
Evans, Rowland: 251, 253n, 256,
307, 319, 326, 331, 356, 369,
421
Evans, Roy: 57n, 125, 210, 221,
222, 223, 227, 228, 231, 234,
237, 239, 254, 325, 341, 356,
392, 411, 416, 417
Executives Club: 415

F

"Face the Nation": 202, 345
Fair Deal: 55, 58
Fairview: 3
Fairview Farms: 66
Family Weekly: 292, 302
Farenthold, Frances: 202n, 396
Fath, Creekmore: 36
Fay, Albert: 153, 324
Federal Bureau of Investigation
(FBI): 195, 257, 259
Federal Reserve Bank: 161n
Ferguson, James: 385n
Finch, Robert: 405, 405n
First City National Bank: 417, 424,
424n
500 Committee for Responsible
Government: 191
Flanagan, Sue: 171, 172
Flores, I. D.: 235n
Floresville: 1, 3, 4, 6, 14, 17, 18,
19, 25, 41, 42, 44, 90, 115,
182, 201, 221, 230, 235n, 249,
327, 362, 363, 401, 423
Fondren, Gene: 382
Ford, Gerald: 400, 433
Ford, Jon: 119
Ford Motor Company: 177
Ford, O'Neil: 6, 169, 170, 173,
389, 390, 391
Fore, Sam Jr.: 41, 241, 242
Formby, Marshall: 89, 91
Forrestal, James: 46
Forsyth, Frederick: 393n
Fortas, Abe: 58
Fort Worth: 5, 35, 56, 58, 60, 63,
64, 65, 66, 69, 109, 188, 215,
297, 300, 301, 307, 325, 359n,
360, 373, 400
Fort Worth *Star-Telegram*: 121,
222, 233, 317, 386
Forty Acres Club: 250, 314
Four C ranch: 6

Francis, Bill: 32
Francis, Charles I.: 57, 58
Franklin: 46
Friars: 30n
Fulbright, Crooker, Freeman, Bates, and Jaworski: 156
Fulcher, Gordon: 243
Fuller, Charlie: 21

G

Gaines, James: 175
Galbraith, John Kenneth: 331
Gallup Poll: 404n, 412
Galveston: 119, 364
Game Conservation International: 387
Gardner, Jim: 56
Gardner, William H.: 379
Garment, Leonard: 388
Garner, John Nance: 207, 347, 426
Garwood, W. St. John: 97, 98, 102
Geddie, John: 429
General Dynamics: 64
General Electric: 170
General Motors: 170, 428n
Giant: 356
Gibbens, Wayne: 261, 261n
Gibralter Savings Association: 417
Gibson, C. C.: 57
Gillespie, Tommye: 114n
Goldwater, Barry: 193, 251, 252, 254, 296, 298, 323, 405, 405n, 427
Gonzales: 2
Gonzales, Antonio: 230, 231, 232, 234
Gonzalez, Henry B.: 169, 176, 219, 220, 221n
Goodman, Scherwin: 390, 391
Good Neighbor Policy: 385
Goodwin, Richard: 212, 213
Gordon, Tom: 214
Goulden, Joseph C.: 239n
Governor's Committee on Education Beyond the High School: 158, 161
Governor's Committee on Public Education: 156, 157
Graham, Billy: 94, 352, 394
Grand Saline: 107, 113
Gray, John E.: 161, 161n
Great Society: 115, 213, 246, 258
Green, Howard: 106, 107
Griago, Tony: 5

Grover, Henry: 107, 327, 327n, 335n
Guadalupe County: 2
Guest, Calvin: 426
Guinn, Jack: 45
Gulf and Western Industries, Inc.: 418
Gulf Resources and Chemical Corporation: 428
Guy, William: 251, 251n

H

Hackerman, Norman: 165, 167
Hackworthe, Johnnie Mae: 113, 114
Halberstam, David: 259
Hale, Bobby: 63, 64
Hale, I. B.: 63n
Haldeman, H. R. (Bob): 331
Haliburton Corporation: 417, 428n
Hall, Jerry: 92
Hall, Morgan: 93
Hall, Ralph: 103
Hall, Walter: 269
Hamer, Frank: 56
Hamilton, Alexander: 387n
Hammer, Armand: 410n, 417
Haney, P. Bert Jr.: 395
Hardeman, Dorsey: 102, 103, 104, 105, 115, 160, 172, 198
Hardin County: 101
Hardin, John Wesley: 2
Harding, Warren G.: 72, 401, 427
Harlandale High School: 17, 23
Harlingen: 236, 362
Harper's: 396, 416n
Harriman, Averell: 68, 72
Harris County: 107, 200
Harris, Ed: 119
Harris, Jerome: 169
Harris, Phil: 386
Harrison, Selig: 263, 268
Harte, Houston: 102
Hartford Insurance Company: 428
Hatcher, Andrew: 250
Hawes, Mrs. Ethel: 64
Haye, Caleb: 400
Hayes, Bill: 198
Headliners Club: 396
Hearnes, Warren: 254
Heatly, W. S. (Bill): 185, 186
HemisFair '68: 119, 126, 168, 169, 170, 171, 172, 174, 175, 176, 177, 179, 210, 219, 220, 230, 235, 237

Lehman, Herbert: 248
Lehrer, Jim: 201
LeMaistre, Charles: 167
Lentz, Zac: 88
Lenz, Mary: 363
Let Us Now Praise Famous Men: 409
Leubsdorf, Carl: 412
Liberty County: 89
Life: 73, 191, 295, 297, 298, 299n, 309
Lindsay, John: 408
Locke, Eugene: 63, 87, 124, 125, 183, 201, 203, 205, 205n, 207, 351, 426
Locke, Mrs. Eugene: 193, 351
Locke, Purnell, Boren, Laney and Neely: 205n
Lockheed Aircraft Corporation: 343
Loeb, Rhodes: 82
Logan, Bard: 114n
Lone Star Gas Company: 156
Long, Russell: 325, 343
Long, Stuart: 92, 102, 108, 113, 122, 223, 347
Longley, Joe: 117, 117n
Longview: 253
Look: 307
Lopez, Mateos: 385n
Los Angeles: 70, 72, 74, 208, 244n, 310, 316, 363n, 364, 372, 404, 432
Los Angeles *Times*: 216, 257, 264, 410
Lower Colorado River Authority (LCRA): 45, 49
Lubbock: 168, 199, 200
Lubbock *Avalanche-Journal*: 92
Lucey, Robert E.: 230
Ludden, Allan: 24
Lufkin: 97, 152
Lyndon Baines Johnson Library: 365

M

Madden, Sam: 397
Madden, Wales Jr.: 152, 156
Magnuson, Warren: 70n
Maguire, Jack: 78, 79
Mahoney, David: 418
Manatt, Charles T.: 411
Manchester, William: 191, 248n, 299, 304, 305, 307, 308, 308n, 309, 314, 323
Mann, Thomas: 201

Marcus, Stanley: 116
Marks, Leonard: 360
Martin, Crawford: 95, 99, 112, 114, 192, 291, 291n, 300n, 309, 354, 395, 405, 426
Maverick, Maury: 388
Mayer, Margaret: 49, 307, 309, 339n, 341, 343, 349, 354
McAllister, W. W.: 357n
McAngus, Mary Jo: 37
McCall's: 299, 301, 305, 309
McCarthy, Eugene: 207, 208, 209, 210, 211, 212, 213, 214, 405, 405n
McCarthy, Joe: 61, 420
McCleskey, H. Clifton: 148
McCrocklin, James H.: 156
McDermott, Eugene: 161n
McDougall, Charles C.: 32
McGovern, Eleanor: 363
McGovern, George: 202, 209, 251, 318, 319n, 331, 332, 333, 359, 359n, 361, 362, 363, 363n, 364, 365, 366, 367, 368, 393, 408, 411, 412, 420, 424
McKnight, Felix: 68, 69
McLean, W. Hunter: 360
McLendon, Gordon: 193
McNamara, Robert: 74, 81, 251, 262
Mead, Mary: 401
Meadows, Algur: 400
Means, Marianne: 246, 409
Meany, George: 239n
"Meet the Press": 387
Mercedes-Benz: 66, 358
Mexico: 38, 125n, 171, 238n, 259, 307, 385, 385n
Mexico City Chamber of Commerce: 259
Midland: 103
Midwestern University: 190
Mier Expedition: 2, 2n
Miller, Joaquin: 17
Miller, Tom: 48
Mills, Wilbur: 214n
Miskell, Frank: 95, 423
Mission: 220
Mitchell, George: 411
Mitchell, John: 329, 364
Mitchell, Martha: 329
Mobley, John: 115
Montand, Yves: 400
Montego Bay: 398
Moody, Dan: 57
Moore, Bill: 160

453

455

River Oaks: 127, 265, 306
Ritter, Tex: 379
Rockefeller, Nelson: 429
Rockwall: 103
Rodarte, J. G.: 235n
Rogers: 389, 390
Rogers, Warren: 329
Rogers, William: 355
Rollins, John: 399
Roosevelt, Elliott: 61
Roosevelt, Franklin: 30, 42n, 54, 61, 101, 251, 347
Roosevelt, James: 364
Roosevelt, Theodore: 387n
Rose, Howard: 95, 104, 109, 150, 224, 225, 423
Rosewood Park: 224
Rowan, Carl: 347
Rowen, Hobart: 345
Ruby, Cecil: 256
Ruckelshaus, William: 409
Rural Electrification Association: 187
Russell, Richard: 67, 75, 415

S

Sager, Lois: 37
St. David's Hospital: 302
St. Joseph's Island: 61, 61n
Salinas, Porfirio: 7
Salinger, Pierre: 71, 213
Salt Water Control, Incorporated: 59n
Samuel Hart Galleries: 8
San Angelo: 102, 260
San Antonio: 4, 6, 15, 16, 19, 23, 87n, 107, 152, 168, 169, 171, 173, 176, 177, 196, 210, 220, 228, 230, 231, 234, 235, 296, 307, 327, 340n, 357n, 360, 378, 408
San Antonio Chamber of Commerce: 177
San Antonio College: 3, 233
San Antonio River: 2
San Antonio Express-News: 119, 169, 175
San Antonio Light: 171
San Clemente: 357, 358, 359
Sanders, Barefoot: 197, 326, 327
Sandhill ranch: 5, 6
San Marcos: 113, 156, 256
Santa Anna: 363
Santa Maria: 77
Sayers, Nancy: 188

Sayers, Scott: 95, 188
Schmidt, Larrie H.: 297n
Schnabel, Charles: 381
Schram, Martin: 428
Schrieber, Flora Rheta: 347
Scott, John Linn: 6
Scott, Wally: 93, 200
Scott, Zachary: 24
Scripps-Howard Newspapers: 371
Seabrook, J. J.: 161n
Secretary of Defense: 216, 373
Secretary of State: 373, 374
Secretary of the Interior: 339n
Secretary of the Navy: 63, 76, 77, 78, 80, 81, 85, 86, 88, 190, 293, 300n, 322, 394, 398, 404, 419
Secretary of the Treasury: 7n, 76, 331, 337, 339, 340n, 341, 346, 348, 349, 349n, 351, 353, 354, 369, 380, 387n, 388, 404, 415, 418, 421
Securities and Exchange Commission: 198n
Seguin: 42n
Seguin, Erasmo: 2
Senate Finance Committee: 339, 342
Senate Foreign Relations Committee: 313
Shannon, William: 366
SHAPE: 61
Sharp, Frank: 197n
Sharpstown State Bank: 197n
Shelly, Jack: 171
Sheppard, Morris: 54
Sheraton-Park Hotel: 343
Shires, Tom: 300
Shivers, Allan: 69, 78, 88, 108n, 111, 148, 198n, 216, 334, 360, 361, 385n
Shriver, Sargent: 214, 255, 257, 314, 362, 363, 368, 412
Shuffler, R. Henderson: 171, 172, 173
Sidey, Hugh: 405
Silber, John: 166, 167
Silsbee: 243
Simons, Pollard: 392, 398, 399, 401
Simpson, Peggy: 332
Sinclair, Harry F.: 427
Singleton, John: 25, 25n, 242
Sinkin, William: 169
Sirhan, Sirhan Bishara: 316
"60 Minutes": 329, 416

Slack, Dick: 105
Small, Clint C.: 57
Smith, Al: 408
Smith, Daniel F.: 81
Smith, Howell E. (Hal): 76, 342n
Smith, Preston: 88, 90, 95, 97, 98, 112, 113, 115, 119, 120, 121, 125, 128, 155, 177, 181, 187, 196, 197, 197n, 198, 199, 200, 201, 202, 202n, 231, 334, 345, 360
Smith, Tony: 177
Sneed, Jerome: 57
Snelson, W. E. (Pete): 103
Sorenson, Theodore: 71n, 213, 314
Southern Governors' Conference: 252
Southern Newspaper Publishers Association: 228
Southwest Texas State College: 156n, 209
Spears, Franklin: 96
Spindletop: 8n
Sportfolio: 386
Sprague, T. L.: 47
Stanton: 93
Starr County: 55
State Department: 108, 373
State Democratic Executive Committee: 27, 54, 55, 57, 69, 98, 111, 112, 193, 206, 252, 324, 416
Stephens County: 245
Stevenson, Adlai: 61, 67, 68, 69, 259, 297, 297n
Stevenson, Coke: 54, 55, 57, 58, 243, 385n
Steves, Marshall: 171
Stockdale: 20
Strauss, Mrs. Robert (Helen): 212, 213
Strauss, Robert: 74, 85, 87, 92, 97, 104, 188, 211, 212, 213, 214, 215, 242, 306, 309, 319, 319n, 331, 334, 337, 340, 343, 372, 392, 405, 411, 412
Strauss, Ted: 351
Stromberger, Ernest: 122, 201, 328
Student Assembly, University of Texas: 27, 30, 31, 32, 33, 35, 36, 37, 38, 41
Sturgeon, L. P.: 155
Sucke, Jack: 26
Sullivan, Ed: 356

T

Taft-Hartley: 54, 55, 228, 256
Talamentes, Esaquel: 5
Tampico: 385
Taniguchi, Alan: 167
Taylor: 382
Teague, Olin: 405
Teapot Dome: 427
Temple, Larry: 95, 175, 188, 327, 328, 329, 351, 360, 392, 419, 423
Templeton, Arleigh: 256
Terry, Joe: 59, 63, 65, 66
Terry, Sarah (Chich): 65
Tettaway, C. D.: 226
Texans for Nixon: 215
Texas A&M: 164, 301
Texas Association of Broadcasters: 403n
Texas Automobile Dealers Association (TADA): 88, 182
Texas Board of Corrections: 222
Texas Board of Medical Examiners: 235n
Texas Brewers' Institute: 88
Texas Chemical Council: 88
Texas Commission on Higher Education: 161n, 162
Texas Constitution: 342
Texas Department of Public Safety: 303
Texas Department of Welfare: 150
Texas Eastern Transmission Corporation: 57
Texas Employment Commission: 47n, 86
Texas Ex-Students' Association: 78, 397
Texas Farmers Union: 194, 255
Texas Fine Arts Commission: 27, 103, 126
Texas Game and Fish Commission: 127, 149
Texas Health Department: 37, 235n
Texas Highway Commission: 89
Texas Highway Department: 16, 303
Texas Hotel: 298
Texas House of Representatives: 29, 182, 255
Texas Industrial Commission: 95, 96, 104
Texas Instruments: 161n, 417
Texas Manufacturers Association: 261n, 382

457

Wright, Phlemon: 13, 16
Wright, S. M.: 236
Wurzbach, Harry: 42n

X

Ximenes, Edward: 220, 221n, 235n

Y

Yancy, Jim: 261n
Yarborough, Don: 91, 92, 100, 101, 125, 190, 192, 201, 206, 221, 223, 227, 228, 229, 244n, 245, 249, 293, 298, 322, 352
Yarborough, Ralph: 69, 100, 108, 125, 168, 175, 176, 181, 188, 189, 190, 191, 192, 193, 194, 195, 196, 197, 207n, 209, 215, 215n, 220, 227, 230, 233, 234, 237n, 248, 249, 252, 255n, 256, 295, 296, 298, 315, 325, 334, 341, 358, 367, 394, 411, 426
Yeagley, Frank: 47n
Young, Stark: 23, 24
Yount, M. F.: 8, 8n
Yucatan: 5

Z

Zavala County: 6, 113
Zeller, Roger: 7
Zeta Tau Alpha: 247
Ziegler, Ronald: 355, 427